Translating the Bible into Arabic: historical, text-critical and literary aspects

BEITRUTER TEXTE UND STUDIEN

HERAUSGEGEBEN VOM
ORIENT-INSTITUT BEIRUT

BAND 131

Translating the Bible into Arabic: historical, text-critical and literary aspects

Edited by

Sara Binay
Stefan Leder

BEIRUT 2012

ERGON VERLAG WÜRZBURG
IN KOMMISSION

Umschlaggestaltung: Taline Yozgatian

Umschlagabbildung: Near East School of Theology Beirut, Bible MS., Box No. III, Booklet 1, Matth. 9:1–6.

Bibliografische Information der Deutschen Nationalbibliothek
Die Deutsche Nationalbibliothek verzeichnet diese Publikation in der
Deutschen Nationalbibliografie; detaillierte bibliografische Daten sind im Internet über
http://dnb.d-nb.de abrufbar.

Bibliographic information published by the Deutsche Nationalbibliothek
The Deutsche Nationalbibliothek lists this publication in the Deutsche Nationalbibliografie;
detailed bibliographic data are available in the Internet at http://dnb.d-nb.de.

ISBN 978-3-89913-909-9
ISSN 0067-4931

 Gedruckt mit Unterstützung des Orient-Instituts Beirut, gegründet von der Deutschen Morgenländischen Gesellschaft, aus Mitteln des Bundesministeriums für Bildung und Forschung.

Ergon-Verlag GmbH
Keesburgstr. 11, D-97074 Würzburg

Druck: PBtisk, Pribram
Gedruckt auf alterungsbeständigem Papier

Contents

Foreword

Arabic translations of the Bible exemplify the complexities of translation as a linguistic operation, and they also illustrate the intricate aspects of their embeddedness in particular cultural and social settings. Translation is informed by premises, facilities and intellectual frameworks, and it results from policies determined by historical contexts. More generally, translations contribute to the appropriation of the foreign and are thus part of a continuous process of modification and reproduction, which keeps cultures alive.

From the outset, Arabic translations of the Bible may be regarded as a classic topic of Oriental Studies concerned with text, its linguistic features and its history, but they are also pertinent to the broadening of horizons which characterise the discipline today. Whatever Oriental Studies may signify today, or whatever they used to signify, it is quite obvious that Arabic Studies, Islamic Studies, the history of the Middle East, the study of Christianity in the Middle East and other region-specific research areas are currently re-engaging in debates and inquiries of more general significance. After a period characterised by rather reclusive specialisation, our study fields are prepared to engage with and – possibly – to contribute to the body of notions, concepts, ideas and methods which are constantly produced in the humanities and social sciences. This development corresponds with the social and intellectual experience of the last decades, at least, as it reflects the interrelatedness of phenomena across cultural boundaries, past and present, and instigates growing interest in common structures and features, as well as in the similarities which interconnect them.

Our interest in Arabic translations of the Bible is therefore related to the broader perspective of translation.

Translation is the "representation of foreign cultures", as the title of a study by Doris Bachmann-Medick suggests.[1] In this vein, translation is a major issue for every student of foreign cultures in practice and theory, since "translation" comprises both the practice of and the discourse about processes produced and structured by cultural encounters. When the Bible and associated religious texts are adapted to new linguistic and cultural contexts via translation, the linguistic interpretation must be understood as a component of a broader concept of translation processes which are especially effective in cross-cultural interaction.

The translation of the Bible into Arabic combines interreligious, intercultural and historical aspects. Translating the Bible is related to multi-confessional and multilingual backgrounds which were – and are – particularly present in Lebanon. The translation of the Bible, again, seems to be part of a broader encounter be-

---

1 Bachmann-Medick, Doris, ed., *Übersetzung als Repräsentation fremder Kulturen*, Berlin: Schmidt 1997.

tween Western and Eastern cultural products which accelerated from the 19th century onwards. The translation here implied agents from various cultures being engaged in cross-cultural transfers.

The conference held in December 2008 explored this fascinating process and its history, premises and achievements.

It is well known that translation cannot produce absolute semantic equivalence. As a consequence, translation may be seen as representing varying degrees of paraphrase[2], because the meaning of words and texts depends largely on the corresponding cultures. The intrinsic syntactic, semantic and pragmatic differences between languages thus necessarily lead to cases of non-equivalence and untranslatability. Translating means in practice, therefore, being shackled by limitations and being obliged to interpret. In terms of cross-cultural relationships, the variation among languages entails non-equivalence which may be a source of misunderstandings among the target-language audience.

Interpretation or decisions and strategies applied in approaching the source text are all the more important, as the source text contains not only linguistic but also rhetorical features. These embrace each other, producing the cohesiveness of texture. How difficult, even impossible, it is to transport the specific texture of the source text to the target language is an experience which most of us probably share. Therefore, translation assumes varying degrees of mutual intelligibility, as well as cases of untranslatability. As a consequence, translation neither consists of, nor results in plain reproduction. It is a creative activity which implies many decisions on the part of the translator, such as, for instance, selection and omission.

Footnotes are one of the many tools used to bridge the gap between complex and inaccessible source texts and the target language. The German translation of the Quran by Rudi Paret, to give but one example, is meant to be read in the light of the footnotes given in a separate volume.

Another school of translation would refuse the employment of such a remedy, as the evidence of the interpretative character of translation approaching but not entirely transporting the source text to the target language is seen as a disturbance to the natural reading flow. Instead, it is preferred to offer a cohesive interpretation, sound and consistent in itself, which makes a reading similar to the reading of the source text in its original cultural environment.

This kind of interpretative reproduction which makes a text migrate to a new cultural environment and – if successful – ensures its survival is the interesting linguistic paradigm of a process of change brought about by migrating ideas, models and artefacts which may all be included in an enlarged concept of 'text'. In this sense, translation, which produces a modification of texts, is similarly applied in the cross-cultural migration of beliefs, ideas, societal models, etc.

---

2 Nida, Eugene A. and Taber, Charles R.: *The Theory and Practice of Translation*, Leiden: Brill 2003 (4th ed.).

The relationship between author and translator, and between original and translation, is situated in specific social and political frameworks, such as mission in the case of religious texts, or colonialism and the confrontation with the Western models of modernity in philosophy and literature. There is an intrinsic relationship between translation and power,[3] and translations express, more or less obviously, cultural policies. Translations may therefore be effective in processes of political and social transformation.

Seen from this viewpoint, translation is more than a vehicle for the diffusion of knowledge. It is a means of creating modes of expression, ideas and concepts on the ground of a mediating process, which starts off from the notion, and the experience, of difference and moves towards the production of similarities.

This overarching broad concept of translation offered a motivational support and a general framework for our proposal to revisit Arabic translations of the Bible in their various linguistic and cultural contexts.

This volume and the conference at the Orient-Institut Beirut in December 2008 owe a lot to Sara Binay without whose dedication and persistence the conference, and the collection and editing of the contributions would not have been possible.

Stefan Leder

---

3 Tymoczko, Maria, and Gentzler, Edwin, eds., *Translation and Power*, Amherst, Mass. 2002.

Introduction

Sara Binay

The first section of this introduction is intended to trace the development of Arabic Bible translations, so far as they are known to us and have already been described in the research literature. This brief account makes no claim to be exhaustive but should give a sketch of the literary history of Bible translation which constitutes the background to the conference "Linguistic and Cultural Aspects of Translation – The Arabic Bible", held in Beirut in December 2008. Some general conclusions arising from the discussions and talks are then presented, particularly with regard to the term "translation", which Stefan Leder has already discussed in his foreword. In the final section, the arrangement of the articles is given and their contents are briefly presented.

The beginnings of the translation of biblical books into Arabic remain historically obscure. The possibility of pre-Islamic translations of the Bible into Arabic is the subject of ongoing discussion.[1] The fact is that at St Catherine of Sinai we have some very ancient Arabic Gospel manuscripts translated from the original Greek text which date back to the end of the 8th century AD.[2]

Later on, one can find fragments of Arabic biblical texts which show the importance of translations over time, and the demands for and uses of Arabic texts for different purposes, e.g. liturgical, polemical and apologetic.[3]

There is considerable evicence for Gospel translations from the Old Syriac into Arabic.[4] Throughout history, several individual scholars have commented on and

---

1 Most recently: Qāshā, Suhayl, "al-Kitāb al-Muqaddas wa-l-lugha al-ʿarabiyya", in: *Tarjamāt al-Kitāb al-Muqaddas fī l-Sharq. Buḥūth bībliyya muhadāt ilā Lūsyān ʿAqqād*, Ayyūb Shahwān, ed., Bayrūt: al-Rābiṭa al-Kitābiyya 2006 (Dirāsāt bībliyya 30), 79–96; Shahid, Irfan, *Rome and the Arabs: A Prolegomenon to the Study of Byzantium and the Arabs*, Washington (DC): Dumbarton Oaks 1984. Badr, Habib, chief ed., *Christianity: A History in the Middle East*, Beirut: Middle East Council of Churches 2005. See also Paul Féghali's article in this volume.

2 Kachouh, Hikmat, *The Arabic Version of the Gospel: the manuscripts and their families*, 3 Vols., Birmingham: University of Birmingham, 2008; idem, "The Arabic Versions of the Gospels: A Case Study of John 1.1 and 1.18", in: *The Bible in Arab Christianity*, David Thomas, ed., (The History of Christian–Muslim Relations, 6) Leiden/Boston 2007, 9–36; idem, "Sinai Ar.N.F. Parchment 8 and 28: Its Contribution to Textual Criticism of the Gospel of Luke", *Novum Testamentum* 50 (2008), 28–57. Hikment Kachouh participated in the Beirut conference and we would like to express our gratitude for his fruitful contribution.

3 Thomas, David, ed., *The Bible in Arab Christianity*, Leiden/Boston: Brill 2007, here: Arbache, Samir, "Bible et liturgie chez les Arabes chrétiens (VIe-IXe siècle)", 37–48.

4 Vööbus, Arthur, *Early versions of the New Testament. Manuscript Studies*, Stockholm 1954, 276ff; Khalıl, Samīr, et al., eds., *Anājīl ʿAbd-Yashūʿ al-Ṣūbāwī al-musajjaʿah*, 2 vols., Bairūt: al-Maktabah al-Bulūsīyah 2007; Brock, Sebastian, *The Bible in the Syriac tradition*, Piscataway, N.Y.: Gorgias Press 2006.

translated biblical texts.[5] Concerning the Old Testament, one finds a milestone in Saadiah Gaon's Arabic Pentateuch, the first five books of the Old Testament, from the 10th century. Saadiah, a famous Jewish scholar from Egypt, was known to Ibn al-Nadīm under the Arabic name Saʿīd b. Yūsuf al-Fayyūmī. The text he produced was primarily intended for the Arabic-speaking Jewish congregations and was written in Hebrew letters. Nevertheless, it was in use among the Copts of Egypt as well. His text may be called a paraphrase rather than a translation of the original. As such, the translator has given his own original spirit to the Arabic text.[6]

There are no physical remains of the 10th century translation of the Septuagint into Arabic by Isḥāq b. Ḥunayn, which is listed by al-Masʿūdī.[7] The Septuagint comprises 72 books of the Old Testament in a Greek version for the use of the Jewish community in Egypt.

A unique translation containing a study of the Gospels with detailed comments on the terminology originated also in Egypt and was composed by the 13th century Copt Hibat Allāh b. al-ʿAssāl.[8]

Walid Saleh shows in this volume, as he has published elsewhere, how a Muslim author used the text of the Bible in his commentary on the Qurʾān.[9]

It is not until the 16th century that one can find efforts to establish new translations of the whole Bible in the Eastern churches, as reported by Georg Graf in his *History of Christian Arabic Literature*.[10] In general, translations of the Gospels and of the other biblical texts were produced as the need arose. The effort to produce complete Bibles containing the Old and New Testaments can be judged as novel and, to my knowledge, has unfortunately not been set in the context of developments in the period's intellectual history. So, in order not to stray into the purely speculative, we must leave open the question of where this trend came from.

---

5 Listed as "Al-Kitāb al-Muqaddas fī l-lugha al-ʿarabiyya. At-tarjamāt al-qadīma", in: *Tarjamāt al-Kitāb al-Muqaddas fī l-Sharq*, Ayyūb Shahwān, ed., Bayrūt: al-Rābiṭa al-Kitābiyya 2006, 317ff.

6 See Graf, Georg, *Geschichte der arabisch christlichen Literatur*, Rom: Bibliotheca Apostolica Vaticana 1944, vol. 1, 101.

7 Al-Masʿūdī, *Kitāb at-tanbīh wal-ishrāf*, M.J. de Goeje, ed., Lugduni Batavorum 1894 (Bibliotheca geographorum arabicorum VIII), 112 (quoted in Graf I, 89).

8 Bailey, Kenneth E., "Hibat Allah Ibn al-ʿĀssāl (sic!) and His Arabic Thirteenth Century Critical Edition of the Gospels (with special attention to Luke 16:16 and 17:10)", *Theological Review (NEST)*, I,1 (1978), 11–26; Abullif, Wadi, "La Traduction des Quatre Evangiles d'al-Asʿad Ibn al-ʿAssāl (XIIIe Siècle)", *Studia Orientalia Christiana* 24 (1991), 216–24; idem, "al-Asʿad Ibn al-ʿAssāl, Introduzioni alla Traduzione dei Quattro Vangeli", *Studia Orientalia Christiana* 33 (2000), 227–249.

9 Saleh, Walid A., "A Fifteenth-Century Muslim Hebraist: Al-Biqāʿī and His Defense of Using the Bible to Interpret the Qurʾān," *Speculum* 83 (2008), 629–654; idem, "Sublime in its Style, Exquisite in its Tenderness: The Hebrew Bible Quotations in al-Biqāʿī's Qurʾān Commentary," in: *Adaptations and Innovations*, Tzvi Langermann and Josef Stern, eds., Paris: Peeters 2007, 331–347.

10 See Graf, I, 89ff.

We then enter the 17th century, which produced the first Arabic Bibles in print. Two of them are products of European scholarly linguistic interest and were published as polyglots in Paris (1629–45) and London (1657).[11] In the polyglots the texts in their original languages were printed beside the Arabic version.

Parallel to these achievements, it is clear that clerics of the Greek Orthodox Church in the East felt the need for a new or better translation of the Bible, and measures were taken to prepare the publication.[12]

It took nearly four decades to complete work on the Bible for the Congregation for the Propagation of the Faith in Rome, for which the Latin text of the *Vulgata* was printed alongside the Arabic text (finished in 1671). Due to the involvement of many scholars and different personalities from Europe and the Near East, the translated text is far from homogeneous.[13] Nevertheless, it must be considered as a very influential edition until the advent of the 19th-century translations.[14]

We now approach a period of very intensive Bible translation activity. The translation projects of the 19th century are closely associated with the foreign missionaries who came to the Near East in that period.

One rarely-mentioned Bible translation is that by Fāris al-Shidyāq. It is assumed that he worked on it, in cooperation with Samuel Lee, on the basis of the London Bible edition dating back to 1657.[15]

Much more attention has been given to the translations initiated by the Protestant missionaries (first parts printed in 1856, completed in 1865) and the Jesuits (3 vols. 1876–1880) of Beirut. Little has yet been said about the literary value of the Protestant and Jesuit editions. In general, the translation effected by the Western Protestants and their Arab colleagues was well received. Supposedly, they tried to imitate the literary style of the original texts.[16] This caused deficiencies which adversely affected the literary quality of the translation. In spite of this, the influence of their translation cannot be exaggerated, because the Orthodox Churches, including the Copts of Egypt, adopted this version.

Some years after the Protestants, the Jesuits published their edition of the Bible in *fuṣḥā*-Arabic, translated by Ibrāhīm al-Yāzijī.[17] He kept away from contempo-

---

11 Ibid., 93f.

12 The contributions of Carsten Walbiner and Hilary Kilpatrick to this volume focus on this topic.

13 Thompson, John Alexander, *The Major Arabic Bibles*, New York: American Bible Society 1956, 16ff.

14 See Paul Féghali's article in this volume.

15 Kahle, Paul, *Die arabischen Bibelübersetzungen*, Leipzig: J. C. Hinrichs 1904, V. See al-Baghdadi, Nadia, "The Cultural Function of Fiction: From the Bible to Libertine Literature. Historical Criticism and Social Critique in Aḥmad Fāris al-Šidyāq", in: *Arabica* 46 (1999), 375–401, here 382f. (We are grateful to Professor al-Baghdadi for her participation in the Beirut conference.)

16 For some evaluations of the literary style, see Thompson, *The Major Arabic Bibles*, 25ff.

17 The procedure was desribed in Khūrī, Sāmī al-, "Al-Shaykh Ibrāhīm al-Yāzijī wa-l-maṭbaʿa al-kāthūlikiyyah, baina 1872 wa 1881", *Al-Mashriq* 65 (1991), 127ff.

rary uses of the Arabic language in the Middle East, trying to reinstall classical ideals. Some reports suggest that he created a translation which is not easy to understand even for people who are well versed in Arabic.[18] Nonetheless, this translation has been used by the Maronite Church of Lebanon until today.

These translations – the Catholic and the Protestant – are the most influential of the 19th century. A cursory comparison of the works shows that the Jesuit translation should not be considered a new one, but rather a revised version of the text edited by the Protestants. Another explanation for the similarity of these versions could be that the translation teams based their work on the same sources.[19] In any case, both versions are very similar to each other compared with the new translations from the 20th century. The differences between the Protestant and Jesuit versions lay in the use of different lexemes which might have certain theological connotations. At the same time, the syntactical structures are identical. In 1997, a study by Tharwat Kades appeared containing a comparison between selected text passages from the Smith–Van Dyck version and from the Jesuit translation as well as from its first revised edition.[20]

The translation by the Dominicans of Mosul, which appeared between 1875 and 1878 in four volumes, should not be forgotten. It may have been of importance for the region of Iraq, but it has been eclipsed by the success of the abovementioned Beirut translations. The Mosul translation was created by the later Catholic bishop of Damascus, Yūsuf Dāwūd. It may be considered a revision of the Roman Propaganda Bible, and is based mainly on the *Vulgate*.[21] This is why it could not compete with the modern translation methods of the Beirut editions.

One of the most interesting Bible translation projects of the 20th century is *al-mutarjama al-mushtaraka*, initiated by the *International Bible Society* and the Jesuit Fr Sami Khoury, chief editor of the journal *Al-Mashriq*. Intellectuals and poets, such as Yūsuf al-Khāl,[22] and scholars of different Protestant and Orthodox denominations, as well as members of the Maronite Church, joined this project.

Because *al-mutarjama al-mushtaraka* has not been officially recognised by the Roman Church, it cannot be termed "ecumenical" (*maskūnī*). The New Testament was published in 1979. The complete edition did not appear until 1993.

---

18 On the literary value of the Jesuits' Bible , see Thompson, *The Major Arabic Bibles*, 30.

19 This remark is quite speculative as long as we have no detailed study of translators' *modus operandi*. Binay in her article mentions the sources used by the Protestants. The paper "Did Van Dyck use the Orthodox Liturgical Biblical Readings for his Arabic Translation of the Bible?", given by Nicolas Abou Mrad during the Beirut conference but not yet published, shed some light on this topic.

20 Kades, Tharwat, *Die arabischen Bibelübersetzungen im 19. Jahrhundert*, Frankfurt/M. u.a.: Lang, 1997.

21 Graf, *Geschichte der arabisch christlichen Literatur*, I, 99f.

22 Hedi Ayadi's article in this volume investigates the biblical citations within the poetry of Yūsuf al-Khāl.

The efforts made by translators of the Bible, who came from different backgrounds, are not confined to the above-mentioned famous translations. Other projects are worthy of mention although they are relatively unknown to the wider public. These include the so-called Būlusiyyah translation of the New Testament in 1953 and Kaslīk's New Testament translation from 1992, as well as *Tarjamat al-Kitāb al-Sharīf*, published between 1990 (New Testament) and 2000 (Old Testament), especially intended for use in North African countries.[23]

Editing or Translating?

The conference "Linguistic and Cultural Aspects of Bible Translation – The Arabic Bible" had as its central theme Bible translations of the 18th and 19th centuries. It was a happy circumstance that contributions focusing on considerably earlier periods led to a broadening of the perspective. Connections between the various contributions even led to the realisation that the meaning of an entirely "new epoch" of Bible translations since the 19th century must be brought into doubt or at least newly defined.[24] The quest to create a uniform and complete edition of the Arabic Bible was probably a modern endeavor which finds a predecessor in the Roman *Propaganda Fide* edition which also displayed this ambition. What must, however, be noted in relation to the editions in question which date back further than the 21st century is the texts' close interdependence. Unfortunately, we cannot always tell with certainty which older versions were used as a template by those preparing a particular compilation.

It has, however, been shown that the so-called "new translations" were in fact in each case based on the older editions, which they naturally sought to improve upon in accordance with the prevailing level of knowledge and theological orientation. This approach seems to apply to the American Mission's and the Jesuits' influential Beirut translations, described in the literature up to now as a new beginning. The echoing of the old manuscripts speaks of a meticulous choice on the part of the translators in each case, who appear to have been well versed in the Bible in the true sense of the phrase and to have mastered their tradition.

Only the 20th-century translations, e.g. the *mushtaraka* edition, which was worked on by the poet Yūsuf al-Khāl among others, break with this tradition and deliver entirely new texts, translated or rather composed by linguists and people from a literary background who were fully aware of their own creative potential.

---

23 Referred to as "Injīl al-sharīf" in *Tarjamāt al-Kitāb al-Muqaddas fī l-Sharq*, Ayyūb Shahwān, ed., 321.

24 So a list of "the modern translations" (*at-tarjamāt al-ḥadītha*) in ibid., 319, begins with Fāris al-Shidyāq's translation, first published in London in 1857. This is followed by the 1865 Beirut edition of the complete Bible by the American missionaries and their Lebanese translators.

A further important result was that during the conference an uncertainty arose regarding the term "translation". Let us begin with the fact that one of the earliest works, that of Saadiah Gaon, was called *tafsīr.* Thus it was made clear on the one hand that the term *tafsīr* is by no means to be found only in the "usual" Islamic milieu. It became clear, moreover, that here we are not yet dealing with the awareness of a "translation", but rather of an "exegesis". This medieval view is compatable with modern translation studies, which have for some years stressed that there can be no "neutral" translation but rather that the translator's individual and cultural cast of mind always have an influence.[25]

The translations, *mutarjamāt*, from the following centuries resemble rather new editions which were based closely on the existing text and only introduced improvements. This applies even to the full translations of the Bible from Beirut, which were generally held to be original new translations. The "Protestant" or, more precisely the Smith–Van Dyck–al-Bustānī–al-Yāzijī translation was based on existing manuscripts (which can be traced back to the Alexandrine Vulgate).

About the contributions

As personalities and manuscripts appear repeatedly in this volume, we chose to create a general bibliography with an Arabic and an English section.

Due to considerations of content and methodology, the contributions are divided into the categories "textual history/history of texts" (تاريخ النص) and "studies on poetry" (الدراسات في الشعر).

The historical section is opened by Ronny Vollandt, who deals with the manuscript copies of the Paris polyglot Bible, which appeared from 1628, using Saadiah Gaon's seminal 10th century translation of the Pentateuch as a basis for his examination.

Paul Féghali traces in his article the origins of the Roman *Propaganda Fide* edition of the Bible. In this connection he names the Arabic Bible manuscripts which can be seen as the precursors or sources of the Roman edition, and deals with the standard of language in various manuscripts.

Carsten Walbiner presents a picture of the Melkite intellectual environment for various translation projects in Syria in the 17th and 18th centuries. With regard to Meletius Karmah's highly ambitious but unfinished project, which had been agreed with the Vatican, he points out that Karmah wanted to engage a multiconfessional team of translators. Hilary Kilpatrick likewise places Meletius Karmah at the centre of her contribution. She examines the linguistic colouring of his extant texts and in doing so uncovers influences in terms of dialect and style.

---

25 See Stefan Leder's foreword to this volume and Trivedi, Harish, "Translating Culture versus Cultural Translation", in: *91st Meridian*, vol. 4, no. 1, Univ. of Iowa 2005.

Ghassan Khalaf (غسان خلف) in his overview of the influences on Bible translations deals in particular with the period since 1850, which he regards as the "Modern epoch" (المرحلة الحديثة) of Bible translation. In contrast, Sara Binay in her contribution stresses the continuity between the older transmissions and the translations of the 19th century, a continuity assured in particular by the Arab contributors to the Protestant translation. How strongly dependent this new translation remains on older works was shown by Nicolas Abou Mrad's talk at the conference.

Issa Diab (عيسى دياب) offers a small concordance of biblical passages from the 19th-century translations as well as of the Masoretic texts and the Septuagint. He outlines the differing theological views, mirrored in these texts, of 19th-century translators.

In their contribution, Walid Saleh and Kevin Casey bring to us the perspective of a Muslim scholar's interest in the text of the Bible. Al-Biqāʿī's astonishing familiarity with the Gospels which he used for his Quran commentary is shown in Walid Saleh and Kevin Casey's concordance.

The literary studies section addresses Arabic poetry, the language's ultimate discipline. Here Hedi Ayadi (الهادي العيّادي) devotes himself to an exciting search for poetic motifs in the work of Yūsuf al-Khāl, where he traces the "game with the sacred and its antithesis".

Adib Saab (أديب صعب) studies the significance of Arabic hymnal Protestant poetry in the broader context of contemporary Arabic literature. He demonstrates inter alia notable metrical similarities between the Arabic version of the Psalms in the 19th-century Protestant Bible translation, produced by, for example, Shaikh Asīr, and Protestant hymns.

The Arabic Pentateuch of the Paris Polyglot: Saadiah Gaon's advent to the republic of letters*

Ronny Vollandt

> "As I perused the translation of the learned Rabbanite Saʿīd al-Fayyūmī, I satisfied myself on account of his style that he is the most preferable of all translators and most eloquent interpreter among the people of his confession."

These words are found in an anonymous preface to Saadiah's Pentateuch translation preserved in MS. Paris BNF Ar. 1 (fol. 1v). It is generally recognised that this very manuscript served as the main basis for the edition of the Arabic portions of the Paris Polyglot. Despite this common knowledge, however, little is known about the manuscript itself, the particular text type it contains and how it made its way into one of the most prestigious printing projects of early modern Europe.

The purpose of this paper is, therefore, multiple. I shall start by summarising our current knowledge of the emergence of Saadiah's *tafsīr*. Next, I shall attempt to deal with its adaptation by the Coptic Church and present a brief description of the textual changes that occurred thus. Although MS. Paris BNF Ar. 1 clearly belongs to that branch of transmission, it exhibits – as will be shown – an inner-Coptic attempt to re-establish the Judaeo-Arabic character of the *tafsīr*.

This stage of transmission is – in my view – also crucial for understanding the early Arabic prints of the Bible, since these are based on existing medieval manuscripts and were produced in a transitional bookish culture that was not clearly demarcated from that of the earlier, chirographic era. Within the confines of the Pentateuch, three distinct – but nevertheless historically interwoven – printing projects belong to that early period of printing Arabic Bibles: Erpenius' *Pentateuchus Mosis Arabicè* (1622); the Arabic portions of the Paris Polyglot (1628–45), which were reprinted in the London Polyglot (1653–57); and *Biblia Sacra Arabica* of the *Congregatio de Propaganda Fide* (1671–73).[1] A new type only emerged with the translations by Aḥmad Fāris al-Shidyāq (Psalter 1850, NT 1851) and Eli Smith and Cornelius van Dyck (entire Bible, 1860–65). Being homogeneous, monographic texts produced in their entirety at one point of time, they were to a certain degree provoked by a strong disapproval of Arabic Bibles printed earlier.[2]

---

* I thank the Syndics of Cambridge University Library for permission to publish images of T-S Ar. 28.144r (see Plate 1) and the Paris Polyglot (see Plates 4–5).

1 In addition, one may add an earlier Judaeo-Arabic Pentateuch that had been printed by Eliezer Soncino in Istanbul in 1546. It features Saadiah Gaon's version in Hebrew letters. It is, however, advisable to treat this print in a separate context.

2 For example, Eli Smith's statement on the *Propaganda Fide* edition: "Of the prophetical and poetical portions of the Old Testament much is either without force, in bad taste, or

The second part of this paper focuses on the transfer of MS. Paris BNF Ar. 1 to Rome with the French ambassador Savary de Brèves, who was involved in the earliest plans for printing it. I shall present how there his attempts were gradually absorbed by the Paris Polyglot project, which eventually concentrated and put into effect all earlier printing aspirations. The Arabic text of the Paris Polyglot held a prominent place in the scholarship of Arabic versions of the Bible for some centuries, which adds to the necessity of research regarding its development. In contrast to the *Propaganda Fide* edition, it had almost no impact on Eastern Churches. In Western contexts, however, it became known as *the* Arabic Bible.

I am well aware that such discussion regarding a number of highly specialised fields makes exhaustiveness unachievable and imprecision inevitable. Still, I hope that this contribution will permit me to point out the problems that deserve further investigation.

1 Saadiah's life and translation enterprise

Saadiah Gaon (882–942) – Saʿīd al-Fayyūmī, as he called himself in Arabic – was the pre-eminent scholar of Judaeo-Arabic culture of his time. His impact included ground-breaking advances in scholarly fields which had barely received any systematic treatment prior to him, such as compendious *halakhic* writing, liturgy, philosophy, grammar, exegesis and Bible translation. The main outlines of his life are well attested.[3] He was born in Dilāṣ, in the Fayyūm district of Upper Egypt, in 882. Despite his prolific writing, very little is known about his family background and his intellectual development. In pursuit of knowledge, Saadiah left Egypt, apparently in his late twenties. He travelled throughout *Bilād al-Shām*, but it was in Palestine that he apparently spent most of the period between his departure and his later career in Babylonia. He resided in Tiberias, which was the cultural centre of Palestinian Jewry at that time.[4] Concrete evidence of his sojourn is furnished by the Muslim historian al-Masʿūdī, mentioning a certain Abū Kathīr Yaḥya al-Kātib as his teacher there.[5] It is likely that Saadiah's intimate ac-

absolutely unintelligible. The whole version is not in classical style. The structure of sentences is awkward, the choice of words is not select, and the rules of grammar often transgressed." ABCFM Annual Reports 1844, 254, as quoted in Leavy, Margaret R., *Eli Smith and the Arabic Bible*, New Haven, CT: Yale Divinity School Library 1993, 15.

3 Still useful is Malter, Henry, *Saadia Gaon: His Life and Works*, Philadelphia: The Jewish Publication Society of America 1921. More recently cf. Brody, Robert, *The Geonim of Babylonia and the Shaping of Medieval Jewish Culture*, New Haven and London: Yale University Press 1998, 235–44; idem, *Rav Se'adyah Gaon*, Jerusalem: Merkaz zalman shazar le-toldot yisra'el 2006.

4 Gil, Moshe, *A History of Palestine, 634–1099*, Cambridge: Cambridge University Press 1992, 175–85.

5 De Goeje, M. J., ed., *al-Masʿūdī: Kitāb at-tanbīh wa-l-ishrāf*, Leiden: Bibliotheca Geographorum Arabicorum 1894, 112–13. On the identification of Abū Kathīr Yaḥya al-Kātib see Polliack, Meira, *The Karaite Tradition of Arabic Bible Translation: A Linguistic and Exegetical*

quaintance with the Tiberian tradition of Hebrew grammar and pronunciation originated in Tiberian scholarly circles.

Through his intervention in the great calendrical dispute with Ben Meir, son of the Palestinian Gaon in the years 921–23, Saadiah gained public recognition. This dispute was ignited by the disagreement of Palestinian and Babylonian scholars over the calculation of the New Year and Saadiah's taking the Babylonian side prompted his appointment as Gaon of Sura in 928. As such, he was the generally recognised religious leader of the early medieval Jewish communities.

About two years later, a bitter quarrel broke out between Saadiah and the Exilarch David ben Zakkai, his political counterpart, when the Gaon refused to confirm a judicial decision by the latter. He was declared to be removed from the post of Gaon and another scholar was installed in his stead. Saadiah, for his part, deposed David ben Zakkai from his post as Exilarch and replaced him with his brother Josiah. The Babylonian elite was divided in two armed camps. Even an attempt to involve the Muslim authorities on his behalf did not resolve the crisis, which lasted for six or seven years. During that period Saadiah had to hide in actual fear of his life and composed – *inter alia* – his commentary to the *Book of Creation*, in Arabic *Tafsīr kitāb al-mabādī*[6], his great philosophical work *The Book of Beliefs and Opinions*, Arab. *Kitāb al-amānāt wa-l-iʿtiqādāt*[7], as well as the *tafsīr*, in secrecy. Reconciliation was finally effected and Saadiah was once again universally acknowledged as Gaon. He died in May 942.

There can be no doubt that the Judaeo-Arabic Bible translation is one of the most influential texts produced by Saadiah.[8] The *tafsīr* could soon be found everywhere throughout the communities in the Near East, North Africa and Muslim Spain, which attests to the fact that it acquired an authoritative, almost canonical, status among all Arabic-speaking Rabbanite communities. Concerning the number of books he rendered into Arabic, he most certainly did *not* translate the en-

---

Study of Karaite Translations of the Pentateuch from the Tenth and Eleventh Centuries C.E., Etudes sur le Judaïsme Médiéval, Leiden and New York: E.J. Brill 1997, 12, no. 39.

6 Lambert, Mayer, ed., *Saadia ben Joseph: Commentaire sur le Séfer Yesira, ou Livre de la Création*, Paris: É. Bouillon 1891.

7 Qāfiḥ, Yosef, ed., *Saadia ben Joseph: sefer ha-nivḥar ba-emunot va-de'ot*, Kiryat Ono: Mekhon mishnat ha-rambam 1998; Altmann, Alexander, *The Book of Doctrines and Beliefs* (Philosophia Judaica), Oxford: East and West Library 1946.

8 Derenbourg, Joseph, Derenbourg, Hartwig, and Lambert, Mayer, eds., *Saadia Ben Joseph: Œuvres Complètes de R. Saadia ben Iosef al-Fayyoûmî*, Paris: E. Leroux 1893–1899. The edition is based on the Constantinople imprint of 1546, the Paris Polyglot and a late Yemenite MS., cf. Mieses, J., "Textkritische Bemerkungen zu R. Saadja Gaons Arabischer Pentateuchübersetzung", *Monatsschrift für die Geschichte und Wissenschaft des Judentums* 63 (1919), 269–90. A new edition is currently being prepared under the auspices of Prof. E. Schlossberg, University of Bar-Ilan. It will be based on MS. St Petersburg RNL Yevr. II C 1. On that manuscript, see Blau, Joshua, "Saadya Gaon's Pentateuch Translation in the Light of an Early-Eleventh-Century Egyptian Manuscript", *Leshonenu* 61 (1998), 111–30.

tire Hebrew Bible. Saadiah produced a translation of the books of Isaiah, Psalms, Proverbs, Job, Lamentations, Esther, Daniel and the entire Pentateuch.[9] Usually, the translation is found attached to a commentary. In the first group of books the translation unit consists of several verses followed by the commentary. The textual unit of the translation roughly equals that of the commentary in length. As for the Pentateuch, each biblical verse is followed by a lengthy commentary (the long *tafsīr*).[10] This arrangement was directed to a scholarly audience and prevented the text from serving a broader, less scholarly public.

In the preface of the short *tafsīr* he gives clear evidence that he was asked to separate the plain text of the Pentateuch (*basīṭ naṣṣ al-tawrāh*) into a separate book (*fī kitāb mufrad*), which would not contain long exegetical discussions.[11] In response to this popular demand, Saadiah disjoined the translation itself (the short *tafsīr*) from the commentary. As is so often the case, the creation of the shorter work caused the near extinction of the longer original: the commentary, in distinction to the wide diffusion of the translation, fell into oblivion and ceased being copied. Already in the Genizah corpus the proportion of fragments containing the commentary is comparably modest.

2 Christian adaptations of the tafsīr and MS. Paris BNF Ar. 1

By the very nature of Judaeo-Arabic, these manuscripts were copied in Hebrew script (see Plate 1). Although a small number of fragments of Saadiah's *tafsīr* in Arabic letters and of Jewish provenance exist in the Genizah collections, the majority of manuscripts in that script were produced for use among Christians.[12] There is no clear evidence when exactly Saadiah's *tafsīr* was transcribed into Arabic script. Although the fragments from the Genizah are datable to the first half

---

9 A version of Ecclesiastes that was transmitted in Saadiah's name among the Yemenites is in fact that of Ibn Ghayyāt. See Abramson, Shraga, "On Isaac Ibn Ghayyat's Commentary to Kohelet", *Kiryat Sefer* 52 (1977), 156–72.

10 Large parts of the first half of Genesis have been edited by Moses Zucker (Zucker, Moses, ed., *Saadia ben Joseph: perushe rav Se'adyah Gaon li-ve-reshit*, New York: Jewish Theological Seminary 1984).

11 It should nevertheless be noted that there are meaningful differences between the separate translation and the one accompanied by a commentary. The differences result from didactic, communal and ideological considerations, which had been explicit in the longer commentary but needed unambiguous emphasis in the short *tafsīr*. On this issue, see Ben Shammai, Haggai, "An 'East Wind' from the South", in: *Studies in the History of Eretz Israel Presented to Yehuda ben Porat*, Yehoshua Ben-Arieh and Elchanan Reiner, eds., Jerusalem: Yad ben Zvi 2003, 288–307; Ben Shammai, Haggai, "Extra-Textual Considerations in Medieval Judaeo-Arabic Bible Translations: The Case of Saadya Gaon", *Materia Giudaica* 8/1 (2003), 53–66.

12 On the Genizah fragments see Vollandt, Ronny, "Some Observations on Genizah Fragments of Saadiah's Tafsīr in Arabic Letters", *Ginzey Qedem: Genizah Research Annual* 6 (2009), 9–44. I hope to furnish a thorough discussion of the Christian adaptations of Saadiah's *tafsīr* in the near future.

of the eleventh century, their scarce attestation does not allow any conclusive and univocal answer to that question. The earliest known dated Christian copy of the *tafsīr* – MS. Leiden Warner 377 – was copied in 1239–40 and would serve as a *terminus ante quem* in that matter. In total, about two dozen manuscripts are extant today, which may be classified into three distinct branches of transmission: a Syrian Orthodox branch (only for the Book of Genesis),[13] a Coptic branch and an independent branch.[14] For the purpose of this paper I shall limit myself to the Coptic branch.

With regard to Arabic versions of the Bible, the Coptic tradition differs from the Syriac and Greek (Melkite) in many ways. The Copts began to translate the canonical Scriptures much later than the others, especially the Melkites. Until well into the twelfth century, the Copts seem to have used Arabic as a written language only very reluctantly and sparsely.[15] Although it cannot be ruled out that partial translations of the Pentateuch – e.g. as part of lectionaries – were written down earlier, manuscript evidence dates from the first half of the 13th century onwards. The first occurrence of an Arabic Pentateuch translation of Coptic provenance is in the form of a later addition on the outer margins of MS. Vatican

13 The group consists of MSS. Leiden Warn. 377, Copenhagen Royal Library Cod. Ar. LXXV, Florence BML or. 57 (olim 12) and Paris BNF Ar. 4. They have distinct approaches towards revision of the Peshitta and employ numerous Syriacisms. MS. Leiden Warn. 377 explicitly mentions the name of the scribe as *al-mardhīnī al-yaʿqūbī* and MS. Paris BNF Ar. 4 features many marginal notes in Syriac. Their attribution to the Syrian Orthodox Church does not necessarily point to a Greater-Syrian provenance in geographic terms. We know that the Parisian and Florentine MSS. were acquired in Egypt, by J. M. Vansleb and Giovanni Battista Vecchietti respectively. They may likely have originated in the Syriac-speaking monophysite communities of Egypt, cf. Den Heijer, Johannes, "Relations between Copts and Syrians in the Light of Recent Discoveries at dayr as-Suryān", in: *Coptic Studies on the Threshold of a New Millennium: Proceedings of the Seventh International Congress of Coptic Studies,* Mat Immerzeel and Jacques Van Der Vliet, eds., Leuven: Uitgeverij Peeters en Dep. Oosterse Studies 2004, 924–38.

14 As represented in MSS. Vatican Borg. Ar. 126 and Istanbul Topkapi 3522. Both are of a yet undetermined provenance, but clearly distinct from the Syrian and Coptic branches. I discovered the latter at the CEDRAC during my stay in Beirut a few days after the conference and am indebted to N. Edelby for his kind assistance. It was copied in 1348. In contrast to the aforementioned branches, they are strictly speaking not adaptations, but rather exhibit an unchanged Arabic transliteration of the Judaeo-Arabic text.

15 This is true for the monastic culture that monopolised manuscript production. The extra-clerical lingual situation is less documented and therefore somewhat difficult to assess. Even so, it appears that the conservative attitude was restricted to the monasteries. Cf. Papaconstantinou, A., "'They Shall Speak the Arabic Language and Take Pride in It': Reconsidering the Fate of Coptic after the Arab Conquest", *Le Muséon* 120 (2007), 273–99; Richter, T. S., "O. Crum Ad. 15 and the Emergence of Arabic Words in Coptic Legal Documents", in: *Papyrology and the History of Early Islamic Egypt*, Petra Sijpesteijn and Lennart Sundelin, eds., Leiden and Boston: Brill 2004; Rubenson, Samuel, "Translating the Tradition: Somc Rcmarks on the Arabisation of the Patristic Heritage in Egypt", *Medieval Encounters* 2/1 (1996), 4–14; Zaborowski, J. R., "From Coptic to Arabic in Medieval Egypt", *Medieval Encounters* 14 (2008), 15–40.

Copt. 1.[16] The marginal text appears to be a faithful translation of the Bohairic version exhibited in the older part of the codex. At a second stage, the translations were featured in bilingual manuscripts that were from the outset designed to contain both languages.[17] On their side, however, Saadiah's translation is found in a large number of manuscripts. The earliest dated among them is MS. Florence BML or. 112 (olim 21), copied 1245/46.[18] It is worth noting that it exceeds the number of bilingual codices by far. In fact, the ratio is almost 2:1.

The integration of Saadiah's *tafsīr* into the Coptic Church, however, entailed a fairly significant revision which allows us to speak of a distinct Coptic adaptation. On the whole, the manuscripts exhibit an attempt to bridge the textual "deficiencies" resulting from the transition into a new cultural context, which concurred with that from one scriptural reference point (i.e. the Hebrew Scriptures) to another (i.e. the Coptic Bible). One detects a tendency to restore literalism: on the one hand, Saadiah's interpretative additions were removed and, on the other, omissions of repetitions were reinstated in accordance with the biblical source text. As we know, both features occur amply in the Saadianic text. In addition, syntax, word order and number of nouns were brought into line with the Coptic text. Albeit only in very particular cases, the manuscripts exhibit an interpolation with Karaite versions as well.[19]

---

16 Rhode, Joseph Francis, *The Arabic Versions of the Pentateuch in the Church of Egypt: A Study from Eighteen Arabic and Copto-Arabic MSS. (IX–XVII Century) in the National Library at Paris, the Vatican and Bodleian Libraries and the British Museum*, Leipzig: W. Drugulin 1921, 36–42. The first dated Copto-Arabic bilingual in a similar fashion is MS. Coptic Patriarchate Bibl. 123 (dated 1215), cf. Takla, Hany N., "Copto (Bohairic)-Arabic Manuscripts: Their Role in the Tradition of the Coptic Church", in: *Coptic Studies on the Threshold of a New Millennium: Proceedings of the Seventh International Congress of Coptic Studies*, Mat Immerzeel and Jacques Van Der Vliet, eds., Leuven: Uitgeverij Peeters en Dep. Oosterse Studies 2004, 639–46. That dating may give a tentative indication of the date of the Arabic portion of MS. Vatican Copt. 1.

17 See Rhode (1921) for a list. MSS. Coptic Patriarchate Bibl. 1–5 are to be added.

18 MSS. Florence BML or. 112 (olim 21); Wolfenbüttel Gudianus Graecus 33; Vatican Ar. 2; Birmingham Mingana Christ. Ar. 7; Coptic Patriarchate Bibl. 18, 19, 22, 24, 25, 30, 31, 38, 51; Cairo Coptic Museum Theol. 193; Vienna Cod. Mixt. 664; London BL Harl. 5475. These manuscripts, especially the copies from Florence and the Vatican, have long been known to scholars. The former was discussed in Adler, J. G. C., *Kurze Übersicht seiner Biblisch-Kritischen Reise*, Altona 1783–4, 67; Bacher, Wilhelm, "Il Manoscritto Fiorentino della Traduzione del Pentateucho di Saadja", *Rivista Israelitica* 2 (1905), 45–49; Chiesa, Bruno, "Un Testimone della Traduzione Araba del Pentateucho di Saadia", in: *Manoscritti, Frammenti e Libri Ebraici nell'Italia dei Secoli XV–XVI*, G. Tamani and A. Vivian, eds., Rome: Carucci 1991. Portions were published in Kahle, Paul, *Die Arabischen Bibelübersetzungen: Texte mit Glossar und Literaturübersicht*, Leipzig: J. C. Hinrichs 1904. Specimens of the latter are found in Rhode (1924), 36*–49*.

19 See Polliack (1997). A fine example is the imitative use of Arab. *adamah* to translate Heb. *ʿaḏāmāh* "ground, earth" in all the manuscripts. This rendering is alien to Saadiah, who commonly uses *al-arḍ*. Unlike him, Karaite exegetes such as Yefet ben ʿElī and Yeshʿuah ben Yehūdah agree on *adamah* as the preferable Arabic equivalent. Also David al-Fāsī (tenth century), the great Karaite lexicographer, records *adamah*. The employment of such

Interesting evidence of an inner-Coptic attempt to return to the Judaeo-Arabic character of Saadiah's *tafsīr* is found in Manuscript MS. Paris BNF Ar. 1 (see Plate 2).[20] It was copied in 1584–85 by four distinct copyists and contains the entire Old Testament according to the Coptic canon, except for the Book of Ruth.[21] It features many prominent Arabic versions: the Pentateuch of Saadiah (fols. 3v–83v), the Psalter of Abū al-Fatḥ ʿAbdallāh Ibn Faḍl of Antioch (232v–267r)[22] and the Prophets of al-Aʿlam of Alexandria (fols. 268r–387v).[23]

---

a Hebraised form is not attested in Saadiah's translation works at all and suggests the involvement of a third party. A similar example is the rendition of *hak-kərūḇīm*, "cherubim", in Gen. 3:24. Saadiah uses *malāʾikah*, whereas the manuscripts exhibit *al-karūbīm*, identical to Yesh'uah ben Yehudah's version. Such a pursuit of imitative affinity to the Hebrew source text is surprising, but nevertheless plays a functional role in adapting thc tcxt to a new context, since the Coptic Pentateuch features a Hebraised form, following the Greek χερουβιμ, cf. Peters, Melvin K. H., *A Critical Edition of the Coptic (Bohairic) Pentateuch* (Septuagint and Cognate Studies Series, 15), Chico: Scholars Press 1983, 10. Similarly, a replacement of Saadianic lexical features in favour of Karaite lexicon can be observed, e.g. *li-l-irshād*, "to guide", for *li-l-ʿaql*, "for the intellect" (Saadiah for Heb. *ləhaskīl*, "to make one wise") in Gen. 3:6. Also this reading is found in Karaite versions and seemed more suitable to reflect the Coptic; idem, 9.

20 One of them, a Muslim copyist named ʿAbd Rabbih b. Muḥammad b. Ahmad b. ʿAbd ar-Raḥmān ash-Shaʿarānī, mentioned his name on fol. 387r. Another, Faḍlallāh b. Tādrus, wrote a colophon at the end of the Book of Proverbs, fol. 404v. The manuscript belongs with a highly interesting set of additional copies, which apparently originated from the same scriptorium. Another copy, apparently made the following year, is preserved in MS. Coptic Patriarchate Bibl. 32, as first mentioned by Samir Khalil Samir in "Trois Versions Arabes du Livre des Juges. Réflexions Critiques sur un Livre Récent", *Oriens Christianus* 65 (1981), 87–101. In contrast to the Parisian manuscript, it contains the Book of Ruth, but dispenses with all Sapiential Books and Major Prophets, except Isaiah and Jeremiah. The observed difference suggests that the choice of books was to a certain degree conditioned by the wishes of commissioners and compiled from different sources. The group consists of MSS. London BL Or. 1326, Vatican Ar. 445, Paris BNF Ar. 25, Coptic Patriarchate Bibl. 79 and Coptic Patriarchate Bibl. 80; a specimen of the last MS. is found in Simaika, Marcus, *Catalogue of the Coptic and Arabic Manuscripts in the Coptic Museum, the Patriarchate, the Principal Churches of Cairo and Alexandria and the Monasteries of Egypt*, Cairo: Government Press 1939, Vol. II, plate XXIV. See also my forthcoming "From the working desks of a Coptic-Muslim workshop: MS Paris–BNF Arabic 1 and the mass production of Arabic deluxe Bibles in early Ottoman Cairo", in: *Patronage and the Sacred Book*, E. Alfonso and J. Decter, eds., Turnhout: Brepols, 2012.

21 There are multiple colophons on fols. 96v, 107r, 122v, 135v, 321r and 345v ranging from Ramaḍān 992 to Muḥarram 993 A.H. For details see Troupeau, Gérard, *Catalogue des manuscrits arabes: Première Partie: Manuscrits Chrétiens Nos. 1–6933*, Paris: Bibliothèque Nationale 1972, 11.

22 Graf, Georg, *Geschichte der christlichen arabischen Literatur*, Città del Vaticano: Biblioteca Apostolica Vaticana 1944 (= *GCAL* I), 116–119.

23 *GCAL* I, 131–133; Löfgren, Oscar, *Studien zu den arabischen Danielübersetzungen, mit besonderer Berücksichtigung der christlichen Texte; nebst einem Beitrag zur Kritik des Peschittatextes*, Uppsala: Almqvist & Wiksell 1936; Vaccari, Alberto, "Le Versioni Arabe Dei Profeti", *Biblica* 2 (1921), 401–23.

Saadiah's *tafsīr* is preceded by a preface (fols. 1v–3r) by an anonymous author.[24] He states (fol. 1v):

> "As I perused the translation of the learned Rabbanite Saʿīd al-Fayyūmī, I satisfied myself on account of his style that he is the most preferable of all translators and most eloquent interpreter among the people of his confession. [...] Thus I copied his version in what follows this preface and intended to transcribe it accurately. For this purpose, I summoned to my aid a notable Jew, whose name is given at the end of this copy. He memorised the text and recalled its words with great sagacity. Further, he was well versed in the study of the expressions, its pronunciation [lit. its recitation; Arab. *tilāwa*] and everything related to the interpretation of its meaning."

Thereupon he enters a long examination of Saadiah's translation features which had been altered or were lost in the Coptic transmission. In order to reinstall them, he introduced a system of rubricated marks which may with some justification be called a proper critical apparatus. First, Saadiah's interpretative additions were reintroduced with the help of his Jewish informant and marked by the letter *zāʾ* (i.e. *ziyādah*). The letter *ʿayn* designates correction by collation with the Hebrew (i.e. *ʿibrānī*), whereas a *khā* (i.e. *nusakh ukhrā*) refers to the readings in the Coptic adaptations of the *tafsīr*. The variants are usually found copied between the lines.

The influence of Saadiah's translation, therefore, is tangible from the very emergence of Arabic translations in the Coptic Church. It was bestowed a semicanonical status and, what is more, the liturgical divisions according to Coptic tradition might indicate that it in fact was employed in liturgy. The importance of the *tafsīr* is underlined by a conservative approach towards it, which is exhibited in the text-critically emended text type found in MS. Paris BNF Ar. 1.

---

24 His approach recalls in many respects that of al-Asʿad Abū al-Faraj Hibatallāh Ibn al-ʿAssāl, who flourished around 1230–60. He accomplished a critical edition of the Arabic Gospels in use among the Copts. The whole enterprise was prompted by the wish to establish a linguistically improved and textually reliable version. Similarly, the variant readings that he retrieved from a collation with Greek and Syriac translation traditions were noted on the margins of the previous Arabic Gospel text, cf. Abullif, Wadi, "La Traduction des Quatre Evangiles d'al-Asʿad Ibn al-ʿAssāl (XIIIe Siècle)", *Studia Orientalia Christiana* 24 (1991), 216–24; idem, "al-Asʿad Ibn al-ʿAssal, Introduzioni alla Traduzione dei Quattro Vangeli", *Studia Orientalia Christiana* 34 (2006); Graf, Georg, "Die koptische Gelehrtenfamilie der Aulād al-ʿAssāl und ihr Schriftum", *Orientalia* 1 (1932), 34–56, 129–48, 93–204; Macdonald, Duncan B., "Ibn al-ʿAssāl's Arabic Version of the Gospels", in: *Homenaje á D. Francisco Codera en su Julibilación del* Profesorado, Eduardo Saavedra, ed., Zaragoza: M. Escart 1904, 375–392; Samir, Samir Khalil, "La Version Arabe des Evangiles d'al-Asʿad Ibn al-ʿAssāl. Etude des Manuscrits et Spécimens", in: *Actes du 4e Congrès International d'études Arabes Chrétiennes (Cambridge, Septembre 1992)*, Samir Khalil Samir, ed., Kaslik: Université Saint-Esprit 1994, 441–551. Whether the anonymous author is in any way affiliated to al-Asʿad Abū al-Faraj Hibatāllah Ibn al-ʿAssāl, an obvious assumption in light of the similarity of the enterprises, requires further research.

3 Savary de Brèves' effort for a printed Arabic Bible

In 1606 a new protagonist was about to enter the stage: François Savary de Brèves, who served as ambassador of France to the Sublime Porte during the years 1591–1604.[25] He had arrived in Istanbul with his uncle and predecessor in office, Jacques de Savary-Lancosme, in 1584 and is well known to have skilfully achieved the famous peace treaty between King Henry IV and Sultan Ahmed I. What is more, the effective diplomat was one of the outstanding Arabic and Turkish scholars of his time, thanks to a twenty-year residency in the East nearly unsurpassed in the Europe of his time.

Upon the cessation of his diplomatic service in Istanbul, however, Savary de Brèves set out on a journey throughout the Levant, Egypt and North Africa.[26] Its purpose, at royal behest, was to inspect the condition of the Christians living in the Ottoman Empire. In the course of the journey, the diplomat visited Lebanon, Jerusalem and Egypt, among many other places. He met the Maronite patriarch Joseph al-Rizzī at the Monastery of Qannūbīn[27] and was welcomed by Mark V, Pope of Alexandria, in Cairo.[28] The journey would determine his future aspirations in many respects: grieved by the inferior social and cultural status of Chris-

---

25 This chapter is much indebted to Duverdier, Gerald, "Les Caractères de Savary de Brèves, Les Débuts de la Typographie Orientale et la Présence Francaise au Levant au 17e Siècle", in: *L'art du Livre à L'Imprimerie Nationale*, Paris: Impr. Nationale 1973; idem, "Les Impressions Orientales en Europe et le Liban", in: *Exposition: le Livre et le Liban jusqu'à 1900*, Camille Aboussouan, ed., Paris: Unesco 1982, 157–73; Lelong, Jacques, *Discours Historique sur les Principales Editions des Bibles Polyglottes*, Paris: Pralard 1713.

26 His journey is well documented. The itinerary of the captain, François Arnaud, is preserved in MS. Paris BNF fr. 19896. His secretaries, Jehan Vuiot de Baron and Jacques du Castel, both left descriptions of the travel. However, only du Castel's was later published in the name of François Savary de Brèves (*Relation Des Voyages De M. De Brèves, Tant en Grece, Terre-Saincte, et Ægypte, qu'aux Royaumes de Tunis & Arger. Ensemble un Traicte Faict l'an 1604, entre le Roy Henry le Grand & l'empereur des Turcs et Trois Discours du dit Sieur. Le tout Recueilly par le S[Ieur] D[u] C[astel]*, Paris: N. Gasse 1628). In addition, the diplomat refers to it in a number of letters.

27 His sojourn in Qannobin is described in his *Relation des Voyages*, 45. He met not only the Patriarch but also George Amira, who had published a *Grammatica Syriaca* at the press of Giaccobo Luna, Rome, in 1596 and Sarkīs al-Rizzī, brother of the Patriarch and later bishop of Damascus. Sarkīs was associated with the printing of the famous Quzhaya Psalter in 1610 and later headed the committee in charge of producing an Arabic Bible at the *Congregatio de Propaganda Fide* in Rome.

28 Cairo and the negotiations with the Coptic Pope Mark V were at the core of the entire enterprise. He abided with him from September 1605 to March 1606. However, they are referred to only briefly in his *Relation des Voyages*. In a letter to Cardinal du Perron he states: "*Je me résous d'avoir vu le Grand Caire pour avoir eu l'occasion de procurer l'union de la nation Cofte à la croire de l'église romaine. J'en ay eu de bonnes arres et pense avoir avancé beaucoup en ce sujet. Le Patriarche de ceste nation écrit à sa Sainteté et au Roy avec promesses de vivre d'ici en avant l'obéissance d'icelle.*" (MS. Paris BNF fr. Dupuy 194, fol. 180). The confession of faith was sent to the Roman authorities by way of the French consul Gabriel Fernoulx. It furnishes important additional details of de Brèves' sojourn, cf. Cattan, Basilio, "La Chiesa Copta nel Secolo XVII: Documenti Inediti", *Bessarione* 34 (1918), 133–61.

tians in the East, he turned himself with zeal to liberating them from the Muslim yoke. The premise of such liberation would, in his view, consist in the union of the Eastern Churches with the Roman papacy that could be effected by missionary publishing through the erection of a printing press. In addition, this "*haute entreprise*", as he would call this printing project in his letters, would likewise serve to supply European Arabists with much-needed textbooks and would thus further Oriental studies. In view of that, Savary de Brèves had actively engaged in obtaining the right material for his enterprise: the manuscripts.

He disembarked at Marseille on 19 November, 1606. After a short interim he was dispatched to Rome in diplomatic service once more. Italy was no less fitting for his ambitions. It had traditionally been the stronghold of early Oriental printing and abounded with an expertise which was sought in vain in the rest of Europe. As early as 1514, Agostino Giustiniani, orientalist and Bishop of Nebbio, had printed a polyglot Psalter comprising Latin, Greek, Hebrew, Aramaic and Arabic side by side.[29] The Medici Oriental Press, under Giovan Battista Raimondi, debuted with an edition of the Arabic Gospels in 1590, intended for dissemination in the Eastern Churches.[30] A second edition, accompanied with a Latin translation and directed to the European market, was published a year later. The establishment of the Medici Press had marked, as had that of the Maronite College in 1584, Pope Gregory XIII's official recognition of the connection between missionary objectives and Oriental studies. Gregory XIII was particularly interested in the publication of a printed Arabic Bible and willingly licensed Raimondi's *magnum opus*, a Polyglot in multiple languages.[31] Although Raimondi

---

29 Giustiniani, Agostino, *Psalterium Octaplum: Hebreum, Grecum, Arabicum, & Chaldeum: Cum Tribus Latinus Interpretationibus & Glossis*, Genuæ: Petrus Paulus Porrus 1516. See Bobzin, Hartmut, "Agostino Giustiniani (1470–1536) und seine Bedeutung für die Geschichte der Arabistik", in: *XXIV. Deutscher Orientalistentag vom 26. bis 30. September 1988 in Köln. Ausgewählte Vorträge*, W. Diem and A. Falaturi, eds., Stuttgart: Steiner 1990, 131–39; Vercellin, Giorgio, *Venezia e l'origine della Stampa in Caratteri Arabi*, Padova: Il poligrafo 2001. In the preface, Giustiniani promises an edition of the entire Bible in this form. The books of the New Testament are said to have been already completed. His departure for Paris on the invitation of the King of France to teach Hebrew at the *Collège Royal* impeded its accomplishment.

30 On Giovan Battista Raimondi and the Medici Press see Jones, John Robert, *The Arabic and Persian Studies of Giovan Battista Raimondi (c. 1536–1614)*, University of London 1981; Jones, Robert, "The Medici Oriental Press (Rome 1584–1614) and the Impact of Its Arabic Publications on Northern Europe", in: *The "Arabick" Interest of the Natural Philosophers in Seventeenth-Century England*, G. A. Russell, ed., Leiden and New York: E.J. Brill 1994, 88–108; Saltini, G. E., "Della Stamperia Orientale Medicea e di Giovan Battista Raimondi", *Giornale Storico degli Archivi Toscani* 4 (1860), 257–308; Tinto, Alberto, *La Tipografia Medicea Orientale* (Studi e Ricerche di Storia del Libro e delle Biblioteche, 1), Lucca: M. Pacini Fazzi 1987.

31 Prior to that, on 25 February, 1578, Pope Gregory XIII had bestowed on Giovan Battista Eliano, whom he dispatched on a mission to the Maronite Church, the special duty of finding manuscripts for editing and printing the Arabic Bible. Cf. Vaccari, Alberto, "Una Bibbia Araba Per Il Primo Gesuita Venuto Al Libano", *Mélanges de l'Université Saint-Joseph de Beyrouth* 10/4 (1925), 79–104. He returned with MS. Vatican Ar. 468, which ultimately

presented the project to the public in the preface to his *Liber Tasriphi*, it never came about for a variety of reasons.[32]

During the first years of his sojourn in Rome, Savary de Brèves took his first steps towards the establishment of a printing press, the *Typographia Savariana*. First, he recruited his collaborators, Gabriel Sionita (Jibrīl aṣ-Ṣaḥyūnī) and Vittorio Scialac Accurensis (Naṣrallāh Shalaq al-ᶜAqūrī) from the Maronite College, Husain, a Turk from Buda[33] and the printer Stefano Paolino, who had previously supervised the print for Raimondi. Further, he arranged the Arabic and Syriac types to be cut and compiled an Arabic–Italian–Latin dictionary (the *Calpin Arabesque*) to facilitate the projected translation enterprises.[34] The first printed work,

---

served as the basis for a revision towards the Vulgate and printed as *Biblia Sacra Arabica* (1671–73) by the *Congregatio de Propaganda Fide*.

For Raimondi's aspirations to print a Polyglot see Saltini, G., "La Bibbia Poliglotta Medicea secondo il Disegno e gli Apparecchi di Gio. Battista Raimondi", *Bollettino italiano degli studii orientali* 22 (1882), 490–5. In addition, he mentions his ambitions in his diary on 12 December, 1592, and 28 January, 1593, comp. Tinto, Alberto, "Un Diario di Giovanni Battista Raimondi (22 Giugno 1592–12 Dicembre 1596)", *Archivo Storico* 151 (1993), 671–84, no. 12, 674, and no. 18, 75. Raimondi had eagerly collected a good stock of Arabic and (Judaeo-) Persian manuscripts of the Bible. On his manuscript delegates to the East cf. Almalgia, R., "Giovan Battista Britti e Gerolamo Vecchietti Viaggiatori in Oriente", *Rendiconti dell'Academia Nazionale dei Lincei* 11 (1956), 313–50; idem, "Giovan Battista Britti Cosentino Viaggiatore in Oriente", *Archivio storico per la Calabria e la Lucania* 25 (1957), 75–101; Richard, Francis, "Les Manuscrits Persans Repportés par les Frères Vecchietti et Conservés aujourd'hui à la Bibliothèque Nationale", *Studia Iranica* 9 (1980), 291–300; idem, "Les Frères Vecchietti, Diplomates, Erudites et Aventuries", in Alastair Hamilton, Maurits Van Den Boogert and Bart Westerweel, eds., *The Republic of Letters and the Levant*, Leiden and Boston: Brill 2005, 11–26.

32 Raimundi, Giovan Battista, ed., *Liber Tasriphi Compositio Est Senis Alemami*, Romae: Ex Typographia Medicæ linguarum externarum 1610. With the death of Pope Gregory XIII and Ferdinando de' Medici's entry into politics, the project was deprived of its benefactors. His last academic print was the *ᶜItiqadāt al-amānah al-urthūdūksiyyah* by Giovan Battista Eliano in 1595, after which he applied himself to the printing of choral books. When Raimondi died in 1614, the Medici Oriental press effectively ceased operation.

33 On Husain, cf. Jones, John Robert, *Learning Arabic in Renaissance Europe (1505–1624)*, London: University of London 1988, 120–23.

34 MS. Paris BNF fr. Dupuy 812, fol. 195, in a letter addressed to Jacque August de Thou, 27 November, 1611: "*Je vous veux entretenir d'une envie grande que j'ai de rendre les langues arabicque et turquesque familières parmi nous, si j'étais aidé du roi ou de quelque autres personnes qui voulussent faire la dépense. J'ai auprès de moi un Turc que vous avez connu qui parle les susdites trois langues et écrit merveilleusement bien icelles. Il sait maintenant notre langue française et entend assez bien le latin. Je puis en recouvrer deux ou trois autres des prisons de Malte ou de celles de Monsieur le grand duc. J'ai retiré chez moi deux chrétiens maronites, de ceux que vivent dans le Mont Liban et qui par conséquent savent la langue arabique avec leur langue paternelle. Ils ont fait leurs études en cette ville dans un collège que les défunts saints Pères les Papes ont fondé à cet effet de façon qu'ils soient passés docteurs en philosophie et théologie […] J'ai aussi eu soin depuis que je suis ici d'apprendre le moyen de faire imprimer des livres des caractères desquelles les dites langues se forment. J'ai dépensé jusqu'à cette heure plus de deux mil écus pour en venir à bout, ce qui m'a réussi.*" MS. Paris BNF fr. Dupuy 812, fol. 107, dated 22 January, 1612: "*J'attendray la réponse de ce que je vous ai écrit sur l'établissement des langues orientales et principalement de l'Arabesque et de la Chaldéenne. J'ay trois*

an Arabic translation of the *Doctrina Christiana* by Cardinal Bellarmin, saw the light in 1613.[35] A year later, he issued a Psalter in Arabic that was printed in two editions, the first in Arabic alone and the second with Latin translation in a separate column facing the Arabic. In the preface we are told that Savary de Brèves secured the very manuscript for this print in Jerusalem during his journey.[36]

The book, however, constituted a mere *coup d'essai* for a much larger project. In a letter dated 15 August, 1612, and addressed to Jacque August de Thou, president of the parliament and custodian at the *Bibliothèque du Roi*, as well as de Brèves' cousin-in-law and long-time correspondent, he first presented the whole extent of his ambitions: "Le Vieux et le Nouvel Testament et quelque Psaumes de David en langues arabesques, traduits en nostre langue latine et imprimés en l'une et l'autre caractère, seront bien venus de nos docteurs."[37] De Thou embraced the printing of a complete Arabic Bible enthusiastically and offered his patronage to the project, albeit advising to concentrate on the Pentateuch first. De Brèves states:

> "*Monsieur, je vous supplie trouvez bon que j'apprenne de vous si le Vieux et le Nouveau Testament et les Psaumes de David en langues arabesque et chaldée, traduits en notre langue latine et imprimés en l'un et l'autre caractère seront bien reçus de nos doctes et si semblables livres se pourraient débiter. J'ai moyen de satisfaire à cette curiosité là.*"[38]

Although he initially demurred on account of time and costs, the project was initiated and assumed shape rapidly. Sionita had commenced editing the manuscript that was eventually to become MS. Paris BNF Ar. 1. In fact, the manuscript preserves many editorial notes by his hand marking lacunae and indicating chapter and verse divisions (see Plate 3).[39] Moreover, the formulaic *incipits* and *excipits* of each biblical book were maintained in the edition. Similar to the text that he had secured in Jerusalem for the print of the Psalms in 1614, it stands to reason that

---

ou quatre hommes avec moi capables de l'intelligence d'y celles et fait faire des lettres pour imprimer." To the best of my knowledge, the *Calpin arabesque* unfortunately has not survived.

35 Similar to the approach of the Medici Oriental Press – and most probably modelled on its example – a bilingual edition followed in 1619. Sionita, Gabriel, and Scialac, Vittorio, eds., *Doctrina Christiana: Illustrissimi & Reuerendiss. D.D. Roberti S.R.E. Card. Bellarmini, Nunc Primùm ex Italico Idiomate in Arabicum, Iussu S.D.N. Pauli V. Pont. Max. Translata per Victorium Scialat Accurensem, & Gabrielem Sionitam Edeniensem, Maronitas e Monte Libano, Philosophiae, ac Sacra Theologiae Professores*, Romae: Ex typographia Savariana. Excudebat Stephanus Paulinus 1619. I have been able to consult only the bilingual edition.

36 Scialac, Vittorio, and Sionita, Gabriel, eds., *Dauidis Regis et Prophetae Psalmi*, Romae: Ex Typographia Savariana. Excudebat Stephanus Paulinus 1619. The preface is reprinted in Balagna Coustou, Josée, *L'imprimerie Arabe En Occident : XVIe, XVIIe et XVIIIe Siècles*, Paris: Editions Maisonneuve & Larose 1984, 16. As demonstrated by A. Vaccari, the manuscript is today found under the class mark MS. Vatican Ar. 584, cf. Vaccari, Alberto, "I Caratteri Arabi della 'Typographia Savariana'", *Rivista degli Studi Orientali* 10 (1923–25), 37–47.

37 MS. Paris BNF fr. Dupuy 812, fol. 237.

38 MS. Paris BNF fr. Dupuy 812, fol. 237, dated 15 September, 1612.

39 E.g. Gen. 19:22–20:2 and Gen. 45:17–46:7 are marked by Sionita as wanting; the text Lev. 9:12 ff. is noted as being superfluous due to an error by the scribe. Sionita indicated the chapter divisions in Latin on the outer margins and in Arabic on the inner.

also the later Parisian copy came into his possession during that journey. Details of the actual acquisition are not known, but it may be assumed that it took place in Cairo. There, the manuscript had been produced twenty years earlier and must have come to de Brèves' attention during his stay.[40] The manuscript was on the whole most apt for the project, since it contained the entire Old Testament with only the minor defect of dispensing with the Book of Ruth. The diplomat, thus, communicated the progress to de Thou in April 1613:

> "*Je suivrai vos louable conseils et ferai travailler aux versions du Vieux et Nouveau Testament le plus diligemment qu'il me sera possible. Mais comme je vous ai ja mandé cela ne pourra pas être fait d'une couple d'années pourvu que je puisse garder avec moi l'un des pères maronites. Le reste se pourra finir en France.*"[41]

In the meantime, as it emerges from the last letter, de Brèves had received notice that his service in Rome was about to terminate in 1614. He had been called back to France by Maria de' Medici, queen consort of France, to attend to the education of her son Gaston, Duke of Orleans and brother of the later king Louis XIII. In June 1613, however, the book of Genesis had been completed and it appears even that the preparation of Saadiah's *tafsīr* was accomplished in its entirety before he departed for Paris.[42]

4 The Paris Polyglot

In 1614 Savary de Brèves returned to Paris, bringing with him not only the printing press, types and manuscripts, but also his collaborators: Gabriel Sionita, Husain of Buda and Stefano Paolino. Vittorio Scialac Accurensis had been replaced by Jean Hesronita (Yuḥanna al-Haṣrūnī), another alumnus of the Maronite College.[43] The press was installed at the *Collège des Lombards* and was prepared for

40 In a letter to de Thou he makes particular mention of Egypt as a source for reliable manuscripts of the Arabic Bible: "*Il faudroit faire venir d'Egypte des livres qui eussent le texte beau.*" MS. Paris BNF fr. Dupuy 812, fol. 255, dated 17 February, 1613.

41 MS. Paris BNF fr. Dupuy 812, fol. 260.

42 MS. Paris BNF fr. Dupuy 812, fol. 265, dated 9 June, 1613: "*Les peres maronites travaillent aux cinq livre de Moise, la Genèse est déjà faite*"; MS. Paris BNF fr. Dupuy 812, fols. 255–257, dated 3 August, 1613, mentions: "*Pour ce qui est du Vieux Testament j'espère bien avant que je parte d'ici qu'il sera traduit, mais non imprimé. Ce sera à mon retour par delà si Dieu plait.*" The most valuable evidence that the Pentateuch had already been completed in Rome, however, is found in Guy Michel Le Jay's later accusations against Sionita, preserved under the title "Raisons de Sr. Le Jay contre le Sr. Gabriel pour la traduction de la Bible Arabique", MS. Paris BNF fr. 18600. In this, he claims that Sionita cannot be credited with having compiled the entire edition of the Arabic Bible, since he arrived in Paris with a complete edition of the Pentateuch in Arabic at hand.

43 Scialac would dedicate himself to the compilation of Arabic grammars at the Maronite College; Vittorio Scialac Accurensis, *Introductio ad Grammaticam Arabicam*, Romae: Excudebat Stephanus Paulinus 1622, idem, *Totum Arabicum Alphabetum, ad unam Tabellam cum suis Vocalibus et Signis, Facilitatis Causa, Reductum*, Romae: Apud Stephanum Paulinum 1624.

operation. Despite the fact that he had been unable to secure the financial means for a *Collège Polyglotte des Langues Orientales*,[44] which had been projected to serve as an academic institution for the accomplishment of the huge task of editing and translating, the work on MS. Paris BNF Ar. 1 resumed with Cardinal du Perron's decision to engage in the reprint of the Antwerp Polyglot in the very same year. The Cardinal had been de Brèves' predecessor as ambassador in Rome and had shown a particular concern for Arabic printing.[45] The reprint was intended to include Oriental versions as well, which were perceived as of utmost value for the clarification of many unclear passages in the Scriptures and to establish an authentic biblical text.[46] In a letter of 3 May, 1615, de Thou informed Sebastian Tengnagel, curator at the Imperial Library, Vienna:

> "Our librarians are currently preparing a new edition of the Bible, which will feature the Chaldaic paraphrases more accurately than the edition of Alcalá and that of Antwerp. It will as well append the Syriac and Arabic versions of the Old and New Testament, with Latin translations. Cardinal du Perron urges the printing and has appointed me as deputy in that project."[47]

Although du Perron was granted the approbation of the General Assembly of Clergy in 1616, he fell short of securing another essential matter: the funding. In

---

44 In a letter to de Thou: "*Moyennant cela j'ai un moyen de faire un collège d'un bon nombre de jeunes gens qui pourraient étudier les dites langues. J'ai aussi eu soin depuis que je suis ici d'apprendre le moyen de faire imprimer des livres des caractères desquels les dites langues se forment. J'ai dépensé jusqu'à cette heure plus de deux mil écus pour venir à bout ce qui m'a réussi, de façon que si vous pouviez induire Sa Majesté à vouloir fonder un collège des dites langues, l'université de Paris en recevrait de l'honneur et le christianisme de l'utile, car par ce moyen nous aurions la communication de toutes les sciences de ces trois nations.*"; MS. Paris BNF fr. Dupuy 812, fol. 195, dated 27 November, 1611. Additional documents are found in Omont, H., "Projet D'un Collège Oriental a Paris Au Début Du Règne De Louis Xiii", *Bulletin de la Société de l'histoire de Paris et de l'Île de France* 22 (1895), 123–27. Sionita and Hesronita, however, received an annual pension by royal order. The grant is published in Bernard, Auguste Joseph, *Antoine Vitré et les Caractères Orientaux de la Bible Polyglotte de Paris. Origines et Vicissitudes des Premiers Caractères Orientaux Introduits en France avec un Specimen de ces Caractères*, Paris: Dumoulin 1857, 5. In addition, Sionita held the chair of Arabic at the *Collège Royal*, replacing Etienne Hubert (1568–1614).

45 As recalled by Raimondi in the preface to his *Liber Tasriphi*.

46 "*Adhuc Sacrorum scriptorium locos tenebris quibusdam, ac fulgine involutos, aut verborum ambiguitate circumseptos, quibus quasi ambagibus, tortuosisque nexibus doctorum ingenia detinentur, in hac eadem lingua claros, immo luce meridiana clariores deprehendes*" (Sionita, Gabriel, and Hesronita, Jean, *Grammatica Arabica Maronitarum*, Paris: ex Typographia Savariana, excudebat Hieronymus Blageart 1616, sig. aii^{r}–aii^{v}). Cf. a similar statement of de Thou in des Maizeaux, Pierre, ed., *Scaligerana, Thuana, Perroniana, Pithoenana, et Colomesiana*, Amsterdam: Covens & Mortier 1740, 94. For a general survey see Bobzin, Hartmut, "Vom Sinn des Arabischstudiums im Sprachkanon der Philologia Sacra", *Hallesche Beiträge zur Orientwissenschaft* 24 (1998), 21–32.

47 "*Librarii nostri novam Bibliorum editionem parant, cui post Hispanam et ultimam Antverpianam, meliorem paraphrasin Chaldaicam sive Syriacam et Arabicam versionem in Vetus et Novum Testamentum addent cum inpretatione Latina peculiari. Illustrissimus Cardinalis Perronus opus urget et vicaria opera nostra ad eam rem ubitur*", published in Lambeck, Petrus, *Commentariorum de Augustissima Bibliotheca Caesarea Vindobonensi*, Vienna: Typis Joannis Christophori Cosmerovii 1665–1679, 160.

consequence, the work on the Arabic Bible came to a standstill. The decision of Stefano Paolino, Raimondi's former printer, to return to Rome was another great loss.[48] The state of affairs worsened further when de Thou, ardent promoter of the project from the beginning, died in 1617, as did Cardinal du Perron a year later. Due to his affiliation with Maria de' Medici, Savary de Brèves fell from political favour after the assassination of Concini, the result of a secret plot organised by Louis XIII. He was forced into retirement from public life and therewith the press effectively ceased operation in 1618.[49] He died in 1627. The project thus lost all of its patrons within two years. Sionita and Hesronita decided to address themselves to different tasks. In 1616 they published an Arabic grammar and furnished a Latin translation of Raimondi's *Geographia Nubiensis* in 1619.[50] Also when Hesronita eventually returned to Lebanon in 1622, Sionita continued to issue books at his own expense.[51]

The work on MS. Paris BNF Ar. 1 gained renewed attention when the Parisian advocate Guy Michel Le Jay offered the much-needed financial means for the accomplishment of the Polyglot printing project. Consequently, it recommenced under his supervision in March 1628. On the whole, as the following list of collaborators shows, the resumption marked a rather drastic rupture in the continuity with earlier stages. Antoine Vitré was made chief printer and ordered to acquire Savary de Brèves' manuscripts and types.[52] Philippe d'Aquin was charged

---

48 Upon his return to Rome, Paolino was employed at the press of the Maronite College and later at that of the *Congregatio de Propaganda Fide*. With some justice, he might be called the eminence of Oriental printing and constitutes the personal link between all important printing projects of the Arabic Bible.

49 Erpenius furnishes evidence on his mental derangement after that event in a letter to Sebastian Tengnagel, dated Leiden, 1 February, 1621; cf. MS. Vienna Österreichische Nationalbibliothek 9737s, fol. 220: "*Dominus de Bréves animum omnino ab illis literis abiecit, me quidquam praestat aut praestiturus est. Vidi nuper cum in Gallia essem hominem. Sed comperi eum ita irritatum et offensum capitie diminutione, ut frustra ego futuros iudicem literatos, qui in re literaria, aliquid porro ab eo volent exspectare. D. Sansium, quod in aula esset semel atque iterum frustra domi eius quaesivi. Nec librorum eius catalogum hactenus nancisci potui.*" Quoted in Jones, *Learning Arabic*, 35–36.

50 Anonymous, *Geographia Nubiensis, id Est Accuratissima Totius Orbis in Septem Climata Divisi Descriptio, Continens Præsertim Exactam Universæ Asiæ Et Africæ Explicationem. Recens Ex Arabico in Latinum Versa a Gabriele Sionita et Joanne Hesronita*, Paris: H. Blageart 1619; Sionita and Hesronita, *Grammatica Arabica Maronitarum*. The latter was designed to have five volumes. However, only the first, dealing with pronunciation, appeared.

51 Sionita, Gabriel, *Liber Psalmorum Dauidis Regis et Prophetæ ex Idiomate Syro in Latinum translates*, Paris: Antoine Vitré 1625; idem, *Veteris Philosophi Syri de Sapientia Divina Poëma Aenigmaticum*, Paris: Antoine Vitré 1628. On Hesronita's return cf. the documents published in Gemayel, Nasser, *Les Echanges Culturels Entre les Maronites et l'Europe: Du Collège Maronite de Rome (1584) au Collège de Ayn-Warqa (1789)*, Beyrouth, Liban: Impr. Y. et Ph. Gemayel 1984, 224, no. 30 and 225, no. 31.

52 As seen above, Vitré had gathered some experience in oriental printing through the publication of Sionita's works in 1625 and 1628. He had also printed Andre Du Ryer's *Rudimenta Grammatices Linguæ Turcicæ* (Paris, 1630). At the urging of Cardinal Richelieu, he purchased the types and manuscripts from de Brèves' heirs in 1632. There is some evi-

with the improvement of the Hebrew and Aramaic portions previously printed in the Antwerp Polyglot and Jean Morin was commissioned to edit the Samaritan Pentateuch, including its Targum.[53] Further collaborators were Jérôme Parent, Godefroy Hermant, Jean Aubert and Jean Tarin. Gabriel Sionita, the only remaining participant, had received the much larger mandate of preparing the Old and the New Testaments in both Syriac and Arabic versions, including their translation into Latin.

By the end of the following year the first four volumes, comprising the Pentateuchal books of the Antwerp Polyglot – predecessor to the Paris Polyglot – rolled off the press. The Masoretic text, the Targum, the Septuagint and the Vulgate were reproduced without many changes. The fifth volume featured the New Testament and was printed between the years 1630 and 1633. Its Syriac version had already been part of the Antwerp Polyglot and Sionita supplied the Arabic text, for which he reused Raimondi's edition and Latin translation of 1592 with minor corrections. In 1632 the sixth volume was accomplished and Saadiah's *tafsīr* printed. The tome exhibits the Peshitta with translation on the left hand page and the Arabic text with Latin facing the Syriac on the right.[54] On the bottom of the page Morin's Samaritan versions are found, Hebrew and Aramaic with one Latin translation for both (see pls. 4 and 5).

The other volumes of the Old Testament, however, remained the sole responsibility of Sionita. Lacking a collaborator, he was overwhelmed by the colossal task and, although the eighth tome was printed in 1635, none of the remaining

---

dence, however, that they remained in Sionita's possession until his imprisonment in 1640. He had been reluctant to deliver them to the printer, who had to get hold of them by means of royal intervention and the assistance of commissar Boissy, cf. Aboussouan, Camille, *Exposition le Livre et Le Liban jusqu'à 1900*, Paris: Unesco AGECOOP 1982, 210–11. There are two different inventories of de Brèves' manuscripts: they are preserved in MSS Paris BNF fr. 15528 and Dupuy 673, fols. 131–32. The first was published as an appendix to Bernard (1857). However, none of them seems to be complete. Sionita was allowed to retain the manuscript he was working on, i.e. MS. Paris BNF Ar. 1. Thus, unlike the other manuscripts, it was not deposited in Richelieu's library. That appears to be the reason why it reached the BNF from the Colbert collection. The history of the de Brèves collection of manuscripts deserves further research.

53 Jean Morin de Blois (1591–1650) was a convert from Protestantism. The manuscripts had been purchased by Pietro della Valle in Damascus in 1616 and procured for the Oratory by Harley de Sancy, de Brèves' successor as ambassador to the Sublime Porte, in 1623. The Pentateuch manuscript is MS. B, in Freiherr von Gall, August, *Der Hebräische Pentateuch der Samaritaner*, Giessen: Verlag von Alfred Töpelmann 1914, III. It was Cardinal de Bérulle who adviced its publication. As did Jean Morin, he considered the Samaritan Pentateuch older than the Massoretic text and free of "rabbanic interpolations". The variant readings were published separately in Paris in 1657. On Morin, cf. Auvray, Paul, "Jean Morin (1591–1659)", *Revue Biblique* 66 (1959), 397–414.

54 So it had been designed by de Thou and de Brèves: "*J'en ai une en arabesque et en recouvrerai une en chaldée. Nous les affronterons?*" BNF MSS. fr. Dupuy 812, fol. 265, dated 9 June, 1613. The manuscript of the Peshitta was furnished by Jean Hesronita, who copied it himself from a *Vorlage* that had been brought to Italy by Sarkīs al-Rizzī. It is preserved as MS. Paris BNF Syr. 6 and bears the sigla 17a6 in the standard Leiden edition.

parts was even close to completion five years later. Consequently, Sionita was urged to vindicate the delay that increasingly presented a severe financial risk to the entire project.[55] Le Jay, with the help of Cardinal Richelieu, had him imprisoned at Vincennes in 1640. Sionita was released under the condition that he finishes the editing of the remaining volumes by Easter that year. Meanwhile, plans were made to replace him and Abraham Ecchellensis (Ibrāhīm al-Ḥāqilānī), another alumnus of the Maronite college and at that time heading the rival printing project of an Arabic Bible at the *Congregatio de Propaganda Fide*, was brought to Paris. He completed work on the Books of Ruth and 2 Maccabees, but returned to Rome a year later. The last two volumes, finally, were printed in 1642 and 1645.

The project led to Le Jay's total bankruptcy. Cardinal Richelieu had earlier offered to bear the printing costs if it were published under his name. Le Jay had declined at that time. The Cardinal, in turn, now commissioned a treatise to point out the errors and inaccuracies of the completed Polyglot. Harsh criticism ensued as a number of pamphleteers sided with him against Le Jay. About this time the English booksellers offered to take 600 copies at half price, which the editor declined. The Paris Polyglot, therefore, did not sell and it is said that a great number of copies were destroyed as waste paper. What is more, it was soon overshadowed by the London Polyglot (1653–57), the last and greatest.

55 In a letter to Le Jay he would stress the technical impossibility of quickening the preparation of the text, cf. in *Paris – Archives du Collège de France, C–XII, Sionite 1*: "*Qu'on n'a jamais imprimé qu'une forme ou demi-feuille par jour, que son ouvrage contient deux mille six cents vingt sept formes, qu'en l'année il n'y a que deux cents soixante et sept jours ouvrables ; conséquemment pour imprimer deux mille six cents vingt sept formes, il faut l'espace de huit années entières. Or, si pour la seule impression il fallu employer huit années, sans considérer le temps pour mettre les voyelles et faire les versions, donc le Sieur Le Jay a grand tort de dire que le dit de Sion pouvait achever l'ouvrage en trois ou quatre ans.*" Or he would compare his work to that of his predecessors of the Alcala and Antwerp Polyglots: "*N'a été fait qu'en quinze années, encore que sept grand personnages y furent employés. A celle d'Anvers, quatre personnes e grand mérite y employèrent douze années, bien que dans l'une et l'autre il n'y a rien qui n'eut été imprimé. Le grec à Venise et l'hébreu à Pesaro et Mantoue. Si ces personnages qui étaient en grand nombre et de très grande érudition ont employé des douze et quinze années pour copier ce qu'ils avaient devant eux, quel sujet a le dit Le Jay de sa plaindre que le dit de Sion seul employé treize années à mettre au net deux textes qui n'avaient jamais été imprimés, pour en faire les versions tout de nouveau, et leur mettre les voyelles, accents, et tous autres point nécessaires à la lecture et intelligence, labeur qui équivolle à celui des Massorètes en l'hébreu?*"

The Holy Books in Arabic: The example of the *Propaganda Fide* Edition

Paul Féghali

Ordered by the Congregation for the Propagation of the Faith, the Holy Bible was published in Arabic in 1671, for the use of the Oriental Churches.[1] It was a major event as, until then, there had not been a complete edition of the Bible in Arabic, let alone a "flawless" version. Thus, Rome took charge of this project, which would take more than half a century to come to fruition.

We will start by analysing the circumstances that helped bring this Bible to completion. We will examine what came before and after it, studying in depth a text that was far from Classical Arabic and had rather what researchers describe as a "Middle Arabic" character. This refers to the Arabic that emerged from monasteries and was directly addressed to the people, impregnated as it was to a great extent with their liturgical languages: Greek, Syriac and Coptic.

1. Circumstances of the Bible's publication.

Long before the 17th century, Rome had taken an interest in the Orient. In 1584, the Roman College was founded on the instigation of Pope Gregory XIII (1572–1585). Before that, two missions were sent to Rome in 1569 at the request of the Maronite Patriarch Mikhāʾīl al-Rizzī, who called for the creation of a school for the priests of this community. The mission, formed by the Jesuit priests Ragio and Eliano along with two students,[2] arrived in Rome on 8 June, 1579. After the Maronite College was founded, the "future" Maronite priests began flocking to Rome, until the College was closed by Napoleon's army.

These students were a key motivation for the papacy to launch the Bible project. Moreover, many legates were fearful of a "heretical" movement in the Orient, and wanted at all costs to ward off this danger, which had actually started in Europe.

For example, the Dutch orientalist, Thomas Erpenius, published the New Testament in 1616 and the Pentateuch in 1622, both in Arabic.

1 *Biblia Sacra Arabica Sacrae Congregationis de Propagande Fide jussu edita ad usum ecclesiarum orientalium: additis e regione Bibia Latinis Vulgatis,* 3 vols., Rome: Typis eiusdum Sacrae Congregat. de Propaganda Fide 1971.

2 جبرائيل سعد الأدنيتيّ من بان (في شمال لبنان)، غسبار غريب من جزيرة قبرص.
Vat. Lat. 5528, fol. 352; Vat. Syr. 410, fol. 772.

Eventually, many translations for the biblical texts were completed in the early 17th century. It was therefore necessary to standardize the different texts and present one complete version that would be in accordance with the Latin Vulgate.[3]

In 1622, the Nuncio appointed four persons to translate the Bible into Arabic. The president of this committee was the Maronite Archbishop of Damascus, Sarkīs b. Mūsā al-Rizzī.[4] He studied in Rome and was in charge of this work until his death in 1638. He copied the largest part of the manuscript Casanatense arab. carsh. 2 (2108).

The committee included another Maronite, Naṣrāllah Shalaq al-ʿAqūrī.[5] He also studied in Rome, where he taught Arabic and Syriac, and died in 1635. As we can see, two initiators of this project died long before the final text was published. As a result, the Arabic Bible would ultimately be much closer to the text of the Latin Vulgate – and less faithful to the manuscripts – than it otherwise would have been, a fact much criticized at the time of publication.[6]

The two other members were Fr Hilarion Rancati, the general abbot of the Cistercian Order, and a Franciscan, Thomas Olicini of Novara, a missionary to Syria and to the Custody of the Holy Land. The latter presented the work plan to the Congregation in 1622.

After the death of Mgr al-Rizzī in 1638, Filippo Guadagnoli took charge of the project. He died in 1656.

---

3 Such was the ruling of the Council of Trent in its fourth session (8 April, 1546): the biblical texts must be in accordance with the Vulgate. See Denzinger, Heinrich, *Enchiridion Symbolorum, Definitionum et Declarationum de rebus fidei et morum*, Freiburg i. Br.: Herder 1991, no. 1505.

4 In Latin: Sergius Risius. He took charge of the printing of the Book of Psalms, published in 1610 at the Monastery of St Antoine of Qozhaya. See:

بولس الفغالي، «طلاّب المدرسة المارونيّة وترجمة الكتاب المقدَّس» في *دراسات في الآداب والعلوم الإنسانيّة*، ١٢، (العددان ١٦-١٧/٨٥) ، بعنوان مدرسة *روما المارونيّة ١٥٨٤-١٩٨٤*، ١٥١-١٧٤.

Here p. 155 (hereafter *Dirāsāt*).

Mgr Rizzī was a hermit at Qozhaya after he came back to Lebanon. His uncle, Patriarch Sarkīs, sent him to Rome to declare the submission of the Maronite community to Pope Paul V after his election in 1605.

5 In Latin: Victorinus (النصر) Scialac Accurensis. In *Dirāsāt*, p. 161, Victorinus has a doctorate in philosophy and theology. He worked with Sionita on the printing of the Book of Psalms and its translation into Latin (*Liber psalmorum Davidis regis et prophetae*, Romae 1614); he also translated Job from Syriac into Latin (*Libri justi Job ex chaldeo sive syro idiomate in latinum interpretatio*, Romae 1618); he also translated on the instigation of Pope Paul V the four Gospels (*Quatuor Jesu Christi Evangelium ex chaldaeo, i diomate in latinum interpretatio,* Jussu Pauli PP V Expleta an. 1617). See Gemayel, N., *Les échanges culturels entre les Maronites et l'Europe; du Collège Maronite de Rome (1584) au Collège de 'Ain-Waraqa (1789),* Beirut 1984, 377–378, 475–477.

6 Lobrichon, G., "Versions anciennes de la Bible, B. La Vulgate", in: *Dictionnaire Encyclopédique de la Bible*, Turnhout: Brepols 1982, 1322–1323: "Elle orienta la polémique contre les Juifs… En fait, les Pélagiens firent bon accueil à cette traduction". ("It directed the polemic against the Jews… In fact, the Pelagians welcomed this translation.")

Fr Thomas died in 1630, leaving his responsibilities to his student, Brother Dominus Germanus of Silesia.[7] Without the help of another eminent Maronite scientist, Ibrāhīm al-Ḥāqilānī,[8] it would have been difficult for him to continue the project. He started his work quite early and carried it on until his death in 1664.

Finally, we have to mention another Maronite, Yūḥannā al-Ḥaṣrūnī,[9] who took on the task. He died in 1632. At the end, a Capuchin, Brother Brice, corrected the translation with the help of Louis Maracci, a researcher known for his analysis of the *Qurʾān*.

The policy of the group changed during these fifty years that were "necessary" to publish the *Propaganda Fide* edition. In the beginning, in 1622, the emphasis was laid upon the examination of the different Arabic manuscripts in order to produce one text, "free of heresies and mistakes". In 1624, however, a decision was taken to translate the Vulgate, meaning that a whole tradition of some centuries was completely overlooked, as if nothing had been achieved in Arabic before the 17th century; more dangerously, the original Hebrew, Aramaic and Greek texts were disregarded. Instead, the work was based on a Latin version that was very polemical in its time. I was even going to say that the text was not compatible with the Bible itself, but rather with theology – the *bête noire* of the Church being "heresy".

In 1628, a new policy was adopted; the translation would follow the Vulgate as much as the Arabic text allowed, and go back to the Hebrew or Greek when the Arabic and Latin were incompatible. At the end, a new revision of the text was made in 1643 and involved tightening the text of the Vulgate as much as possible, from the end of Ezekiel.[10]

In 1632, al-Rizzī started printing Genesis. The group completed the text of the Pentateuch in 1635. In 1647, the Old Testament was completed, followed by the New Testament in 1649. However, they included some "mistakes" that had to be rectified, and some passages that did not follow the text of the Vulgate. Hence a last revision, after which the text finally appeared in 1671, meaning that neither al-Rizzī nor the first collaborators would see the fruit of their labour.[11]

---

7 See: de Gonsague, L., in *Collectanea Franciscana* 1 (1931). Quoted in Graf, Georg, *Geschichte der christlichen arabischen Literatur,* Vatican, vol. I, 97.

8 In Latin: Abraham Ecchelensis. He taught Arabic and Syriac in many European cities, and was the interpreter for the Congregation for the Propagation of the Faith.

9 In Latin: Johannes Leopardus Esronite. In Arabic: يوحنّا بن دايس بن يعقوب بن فهد الحصروني
He entered the Dominican Order and took the name of John the Baptist.

10 This Bible followed the sequence of the Vulgate (Denzinger, 1502), meaning that the Pentateuch, the historical books, the Psalms, and the Books of Wisdom, Jeremiah, Isaiah and a large part of Ezekiel were not subject to this new policy.

11 This approach can be read in the double introduction to the work, which was printed in three volumes. The first volume starts with Genesis and ends with 2 Chronicles (472 pages). The second starts with Ezra and ends with 2 Maccabees (526 pages). The third encompasses the New Testament (283 pages). At the end are three appendices. The Latin is

Marhaj al-Bānī,[12] nephew of Ibrāhīm al-Ḥaqilānī, wrote the preface. "Most of the nations went astray from the right track, deviated toward different errors, and took false, rotten paths; but God did not allow that the books that contain his Word be lost, so that every language on earth admits that in his Word is the right path toward salvation and happiness."

Marhaj writes further: "As for the Word that God revealed, it was first written by the prophets and apostles, each one in the language of his land or of his people. It was then transmitted in other languages, so that all nations know the Word of God for the salvation of all."

The preface underlined the importance of the Latin used by the Holy Roman Catholic and Apostolic Church. "This Latin version," says al-Bānī, "is in harmony with the meaning and most of the terms used in the original texts, namely the Hebrew and Greek."

But that was not the case in other languages, especially Arabic. "Things changed because of the different orders and heretics, due to a lack of education and faith…" Thus, only a few manuscripts laden with mistakes remained. At that point, the wish of Pope Urban VIII (1623–1644) converged with that of the archbishops and bishops of the Orient. Archbishop Sarkīs was asked to gather at his residence many scientists, theologians, monks, priests, laymen and professors of Arabic, Hebrew, Greek and other languages, to assist them in correcting the Arabic text.[13]

Al-Bānī described the method of work that started, according to him, in 1625. The group read the Arabic manuscripts, compared them with the Hebrew and Greek original texts, and chose what sounded correct and in accordance with them. Afterwards, they added what was missing and corrected what was erroneous in the light of the Vulgate.

And what about the language? It is definitely Middle rather than Classical Arabic. Even some vowels were dropped, especially at the end of the words. Arabic was actually for Christians "another language, if not a *second* language".[14] As a matter of fact, this *Propaganda Fide* edition was written between two epochs: the

---

that of the Vulgate and does not always correspond to the Arabic. But as the work progresses, the Arabic text is brought nearer to the Latin. See Vaccari, A., "Una Bibbia Araba per il primo Gesuita ventuto al Libano", *Mélanges de l'Université Saint-Joseph (MUSJ)* X (1925), 79–104.

12 In Latin: Fauste Nairon. He studied in Rome. In 1650, he was ordained a priest by Patriarch Yūḥannā al-Ṣafrāwī, who sent him to Rome to prepare the ordinal التعبدات. For that purpose, he needed the texts of the New Testament, he printed in 1703 – the Syriac and facing it the Arabic in Karshuni – in two volumes: the Gospels and the rest of the New Testament.

13 *Dirāsāt*, 163.

14 Griffith, S., "Les premières versions arabes de la Bible. Les liens avec la langue syriaque", in: *L'ancien Testament en syriaque* (Études Syriaques, 5), Paris: Geuthner 2008, 221–245, here 239. See also Blau, J., *A Grammar of Christian Arabic 9* (CSCO, vols. 267, 276, 279), Louvain: CSCO 1966–1967.

Abbasid epoch, which produced prose rhymed texts such as that of ʿAbdishūʾ; and the modern epoch, characterised by a return to Classical Arabic in what was called the "Arabic Renaissance" in the 19th century. One of its pioneers was Ibrāhīm al-Yāzijī who wanted to pit himself against the text of the Qurʾān and even outshine it.

But before reading the texts that preceded or followed the *Propaganda Fide* edition, I would like to have a look at the manuscripts that were read or consulted, at those that were chosen as a basis for work.

Fr Vaccari gives us a helpful hint when he cites MS. Vat. Ar. 468, which includes all the Old Testament except the Book of Baruch.[15] What is interesting here for us is that MS. 419, which resembles the *Propaganda Fide* edition to a great extent with its grammatical mistakes,[16] can be found in the *Bibliothèque Orientale* of Beirut.

MS. Vat. Ar. 468 was copied in Tripoli, in northern Lebanon, under the watchful eye of Fr Jean-Baptiste Eliano, the first Jesuit sent by the Pope to Lebanon. According to the colophon, it is a copy done in Damascus in 1238, and the copy was written in Antakya (Antioch) in 1021.[17]

Where does this manuscript come from? We deal here with two theories: Fr Vaccari believes that the Pentateuch is based on the Septuagint (LXX), with an influence of the *Peshiṭta*; whereas Graf considers it to have been taken first from the *Peshiṭta*. His argument is based among other things on the way proper names are written.

For the historical books, from Joshua to Nehemiah, there is no doubt: it is the text of the *Peshiṭta*. The same goes for the Books of Esther and Job. Tobias was taken from the Vulgate, which differs greatly from the Septuagint, and Judith was taken from the Septuagint.[18]

---

15 "Una Bibbia Araba", 94ff. We find at the end of the article a page from Deuteronomy
بسم الله الرحمن الرحيم، السفر الخامس من التورية (التوراة) المسمّى تثنية الاشتراع وهو عشرون إصحاحًا. الإصحاح الأوّل: «هذا القول الذي قاله موسى لبني إسرائيل كلّهم وهم في عبر الإردنّ... »

16 Cheikho, Louis, *Catalogue raisonné des manuscrits de la Bibliothèque Orientale*, vol. 4: *Philosophie et Écriture Sainte* (*Mélanges de l'Université Saint Joseph*, 10,5), Beyrouth: Impr. Catholique, 1925 (Kraus Reprint 1973). An example is given on pp. 149–151 (Gen. 49):
دعا يعقوب بنيه وقال لهم: اجتمعوا فأنبّيكم بما يصير بكم في آخر الأيّام، أنصتوا يا بني يعقوب واسمعوا إسرائيل أبيكم: روبيل بكري، قوّتي، ورأس عنائي. أوّلاً في العطايا وأعظم في العزّة. ظللتُ (= ضللت) مثل الباب لا تلبث، لأنّك ارتقيت إلى مضجع أبيك .
However, the Ben Sirach/Ecclesiasticus text no. 420 of the *Bibliothèque Orientale* is not in the slightest different from the second volume of the *Propaganda Fide* edition. We read on page 2:
المقدِّمة عن مصنَّف مجهول. هذا يشوع كان ابن سيراخ ابن يشوع وكان لهما اسم واحد... (ص ١٥١-١٥٢)

17 Graf, Georg, *Geschichte der christlichen arabischen Literatur*, Città del Vaticano: Biblioteca Apostolica Vaticana 1944, vol. I, 89–92. Since this colophon was placed at the end of 2 Maccabees, the question was asked if it relates to the whole Bible or only to that particular book.

18 Thompson, J. A., *The Major Arabic Bibles, Their Origin and Nature*, New York. American Bible Society 1956, 17–18.

The Book of Psalms, according to Graf (II, pp. 52–64), is the text of Abū-l-Faṭh ʿAbdallāh b. al-Faḍl al-Muṭrān al-Anṭākī.[19] The Books of Proverbs, Ecclesiastes, Canticles, Wisdom and Ecclesiasticus were taken from the Septuagint. The Prophets paraphrased the *Peshiṭta* with the Septuagint in mind. According to Löfgren,[20] Daniel is based on the Greek with a revision of the Syriac. Finally, 2 Maccabees is based on the Greek.

As we can see, this manuscript is not homogeneous, as it contains texts taken from various sources – Greek, Syriac and Syriac–Greek. Vaccari mentions in this same context two Arabic manuscripts (Vat. Ar. 489 and 490), from which he quotes short passages.[21]

Another MS. was largely copied by Sergius Risius from Vat. Ar. 606 (1344). It is Casanatense arabe. Carsh 2 (no. 2108),[22] which contains the Pentateuch. It is based on the *Peshiṭta*, but reviewed according to the Septuagint, be it directly from the Greek or indirectly from a Coptic copy based on the Greek. Vaccari gives an example from Gen. 41:43, concerning Joseph:

- "They mounted him on a second chariot."[23] This text is taken from the Septuagint, not from the *Peshiṭta*, where we can read: they sat him.[24] This is Vat. Ar. 468.
- "And the town crier shouted ahead of him."[25] This is in Vat. Ar. 404 and the Septuagint, with the use of an objective complement (*al-muṭlaq*).

---

19 This deacon lived in Antioch in the eleventh century. He claimed to have translated his text from the Septuagint, but it seems that he used an old version. An article on this is to be published by P. Féghali and ʿAbdallāh b. al-Faḍl.

20 Löfgren, O., *Studien zu den arabischen Danielübersetzungen*, Uppsala : Almqvist & Wiksell 1936, 52.

21 Vaccari, A., "Una Bibbia Araba per il primo Gesuita venuto al Libano", *MUSJ* X (1925), 79–104. We read in the appendix of "Una Bibbia Araba" plate V of the Canticle:

ضعني على قلبك كختم وعلى ساعديك كخاتم فإنَّ المحبَّة معتزمة كالموت، والغيرة قاسية كالجحيم تبسط أجنحتها كانبساط أجنحة النار".

The colophon speaks about the Books of Wisdom, Proverbs, Ecclesiasticus and Canticles.

قص كتاب سليمان ابن داوود الذي تملَّك على إسرائيل بعون الله تعالى وحسن توفيقه... وذلك نهار الاثنين التاسع من شهر شباط سنة ٧٠٨٧ لأبينا آدم عليه السلام، بيد العبد الحقير الخاطي داوود... ابن تادرس القس وهبه من قرية بطران من كورة طرابلس المحروسة غفر الله له ولوالده ولساير بني المعموديَّة الأرثوذكس. آمين. كُتب برسم خزانة الأب البارّ البتول القس جوان باتشتا أي يوحنّا المعمدان من محروسة البندقيَّة هنَّأه الله تعالى به زمان طويل بامتداد العمر المسرور واستقامة الأحوال والأمور بشفاعة العذرى الطاهرة أمّ النور وجميع القدّيسين. آمين

22 Vaccari, A., "Un codice carsciunice della Casanatense e la Bibbia araba del 1671", *Biblica* IV (1923), 96–107.

23 και ανεβιβασεν αυτον επι το αρμα το δευτερον των αυτου.

24 ܘܐܘܬܒܗ ܒܡܪܟܒܬܐ ܐܚܪܝܬܐ ܕܝܠܗ

In Greek, the plural is used: *those* who are around the king. But in Syriac, the singular: the king made *him* sit, in line with the masoretic text (=MT) וירכב אתו

25 και εκηρυξεν εμπροσθεν αυτου κηρυξ: and the town crier shouted ahead of him. The Hebrew says only: ויקראל פניו: they shouted ahead of him. In Syriac, the singular form is used: ܘܩܪܐ ܩܕܡܘܗܝ : and he shouted ahead of him.

- "You are the master and the governor."[26] This is in the text of the *Peshitta* and of Vat. Ar. 468 or 606.
- "And they knew he was the governor." This is in the text of the Vulgate.[27] It is a paraphrase of the Hebrew and of the Greek: "He governs…". This fits with the Syriac and with Vat. Ar. 468.

We took this example chosen by Fr Vaccari (*Biblica* IV, 107) without fully following it. This gives us an idea of the text of the *Propaganda Fide* edition. It was subject to so many influences that one cannot say accurately from which manuscript it was taken. Moreover, this project used material in many languages – Latin, Greek, Syriac – which could only detract from the cohesion of the final text.

As for the Gospels, the work was less complicated. A codex from Cyprus, which we could identify with Borg. syr. 49 dating back to 1398, was classified by Ignazio Guidi as the Alexandrian Vulgate of Syriac origin.[28]

We could not identify the manuscripts of the Acts and the Epistles. But it is likely that they are of Syriac origin. As for the Book of t he Apocalypse, which was only later added to the Syriac canon of the New Testament, it seems to be a version of the Buhairic Coptic,[29] with an attempt to adapt it to the Latin Vulgate.

Despite the political disparity, the number of manuscripts, the flaws that one detects here and there and the different hands that worked on it, one must say that the *Propaganda Fide* edition was for two centuries a great help to all communities living in the Orient. Only in the second half of the 19th century did it give way to the new translations that spread in the Near and Middle East.

2. *Before and After*

The *Propaganda Fide* edition was not a secluded island cut off of what preceded and followed its publication in 1671. A whole biblical work in Arabic paved the way for this edition, which soon became a reference Bible for the Catholics of oriental rite as well as for the Protestants.

a. The first biblical texts in Arabic

Did biblical texts exist before Islam? This question has often been asked. Some have suggested that they did. But I believe that there were no biblical texts in the

26 In Syriac ܐܒܐ ܘܫܠܝܛܐ: the father and the governor; in Hebrew אברך: to kneel down.
27 Et praepositum esse scirent. In Syriac: ܐܫܠܛܗ
28 Guidi, I., *Le traduzioni degli Evangelii in arabo e in etiopico* (Atti della R. Accademia dei Lincei, anno 295 [1888], Series Quarta Classe di Scienze morali, storiche e filologiche, Vol IV, Parte I, Memorie, 32).
29 It was adopted for the 1616 New Testament in Arabic, in the Erpenius text.

Arabian Peninsula before Islam. The Jews listened to the Word of God in Hebrew or Aramaic,[30] Christians resorted to Aramaic (or Syriac) or to Greek.[31] This is why the Bishop of Arabs, St George (d. 724), wrote in Greek and not in Arabic.[32]

So the Christians of the Arabic Peninsula knew the Bible and could hear and understand the text of the *Qur'ān*. Besides, their world was not closed as one might think; the caravans moving from north to south allowed them to come into contact with their co-religionists.[33]

But even if a Bible translation did not exist in the pre-Islamic period, we can talk about orally transmitted traditions – texts for liturgy and preaching chosen, for example, by Qass b. Sāʿida[34], Bishop of Najrān, who died around AD 600. Syriac remains the background of these texts, because the priests and monks were Syriac speakers, as was Baḥīrā; tradition has it that this Christian monk met Muhammad when the latter was still a child.[35]

What happened then to the early translations? Some parts of the Bible were used for liturgical purposes,[36] as Arabic spread more and more among Christians, who left with time their indigenous languages, Syriac and Coptic. One must wait until the ninth century to see the oldest Arabic manuscripts of the Bible, which can be found today in St Catherine's Monastery at Mount Sinai.

- Sinai Arabic Codex 151. It contains the version of the Epistles of St Paul, the Acts of the Apostles and the Catholic Epistles. It dates back to 253 HA/AD 867.[37] Bishr b. al-Sirrī translated it from Syriac. Here we make a definitive de-

---

30 Newby, G.D., *A History of the Jews of Arabia. From ancient Times to their Eclipse under Islam*, Columbia (SC): University of South Carolina 1988.

31 Hainthaller, T., *Christliche Araber vor dem Islam* (Eastern Christian Studies, 7/2007), Leuven: Peeters; Montgomery, J.E., "The Empty Hijaz", in: *Arabic Theology, Arabic Philosophy: From the Many to the One. Essays in Celebration of Richard M. Frank*, J.E. Montgomery, ed., Leuven: Peeters 2006, 37–97 (Orientalia Lovaniensia Analecta, 152).

32 Rilliet, F., "Georges des Arabes", in: *Dictionnaire Encyclopédique du Christianisme Ancien*, Paris: Cerf 1990.

33 Shahid, I., *Rome and the Arabs: A Prolegamenon to the Study of Byzantium and the Arabs*, Washington (DC): Dumbarton Oaks 1984. This book had been expanded upon by a work studying in depth the fourth, fifth and sixth centuries.

34 حنّا الفاخوري، *تاريخ الأدب العربيّ* (ط ١٢)، المكتبة البولسيَّة، جونيه، ١٩٨٧، ص ٢٠٤. قس هو أسقف نجران. توفّي نحو سنة ٦٠٠م: "أيُّها النّاس اسمعوا وعوا، وإذا وعيتم فانتفعوا. إنَّه من عاش مات، ومن مات فات.

35 Addas, C., "Baḥīrā", in: *Dictionnaire du Coran*, Robert Laffont, ed., 2007, 105.

36 Blau, J., *Grammar* I, 31, speaks of a bilingual fragment of Psalm 78 (77 in the Septuagint) translated from the Greek and dating back to the eighth century. It had been published in Violet, B., *Ein zweisprachiges Psalmfragment aus Damaskus*, (Berichtigter Sonderabzug aus der Orientalischen Literaturzeitung), 1901.

37 Staal, Harvey, ed., *Mt Sinaï Arabic Codex 151. I, Pauline Epistles* (CSCO 452–453), Louvain 1983. We read on page 248 of CSCO 452 the colophon:

ترجم هذه الرسائل وهي أربع عشرة من السريانيَّة إلى العربيَّة وشرح تفسيرها بما أمكنه من الإيجاز، الضعيف الخاطئ المسكين بشر بن السرّيّ لأخيه الروحانيّ سليمن (سليمان) وأكمل ذلك في شهر رمضان من سنة ثلث وخمسين ومائتين في مدينة دمشق.

parture from Classical Arabic to engage with the Arabic of the monasteries and the Christian communities.[38]

- Sinai Arabic 72 encompasses the four Gospels as read according to the Calendar of the Church of Jerusalem. According to the colophon, it was written by Stephen of Ramleh[39] in 284 HA/AD 897.[40] It is an unpublished text that apparently belongs to a family of six manuscripts containing a version of a Greek original text.
- Vat. Ar. 13. It comprises the text of the Psalms, the four Gospels, the Acts of the Apostles and the Epistles. Only the Epistles of Paul and some portions of the Bible are left out. This manuscript comes from St Sābā Monastery and was most probably copied in the ninth century.
- Sinai Ar. 1 dates back to the ninth century. "It encompasses Arabic translations of the books of Job, Daniel, Jeremiah and Ezekiel,"[41] says Juan Pedro Monferre Sala[42] speaking of a translation from the syro-hexaplar with references to some other Syriac versions.

In this way, many texts are tinged with this "Middle Arabic" which produced the texts of the *Propaganda Fide* edition. I previously mentioned the Epistles of Paul published by Harvey Staal in 1983. In 1984, we have access to the Acts of the Apostles and the Catholic Epistles (*Corpus Scriptorum Christianorum Orientalium* [CSCO] 462–463). The text starts as follows: "In the name of the Father and the Son and the Holy Spirit, One God. Book of the Epraxis, Acts of the Apostles."[43]

---

38 What follows is the beginning of the Epistles to the Roman:
(١) بولس عبد يسوع المسيح، مُدعى رسول مختصّ لبشرى إنجيل الله (٢) الذي منذ القديم أنذرت به أنبيائه في كتبه المقدَّسة (٣) من أجل ابنه المولود من ذرّيّة آل داود بالجسد".
This is a translation from Syriac that does not take the declension of the words into consideration. Here is the literary text:
بولس عبد يسوع المسيح المدعوّ رسولاً مختصًّا ببشرى إنجيل الله الذي به أنذرت (أنذر) أنبيائه (أنبياؤه) منذ القديم في كتبه المقدَّسة.

39 Griffith, S., "Stephen of Ramleh and the kerygma in Arabic in 9th-century Palestine", *Journal of Ecclesiastical History* 36 (1985), 23–45.

40 Idem, *Arabic Christianity in the Monasteries of Ninth-Century Palestine*, 132, nos. 18–20. Photograph of the colophon in: Padwick, C.E., "Al-Ghazali and the Arabic Versions of the Gospels", *Moslem World* (1939), 134 (cf. Graf, *Geschichte*, vol. I, 142–147); Garland, A.G., "An Arabic Translation of the Gospel According to Mark", unpublished PhD–thesis (1979).

41 Grifftih, "Les premières versions arabes de la Bible", 225.

42 "Liber Job detractus apud Sin. Ar. 1: Notas en torno a la *Vorlage* siriaca de un manuscrito arabe cristianeo (s. IXe)", *Collectanea Christiana Orientalia* 1 (2006), 119–142.

43 P. 1. We notice the orthography: الالاه instead of الإله. In the Syriac tradition, the Greek word πραξεις used to be translated in Syriac as: ܦܪܟܣܝܣ ܕܫܠܝܚܐ. The beginning of the text is:
1: 1 ...قد كتبت إليك كتابًا أوّلاً (والأصح: أوّل) يا ثاوفيلا، في جميع الأمور التي بدأ ربُّنا يسوع المسيح يفعلها ويعلِّمها
١: ٣ أولائك (والأصحّ: أولئك) الذين أراهم نفسه... إذ كان يتراء (والأصحّ: يتراءى) لهم ويقول على ملكوة (بل: ملكوت) السماء.

The text of the Acts is divided into 25 sections,[44] which extend with the Epistle of James the Apostle[45] (sections 26–28), 1 Peter (29–30), 1 John (31–32), 2 Peter, 2 John, 3 John and Jude.[46]

What we said about the second volume edited by H. Staal (CSCO 462) applies also to the first volume (CSCO 452). It is as well divided into sections starting from the Epistle to the Romans (sections 1–10), and so on until section 55, which starts with Heb. 12:3.[47]

Another text was published in 1997 by Adriana Drint.[48] This manuscript, which originated at St Catherine's Monastery at Mount Sinai, is the Codex Ar. 589. According to A.S. Atiya, it could date back to the ninth to eleventh centuries,[49] but a closer look at the data shows that this manuscript could be older.[50]

What we can notice in this text is the almost complete absence of the *hamzah*. وتسايل = وتساءل (5, 11)واايمروا= وائمروا. (13, 41) القايمة = القائمة. (14, 19). In 10, 35: شيا instead of شيئًا. In 5, 16: ريّس instead of رئيس[51]. Then the *alif* at the end of the verb: يبدوا لك instead of يبدو لك. And the *scripta plena*: هاكذا (3, 35) instead of هكذا. الالاه instead of الإله.

The text of 4 Ezra is a concise translation from the Syriac[52] that can be read entirely in the Codex Ambrosianus, and in fragments at the *Bibliothèque Nationale* in Paris. For example, in 4:48: نظرتُ فإذا دخان كثير / the Syriac: ܚܙܝܬ ܘܗܐ ܬܢܢܐ ܣܓܝܐܐ. Or in 7:28: وينعم الذين بقوا ثلثين سنة / the Syriac: ܘܢܚܕܘܢ ܠܗܠܝܢ ܕܐܫܬܚܪܘܗ ܬܠܬܝܢ ܫܢܝܢ.

---

44 In Syriac ܨܚܚܐ, in Arabic إصحاح. This corresponds to the liturgical readings. In fact, the first five *ṣḥoḥō* are not marked. The sixth starts with Acts 7:11.

45 The text starts with: بسم الله الرحمن الرحيم. We speak of الإصحاح الأوّل, then it is said in 1:1: من ها هنا يُقرأ يوم الخميس خامس الفصح.; and at the end of 1:12: إلى ها هنا يُقرأ يوم الخميس.

46 Each epistle starts with: بسم الله الرحمن الرحيم. Peter is فطروس, equivalent to πετρος. In 2 Peter 1, we read: من ها هنا يقرأ في عيد التجلّي، وقت القدّاس. And at the end of verse 18, we read: إلى ها هنا يُقرأ. At the beginning of verse 10, the plural imperative should be واعنوا (or واعتنوا). But in the text, we read: واعنو.

47 In the Antiochian tradition, the Epistle to the Hebrews is an Epistle of Paul. Féghaly, P., "Les épîtres de saint Paul dans une des premières traductions en arabe", *Parole de l'Orient* 30 (2005), 103–129. See Brock, S., "A neglected Witness to the East Syriac New Testament Commentary Tradition; Sinaî, Arabic MS. 151" in: *Studies on the Christian Arabic Heritage* (Eastern Christian Studies 5), R. Ebied, H. Teule, eds., Leuven: Peeters 2004, 205–215.

48 *The Mount Sinaï Arabic Version of 4 Ezra* (CSCO 563, 564), Louvain: Peeters 1997.

49 Atiya, A.S., *The Arabic Manuscripts of Mount Sinaï. A hand-list of the Arabic manuscripts and scrolls microfilmed at the Library of the Monastery of St Catherine Mount Sinaï*, Vol. I, Baltimore: John Hopkins 1955, 24.

50 The foreword:

الأدمه، كتاب أسفار عزرة (عزرا) المعلّم الكاتب، قلم الرب. بسم الله الرحمن الرحيم، نبدا (نبدأ) بعون الله بكتاب عزرة المعلّم الكاتب قلم الربّ الذي قذفه الله في قلبه وأملاه عزرة على الخمسة نفر (أشخاص) الذين أمره الله أن يأخذهم معه إلى الصحرا (الصحراء).

51 Hopkins, S.A., *Studies in the Grammar of Early Arabic. Based upon Papyri Datable to before 300 AH/ AD 912*, Oxford: Oxford University Press 1984, 19–20.

52 Stone, E., "A New Manuscript of the Syro-Arabic version of the Fourth Book of Ezra", *Journal for the Study of Judaism* 8 (1976/77), 183–184; Drint, A., "The Mount Sinaï Arabic Version of IV Ezra. Characteristics and Relevance of an Early Arabic Translation of the Syriac Text", *Orientalia Christiana Periodica* 58 (1992), 401–422.

The wisdom of Jesus ben Sirach (Ecclesiasticus), Sinai Ar. 155, which dates from the ninth or tenth century, was edited by Richard M. Frank in 1974 (CSCO 357–358) with an English translation. This text, which translates the syro-hexaplar, starts with 1:26 b[53] and ends with 42:8: "Do not be ashamed to correct the insane, the foolish, the stupid, or to judge an old man at the end of his days because of adultery. Then you shall be respectful, just, experienced in all matters more than any other living being."[54] It then ends with 43:33: "I glorify the Lord who created everything and bestow wisdom on believers."[55] We notice the flawed construction compared with the Classical Arabic. One should say خالق كلّ شيء instead of الخالق لكلِّ شيء.

And the colophon: "Ended and completed is the wisdom of Ibn Sirach, wise in his behaviour towards those who need to be led, by the strength of Jesus Christ, Our Lord. Glory to him forever. Amen."[56]

In *Translation Techniques in two Syro-Arabic Versions of Ruth*, a text published in 2003, Per A. Bengtsson uses two texts to show to what extent the Arabic version is influenced by the Syriac original. The first is Melkite and stems from St Petersburg (1235–1238) and from Damascus (1690). The other is Coptic and encompasses five manuscripts dating from the 14th to the 16th centuries.

Here are some examples:

- ܐܫܟܚܬ ܪܚܡܐ ܒܥܝܢܝܟܝ: I found mercy in your eyes. وجدتُ رحمة في عينيك. But, searching for another turn of phrase, the second says: ظفرتُ منك برحمة. (Ruth 2:10).
- ܠܡܠܩܛ ܠܡܠܩܛܐ: Pick up. لتلتقط التقاطًا. Or: لتلتقط. (2:3).
- ܘܬܗܘܝܢ ܐܙܠܐ ܒܬܪܗܘܢ: You shall follow them. وتكونين تذهبين) وتكوني تذهبين وراهم وراءهم). The second: واتبعيهم والتقطي. (2:9).
- ܕܠܐ ܐܙܠܬܝ ܒܬܪ ܥܠܝܡܐ: You did not follow the young men. إذ لم تذهبي وراء الغلمان. Or: لأنّك لم تطلبي الشباب. (3:10).
- ورفعن أصواتهنّ بالبكاء. The women in question are Naomi and her daughter-in-law Ruth. There is an attempt to improve the text with the dual form ورفعتا أصواتهما بالبكا, but the correct form is: ورفعتا صوتيهما وبكتا (أو: بالبكاء). (1:9).

A last text gives us an idea about the evolution of the translation. It relates the events when Ruth comes to Boaz (Ruth 3:7). Here is the first text, which is a slavish copy of the original:

---

53 ...فإنَّ الربَّ يرزقك إيّاها. (٢٧) إنَّما الحكمة والموعظة خشية الربّ. إنّما مسرَّته الأمانة والدعة.
Féghaly, P., "Versions arabes de Ben Sira", *Parole de l'Orient* 30 (2005), 65–78.

54 CSCO 357, 76: ولا من أن تؤدِّب وتوبّخ الجاهل الأحمق المائق، ولا من مدينة شيخ عند آخر كبره بزناه، وتكون أديبًا، محقًّا، مجرَّبًا بكلِّ شيء أكثر من كلِّ حيّ".

55 Ecclesiasticus 43:33 وأمجِّد الربَّ الخالق لكلِّ شيء المعطي الحكمة للمؤمنين.

56 تمَّت وكملت حكمة ابن سيراخ الحاكم في الأدب للذين يحتاجون إلى الأدب، بقوَّة المسيح ربّنا الذي له مجد (بل: المجد) إلى الأدهار كلِّها. آمين.

فلمّا أكل وشرب وطاب قلبُه جا (أو: جاءت) تنام في جانب الأندر (ܐܕܪܐ= البيدر)، وفي أحلا (أحلى) نومه حين نام في الأندر، جاء (= جاءت) هي خفيا (= خفية) فكشف (ܚܠܗ. بل هي كشفت) ملتحفة (ܡܬܥܛܦܐ) فسقطت عند رجليه..

And the second text:

فلمّا أكل وشرب وطابت نفسه، جا (جاء) إلى البيدر فرقد. فجات (فجاءت) إليه ورقدت إلى جانبه. وفي أطيب نومه وهو راقد إلى البيدر أتت خفيًا (خفية) وكشفت طرف كساه (= كسائه) ورقدت عند رجليه.

Knowing that these texts were written by Christians for their communities, in what was called "Middle Arabic", it is worth remembering that Classical Arabic was in its golden age in Baghdad, especially in the Abbasid period and beyond. In this context I will mention only three texts; the first was written by a Muslim, al-Yaʿqūbī (d. 897), an Arab historian and geographer with Shiite leanings.[57] He wrote a universal history, the first part of which is dedicated to the beginning of humanity and in which he quotes texts from the Old and New Testaments. The following extract is a summary of the Gospel of Matthew (chapters 1 & 2).

«فأمّا متّى فإنّه قال في الإنجيل في نسب إيسوع (= يسوع) بن داود بن إبراهيم إلى أسفل، حتّى انتهى إلى يوسف بن ماثن بعد اثنين وأربعين أبًا، ثمّ قال: وكان يوسف بعل مريم، وإنّ المسيح وُلد في بيت لحم من قرى فلسطين، وملك فلسطين يومئذ هيرودس. وإن قومًا من المجوس ساروا إلى بيت لحم، وعلى رؤوسهم نجمٌ يهتدون به، حتّى رأوه فسجدوا له».[58]

The author also quotes the Sermon on the Mount (chapters 5–7) with some interpolations:

وكان أوّل ما تكلّم به من الإنجيل، على ما في إنجيل متّى: طوبى للمساكين القائمة قلوبهم بما عند ربّهم، بحقٍّ إنّ لهم ملكوت السماء. طوبى للجياع العطاش في طاعة الله. طوبى للصادقين في قولهم، التاركين للكذب، الذي هم ملح الأرض ونور العالم. لا تقتلوا. لا تُسخطوا أحدً، وأرضوا من سخط عليكم، وصالحوا خصمكم، ولا تزنوا، ولا تنظروا إلى غير نسائكم. فإن كانت عينك اليمنى تدعوك إلى الخيانة، فاقلعوها حتّى تنجوا بأبدانكم، ولا تطلّقوا نساءكم من غير زنية.[59]

The second ("Classical") example is the Diatessaron.[60] This Gospel, put together by Tatian (second century) and combining the four Gospels, was translated into Syriac by Abū-l-Faraj 'Abdallāh b. al-Ṭayyib (d. 1043). This Iraqi doctor, philosopher and priest was renowned for his "knowledge of Christianity" (*Fiqh al-naṣrāniyyah*). I would like here to quote section (*iṣḥaḥ*) IV:

57 *Dictionnaire historique de l'Islam*, Paris: PUF 2004, 853.

58 *تاريخ اليعقوبي*، وهو تاريخ أحمد بن أبي يعقوب بن جعفر بن وهب ابن واضح الكاتب العبّاسيّ المعروف باليعقوبيّ، النجف، ١٩٤٩، ص ٦٨.

59 *المرجع السابق*، ص ٧٠.

60 *الدياطسّرون أي الرباعيّ*، نشره الأب إ- س مرمرجي الدومنيكيّ، المطبعة الكاثوليكيّة، بيروت، ١٩٢٥

(١٨) الله لم يبصره أحدٌ قطّ. الوحيد الله الذي هو في حضن أبيه هو خبَّر. (١٩) وهذه هي شهادة يوحنّا، إذ أرسل إليه اليهود من أورشليم كهنة ولاويّين ليسألوه: «أنت من أنت؟» (٢٠) وأقرَّ ولم يجحد، واعترف بأنّه ليس هو المسيح. (٢١) وسألوه أيضًا: «ماذا الآن، إيليّا أنت»؟ فقال: «لستُ هو». «أنبيّ أنت؟». قال: «لا». (٢٢) فقالوا له: «من أنت حتّى نجيب الذين أرسلونا؟ ماذا تقول عن نفسك؟» (٢٣) فقال: «أنا الصوت الصارخ في القفر، أصلحوا طريق الربّ، كما قال إشعيا النبيّ».[61]

Such a language could have been that of the *Propaganda Fide* edition, if the whole Bible had been preserved. Besides, the text of the Diatessaron was not published until 1888, based on two manuscripts from the Vatican Library.[62]

The third text written in Classical Arabic is the *Arabic Rhymed Evangeliary of 'Abdishu' of Nisibis* (d. 1318),[63] subtitled: "The pure Gospel from which this book was written. Commented by its writer Mar 'Abdishu', and its translator … the Holy Gospel taken from the four Gospels of Matthew, Mark, Luke and John". It is ordered in a way to be read all the year long, on Sundays and holidays, during Lent and the different commemorations.[64] The author, Bishop of Nisibis and Armenia, had a double purpose – pastoral and literary – in presenting his work. The pastoral purpose was to assign liturgical texts for Sundays, feast days, etc. The literary purpose was to write in an Arabic that would compete with the eloquent style (*iʿjāz*) of the *Qur'ān*, which is why he followed the style prevailing in his century and presented his work in rhymed prose (*al-sajʿ*), as did other Arab writers such as al-Ḥamadhānī and al-Ḥarīrī.

I would like here to quote the Gospel for the second Sunday of the Annunciation:[65]

١: ٢٦ وفي الشهر السادس من الحبل بيحيي الغسول (غسل، عمَّد)
أُرسل جبرائيل الملك (الملاك) من لدن الله إلى الجليل
إلى مدينة اسمُها ناصرة، فجاء بالتنزيل.
٢٧ إلى عذراء مُملَكة (ملك أو زوجة) برجل اسمه يوسف الأصيل
من بيت داود ومن آله العُدول
واسم العذراء مريم البتول.
٢٨ فدخل عليها الملك (الملاك) وهو يقول:
«السلام لك، أيّتها الملأى من النعمة والخير المبذول
مولانا معك، أيّتها المباركة في النساء وربّات الحجول (النساء) »

---

61 المرجع السابق 30, 32

62 *Tatiani Evangeliorum harmoniae arabicae. Edidit et translatione latina donarit* P. Augustinus Ciasca, Romae: Typ. Polyglotta S.C. de Propaganda Fide, 1888.

63 See Fr Sami Khoury's critical edition in *Patrimoine Arabe Chrétien* (2007), 19–20.

64 First part, p.7. الإنجيل الطاهر الذي انكتب منه هذا الكتاب، أن يقول فيه مار عبد يشوع كاتبه ومترجمه انكتب برسم خزانة الملك المعظَّم العالم العادل المؤيَّد المظفَّر المنصور فخر الدين أدام الله سعادته وخلَّد ملكه ودولته إلى الأبد. آمين.

65 First part, p. 118. We read السبار, in Syriac ܣܘܒܪܐ, which means the awaited time, the Advent. The first Sunday presents the Annunciation to Zachariah (Luke 1:1–25). This second Sunday presents the Annunciation to Mary (Luke 1:26–56).

٢٩ وهي، لمّا لمحته، جزعت وارتهبت لكلام الرسول
وظلّت مفكِّرة أن «من هو هذا السلام بالغرائب والإكرام موصول؟»

The same rhyme is repeated in each pericope, as in every Arabic poem. But this practice had its predecessors, such as Elijah of Nisibis, Moses Bar Kepha and Yūḥannā b. al-Maʿdanī. Those who followed it included Yaʿqūb al-Dibsī (d. 1692), a Tripolitan born in Aleppo, who translated the Gospels in rhymed prose. He was a near contemporary of the *Propaganda Fide* Bible.

b. The heirs of the Propaganda Fide *edition*

The Anglicans were the first to profit from the *Propaganda Fide* edition. They adopted the protocanonical books of the Old Testament and left out the deuterocanonical (Tobias, Judith, 1 Maccabees, 2 Maccabees, Baruch, Wisdom and Ecclesiasticus).

In 1821 they published a Bible with the subtitle: "Book of the New Testament, i.e. the Holy Gospel of Our Lord Jesus Christ, edition of God's poor servant Richard Watts in London – the city that God preserves – from the copy printed in Rome, the Great city, in 1671, in aid of the Oriental Churches."[66]

The subtitle of the Bible printed in 1833 was:

كتاب المقدَّس المشتمل على عهد العتيق الموجودة في الأصل العبرانيّ، وأيضًا كتاب العهد الجديد لربّنا يسوع المسيح. طبعة العبد وليم واطس في لندن المحروسة سنة ١٨٣٣ على النسخة المطبوعة في رومية العظمى سنة ١٦٧١، لمنفعة الكنائس الشرقيَّة.

The New Testament was printed in 1820, 1821, 1833, 1850 and 1858; the Old Testament in 1822, 1833 and 1860.[67]

An English Bible society known for its efforts to foster the knowledge of Christianity[68] turned to Fāris al-Shidyāq, an eminent Arabic writer. He adopted the text of the *Propaganda Fide* edition as a starting point and tried to improve its wording, but did not get very far.[69]

In the Maronite community, the New Testament was mostly printed from the *Propaganda Fide* edition: the Arabic text (in Karshuni) facing the Syriac text.

Late in the 17th century, Bishop Germanus Farḥāt (1670–1732) used the *Propaganda Fide* edition, corrected it and brought it closer to the Syriac text. The Epistles had four editions, all printed in the Monastery of Qozhaya, the last two of them in 1854 and 1864. Moreover, two editions were printed at the Maronite

66 كتاب العهد الجديد يعني إنجيل المقدَّس لربّنا يسوع المسيح. طبعة العبد الفقير رجارد واطس في لندن المحروسة سنة ١٨٢١ على النسخة المطبوعة في رومية العظمى سنة ١٦٧١، لمنفعة الكنايس الشرقيَّة.

67 Graf, *Geschichte*, vol. I, 198.

68 الجمعيَّة الإنكليزيَّة المعروفة بجمعيَّة ترتية المعارف المسيحيَّة.

69 *Dirāsāt*, 165, no. 64: it draws up a comparison between the two texts of the *Propaganda Fide* edition and that of Shidyāq.

printing house of Aleppo in 1862 and 1874.[70] With the exception of the 1897 edition, which was printed in Arabic letters, all the editions of the Epistles were printed in Karshuni.

What we have said about the Lectionary goes for the Evangeliary. Farḥāt first corrected the Roman edition and then undertook the translation of the Gospels directly from the Syriac text.

The Lectionary was the work of Farḥāt. The first edition was printed on the orders of Patriarch Ḥubaysh in 1841; first in Karshuni and in 2007 in Arabic letters with the help of Marsīl Hadāyā.[71]

Concerning the Syrian Catholic Church, I will only quote the introduction by Fr Yūsuf Dawūd from Mosul:

فاعلم أنّي قد جعلتُ أساسًا لنصّ الذي حرَّرتُه الترجمة العربيّة المطبوعة برومية سنة ١٦٧١ بهمّة سركيس الرزّي مطران دمشق المارونيّ لسبب أنّها هي التي تداولتها أيدي الناس في كلِّ مكان، وتعدَّدت آذانُ القارئين والسامعين عليها.[72]

So the basis of this Dominican Bible was the text of the *Propaganda Fide* edition, after some rectifications were made in its content and form.

But the Bible of the Jesuit Fathers printed with the collaboration of Ibrāhīm al-Yāzijī was characterised by a total return to Classical Arabic, if not to Quranic. As for the Protestant Bible, the so-called Van Dyck Bible, it is considered a semi-classic, as its collaborators wanted the Word of God to be understood by the people.

Conclusion

Such was our approach to reading the *Propaganda Fide* Bible published in 1671. This text, which stemmed from Rome in order to correct the mistakes that had infiltrated the biblical treatises, took a long time before it saw the light of day. Between Classical Arabic, the typical style in Baghdad in the Abbasid epoch, and Middle Arabic, the typical style in monasteries and churches at that time, the *Propaganda Fide* edition eventually opted for the latter. This text, adopted by different churches, rendered much service during two centuries. Yet it was superceded in the 19th century by other Bibles that were based on it, but which tried to present the holy text in a classical Arabic worthy of the Arabic Renaissance that started in the 19th century and left us a splendid heritage to profit from.

---

70 Dib, P., *Etude sur la liturgie maronite*, Paris: Lethielleux 1919, 88.

71 *ريش قريان قزحيا ١٨٤١*، نصّ وملاحق، إعداد ونشر الأخت مرسيل هدايا، الكسليك، ٢٠٠٧.
See "Germanos Farhat, Bishop of Aleppo and Arabist (1670–1732)", *Melto* 2 (1966), 115–129.

72 *الكتاب المقدّس أي العهد القديم والعهد الجديد*، الآباء الدومنيكان، ١٨٧٥، أعيد تصوير الكتاب سنة ٢٠٠٠ في بيروت بهمّة جمعيّات الكتاب المقدّس.

Melkite (Greek Orthodox) approaches to the Bible at the time of the community's cultural reawakening in the early modern period (17th–early 18th centuries)*

Carsten Walbiner

Introduction

The 17th century witnessed an impressive intellectual revival within both the main Christian Churches of Bilād al-Shām, and it is not wrong to call this period a pre-*nahḍah*, as it prepared the way for many later developments and even anticipated some of them. Maronites and Melkites – who in this century were still exclusively the Greek Orthodox – developed manifold cultural, scientific and literary activities. In the case of the Maronites, these activities resulted mainly from their close relations with the Vatican and were largely carried out by the graduates of the Maronite College established in Rome in 1584 by order of the Pope. Often Europe, and not the Near East, was the setting for the scholarly undertakings of Maronite men of learning. It may suffice here to mention John Sionita and Abraham Ecchellensis, who both became involved in the project of the Paris Polyglot Bible.[1] The Melkite intellectual revival, which happened chiefly in Syria, and here especially in Aleppo, resulted from a more diverse set of influences. Besides the encounter with the Western European world of thought – mediated by the contacts with missionaries, diplomats and merchants residing in Syria, but also visits to Europe by Near Easterners and the reading of books of European origin – there was an obvious impact from the Greek-speaking world as well as from other Orthodox regions such as the Romanian principalities and Russia.[2]

* I am most grateful to Dr Hilary Kilpatrick of Lausanne for her valuable advice in certain questions of language and content. I would likewise like to thank Dr Sarjoun Karam of Heidelberg for his kind support.

1 On the cultural and literary activities of the Maronites in early modern times see Gemayel, Nasser, *Les échanges culturels entre les Maronites et l'Europe. Du Collège Maronite de Rome (1584) au Collège de ʿAyn-Warqa (1798)*, 2 vols., Beyrouth: Impr. Y. et Ph. Gemayel 1984; Graf, Georg, *Geschichte der christlichen arabischen Literatur*, vol. 3, Città del Vaticano: Biblioteca Apostolica Vaticano 1949, 299–476; on the Parisian polyglot Bible see also Ronny Vollandt's contribution in this volume.

2 On Melkite literary and cultural production during the 17th and early 18th centuries see Nasrallah, Joseph, *Histoire du mouvement littéraire dans l'Eglise melchite du Ve au XXe siècle*, vol. IV/1, Louvain 1979; Idlibī, Nāwufiṭūs (Edelby, Neophytos), *Asāqifat al-Rūm al-Malikīyīn bi-Ḥalab fī l-ʿaṣr al-ḥadīth*, Ḥalab 1983, 36–37, 48–52, 67–70, 94–96, 116–119, 130–132.

Both Churches took a lead in Arab Christianity's approach towards modernity and thus became pioneers for the Arab world as a whole.

The Bible was amongst the subjects which met with intensified interest among Maronites and Melkites alike. In the following, the approach of the Melkites towards the Holy Scriptures shall be portrayed. For them, as for all other Christians, the Bible occupied a central place within theological thinking and spiritual life. Although the Orthodox Church by no means prevented private reading of Scripture and individual reflection on it, the Liturgy and other services had become the usual place where the ordinary believer came into contact with the text of the Bible. The intellectual decline of the Orthodox Church in the later Middle Ages, which resulted amongst other things in a widespread neglect of theological education of the clergy, meant that the services were the only occasions where many priests, too, encountered the Bible.[3] What Astérios Argyriou has observed of Greek-speaking Orthodoxy also holds true for the Orthodox of the Arab lands: "Le culte devient ainsi le centre de toute la vie religieuse, spirituelle et théologique. Il devient aussi le lieu privilégié sinon unique de la lecture et de la méditation des [Saintes] Ecritures."[4] Accordingly, the Bible existed predominantly in versions for liturgical use which were arranged according to the needs of worship and acquired a kind of sacred dignity. Complete texts of the Bible, which "could have served for knowledge and teaching" were mainly absent.[5]

The Melkites went through a long and not entirely recognisable process of Arabisation.[6] The earliest activities of translation, which included Bible texts, can be traced back to the eighth century. This process, which happened on two levels – the vernacular and the liturgical – came to an end in early modern times[7] and with the beginning of the 17th century the Greek Orthodox Meletius Karmah,

---

3 Argyriou, Astérios, "La Bible dans le monde orthodoxe au XVIe siècle", in: *Le temps des Réformes et la Bible*, Guy Bedouelle, Bernard Roussel, eds., Paris: Beauchesne 1989, 385–400, here especially 388; Onasch, Konrad, arts. "Evangelium"; "Lesebücher"; "Lesungen", in: idem, *Lexikon Liturgie und Kunst der Ostkirche*, Berlin: Buchverlag Union 1993, 115–116, 245–247, 247–249.

4 Argyriou, "La Bible dans le monde orthodoxe", 390.

5 Graf, *Geschichte*, vol. 1, Vatican City 1944, 138; Onasch, *Lexikon Liturgie und Kunst*, 246.

6 On several aspects of this process see Nasrallah, Joseph, "La liturgie des Patriarcats melchites de 969 à 1300", *Oriens Christianus* 71 (1987), 156–181; Cannuyer, Christian, "Langues usuelles et liturgiques des Melkites au XIIIe s.", *Oriens Christianus* 70 (1986), 110–117.

7 As late as 1594 two bishops from the Patriarchate of Antioch signed a letter, written in Greek to the Tsar of Russia, in Syriac letters while the other signatories put their names in Greek or Arabic (Pančenko, K. A., and Fonkič, B. L., "Gramota 1594 g. antiochijskogo Patriarcha Ioakima VI Zarju Fedoru Ivanoviču", in: *Monfokon. Issledovanija po paleografii, kodikologii i diplomatike / Montfaucon. Etudes de paléographie, de codicologie et de diplomatique*, Rossijskaja Akademija Nauk, Institut vseobščej istorii, Zentr "Paleografija, Kodikologija, Diplomatika", ed., vol. 1, Moscow and St Petersburg: Al'jans Archeo 2007, 166–184, here 183).

soon to be discussed, could state with every justification: *inna al-ʿarabīyah lisānunā* ("our language is Arabic")[8].

In the 17th century the Arabic lectionary in use amongst the Orthodox was generally attributed to ʿAbdallāh b. Faḍl al-Anṭākī, the famous eleventh-century translator and author. Thus Macarius b. al-Zaʿīm, who will be introduced later, said of "the Deacon ʿAbdallāh b. Faḍl al-Anṭākī" that "he was very learned in Arabic, Greek and Syriac and [...] translated the New and the Old Testament together with their commentaries into Arabic for the [Arab] Christians, ordering them to read them on all Saturdays, Sundays and feasts of the Lord."[9]

Meletius Karmah's translation project

But there was also an awareness that many other versions of the Bible were in circulation. Meletius Karmah, who was from 1612 until 1634 Metropolitan of Aleppo and then for one year until his death Patriarch of Antioch, and who must be regarded as the *spiritus rector* and a main protagonist of the intellectual awakening amongst the Orthodox of Syria in the 17th century[10], was well aware of the multitude of existing Arabic Bible translations, in which he saw a reason for the corruption and defectiveness of the Bible text in use by Arab Christians. In a letter to Rome he says:

> "Concerning the books in the churches of the Arab Christians, not a single one is correct and contains the right writing (*kitābah qawīmah*), because some were translated from Syriac, others from Greek, Armenian or Coptic. The Bible which lately appeared in Rome[11] and had been translated from Coptic into Syriac is taken there [i. e. in Rome]

---

8 Cf. Walbiner, Carsten-Michael, "'Und um Jesu willen, schickt sie nicht ungebunden!' Die Bemühungen des Meletius Karma (1572–1635) um den Druck arabischer Bücher in Rom", in: *Studies on the Christian Arabic Heritage in Honour of Father Prof. Dr. Samir Khalil Samir S.I. at the Occasion of his Sixty-Fifth Birthday*, Rifaat Ebied, Herman Teule, eds., Leuven, Paris and Dudley: Peeters 2004, 163–175, here 168.

9 Introduction to *Kitāb al-Naḥla*, published by Ḥabīb al-Zayyāt in *Khazāʾin al-kutub fī Dimashq wa-ḍawāḥīhā*, al-Fajjāla: Maṭbaʿat al-Maʿārif 1902, 144–151, here 150; see also Walbiner, Carsten, "Preserving the past and enlightening the present. Macarius b. al-Zaʿīm and Medieval Melkite literature", *Parole de l'Orient*, 24 (2009), 433–441, here 437–438, 440–441. This attribution of the common lectionary to b. Faḍl has not been substantiated by modern research: "Die bisher bekannt gewordene handschriftliche Bezeugung dieser Tradition ist sehr gering" (Graf, *Geschichte*, vol. 1, 188).

10 On Karmah's life and work see Idlibī, *Asāqifat al-Rūm*, 31–48, 52–55; Nasrallah, *Histoire*, vol. IV/1, 70–76.

11 Karmah refers to the so-called Medici Bible, which is based on the Egyptian or Alexandrinian Vulgate: *al-Injīl al-muqaddas li-Rabbinā Yasūʿ al-Masīḥ al-maktūb min arbaʿ al-injīlīyīn al-muqaddasīn yaʿnī Mattā wa-Marqus wa-Lūqā wa-Yūḥannā*, Giovanni Battista Raimundi, ed., Roma: Typographia Medecea 1591. On the Egyptian Vulgate see Graf, *Geschichte*, vol. 1, 155–162.

> to be correct, as Arabic is not your language. But it turns out that it is not correct and true, [but] a weak version, and its publication has been in vain."[12]

In another place Karmah speaks of the "weeds [...] which the heretics sowed [in the Bible texts]" and which must be extracted.[13] It is interesting to observe that Karmah included the Medici Bible printed in Rome in 1591 in his critique as he had found in it "many mistakes".[14]

Karmah made a revision of the liturgical books in use in his Church the main field of his own intellectual activities, and the Bible was naturally included. So Karmah composed a revision of a commentary of the Gospels by John Chrysostom in the translation of ʿAbdallāh b. Faḍl al-Anṭākī[15]. More interestingly, he conceived an ambitious project for a new translation of the whole Bible into Arabic, for which he designed an approach that sounds very modern. By proposing the inclusion of a Roman Catholic and a Maronite scholar he transgressed confessional boundaries, a most remarkable attitude for his time. Furthermore, the project bears multidisciplinary features as Karmah opted for a cooperation between linguists and theologians.[16] It remains open to debate to what extent this concept was really Karmah's own and whether and how it had been influenced by Tommaso Obicini,[17] an orientalist and missionary whom Karmah proposed as the head of the undertaking. As remarkable as the design of the project is Karmah's endeavour to have its outcome printed. He clearly recognised that the new medium of book printing offered the previously unavailable opportunity to multiply an identical text in hundreds, if not thousands of copies. Thus, there existed the possibility of unifying the different versions of the Bible in use.

But Rome decided against the proposal from Karmah, who obviously did not see any alternatives for the realisation of his project, which thus remained unaccomplished. But as Hilary Kilpatrick has rightly observed, Karmah's efforts for a new translation of the Arabic Bible deserve a place of honour in the history of Arabic Bible translations.[18]

The historical studies by Macarius b. al-Zaʿīm

None of those around Karmah possessed the ambition or opportunities to realise his Bible project. Macarius b. al-Zaʿīm, Karmah's most faithful disciple, who like

12 Walbiner, "'Und um Jesu willen!'", 169.
13 Ibid., 167.
14 Ibid.
15 Nasrallah, *Histoire*, vol. IV/1, 78; Idlibī, *Asāqifat al-Rūm*, 50.
16 For details see Walbiner, "'Und um Jesu willen'", 165–170, and the contribution by Hilary Kilpatrick elsewhere in this volume.
17 On Obicini see Bottini, Giovanni-Claudio, "Tommaso Obicini (1585–1632) Custos of the Holy Land and Orientalist", in: *The Christian Heritage in the Holy Land*, Anthony O'Mahony et. al., eds., London: Scorpion Cavendish 1995, 97–101.
18 See the conclusion to her contribution to this volume.

his mentor became first Metropolitan of Aleppo and then Patriarch of Antioch and who has to be regarded as the most prolific Arab Orthodox writer in early modern times, focused in his work on other issues.[19] Macarius was deeply interested in history and concentrated on providing his community with knowledge about a diversity of subjects. He derived this information mainly from Greek manuscripts and printed books, but also from other sources. It was especially during his two long journeys to the Balkans, Russia and Georgia that Macarius came across the material for his compilations and translations. His notebook-like collections, which are a typical feature of his work as an author, contain a number of entries on the Bible. Besides more "technical" information on the Bible, for instance on "The names of the books of the Old and the New Testament according to the arrangement in the Greek copies"[20] or "The number of the chapters and sections of the Gospels"[21], one finds explanations of the biblical stories and their protagonists. Here only a few examples will be mentioned. In his collection *Majmūᶜ laṭīf*, Macarius tells his readers "Why Joseph [of Arimathaea] took down the body of Christ [from the cross] already on Friday and did not wait until Saturday".[22] Another entry sets out "How God in the beginning created 22 innovations within six days".[23] The *Majmūᶜ mubārak* contains amongst others a concise "Explanation of the Gospel of Matthew"[24] and a short "Explanation of sayings and parables from the Gospels"[25]. In the *Kitāb al-Naḥlah* Macarius provides short entries "On the fourfold occurrence of biblical things, amongst them the four Evangelists"[26], "On Moses' staff and other stories about him"[27], "On the three holy kings"[28], "On the 30 pieces of silver for which Judas sold the Lord"[29], "On the language that Adam spoke"[30] and other matters. In another work there is a longer treatise on place names mentioned in the Bible and other works of Christian provenance which

[19] On Macarius' life and work see Walbiner, Carsten-Michael. "Die Mitteilungen des griechisch-orthodoxen Patriarchen Makarius b. az-Zaᶜīm von Antiochia (1647–1672) über Georgien nach dem arabischen Autograph von St. Petersburg." Ph.D. thesis, Leipzig, 1995, 8–38; Idlibī, *Asāqifat al-Rūm*, 57–71, 81–97; Nasrallah, *Histoire*, vol. IV/1, 87–127.

[20] MS. London, British Museum, ar. chr. 28 [Add. 9965], fols. 158a–158b (cf. Slīm, Suᶜād Abū al-Rūs, "Makhṭūṭ majmūᶜ mubārak li-l-baṭriyark Makāriyūs al-thālith al-Zaᶜīm", *al-Mashriq* 68 [1994], 175–196, here 190).

[21] MS. Ṣarbā, Dayr al-Mukhalliṣ, Collection Dayr al-Šīr 600, p. 488 (cf. Abraṣ, Mišāl, "Makhṭūṭat majmūᶜ laṭīf li-l-baṭriyark Makāriyūs al-thālith Zaᶜīm", *al-Mashriq* 68 [1994], 421–448, here 439).

[22] Ibid., pp. 393–394 (cf. Abraṣ, "Makhṭūṭat majmūᶜ laṭīf", 436).

[23] Ibid., pp. 399–400 (cf. Abraṣ, "Makhṭūṭat majmūᶜ laṭīf", 436).

[24] MS. London, British Museum, ar. chr 28, fols.161a–161b (cf. Slīm, "Makhṭūṭ majmūᶜ mubārak", 190).

[25] Ibid., fols. 239b–240b (cf. Slīm, "Makhṭūṭ majmūᶜ mubārak", 195).

[26] MS. Homs, Greek Orthodox Metropolitanate 27, fols. 23b–24b.

[27] Ibid., fols. 24b–27b.

[28] Ibid., fol. 30b.

[29] Ibid., fol. 33a.

[30] Ibid., fols. 51a–51b.

many people were no longer able to identify.[31] Finally, it is worth mentioning a little tract in which for each letter of the Arabic alphabet Macarius has collected five verses of the Bible (*istīkhūnāt*) starting with the letter concerned.[32] He has done so because, as he observes, many teachers of the Church had done likewise in their liturgical canons and because "many Christian poets have composed verses and poems beginning with the letters in the Arabic alphabetical order".[33]

As these examples show, Macarius strove mainly for a deeper understanding of biblical events and an illumination of the background to them. Although his approach was unsystematic and purely descriptive and lacked a critical and theological attitude, Macarius nevertheless inspired his readers to think more thoroughly about the Bible, which he saw as a historical document amongst other things, and which he therefore made a subject of his own research.

The printing of the Gospels by Athanasius al-Dabbās

The Melkite approach towards the Bible reached its climax in early modern times with the activities of Athanasius al-Dabbās (1647–1724). The Damascus-born al-Dabbās lived for a while as a monk in the monasteries in and around Jerusalem, which gave him the opportunity to acquaint himself with the Greek world of thought and to enter into close contacts with the Western missionaries stationed in the Holy Land. In 1686 the Aleppans chose him as anti-patriarch against the ruling incumbent Cyrillus al-Zaᶜīm. Also supported by Rome, al-Dabbās was able to challenge his opponent successfully for some years. But finally, in 1694, he had to back down and content himself with the diocese of Aleppo for a quarter of a century until, in 1720, after Cyrillus' death, he became the rightful patriarch of Antioch, a post he held until 1724.[34] In Aleppo al-Dabbās engaged in lively intellectual activities. A long sojourn in Walachia at the turn of the 17th/18th centuries not only provided him with many intellectual impulses but also gave him a deeper understanding of a medium which had not so far found a home in the Arab world – the printing of books with moveable type. Financed by the ruler of Walachia, in 1701 and 1702 two Arabic liturgical books were printed "at the request and under the supervision" (*bi-iltimās wa-mushārafah*) of al-Dabbās.[35] It seems al-Dabbās learned the

---

31 MS. St Petersburg, Institute of Oriental Studies, B 1227, fols. 40a–50a.

32 Ibid., fols. 122a–126b.

33 Ibid., fol. 122a.

34 On the life and work of al-Dabbās see Idlibī, *Asāqifat al-Rūm*, 107–132; Nasrallah, *Histoire*, vol. IV/1, 132–146.

35 On al-Dabbās' Romanian prints see Gdoura, Wahid, *Le début de l'imprimerie arabe à Istanbul et en Syrie: évolution de l'environnement culturel (1706–1787)*, Tunis: Institut Supérieur de Documentation 1985 (Publications de l'Institut Supérieur de Documentation, 8), 135–137, 271; Dabbās, Anṭuwān Qayṣar, and Rashshū, Nakhla, *Tārīkh al-ṭibāᶜa al-ᶜarabīya fī al-mashriq. Al-baṭriyark Athanāsiyūs al-thālith Dabbās (1685–1724)*, Bayrūt: Dār al-Nahār 2008, 55–60.

craft of printing and was, when departing from the Balkans, awarded the necessary equipment for a printing shop. Back in Aleppo, where he returned in 1705, he installed the press and in 1706 the first two books ever printed in Arabic letters in the Arab world came out – the Psalms and the Gospels.[36] It is the edition of the Gospels that interests us in the present context.

There exists some confusion about the character of the 1706 Bible edition. Georg Graf – most likely following Cyrille Charon (Karalevsky) – describes it as the Four Gospels, with the text of the Gospels in its "natural" order but with the readings in the services marked. According to Graf, another edition followed in 1708, with the text arranged according to the readings during the Church's year, thus a mixture of the four Gospels.[37] But the copy of the 1706 edition examined for this article[38] is clearly of the type ascribed by Graf and Charon to the 1708 edition.[39] It contains the text of the Bible portioned into readings for all the Sundays and Saturdays as well as for the feasts of the Church and must thus be classified as an Aprakos Gospel, meaning that the readings are arranged according to the ecclesiastical year, starting with Easter Sunday. Each reading is followed by a commentary by an unspecified author, introduced by the words *qāla 'l-mufassir* ("the commentator says"). Al-Dabbās added an introduction (*fātiḥat al-injīl al-sharīf*)[40] of five pages to which I will refer later. Georg Graf describes the text as a revised version of the "Egyptian Vulgate"[41], a view that can be supported by the classification of

36 On the Aleppo printing press see Gdoura, *Le début de l'imprimerie arabe*, 138–152; Dabbās, Rashshū, *Tārīkh al-ṭibā^ca al-^carabīya fī al-mashriq*, 63–79.

37 Graf, *Geschichte*, vol. 1, 159–160, 188; cf. Charon, Cyrille, *Histoire des Patriarcats Melkites*, vol. 3, Rome and Paris: Forzani 1909, 98. Joseph Nasrallah (*Histoire*, IV/1, 144–145; *L'imprimerie au Liban*, Harissa 1948, 23) takes the same view. A short description of Dabbās' 1708 edition of the Gospels, at that time in the possession of the Imperial Public Library at St Petersburg, leads one to assume that Graf and the others simply confused the 1706 with the 1708 edition, as the latter is described as containing the four Gospels consecutively and not arranged according to the readings of the Church year (cf. Dorn, Bernhard, "Ein Nachtrag zu Schnurrer's Bibliotheca Arabica aus den Schätzen der Kaiserlichen öffentl. Bibliothek zu St. Petersburg", *Zeitschrift der Deutschen Morgenländischen Gesellschaft* 8 [1854], 386–389, here 389).

38 *Kitāb al-injīl al-sharīf al-ṭāhir wa-l-miṣbāḥ al-munīr al-zāhir*, Aleppo 1706 (University and Research Library Erfurt/Gotha, Gotha branch, Theol. 2 F 58/3). For a general description of this copy see Walbiner, Carsten, "Kitāb al-injīl al-sharīf al-ṭāhir wa-l-miṣbāḥ al-munīr al-zāhir (The Book of the honourable pure Gospel and the illuminative lamp)", in: *The Beginnings of Printing in the Near and Middle East: Jews, Christians, Muslims*, Klaus Kreiser, ed., Wiesbaden: Harrassowitz 2001, 24–25.

39 This is also stated on fol. 4a of the 1706 edition, where the title of the Gospels is repeated, this time followed by the words: *murattaban tartīban kanā'isīyan* ("arranged in the ecclesiastical order") as well as on fol. 5a, where it is stated that the book is "subdivided according to the course of the days of the year" (*mufaṣṣalan ^calā madār ayām al-sanah*). On the partly contradictory descriptions of the (several?) 1706 and 1708 editions see Morozov, D. A., "Arabskoje Evangelije Daniila Apostola (K istorii pervoj arabskoj tipografii na Vostoke)", *Arkhiv russkoj istorii* 2 (1992), 193–203.

40 *Kitāb al-injīl al-sharīf*, fols. 1b–3b.

41 Graf, *Geschichte*, vol. 1, 185, 188.

Bible families established by Hikmat Kachouh on the basis of two verses from the Gospel of John (1.1 and 1.18). Regarding these verses, the 1706 edition shows a complete correspondence with two manuscripts of the Egyptian Vulgate from the 16th and 17th century respectively.[42] This means that al-Dabbās chose for his edition a form of the Bible text which in its phrasing was familiar to the readers of his time. He claims in his introduction to have revised the text "according to the Greek language sentence by sentence" and to have "corrected its syntax word by word" (*baʿda an ḥarrartuhu ʿalā al-lughah al-yūnānīyah bi-waḍʿihi jumlah fa-jumlah wa-aṣlaḥtu iʿrābahu lafẓah fa-lafẓah*).[43] To what extent this revision led to any substantial changes to the text current in the 17th century remains to be established.[44]

Several authors – amongst them the present speaker – have described the Aleppo Gospels of 1706 as meant for liturgical use.[45] But a thorough reading of the introduction, which in rhymed prose (*sajʿ*) praises the Bible at length as the central text of Christianity, reveals that al-Dabbās had something else in mind. Hidden in this encomium are some most interesting views of the editor concerning the question of who should read and possess the Book of Books. He believes that possessing the Gospels is "a duty for all believers" (*wājibun ʿalā kulli min al-muʾminīn*) as "it contains ample truths for all ranks of people, be they scholars or illiterates" (*li-taḍammunihi maʿānīyan kāfiyatan li-kulli rutbah min al-nās, ʿulamāʾ kānū am ummīyīn*)[46], married or single, priests or monks (*muzawwajan kunta am aʿzaban, ilklīrīkīyan am rāhiban*)[47]. People should have the Gospels in their homes as "a preventive weapon and a sharp sword" (*silāḥ māniʿ wa-muhannad qāṭiʿ*).[48] And, "to facilitate its possession", al-Dabbās "set about printing it" (*wa-li-kayy yusahhila ʿalaika imtilākahu wa-yahūna ladaika iqtināʾuhu fa-sharaʿtu ḥīnaʾidhin bi-ṭabʿihi*).[49]

One can only speculate about the reasons for al-Dabbās' obvious aim to make the Bible a book read by all strata of people, an approach that contradicted not

42 Compare fols. 5a and 7b of the Aleppo edition with Kachouh, Hikmat, "The Arabic Versions of the Gospels: A Case Study of John 1.1 and 1.18", in: *The Bible in Arab Christianity*, David Thomas, ed., Leiden and Boston: Brill 2007 (The History of Christian-Muslim Relations, 6), 9–36, here 19.

43 *Kitāb al-injīl al-sharīf*, fol. 3b.

44 For some readers al-Dabbās created with his printed edition a textual authority that was regarded superior to handwritten manuscripts (cf. Walbiner, Carsten, "Some Observations on the Perception and Understanding of Printing amongst the Arab Greek Orthodox [Melkites] in the Seventeenth Century", in: *Printing and Publishing in the Middle East. Papers from the Second Symposium on the History of Printing and Publishing in the Languages and Countries of the Middle East, Bibliothèque nationale de France, Paris, 2–4 November, 2005*, Philip Sadgrove, ed., Oxford: Univ. Press 2008, 65–76, here 72). However, this opinion was not universally held (see ibid., 74).

45 Graf, *Geschichte*, vol. 1, 160; Charon, *Histoire*, 98; Nasrallah, *Histoire*, vol. IV/1, 144–145; Walbiner, "Kitāb al-injīl al-sharīf", 24.

46 *Kitāb al-injīl al-sharīf*, fol. 2a.

47 Ibid., fol. 3a.

48 Ibid., fol. 3b.

49 Ibid., fol. 3b.

only Orthodox conceptions but the reality in early modern Syria. The idea sounds very Protestant, and such an impact cannot be excluded totally as al-Dabbās had come in contact with Protestant thinking – although perhaps unconsciously – while in the Balkans.[50]

There is another striking feature of al-Dabbās' introductory words to his edition of the Bible. More then once he uses expressions which have a very strong Muslim connotation. So he speaks of the revelation in the Gospels as *tanzīl*,[51] a term normally used for God's sending down of the Qurʾān. The Bible is called by al-Dabbās a *muṣḥaf sharīf*,[52] in Muslim circles a very common designation for the Qurʾān. And the recitation of the Bible, normally called *qirāʾah*, is described by al-Dabbās as *tilāwah*,[53] a term describing the recitation of the Qurʾān.[54]

What has been said above proves that the 17th and early 18th centuries saw a number of remarkable approaches of Orthodox men of learning to the Bible. Although developed in close contact and exchange with non-Arab traditions, these different ideas and projects must be described as indigenous in inspiration and realisation. Unfortunately, the schism of 1724 in the Melkite Church, which resulted in a great waste of potential, prevented the Orthodox for many generations from following the lead taken by Meletius Karmah, Macarius b. al-Zaʿīm and Athanasius al-Dabbās and approaching the Bible with new questions and concepts.

---

50 One of the sources for Dimitrie Cantemir's *Divan*, which al-Dabbās translated from Greek into Arabic while in Romania, is the Unitarian theologian Andreas Wissowatius (cf. Cantemir, Dimitrie, *The Salvation of the Wise Man and The Ruin of the Sinful World / Ṣalāḥ al-ḥakīm wa-fasād al-ʿālam al-dhamīm*, Ioana Feodorov, ed., Bucharest: Acad. Romane 2006, 29).

51 *Kitāb al-injīl al-sharīf*, fol. 2a.

52 Ibid.

53 Ibid., fol. 3a.

54 Accordingly, none of the three terms quoted above are listed in Georg Graf's *Verzeichnis arabischer kirchlicher Termini* (Louvain: Durbecq 1954 [CSCO, 147]).

Meletius Karmah's Specimen Translation of Genesis 1–5*

Hilary Kilpatrick

On becoming Archbishop of Aleppo in 1612, Meletius (ʿAbd al-Karīm) Karmah[1] embarked on a programme of revision, translation and, as he hoped, printing of religious books for the Greek Orthodox faithful in his diocese and more generally in the Patriarchate of Antioch. This "spiritual nourishment", as he termed it, for his hungry flock included not only service books, the Euchologion and Horologion[2], but also the Bible. Unlike his fellow Orthodox in the Greek-speaking world, who could turn to the Greek colony in Venice for financial support and help in printing books, Meletius Karmah had to appeal to other Christians for assistance. He had good contacts with some of the Catholic priests sent to care for the welfare of the Italian and French Catholic merchants in the city and later to work as missionaries, and he knew Rome as a source of printed books in Arabic as well as other languages. Several letters of his to the Vatican authorities, notably the Congregation for the Propagation of the Faith (*de Propaganda Fide*), mention books he had received or hoped to receive.[3] It was, therefore, logical for him to enter into

---

* I am most grateful to Dr Carsten Walbiner (Bonn), Mr Ronny Vollandt (Cambridge) and Professor Irene Backus (Geneva) for their help and advice at various stages of preparing this paper.

1 Meletius Karmah, whose baptismal name was ʿAbd al-Karīm, was born in Hama around 1572. After spending some time at St Saba's monastery in Palestine, where he got to know the tradition of the Orthodox Church, learned Greek and became a monk, he returned to his native town and was ordained deacon and then priest. A mission to negotiate a decrease in the tax assessment of the Greek Orthodox of Hama with the Ottoman authorities brought him to Aleppo, where he quickly became known as an inspiring preacher. The see of Aleppo was vacant at the time, and the community proposed him to fill it. He was consecrated in 1612 and remained in Aleppo until April 1634, when he was chosen as Patriarch of Antioch with the name Euthymios II. He died in January 1635. For his biography see Idlibī, Nāwifiṭūs, *Asāqifat al-rūm al-malakīyīn bi-Ḥalab fī l-ʿaṣr al-ḥadīth*, Aleppo: Maṭbaʿat al-Iḥsān 1983, 31–55, and Nasrallah, Joseph, *Histoire du mouvement littéraire dans l'église melchite du Ve au XXe siècle*, vol.4, 1: *Période ottomane, 1516–1724*, Louvain: Peeters 1979, 70–76.

2 The Euchologion contains the texts and rubrics of the three Eucharistic rites in use in the Orthodox Church, the prayers required for the administration of the Sacraments and the fixed parts of the Divine Office. The Horologion contains the recurrent portions of the Divine Office extending through the year.

3 In *SOCG* (= *Scritture Originali riferite nelle Congregazione Generali*, Archives of the Congregation *De Propaganda Fide*), vol. 181 (*Lettere in Diverse Lingue dall'anno 1622 a 1629*), fol. 36, Meletius mentions seven titles he hoped to receive. Among them is a copy of *Varinos*, the dictionary of the Greek language compiled by the Latin humanist Guerrino Favorino da Cameriono (also known as Varinus Phavorinus; d. 1537) and published in Rome in 1523. The others are reliable texts of the Greek Old and New Testaments; an unspecified *Lessico*

correspondence with the Vatican to gain support for his project to produce and print a revised Arabic translation of the Bible.

It is striking that in his correspondence with the Vatican, Meletius never mentions the involvement of any other Antiochian Orthodox hierarch in his projects. One wonders whether he informed the Patriarch of Antioch, Ignatios III ʿAṭīyah (1618–1634),[4] or whether he asked his fellow bishops for help, for instance in collecting texts. Since the Patriarchate's archives for this period of its history have apparently been lost, there is no way of knowing whether Meletius was truly an *Einzelgänger* or whether he simply found it advisable to present this project to the Vatican as his own brainchild.[5]

In a letter preserved in the Archives of the *Propaganda Fide* which summarises his thinking,[6] Meletius sets out in detail why a new translation of the Bible into Arabic is necessary and explains his ideas of how it should be made. He points out that Arabic versions of the Bible vary greatly among themselves. He distinguishes seven different "copies" (*nuskhah*), presumably representing different traditions of textual transmission, those of Damascus, Tripoli, Beirut, Cairo, Sinai, Jerusalem and Aleppo. They each have lacunae and additions and are not in agreement with one another.[7] To a modern reader, and perhaps to the Cardinals of the *Propaganda Fide*, that might simply seem inevitable in a manuscript tradition; the Vulgate, too, suffered from textual deviations before the introduction of printing. But the case with the Arabic Bible was more complicated, as Meletius stresses. Different versions had been translated from different languages: Hebrew, Syriac, Greek, Armenian, Coptic. Moreover, heretics had sown their "mildewed corn" in

---

Greco; the Greek texts of Basil the Great's *Commentary on the Six Days of Creation* and John of Damascus' *Miʾat maqālah*, the Arabic title of *De fide orthodoxa*; and two unspecified Greek grammars. Meletius asks for printed copies of all these texts apart from the *Miʾat maqālah*. Summaries of this and other letters from Meletius and other Orthodox clergy preserved in the archives of the *Propaganda Fide* have been published: Jabbūr, Makāriyūs, and al-Khūrī, Ziyād Tawfīq, *Wathāʾiq hāmmah fī khidmat kanīsatinā al-anṭākīyah. Man ṣanaʿ al-infiṣāl sanat 1724?*, Beirut: Manshūrāt al-Nūr 2000. This publication will be referred to as *Wathāʾiq hāmmah*. More or less precise requests for books are also found in *SOCG*, vol. 181, fols. 35 and 208, and *SOCG*, vol. 180 (*Lettere di Lingua straniera dall'Anno 1631 sino al 1645*), fols. 75 and 35, and thanks for books received in *SOCG*, vol. 181, fol. 36, and *SOCG*, vol. 180, fol. 75.

4 Until 1628 Ignatios was engaged in imposing his authority as against the anti-Patriarch Cyril Dabbās, a conflict in which Meletius consistently supported him.

5 That Meletius could take such initiatives without referring to his Patriarch's approval of them shows how loose the organisation of the Patriarchate of Antioch was at the time – in marked contrast to the centralisation of the Vatican.

6 These letters and the copies of the letters sent by Vatican authorities, which are also in the Archives, represent the only evidence extant about Meletius' ideas on revising and translating religious books. Any correspondence he might have had on the subject with the Patriarchs of Antioch or Constantinople, with fellow bishops or with like-minded reformers has not come to light.

7 *SOCG*, vol. 181, fol. 208 (dated 1629); cf. *Wathāʾiq hāmmah*, 6.

the text, and this needed to be weeded out.[8] (The "heretics" Meletius meant, non-Chalcedonian Christians, were probably not those who would immediately occur to Vatican officials confronting Calvinists, Lutherans and other Protestants.)

To remedy this confusion, Meletius suggested a carefully thought-out project.[9] The different versions should be bought and brought to Aleppo. A team of six men should be put to work: two secretaries, one for Arabic, the other for Greek; two scholars, one knowledgeable about Arabic, the other about Greek; and two collators of the different versions. Their task would be to compare the Arabic versions with the Greek and Latin ones and establish the correct text. Meletius made no estimate about the time the work would take: the project was open-ended.

The question arises how Meletius came to formulate this project. Revision of the Arabic Bible had certainly been occupying his thoughts for years, for a letter from Tommaso Obicini[10] to Cardinal Roberto Ubaldini in 1622 mentions his having already written to Paul V about it.[11] Was the final proposal entirely his own idea? Did it take shape in conversations with the Catholic missionaries he knew in Aleppo?[12] Was he inspired by the editors of texts, religious and otherwise, in the Greek-speaking world[13] and the activities of that foremost exponent of Orthodox "religious humanism",[14] Cyril Loukaris? He met Loukaris twice in Constantinople, first in 1615 and then, when the latter was Patriarch of Constantinople, during a stay of several months in 1626–7?[15] In the absence of further documentary evidence these questions cannot be answered.[16]

---

8 *SOCG*, vol. 181, fol. 36 (undated, but the Latin translation bears the date 4 October, 1623). Dozy, *Supplément aux dictionnaires arabes*, [1881], repr. Beirut: Libraire du Liban 1968, vol. 1, s.v. *z-w-n*, translates *zīwān/ziwān* as "du froment mal réussi, p.e. celui qui [...] a souffert de pluies trop abondantes". He identifies it as a specifically Aleppan word.

9 See also the paper by Carsten Walbiner in this volume on Melkite approaches to the Bible.

10 For the life of this Franciscan friar see Bottini, Giovanni-Claudio, "Tommaso Obicini (1585–1632), Custos of the Holy Land and Orientalist", in: *The Christian Heritage in the Holy Land*, Anthony O'Mahony with Göran Gunner and Kevork Hintlian, eds., London: Scorpion Cavendish 1995, 97–101, and the literature mentioned there.

11 I rely on the summary of this letter (*SOCG*, 382, *Memoriali 1622*, fols. 68–69) given by Kowalsky, Nikolaus, "Zur Vorgeschichte der arabischen Bibelübersetzung der Propaganda von 1671", *Neue Zeitschrift für Missionswissenschaft* XVI (1960), 268–9. Interestingly, as the letter makes clear, Tommaso Obicini thought that the edition could be prepared in Rome, using the Arabic manuscripts there.

12 As suggested by Carsten Walbiner in his paper in this volume.

13 Lassithiotakis, Michel, "Le role du livre imprimé dans la formation et le développement de la littérature en grec vulgaire (XVIe–XVIIe siècles)", *Revue des Mondes Musulmans et de la Méditerranée* 58/59 (1999), 196.

14 The expression is Podskalsky's (Podskalsky, Gerhard, *Griechische Theologie in der Zeit der Türkenherrschaft (1453–1821). Die Orthodoxie im Spannungsfeld der nachreformatorischen Konfessionen des Westens*, Munich: C.H. Beck'sche Verlagsbuchhandlung 1988, 117 ff.).

15 This was during the longest of Patriarch Cyril Loukaris' (1572–1638) occupations of the throne of Constantinople, when he was fully engaged in raising the educational level of the Greek Orthodox by reorganising the Patriarchal Academy, setting up a printing press and having the New Testament translated into modern Greek (Podskalsky, *Griechische The-*

As with a modern application for a research project, Meletius thought about the funding. His hope was that the Vatican would finance the collecting of the various versions and pay the team of six who would prepare the sound text. He himself was ready to assist them for nothing. He asked that the Custodian of the Holy Places in Jerusalem, Tommaso Obicini, be sent to work with them, for he already knew about this project and was generally well-liked among the Christians in Aleppo; he could also administer the Vatican's grant, so the Cardinals might be sure it did not end up in the wrong hands. And if for whatever reason he could not come, Meletius invited the Cardinals to nominate an administrator of the funds who would come to Aleppo. In this case, too, Meletius would do all he could to help him, asking no reward for himself.

Meletius was keen that the translation should be carried out in Aleppo, for "Arabic is our language" and thus mistakes would not creep into the resulting version, as they had to the printed Gospels he had received from the Vatican. He appreciated the effort made in Rome to translate the Bible, praising the knowledge of the Arabic language which the translators had acquired, although it was foreign to them. But the Christians in Arab lands had readers over their shoulders: "The Muslim scholars in our countries love honour and vie with each other in ornate style. When they saw [this translation], they discovered some formulations which they disapproved of on the grounds that they were incorrect (*ghayr murattab*)." Moreover, some words it used were unacceptable in *fuṣḥā*.[17]

Well aware of the weaknesses of the translation received from Rome,[18] Meletius decided to propose an alternative. Without waiting any longer for the project he had outlined to be accepted by the Vatican (in fact his offer of cooperation was never taken up), he gathered around him some local scholars[19] and Father

---

ologie, 166–171; Vaporis, N.M., "Patriarch Kyrillos Loukaris and the Translation of the Scriptures into Modern Greek", *Ekklēsiastikos Pharos* 59 (1977), 227–241).

16 Meletius' correspondence with the Vatican about printing Arabic books is set out and discussed in Walbiner, Carsten-Michael, "'Und um Jesu Willen, schickt sie nicht ungebunden!' Die Bemühungen des Meletius Karmah (1572–1635) um den Druck arabischer Bücher in Rom", in *Studies on the Christian Arabic Heritage in Honour of Father Prof. Dr. Samir Khalil Samir S.I. at the Occasion of his Sixty-Fifth Birthday*, Rifaat Ebeid and Herman Teule, eds., Leuven: Peeters 2004, 163–175.

17 *SOCG*, vol. 180 (*Lettere di Lingua straniera dall'Anno 1631 sino al 1645*), fol. 59 (1 March, 1632), and fol. 69 with the identical text.

18 This was presumably the Four Gospels, printed at the Medici Press in 1590–91, based on Hibatallāh b. al-ʿAssāl's (fl. 1231–1253; *GCAL* II, 403) Coptic version (*GCAL* I, 157–159; van Esbroeck, Michel, "Les versions orientales de la Bible: une orientation bibliographique", in: *The Interpretation of the Bible. The International Symposium in Slovenia*, Jože Kražovac, ed., Ljubljana and Sheffield: Slovenska akademija znanosti in umetnosti and Sheffield Academic Press 1998, 411–412). It is interesting that Meletius seems to think that the translation was made by non-Arabs.

19 "*Baʿḍ al-ʿārifīn ʿindanā*"; whether Muslims are meant is not explicit, *pace* Walbiner, "'Und um Jesu Willlen'",170, no. 27.

Agathangelos,[20] who was by then thoroughly familiar with Arabic and who had with him a Latin and a Hebrew text, and together they translated the first five chapters of Genesis.[21] In the covering letter to the Pope's adviser and the *Propaganda Fide* which accompanies the specimen Genesis translation, Meletius excuses himself and his team for proposing an alternative version to the Roman one, stressing that they have not done so out of arrogance but for the good of the local Christian community. As he explains, it is a general rule that each language has its own conventions, and a word for word translation will be faulty, needing correction and polishing up.[22] Where the Arabic language is concerned, one of its distinguishing traits which the translator must respect is word order. It may differ from that of the original version, but this must be accepted.[23]

It emerges, then, that the five chapters sent to the Vatican are not the product of Meletius' ambitious original plan but the modest result of the ad hoc working group he assembled in Aleppo. What can be said about this translation, and how does it differ from the one published 40 years later by the *Propaganda Fide*?[24] In what follows I point out some important features specific to Meletius' translation without, however, proposing a final judgement about its value compared with that of the Propaganda.

Although Meletius does not say which manuscripts he has used for his version, the observations in his letters give an idea of the range of sources he may have had at his disposal. They do not tell us which Arabic version he took as a basic text to be revised, but an idea may be formed of it from MS. Bodl. Ar. Hunt. 424.[25] This is one of the many Christian Arabic manuscripts donated to the Bodleian by Robert Huntington, for some ten years (1671–1681) chaplain to the merchants of the Levant Company in Aleppo. The only detailed discussion of it identifies it as a Melkite version of Genesis of unknown provenance and age, agreeing in many respects with the Septuagint but also showing decided affinities with the Hebrew Bi-

20 Agathangelo de Vendôme (1598–1638), a Capuchin, was in Aleppo from 1629 to 1633 before he was transferred to Cairo. He died as a martyr in Ethiopia (*GCAL* IV, 195).

21 *SOCG*, vol. 180, fols. 67, 68, 70, 71, 72 (see Plates 6 and 7).

22 *SOCG*, vol. 180, fols. 59 and 69.

23 *SOCG*, vol. 180, fol. 41 (May 1634); Walbiner, "'Und um Jesu Willlen'", 172 (as part of Meletius' recommendations for printing the Bible, translated in full, ibid. 171–173).

24 In preparing the first draft of this paper I could not consult the original print, *Biblia Sacra Arabica Sacrae Congregationis de Propagande Fide Iussu Edita. Al-Kutub al-muqaddasah bi-l-lisān al-ʿarabī*, Rome: Typis Sacrae Congretaionis de Propaganda Fide 1671, and had to rely on a reprint by Richard Watts (*Kitāb* [sic] *al-muqaddas*, London 1831). Just before the conference Father Makāriyūs Jabbūr, the librarian at Dayr al-Mukhalliṣ in Ṣarbā, kindly gave me a photocopy of the digitalised Rome 1671 edition, for which I am most grateful. As I discovered, the London reprint has some changes, mainly of orthography, but also more important ones, such as omitting the *Propaganda*'s indication of the Hebrew name of Genesis.

25 The similarities between Meletius' sample translation and MS. Bodl. Ar. Hunt. 424 were detected and pointed out to me by Ronny Vollandt, who also provided me with a copy of the relevant passage of this MS. I gratefully acknowledge his help.

ble and the Syriac Peshitta.[26] It is mostly written on paper, but has folios of parchment at the beginning and end; Genesis 1:1–5:10 (ff. 7r–13v) is written on parchment. The parchment sections represent versions made from the Septuagint, although they differ considerably in style from other Septuagint versions.[27]

In its original Greek, the Septuagint, still today the authoritative version of the Old Testament for liturgical use in the Orthodox Church, must have been an important point of reference for Meletius;[28] it will be seen that his version reflects the Septuagint text more closely than does Bodl. Ar. Hunt. 424. By contrast, when the Vatican authorities in 1622 decided to prepare their own text, they sought to base it on Vatican Arabic manuscripts and the Vulgate, whose version of the Pentateuch goes back to the Hebrew text. Although disagreements arose in Rome about whether a new translation should be made or an existing translation revised, and about which manuscripts should be consulted, comparison of the Arabic text with the authoritative Vulgate text and assimilation to it remained of prime importance, as can be seen from the final edition, where the Arabic and Latin texts are printed next to each other.[29] This difference in textual traditions needs to be borne in mind when Meletius' specimen translation and the *Propaganda Fide* translation are compared.

In the following discussion of the different versions, I shall refer to the specimen translation Meletius made in Aleppo as A, the *Propaganda* translation as P, and MS. Bodl. Ar. Hunt. 424, which seems to offer a backdrop for Meletius' revision, as H. Divergences manifest themselves from the very beginning. [30] In A, Genesis is entitled "*Sifr kawn al-dunyā, wa-yuqāl lahu bi-l-ʿibrānī barāsīt*",[31] and H has "*Sifr al-khalīqah wa-huwa sifr kawn al-dunyā*", while P has "*Sifr takwīn al-khalāʾiq,*

[26] Rhode, Joseph Francis, *The Arabic Versions of the Pentateuch in the Church of Egypt. A Study from Eighteen Arabic and Copto-Arabic MSS (IX–XVII century) in the National Library at Paris, the Vatican and Bodleian Libraries and the British Museum*, Leipzig: W. Drugulin 1921, 118.

[27] Ibid., 89–90.

[28] Meletius' frequent requests in his letters to the Vatican for Greek reference works (cf. note 3 above and the titles mentioned there) reflect the importance he accorded to the Greek textual tradition. Requests for books, mostly in Greek, also occur in *SOCG*, vol. 181, fols. 35 and 208, and vol. 180, fols. 75 and 35; and thanks for books received in *SOCG*, vol. 181, fol. 36, and 180, fol. 75.

[29] The details of the various decisions are given in Kowalsky, "Zur Vorgeschichte", 268–274. From the documents he quotes, it emerges that the first pages of the translation of Genesis were not printed before 1632, and that the translation was made by a committee, *pace* the introduction to the digitalised copy of the *Propaganda* edition in Dayr al-Shīr (OBARL 00001), which gives the translator as Father Sarkīs al-Rizzī and the date of printing as 1625. In fact Sarkīs al-Rizzī, Maronite Archbishop of Damascus but resident in Rome from 1622 until his death in 1638, chaired the committee of five translators.

[30] In the following discussion the vowelling follows the rules of Classical Arabic as much as possible, since very little is known about pre-modern Middle Arabic vowelling and pronounciation.

[31] So, at least, it appears in the photocopy of the text provided by the Vatican archives, though a mark over the *sīn* might be intended for the three dots of *shīn*.

wa-yuqāl lahu bi-l-ʿibrānī barāshīth". Although in modern Arabic *kawn* expresses "a state of being", there are instances in classical Arabic of its meaning "coming into being, genesis".[32] Why P has preferred *al-khalāʾiq* to *al-dunyā* calls for an explanation which I cannot provide. There is nothing corresponding in H to A's and P's indication of the Hebrew name of Genesis, but H introduces the entire Pentateuch with the heading *Kitāb al-tawrāh al-munzalah ʿalā ṣafī Allāh Mūsā al-nabī wa-huwa khams al-asfār*.

Another difference concerns the designation of chapters and verses. H does not indicate chapter or verse divisions at all. A indicates chapters with *faṣl*,[33] a standard term in Arabic also found, for instance, in Saadiah Gaon's translation of the Pentateuch[34] and in the London Polyglot, but it does not mark verses. P gives chapter headings with the typically Christian *aṣḥāḥ*, and adds the verse numbers in the margin.

I now present some significant textual variants in the two versions A and P, referring also to H where A, or far more rarely P, agrees with it. One category of variants can be explained by the attempt to follow the Greek Septuagint (LXX) text as faithfully as possible in Arabic.[35] In three-quarters of the some 200 instances where A and P differ and one of them reflects the LXX, it is A which does so. This may concern grammatical forms: defined as against undefined or vice versa (1:6: *bayna māʾin wa-māʾ*; P and H: *bayna l-māʾi wa-l-māʾ*; 1:21: *al-ḥīthāna* [sic] *l-ʿiẓāma*; P: *ḥīṭānan ʿiẓāman*; cf. H: *al-ḥiyāt* [sic] *al-ʿaẓīmah*); participle instead of relative clause (1:26: *al-mutaḥarrikah*; P: *alladhī yataḥarriku*) or the reverse (2:22: *allatī akhadhahā*; P: *al-maʾkhūdhah*; cf. H: [*al-ḍilʿ*] *alladhī akhadhahu*); *maṣdar* instead of verbal form (3:24: *li-ḥifẓi*; P and H: *li-yaḥfuẓa*; 1:15: *li-l-ḍiyāʾi ...li-l-ishrāqi*; P: *li-tunīra....wa-li-yuḍīʾa* [sic]; cf. H: *li-l-ḍiyāʾi ...li-yaẓhura*). An instance where P is closer to the LXX is 3:8, where Adam and Eve hear *ṣawta l-rabbi māshiyan* in the garden; in A they hear *ṣawta mashyi l-rabbi*. Undoubtedly, echoing the LXX may lead to some strange or unidiomatic results. In A, God takes from Adam *wāḥidatan min aḍlāʿihi* (2:21 = LXX *mian tōn pleurōn autou*) where P has the stylistically preferable *ḍilʿan min aḍlāʿihi*. God rests from *kulli ʿamalihi lladhī ʿamalahu* in P (= LXX *pantōn tōn ergōn*

---

32 *Wörterbuch der klassischen arabischen Sprache*, Band I: *Kāʾ*, Wiesbaden: Otto Harrassowitz 1970, s.v. *k-w-n* (with an instance in al-Jāḥiẓ where it is parallel with *khalq*).

33 The heading "*Al-faṣl al-khāmis*" is omitted, but the translation continues to the end of Genesis 5. This omission should, I believe, be seen as one of a number of scribal errors in the text (for others, see below), rather than as a radical attempt to renumber the chapters of Genesis.

34 The Arabic translation by Saadiah Gaon (Saʿīd b. Yūsuf al-Fayyūmī) (269/882–331/942) of the first four chapters of Genesis is printed in Arabic script in Kahle, Paul, *Die arabischen Bibelübersetzungen. Texte mit Glossar und Literaturübersicht*, Leipzig: J.C. Hinrichs'sche Buchhandlung 1904, 13–23.

35 For the LXX text with an extensive commentary I have drawn on Alexandre, Monique, *Le commencement du livre Genèse I–V. La version grecque de la Septante et sa réception*, Paris: Beauchesne 1988, which was undertaken as part of the project directed by Marguerite Harl of translating the Septuagint into French.

autou hōn epoiēsen), while A has *kulli l-ʿamali lladhī ʿamalahu* (2:2). A phrases God's recommendation to Adam to eat of the trees of the garden *Li-l-akli taʾkul* (2:16; = LXX *brōsei phagē*) where P has *kul aklan*.

A large number of variants concern vocabulary. The light that God creates on Day One is *ḍawʾ* in A and H, *nūr* in P. In A and H, Cain kills Abel in a *buqʿah* (4:8; cf. LXX *pedion*) but in P the deed is done in a *ḥaql*. "Tree" in A is usually *ʿūd* (= LXX *xulon*) following H, which has *ʿūd* consistently, whereas P and occasionally A have *shajarah*. As this example shows clearly, some of the variants reflect LXX usage. God *jabala* (created) living creatures in A (2:19), whereas in P he *ṣawwara* them. To prepare Adam for the removal of his rib, God cast a *subātan* on him *fa-nāma* according to A (2:21), while P has God cast a *subāta nawmin* on him *fa-raqada*; here both versions partly follow H, where Adam is overcome by a *subāta nawmin fa-nāma*. A renders the bdellium (LXX *anthrax*) found in the land of Havilat as *laʿl* (2:12) in contrast to P's *lūlū*. The preposition *kata* in the sense of "according to" is rendered in A by *ʿalā*, *ḥadwi* or *ḥasaba* (e.g. 1:21, 25); in P by *ka-* or *ka-mithli*. God's exhortation to mankind to fill the world, *imlayā l-arḍ* according to A and H (1:28), becomes *ishḥanā l-arḍ* in P; the same difference is found in the exhortation to marine life (1:22).

Many other instances of alternative translations could be given. For instance, A's serpent is *aktharu makran* (cf. H's *aktharu fiṭnatan*) than all the animals, while P's is *akhbathu* (3:1). Describing his reaction to hearing God call him, A's Adam says "*khiftu*" while P's says "*faziʿtu*" (3:10). Abel's offering of the firstlings of his flocks includes their fat, *shuḥūm*, in A (4:4; cf. H's *shuḥūmah* [sic]), but their *simān* in P. After Abel's death, Eve bears Seth, saying: "[*Allāhu*] *aqāma lī zarʿan*" (A, H), or "*waḍaʿa lī zarʿan*" (P) (4:22). Lamech will be avenged *sabʿatan fī sabʿīna* (A) but *sabʿatan bi-sabʿīna* (P) (4:21).[36] When Cain invites Abel to go out with him into the field (4:8), A has the idiomatic *halummā bi-nā ilā khārij* for P's *li-nakhruj ilā l-ḥaql*. In 2:3, where God is mentioned twice ("So God blessed the seventh day and hallowed it, because on it God rested from all his work which he had done in creation"), A cleverly gets around this un-Arabic repetition of the subject as follows: "*li-an* [sic] *fīhi kaffa min kulli ʿamalin abdaʿahu taʿālā li-l-ʿamal*", whereas P has: "*li-annahu fīhi starāḥa min jamīʿi ʿamalihi lladhī khalaqa llāhu li-yaʿmal*". But P's rendering of God's "It is not good (that the man should be alone)" (2:18) as *lā yaḥsunu* is preferable to A's *laysa huwa jayyidun* [sic], which echoes LXX. A few variants can be explained by H's and A's awareness of possible Muslim readers' sensitivities. On the fourth day of the Creation God puts lights in the firmament for signs (1:14) which P renders *āyāt*, while A and H prefer the more neutral *ʿalāmāt*. Cain's bringing an offering of the first-fruits of the earth (4:3) is expressed by *qaddama… ḍaḥīyatan* in A and H, rather than *qarraba… qurbānan*, as in P.[37]

[36] The verse numbers at the end of Genesis 4 in the *Propaganda Fide* text differ slightly from those in modern Bibles. Meletius' text has no verse divisions.

[37] In vol. 5, however, A also has *qarābīnihi* for Cain's offerings, while H has retained *ḍaḥāyāhu*.

A locates the third river of Paradise, the Tigris, in a way easily comprehensible to Arab readers: *wa-huwa al-jārī muqābila l-ʿIrāq* (cf. H: *wa-huwa al-jārī muqābila ahli l-ʿIrāq*), while P, retaining the conventional designation, also found in LXX, writes *wa-huwa yamḍī qibāla l-Athūrīyīn* (2:14). A somewhat similar approach to A's can be found in Saadiah Gaon's translation, for he renders the same passage *wa-huwa al-sāʾiru sharqīya l-Mawṣil*.[38]

Where orthography and *iʿrāb* are concerned, the Aleppo translation by and large reveals more characteristics of Middle Arabic than does the *Propaganda* translation. *Hamzah* is often left out, for instance in *al-samā* or *al-ḍawʾ*, but there are also examples of these words where it is included, e.g. in 1:8 and 18. The dots of *tāʾ marbūtah* may be omitted, particularly at the end of a phrase. This is carried even further in the name of the river *al-Furāt*, which A spells *al-Furāh* (2:14).[39] Two cases of perfect feminine second person endings with long *ī* occur in 3:14, when God addresses the serpent: *faʿaltī* and *antī*. In the form *fāʿilun* with middle radical *wāw* or *yā*, *hamzah* is replaced by *yāʾ*: e.g. *qāyilan*; this, however, is also standard in P. *Alif maqsūrah* is replaced by *alif*, as in *sammā*, *alqā*; combined with the absence of *hamzah* this gives *rā* for *raʾā*. *Kāna* and *laysa* may be followed by the nominative, as in the example quoted above; *laysa huwa jayyidun*, and the particles *inna* and *anna* may introduce subjects in the nominative. By contrast, P seems ill at ease with the dual; it has Lamech address his two wives "*Ismaʿā ṣawtī yā nisāʾa Lāmikh wa-anṣitā li-qawlī…*" (4:21).

In chapter 5, with its list of Adam's descendants, A's syntax of numerals, which all qualify *sanatan/sinīna*, is partly Classical. In the case of numerals between 11 and 99, however, Middle Arabic intrudes, as in *khamsata ʿashara*, *khamsata wa-sittīna*. When hundreds are mentioned too, an unusual phenomenon is the omission of *wāw* between the hundred and the unit: *mīyah ithnayn wa-sittīna*, *thamānimīyah khamsah wa-tisʿīna* (but *thamānimīyah wa-arbaʿīn sanah*).

Some features which only occur once or twice may be explained rather as scribal errors than as traces of Middle Arabic. I would put *ʿaḍman min ʿiẓāmī* (2:23) in this category; A does not normally confuse homophonic consonants. Likewise, *lam tamūtā* for *lan tamūtā* (3:4), *ablasahumā* for *albasahumā* (3:21) and, most strikingly, the omission of the heading *al-faṣl al-khāmis* are the result of oversights. All in all, the presence of Middle Arabic in Meletius' translation is limited. It may not, however, have been unintentional. Attitudes to Middle Arabic among both Muslim and Christian writers in the 17 th century were far less purist than those that developed later.[40] Moreover, the desire to make the Bible and service books accessible to

---

38 Kahle, *Die arabischen Bibelübersetzungen*, 18.

39 P has overcorrected here, writing *al-Furāth*.

40 See the examples in Jérôme Lentin's extensive study, *Recherches sur l'histoire de la langue arabe au Proche-Orient à l'époque moderne*, unpublished Thèse de Doctorat d'état, Université de Paris III 1997. The introduction of printing seems to have encouraged the trend towards linguistic purism – as it did the reference to a "classical" period of Arabic literature. This

the (literate) faithful precluded the use of too elevated a language. A parallel exists in Greek literature of the early Ottoman period. A trend towards employing the spoken language in written texts can be observed, for instance, in the works of Nikolaos Sophianos (c. 1500–after 1552), who sought to spread education in the vernacular,[41] and, where Scripture was concerned, in Ioannikios Kartanos' *Anthologion*, compiled from the Old and New Testaments, which also included an outline of popular theology, sermons and an explanation of the Liturgy.[42] Patriarch Cyril Loukaris' bilingual New Testament with modern Greek, already referred to, which was ultimately printed in Geneva by Pierre Aubert, the official publisher to the Republic, in 1637 or 1638 after an earlier attempt to bring it out in Amsterdam failed, belongs to the same trend. [43]

To conclude: without wishing at this point to give an overall judgement on the value of the Aleppo translation in comparison to that of the *Propaganda*,[44] I believe that it has its place in the history of Arabic Bible translations. Meletius' conception of an ecumenical translation project was extraordinarily far-sighted, and his desire to take into consideration the various versions derived from different language traditions was commendable. One may wonder how far his team followed the principles he had put forward when working on these five chapters of Genesis. Yet for readers and listeners in Syria, his incorporation of many expressions from an indigenous tradition of Bible translations represented by Bodl. Ar. Hunt. 424 was–or would have been–likely to smooth the way for his own translation, more scholarly and more closely aligned with the Septuagint, to gain acceptance. In any event, the decision of the *Congregatio de Propaganda Fide* to ignore his vision of Bible translation and his specimen translation and to give so much weight to the Vulgate can only be regretted.

---

trend has been labelled "Klassizismus der arabischen Druckkultur des 19. Jahrhunderts" (Reichmuth, Stephan, and Schwarz, Florian, eds., *Zwischen Alltag und Schriftkultur: Horizonte des Individuellen in der arabischen Literatur des 17. und 18. Jahrhunderts*, Beirut and Würzburg: Ergon Verlag 2008, XVI [editors' introduction]).

41 Dimaras, C. Th., *Histoire de la littérature néo-hellénique des origines à nos jours*, Athènes: Institut Français d'Athènes 1965–1966, 99–100; Lassithiotakis, "Le role du livre imprimé", 202–203.

42 Argyriou, Astérios, "La Bible dans le monde orthodoxe au XVIe siècle" in *Le temps des Réformes et la Bible* (Bible de tous les temps, vol. V), Guy Bedouelle and Bernard Roussel, eds., Paris: Beauchesne 1989, 396–398.

43 Staikos, Konstantinos Sp., and Sklavenitis, Triantaphyllos E., *The Publishing Centres of the Greeks. From the Renaissance to the Neo-Hellenic Enlightenment*, Athens: National Book Centre of Greece 2001, 94–95; Reverdin, Olivier, "Livres grecs imprimés à Genève au XVIe et au XVIIe siècle", in *Cinq siècles d'imprimerie genevoise. Actes du Colloque internationale sur l'histoire du l'impression et de livre à Genève, 27–30 avril 1978*, Jean-Daniel Candaux and Bernard Lascaze, eds., Geneva: Société d'histoire et d'archéologie 1980, 238.

44 A systematic comparison of the Aleppo translation with that of the *Propaganda* and older, probably Syrian, versions such as Bodl. Arab. Hunt 424 could be rewarding for the study not only of the Arabic Bible but also of the Arabic language in the Mamluk and early Ottoman period.

A final question: could it be that the *Propaganda Fide* translation imposed itself for more than a century not so much because of any text-critical or literary superiority but because it was not an individual effort? On the contrary, it was backed by an organisation and could thus be completed. The Congregation for the Propagation of the Faith took 40 years to produce an entire Bible in Arabic, with various scholars being involved in the enterprise as time passed. When Meletius outlined his project to the Vatican, he was already in his late fifties. By analogy, he would have needed to live to be a hundred to see his translation finished.

Revision of the manuscripts of the "so-called Smith-Van Dyck Bible"

Some remarks on the making of this Bible translation[1]

Sara Binay

The Near East School of Theology (NEST) in Beirut is home to a largely forgotten treasure that has long ceased to be consulted by researchers. The manuscripts of the so-called Smith–Van Dyck Bible are stored in tin boxes which are kept in a special room. Concerning the valuable contents of the boxes, some reports about the process of this translation seem to me sometimes confusing or contradictory.

As a matter of fact, we know that in 1844 the American Mission in Syria voted for the complete and new translation of the Holy Scriptures based on the manuscripts in the "Original Languages". Eli Smith, who ran the American Press at Beirut, was appointed to lead the work on the project. Until then, the Protestant missionaries had used prints of the Roman *Propaganda Fide* Edition finished in 1671 without the books which they considered to be apocryphal[2], but this translation was now seen as partly "unintelligible". Or, in the words of Eli Smith:

> "The whole version is not in a classical style. The structure of the sentences is awkward, the choice of words is not select, and the rules of grammar are often transgressed. We have been ashamed to put the sacred books of our religion, in such a dress, into the hands of a respectable Muhammedan or Druze, and felt it our duty to accompany them with an apology; and some of us never think of reading a chapter in public without previously revising it."[3]

My interest in the matter was aroused by a discussion in the *Journal of the American Oriental Society* from the years 1885–1889, where one can find contradictory reports about the supposed destruction of Eli Smith's translation.

Prof. Hall reported that

> "It is clear that in the Old Testament Dr. Smith left a MS translation of the Pentateuch, the prophetical books of Hosea, Joel, Amos, Obadiah, Jonah, Micah, Nahum, and 52 chapters of Isaiah. Likewise, he had printed 16 chapters of Matthew, besides translating

---

1 I owe thanks for their help, discussion and encouragement in my work to Dr. George Sabra, Rima M. Fakhri, Matthias Fuhst, Syrinx von Hees and Dónall Ó Mearáin.

2 Tibawi, A.L., *American Interests in Syria 1800–1901. A Study of Educational, Literary and Religious Work*, Oxford: Clarendon 1966, 122.

3 "Report of E. Smith, in March 16th 1844, on the existing Arabic Versions of the Scriptures", in: *Brief documentary history of the translation of the Scriptures into the Arabic Language by Rev. Eli Smith, D.D., and Rev. C.V.A. Van Dyck, D.D.*, Presbyterian Church in the U.S.A., Syrian Mission, ed., Beirut: American Presbyterian Mission Press 1900, 1f.

> the entire New Testament. It is also true that these printed chapters of Matthew were destroyed; but it is the opinion of the librarian that all Dr. Smith's MSS. of all the work that he did on the translation of the Bible are preserved in the Mission Library, "under lock" in tin boxes, and highly valued by the Mission. If this opinion is correct, the story that Dr. Smith's MS translation of the New Testament was destroyed is untrue, and grew out of the fact of the destruction of the printed sheets of Matthew – which, of course were destroyed only because of their following a Greek text different from the *ignis fatuus* of the *textus receptus*."[4]

This passage deals with Eli Smith's legacy and questions his competence or, to be more precise, his orthodoxy.

For sure, Eli Smith must be considered the father of Protestant Bible translation into Arabic. The reasons for the urgent need for a new intelligible edition have already been mentioned. Of course, the idea of the project for a new translation was not born from his mind only; its necessity had become apparent from the beginnings of Protestant missionary activity in the Middle East.[5]

Reverend Dr. Eli Smith came to the Near East in 1827[6] and lived mainly there until his death. He was the founder and promoter of the American Press in Beirut. He was the natural choice for the Board of the Syrian Mission to appoint to supervise the new translation in 1844.

My suspicions were aroused by a letter from him to Emil Rödiger, first secretary of the DMG (German Oriental Society) at this time, quoted in the *Zeitschrift der Deutschen Morgenländischen Gesellschaft* (*Journal of the German Oriental Society*) in 1856, where he writes about his own work.

> "Meine eigene Arbeit, die arabische Bibelübersetzung [Ztschr. IX, 269], bleibt in ihrem gemessenen Gange. Als Styl- und Druckprobe lege ich Ihnen ein Blatt von dem Exodus und eins vom Ev. Matth. bei. Sie werden daraus ersehen, dass die Herausgabe bloss des Pentateuchs nicht wenig Mühe macht. Was die Arbeit besonders aufhält, ist, dass wir von jedem Correcturbogen Exx. an alle Missionsstationen in Syrien versenden; aber der Zeitverlust wird mehr als aufgewogen durch den Gewinn, den die Uebersetzung selbst davon zieht. Ungelehrte, aber verständige Eingeborene verschiedener Landestheile lesen die Correcturbogen und merken alle Wörter und Redensarten an, die sie nicht verstehen. Dies zeigt uns, welche Veränderungen im Interesse allgemeiner Verständlichkeit zu machen sind, bevor der Bogen abgezogen wird."[7]

My translation, possibly a back-translation,[8] of his letter reads as follows:

---

4 *Journal of the American Oriental Society* (*JAOS*) 13 (1889), VIII–IX.

5 Tibawi, *American Interests*, 121.

6 Salibi, Kamal and Khoury, Yusuf K., eds., *The Missionary Herald. Reports from Ottoman Syria. 1819–1870*, 5 vols., Amman: The Royal Institute for Interfaith Studies 1995, vol. I, 270.

7 "Aus einem Briefe von Dr. E. Smith", *Zeitschrift der Deutschen Morgenländischen Gesellschaft* (*ZDMG*) 10 (1856), 813.

8 We know that Smith wrote notes in English to Fleischer in Leipzig. Cf. Glass, Dagmar, *Malta, Beirut, Leipzig, and Beirut again. Eli Smith, the American Mission and the Spread of Arabic Typography*, Beirut: Orient-Institut Beirut 1998, 16, pl. 8. One would have to check the archive of the DMG to ascertain the original language of the quoted letter, but this does not concern us here.

"My own work, the Arabic Bible translation, is still ongoing. As an example of the style and the typesetting, I am enclosing for you one sheet from Exodus and one from the Gospel according to Matthew. You will see from this that the publication of the Pentateuch alone takes much effort. What particularly holds up the work is that we send copies of each printed sheet to all missionary stations in Syria. But the loss of time is more than made up for by the benefits to the translation. Uneducated but intelligent natives from different parts of the country read the proofs and indicate all words and expressions which they can not understand. This shows us which corrections have to be done in the interest of general comprehensibility before the sheet is printed."

There is not a single mention of his "native helpers" in Beirut on this occasion. We find the same silence in the *Missionary Herald*, a journal which reported from all mission stations around the world. When it speaks about the Arabic Bible translation, the focus is on Eli Smith alone.[9] Later on, Van Dyck summarised that

"As Arabic scholars, Dr. Smith associated with him Sheikh Nasîf al-Yazigi and M[uallim] B[utrus el-] Bistani, both Christians. I had with me Sheikh Yusuf el-Asīr, a Muslim, and a graduate of the college of the great Mosque of El-Azhar in Cairo."[10]

Buṭrus al-Bustānī, born in 1819, was one of the most famous personalities of the intellectual scene in Ottoman Syria during the 19th century. There are some valuable papers focusing on his life and work[11] as well as the great number of books about the period which can not avoid mentioning his name for one reason or another. I will look only at his engagement with the Bible translation by the Protestant mission to Syria.

I think one can consider the young (and also the older) Buṭrus al-Bustānī a stroke of good luck for the American missionaries. He embodied many different virtues and personal skills. A well-educated, civilised man from a good family, open-minded and a good social networker, he was also gifted in languages. Apart from his mastery of Arabic, his knowledge of Syriac originating from his years of study at ʿAin Waraqa, which was a sort of academy for the Maronite elite, was supplemented by learning Greek and Hebrew with the missionaries. We should not overlook in our context that he mastered English, which allowed him, besides his job with the American mission, to work as a dragoman for the American consulate in Beirut. All of these skills enabled him to prepare the first draft of the Holy Book in Arabic during his work with Eli Smith on the Bible translation. I will not claim that Eli Smith was not a good Arabist; we have no proof

9 Cf. *The Missionary Herald*, vol. IV, 185, 214.

10 *JAOS* 11 (1885), 280.

11 *Encyclopaedia of Islam* (*EI*[1]), vol. I, 805; *EI*[2], Suppl., 159f; Tibawi, A.L., "The American Missionaries in Beirut and Buṭrus al-Bustānī", in: *Middle Eastern Affairs* 3 (1963), 137–182; Zachs, Fruma, *The Making of a Syrian Identity. Intellectuals and Merchants in Nineteenth Century Beirut*, Leiden: Brill 2005, 222f.

for such a conclusion. But he confessed to al-Bustānī's "giving to the work a native coloring which a foreigner could not so easily accomplish".[12] Besides the fact that Smith used the Roman edition[13] as "help"[14] for the translation project, the similarity between the "new" Protestant translation and older manuscripts[15] may partly originate in al-Bustānī's familiarity with older versions since the time of his study in ʿAin Waraqa.

The contract between Smith and al-Bustānī included the condition "that in case of the death of either party, the contract became null and void."[16] The two men worked together for nearly ten years, until Smith died in January 1857, leaving behind a complete translation of the four Gospels and several books of the Old Testament. Afterwards, the Protestant mission was not committed to working with al-Bustānī further on the project.

In Eli Smith's time, al-Bustānī was not only in charge of translating, but was also responsible for the Bible at the printing stage. As Eli Smith put it:

> "...an arrangement has been made with Mr. Bistany by which he becomes responsible for the correct printing of the book. He is to attach the references to the proper words in the translation by looking them all out in their places, to verify them by looking them out again when in type, to read at least four proofs, and to see that the division and numbering of the chapters and verses correspond to the same in the English version."[17]

Let us now turn to the manuscripts stored at NEST in Beirut. In my opinion, there is no material trace of al-Bustānī's work in the MSS. This opinion contradicts a handwritten note probably added by Van Dyck to the MS. boxes. There, he suggests that the red notes put on the right page of the MS. booklets were by al-Bustānī.[18] For me it seems more likely that these were suggestions by Naṣīf al-Yāzijī. I come to this conclusion based on various facts.

Van Dyck was reporting about the translation process about a decade after it took place and may have been confused. He stated that

---

12 "Dr. Smith's Report on the translation of the Scriptures, April 1854", in: *Brief documentary history of the translation of the Scriptures into the Arabic Language by Rev. Eli Smith, D.D., and Rev. C.V.A. Van Dyck, D.D.*, Presbyterian Church in the U.S.A., Syrian Mission, ed., Beirut: American Presbyterian Mission Press 1900, 8.

13 On the genesis of this edition see the article by P. Féghali in this volume.

14 "Smith's Report, 1854", 6, where he names other "helps" such as Saadiah Gaon's and Erpenius' translation as well as different readers used by the churches in Lebanon at his time.

15 Dr. Nicolas Abou Mrad emphasised this fact during the Beirut Conference on Bible translation.

16 "Dr. C.V.A. Van Dyck's Report on the translation, April 29th, 1863", in: *Brief documentary history of the translation of the Scriptures into the Arabic Language by Rev. Eli Smith, D.D., and Rev. C.V.A. Van Dyck, D.D.*, Presbyterian Church in the U.S.A., Syrian Mission, ed., Beirut: American Presbyterian Mission Press 1900, 14.

17 "Smith's Report, 1854", 12f.

18 See Plate 8 in the Appendix.

> "A clear copy of each book [of the Bible], as soon as it was finished, with lines wide apart, and with different readings in red ink under such words or passages as admitted of more than one meaning, was put by Mr. Bistany into Dr. Smith's hands."[19]

If this were true, then we would be holding in our hands the very first draft done by al-Bustānī and Smith. Actually, we have found in the tin box, among the papers of the Genesis translation, an envelope probably containing the true *first* draft[20] written by al-Bustānī and Smith, which differs very much from the text that was printed in the end.

Apart from this, the assumption that these "clear copies" would be al-Bustānī's work contradicts the further report by Van Dyck that

> "This work [the first draft] was then put into the hands of Nasif al-Yazigi (corrector of the press), who copied it with Dr. Smith's corrections, and made such of his own as he thought the grammar rhetoric of the language required; but being with no language besides the Arabic, and often prone to sacrifice the meaning to a grammatical or rhetorical nicety, the work was not to be trusted until it had another revision. This Dr. Smith gave about to put the work to press."[21]

The second option, which has been the most widely believed until today, is that the booklets contain the text copied by al-Yāzijī. Either the corrections in red are by al-Yāzijī using the same method as was established for the lost drafts by Smith and al-Bustānī, or al-Bustānī went over the text a second time. But we have no evidence for this possibility apart from Van Dyck's handwritten note. This contradicts the heretofore assumed sequence of events: that Eli Smith worked first *only* with al-Bustānī and afterwards *only* with al-Yāzijī on the text.

A very unlikely option would be to conclude that the right page is the draft by al-Bustānī, which was then copied on the left page by al-Yāzijī. It is very obvious that the copies are from the one hand. We can clearly see the corrections made by the pencil of Eli Smith.

If we examine the suggestions in red, we can see that they are mostly not accepted. This finding might help us with our investigation because it corresponds with statements by the American missionaries regarding al-Yāzijī, criticising his taste and style in Arabic.[22]

This brings us to the third person to be part of the translation team. Naṣīf al-Yāzijī (1800–1871), another well-known personality in the literary life of the late Ottoman period,[23] differed from al-Bustānī. Belonging to a Greek-Catholic family, he dedicated most of his life to studying and producing Arabic literature, a

---

19 "Van Dyck's Report, 1863", 14.

20 A comparison between this draft and older versions of the Bible in Arabic is still a *desideratum*.

21 "Van Dyck's Report, 1863", 14.

22 "Van Dyck's Report, 1863", 14 (quoted above, cf. note 20). Cf. note 23.

23 *EI*[1], vol. IV, 1170f; von Kremer, A., "Nâṣîf aljâziǵî", *ZDMG* 25 (1871), 244f; Zachs, *The Making of a Syrian Identity*, 243.

good deal of this output being poetry. For twelve years he worked as a scribe at the office of Emir Bashir in Beiteddin. As far as I know he did not speak any European language (although he may have spoken French). The quotation from Van Dyck's report indicates that he had no knowledge of any Semitic language other than Arabic.

From both Smith's and Van Dyck's statements, we learn that, despite al-Yāzijī's authority in terms of the Arabic language, he also posed a problem to the missionaries. Quoting Smith:

> "Finally, I sit down over the work with Sheikh Nasīf, and receive his criticisms upon it, as an Arabic composition, in reference to grammar, lexicography and taste, after which he copies the work anew. His criticisms undergo a thorough discussion, often consuming much time, and special caution is constantly observed lest he sacrifice any important shade of the inspired idea to the niceties of Arabic grammar or taste, which, after all, are not essential. Yet it is my aim to let no phrase finally pass which does not receive his approbation. Master as he is of Arabic grammar, and richly as his mind is stored with Arabic words, it was soon found that in the terms of natural history and certain other sciences, as well as in the technicalities of different trades and professions, and in other like matters, his knowledge was indistinct and often very dejective. [...] Unfortunately, also, for the last year, his mind has been under a cloud, and his health delicate, giving me much anxiety lest he may fail entirely. Yet my sessions with him are often invaluable, and I never cease to feel that his aid is essential to the best success of the work."[24]

One can notice here a very ambivalent attitude on the part of the Americans towards their native colleague. On the one hand, they could not do the work without his experience and profound knowledge in language matters; on the other, he was not a simple tool fulfilling the wishes of an American missionary, as at least Eli Smith seemed to expect.

So far, I have introduced the first Bible translation team I am examining. Let us sum up until this point: Al-Bustānī created the first draft, translating from the original texts, mainly Greek and Hebrew. As stated before, we must bear in mind that he was familiar with older translations, at least with the contentious *Propaganda Fide* Edition. The work done by al-Bustānī was reviewed by Smith, who compared it to older Arabic translations and applied to it his linguistic "critical apparatus", a collection of dictionaries and books on grammar, etc.[25] This version was put into the hands of al-Yāzijī, who copied it a first time and then, after a further revision by Smith based on a discussion of the text between the two men, copied it a second time. Then the booklet went to press. The galley proofs were sent to the other missionaries in Syria, proofread and corrected once more before the final printing, which was monitored by al-Bustānī.

---

24 "Smith's Report, 1854", 9.

25 Cf. "Smith's Report, 1854", 5 ff, on his "helps".

Regarding the share of the work done by al-Bustānī, a very paternalistic remark by Eli Smith summarises: "Yet no doubt there does remain, in the end, a decided coloring given by the first hand through which the work passes."[26]

Anyhow, we proceed now to the role of Reverend Dr Cornelius Van Dyck (1818–1895). He was a medical doctor with a lifelong dedication to the study and teaching of secular and scientific subjects. He was fluent in Arabic and had to a great degree adopted the late Ottoman lifestyle. From the point of view of his Lebanese contemporaries he was a beloved fellow.[27] Before he replaced the deceased Eli Smith at the Beirut mission, he lived in Sidon.

He also succeeded Eli Smith in the Bible translation project. His account of the work done by his predecessor raises some questions: "He [Smith] left a basis of the entire New Testament, but nothing was put in type."[28] This is not true, as we have already stated and as Van Dyck himself later confirmed. However, he gives evidence that Smith translated the whole New Testament and at the same time mentions the real obstacle to this invaluable work. Because he and al Bustānī used for their translation some manuscripts of the original scriptures which were not acknowledged as the "canonical" *textus receptus*,[29] the first prints of Matthew up to chapter 16 were burnt after his death. "[W]herefore," Cornelius Van Dyck informs us, "the whole New Testament had to be done over".[30]

Carefully comparing the printed Gospels with the manuscripts left by Smith, one can conclude that the printed edition follows to 95 %, if not more, the al-Bustānī–Smith–al-Yāzijī translation. There is proof that Cornelius Van Dyck really reread their translation but only in a few cases did he have to implement corrections, some based on his comparison with the recognised Greek text and some in matters of Arabic style.[31]

Therefore, one can surely argue that Smith and his colleagues did not leave only a "basis" translation behind: it was a nearly perfect or, let us say, complete translation of the New Testament.

Van Dyck had to continue translating the remaining books of the Old Testament in 1860. Unfortunately, we know nearly nothing about his "helpers" for the translation. Anyhow, one can follow his method through the NEST manuscripts, which show us a personality different from the very fastidious Eli Smith.

---

26 Ibid., 9.

27 We can infer this from the so-called "Cabinett of Van Dyck", a wooden sideboard containing his books in Arabic presented to him as a gift by "the Beirutis" in 1890 on the occasion of the 50th anniversary of his arrival in the Near East.

28 *JAOS* 11 (1885), 279.

29 Cf. "Van Dyck's Report, 1863", 15; *JAOS* 11 (1885), 279.

30 Ibid., 279.

31 See Plate 9 in the Appendix.

At least one must ask whom Van Dyck employed as a scribe. If we compare the main manuscripts left by Van Dyck with his handwriting in Arabic, it becomes quite obvious that the manuscripts were not copied by himself.

Now we come back to a previous quotation:

> "As Arabic scholars, Dr. Smith associated with him Sheikh Nasîf al-Yazigi and M[uallim] B[utrus el-] Bistani, both Christians. I had with me Sheikh Yusuf el-Asīr, a Muslim, and a graduate of the college of the great Mosque of El-Azhar in Cairo. *I preferred a Muslim to a Christian, as coming to the work with no preconceived ideas of what a passage ought to mean, and as being more extensively read in Arabic.*"[32] (My italics)

Sheikh Yūsuf al-Asīr's is the last name to mention in association with the Bible translation team. He was a learned Muslim scholar from a Sidonian family, who spent long years of study in Egypt, worked for the Ottoman administration and taught Arabic at the Maronite school of *al-Ḥikma* and al-Bustānīs *National School*.[33] Yūsuf al-Asīr was also an editor of the first Muslim weekly in the Near East, *Thamarāt al-Funūn*, a fact often ignored in publications on the period.[34]

Since we have hardly any information from other sources in relation to his part in the translation of the Scriptures, it was not easy to identify his contributions to the material stored in the once-famous tin boxes. Van Dyck noted in his report on the Bible translation in 1863 that "during the progress of his work the translator was assisted by Sheikh Yusuf el-Asîr"[35], without explaining more on the nature of this assistance. We know that he composed, besides his classical *Dīwān*, hymns which can be found in the contemporary hymn book used by the Lebanese Protestant congregation, better known as the *National Evangelical Church*.[36]

So, in the end one can find traces of al-Asīr's contribution in the manuscripts of the translation of the Psalms. Here, we have a new hand not only providing vocalisation and the like but also adding remarks on grammar, syntax or lexicography.[37]

Apart from this, the fifth tin box at the NEST contains the first printed versions of the New (1860) and Old (probably 1865) Testaments, originally without vocalisation, which someone, in my view most probably Yūsuf al-Asīr, has vowelled by hand.[38] In some remarks on the margin we recognise the same handwriting as in the Psalms. Van Dyck wrote in 1885 that the vowelling for the NT was done by himself and "then submitted to Sheikh Yusuf el-Asîr el-Azhari" and other schol-

---

32 Ibid., 280.

33 De Ṭarrāzī, Fīlīb, *Tārīḫ aṣ-ṣiḥāfa al-ʿarabīya*, Bairūt 1913–1933, vol. I (1913), 135ff.

34 Ibid., vol. I (1913), 138; vol. II (1913), 35.

35 "Van Dyck's Report, 1863", 16.

36 Adib Saab's contribution to the Arabic section of this volume contains an example of al-Asīr's poetry for liturgical use.

37 See Plate 10 in the Appendix.

38 See Plate 11 in the Appendix.

ars.[39] In the fourth volume of *History of the Missions of the American Board of Commissioners for Foreign Missions to the Oriental Churches* (1872) we read the remark that "Dr. Van Dyck was preparing a vowelled edition of the New Testament, suitable for Mohammedans, written in the style of the Koran, which required much care and labor."[40] We can only infer the role of Yūsuf al-Asīr in this.

Having identified the translation team through investigation of the NEST manuscripts, we can come to a conclusion.

Even if it is not possible to single out every individual contribution to the translated text by the members of the first group (Smith–al-Yāzijī–al-Bustānī), it seems to me beyond question that the influence of al-Bustānī and al-Yāzijī must be considered very great. Even after the revision by Cornelius Van Dyck, the changes which he made to the text produced by this group are very minor. In general, it is the Smith–al-Yāzijī–al-Bustānī text which was printed, at least for the New Testament.

According to his report, the identities of Van Dyck's "helpers" remain mainly – with the exception of Yūsuf al-Asīr – unknown.[41]

I would like to speculate briefly on some of the cultural influences brought to bear on the translations by the team.

The missionaries, having received a Protestant education in America and Europe, came to the Orient, learned Arabic and gathered long years' experience in their late Ottoman environment. Of course, they were influenced by this experience. Within their personalities they brought together aspects of their education and their life experience.

Al-Bustānī joined the Protestants with his background of a famous Maronite family. He was aware of the missionaries' contribution to his education and that this period of his life had helped shape his world view. Despite this, he never allowed his thinking to be monopolised by the missionaries and he remained an absolutely independent thinker and actor.

The case of al-Yāzijī is quite different. He did not convert but lent his outstanding knowledge of the Arabic language to the missionaries. I suspect that, of the members of the translation team, he was the least culturally transformed or, so to speak, "translated" during his life. Interestingly enough, his famous son Ibrāhīm worked for the Jesuits' press and "helped" the Jesuit fathers with their edition of

---

39 "Dr. Van Dyck's History of the Arabic translation of the Scriptures, March 7th, 1885", in: *Brief documentary history of the translation of the Scriptures into the Arabic Language by Rev. Eli Smith, D.D., and Rev. C.V.A. Van Dyck, D.D.*, Presbyterian Church in the U.S.A., Syrian Mission, ed., Beirut: American Presbyterian Mission Press 1900, 29. Adib (in this volume) also lists other poets who were involved in the Arabic adaptation of the Psalms. But they are not mentioned in the sources consulted for this paper.

40 Anderson, Rufus, *History of the Missions of the American Board of Commissioners for Foreign Missions to the Oriental Churches*, Boston: Congregational Publ. Soc. 1872, vol. IV, 354.

41 Cf. note 32.

the Arabic Bible. This way, two men of one family played an important role in the establishment of the two rival translations, Catholic and Protestant, and did not show many ideological scruples in doing so.

And finally there is the very interesting Muslim scholar Yūsuf al-Asīr, graduate of al-Azhar, who involved himself in the cultural life of his period without regard for religious barriers. My impression is that his engagement with Christian schools and other activities did not harm his reputation as a Muslim judge and *mufti*. The question of whether these contacts influenced his fulfilment of his "Muslim duties" has not yet been researched.

All five men were remarkable personalities. One should never belittle the merits of Smith and Van Dyck but here I would plead for recognition also of the merits of the indigenous scholars, al-Bustānī, al-Yāzijī and al-Asīr, which came into play in the Bible translation under discussion. Looking back to the title of this paper, I think that we are mistaken to speak about a "Smith" – or "Van Dyck" – Bible only, or – considering the different religious backgrounds of the scholars – to speak about a "Protestant" Bible translation at all![42]

---

42 An interesting and very critical account of the role of the American missionaries in the Near East can be found in Makdisi, Ussama, *Artillery of Heaven. American Missionaries and the Failed Conversion of the Middle East*, Ithaca: Cornell University Press 2008.

An Islamic Diatessaron: Al-Biqāʿī's Harmony of the Four Gospels*

Walid A. Saleh and *Kevin Casey*

Al-Biqāʿī: a Muslim Defender of the Bible

The encounter between al-Biqāʿī (809–85/1407–80), a late Mamluk scholar, and the Hebrew Bible is now well documented.[1] Al-Biqāʿī wrote a massive Qurʾān commentary, *Naẓm al-durr fī tanāsub al-āyāt wa-l-suwar*, in which he uses the Hebrew Bible to interpret biblical material in the Qurʾān.[2] Al-Biqāʿī extensively quotes the Hebrew Bible, copying from the official Jewish Arabic translations (both the Karaite and Rabbinic translations). His handling of the material shows a remarkable familiarity with the world of the Hebrew Bible. The spirit in which these quotations are made is one of reverence. Rarely, if ever, does al-Biqāʿī attack the Bible or its textual integrity. To him it is a divine book, a scripture worthy of respect and a reliable source of information about Israelite history. The Bible is also a source of moral edification for the Muslims; when the Bible contradicts Islamic traditions on biblical material, al-Biqāʿī sides with the Bible considering it more trustworthy on these issues than transmitted Islamic biblical lore.[3]

Al-Biqāʿī was a combative scholar, eager to pick fights with his colleagues. He was always on the lookout for any infringements on the *sunna* (the practices of Muhammad). He considered himself to be one who "enjoined people to do good and preached against committing evils" (*yaʾmur bi-l-maʿrūf wa-yanhā ʿan al-munkar*) and was not hesitant to campaign against any innovations in religious matters. He embroiled himself in at least three major controversies. Al-Biqāʿī led the attack on the reputation of the poet Ibn al-Fāriḍ.[4] He went after Ibn al-ʿArabī.[5] Nor did he

---

* We are grateful to Professor John Kloppenborg for his detailed comments on al-Biqāʿī's Diatessaron and for his help with secondary literature on post-Reformation harmonies.

1 Saleh, Walid A., "A Fifteenth-Century Muslim Hebraist: Al-Biqāʿī and His Defense of Using the Bible to Interpret the Qurʾān", *Speculum* 83 (2008), 629–654.

2 Idem, "Sublime in Its Style, Exquisite in Its Tenderness: The Hebrew Bible Quotations in al-Biqāʿī's Qurʾān Commentary", in: *Adaptations and Innovations*, Tzvi Langermann and Josef Stern, eds., Paris: Peeters 2007, 331–347.

3 For an example of where al-Biqāʿī sides with the information from the Gospels see his *Naẓm al-durar fī tanāsub al-āyāt wa-l-suwar*, Bairūt: Dār al-Kutub al-ʿIlmīyah 1995, vol. 2, 603 (Indian edition, Dār al-Maʿārif al-ʿUthmānīyah, 1976–1982, vol. 7, 48). For a detailed analysis of his Hebrew Bible quotations see Saleh, "Sublime".

4 Homerin, Th. Emil, *From Arab Poet to Muslim Saint: Ibn al-Fāriḍ, His Verse, and His Shrine*, Cairo: The American University in Cairo Press 2001 (reprint of 1994 edition), 62–75.

5 Knysh, Alexander D., *Ibn ʿArabi in the Later Islamic Tradition: The Making of a Polemical Image in Medieval Islam*, New York: State University of New York Press 1999, 209–223.

spare al-Ghazālī.[6] Each of these controversies convulsed the scholarly communities of Cairo and Damascus. What made him a formidable opponent was his eagerness to write polemical pamphlets defending his position and attacking his enemies. His use of the Bible in his Qurʾān commentary thus did not go unnoticed and his enemies saw an opportunity to question his Islamic credentials. A concerted attack on his practice was mounted by his enemies, forcing him to write an *apologia*.

Al-Biqāʿī's *apologia*, *al-Aqwāl al-qawīmah fī ḥukm al-naql min al-kutub al-qadīmah*, is the most extensive discussion of the status of the Bible in Islam.[7] It is a resolute defence of the Bible from an Islamic perspective. The Bible's textual integrity is of sufficient calibre, al-Biqāʿī argues, that Muslims can safely use it in religious context. We thus have two angles from which to observe al-Biqāʿī's engagement with the Bible: the theoretical perspective in his *apologia*, and the practical perspective of his citations of biblical quotations in his Qurʾān commentary.

Of all the disputes al-Biqāʿī involved himself in, it was only his position regarding the integrity of the Bible and the permissibility of using it by Muslims that was widely supported by the most prominent scholars of Cairo and Damascus. Al-Biqāʿī managed to get the scholarly elite behind him and obtained *fatwas* supporting his position, which proved effective in allowing him the liberty to continue his work.[8]

The Four Gospels' Harmony in al-Biqāʿī's Qurʾān Commentary

This article will document another important aspect of al-Biqāʿī's openness to the scriptures of other religions, namely his quotation from the four Gospels. Indeed, that al-Biqāʿī should have quoted the four Gospels is a far more compelling example of his openness to the scripture of other religions than his quotations from the Hebrew Bible. Nothing in Rabbinic Judaism was offensive to al-Biqāʿī's sensibilities. The Jews were chosen by God, as the Qurʾān attested; they received a revelation, the Torah, and they were strict monotheists like the Muslims. With Christianity, however, the situation was different. The Qurʾān was unequivocal in its rejection of central Christian doctrines including the divinity of Jesus, his crucifixion, and the nature of God (the Trinity). Thus, it is remarkable that al-Biqāʿī did not hesitate to quote what was, in the end, a full version of the life of Jesus as presented in the Gospels. Once more the motivations behind al-Biqāʿī's quotations were not polemical. It is clear that al-Biqāʿī wanted a comprehensive narrative of the Jesus story and wanted to make it available to his

---

6 Ormsby, Eric L., *Theodicy in Islamic Thought: The Dispute over al-Ghazālī's "Best of All Possible Worlds"*, Princeton: Princeton University Press 1984, 135–181.

7 Biqāʿī, Ibrāhim b. ʿUmar al-, *In defense of the Bible. A critical edition and introduction of al-Biqāʿīs Bible treatise*, Saleh, Walid (ed.), Leiden: Brill 2008.

8 For details on this controversy and the *fatwas* see Saleh, "Muslim Hebraist" and *In Defense of the Bible*, 21–35.

Muslim readers, fully cognisant of the fact that most of them had no access to this story and that his would be the only accessible narrative.

In *Naẓm al-durar* al-Biqāʿī quotes the Gospels because he believes they prove the Qurʾān's claims that Jesus was a sign (*āyah*) and a man full of wisdom (*ḥikmah*). As such the miracles and teachings of Jesus (both his sayings and the parables) are admitted into an Islamic meta-narrative as *the* referent of the Qurʾanic story of Jesus. The Qurʾān, in light of al-Biqāʿī's usage of the Gospels, is speaking of the Jesus of the Gospels. Al-Biqāʿī, moreover, presents the Jesus of the Gospels to his Muslim readers using the phraseology of the Arabic translation, with all its characteristic Christian inflections. This is in marked distinction to the usual approach to the image of Jesus of the Qurʾan. We have to remember that the Islamic tradition had already elaborated an image of Jesus that was at variance with the Jesus of the Gospels.[9]

Although most of the quotations are made in a positive spirit, there are instances where al-Biqāʿī is compelled to engage in polemics against certain Christian doctrines, namely the divinity of Jesus. Yet, even in such cases, al-Biqāʿī accepts the textual integrity of the Gospels and argues by using them against the Christian doctrine in question.[10] In this sense he is accepting the Gospels while rejecting Christian theology. This mode of argument is thus more in the manner of biblical interpretation rather than polemical argumentation. To al-Biqāʿī the Gospels do not support the elaborate Christian theology of the Trinity or the divinity of Jesus or conclusively prove the veracity of the crucifixion. The seriousness with which he takes the integrity of the Gospels' language is clear from his handling of their filial language. Al-Biqāʿī addresses the language of sonship and fatherhood. On the one hand, he can see that it was used metaphorically and that, as such, that usage reflected a certain religious sensibility that Muslims, though not allowed to indulge in, should be capable of understanding; on the other hand, he edits some of this language in his quotations.[11] Al-Biqāʿī is even willing to do some Gospel exegesis in support of a cherished Christian institution that is praised in the Qurʾān, namely monasticism. He manages to find vindication in the Gospels for the monastic life.[12]

Despite al-Biqāʿī's openness to the scripture of Christianity, he is interested only in the Gospels. Nothing of the rest of the New Testament leaves a trace in his thinking or in his Qurʾān commentary.

Finally, al-Biqāʿī did not quote from just one Gospel. He actually managed to present a Diatessaron of the four Gospels using Matthew as the scaffold on which to build his composite narrative. He was fully conscious of what he was doing (*wa-*

9 On the Muslim Jesus see Khalidi, Tarif, *The Muslim Jesus: Sayings and Stories in Islamic Literature*, Cambridge: Harvard University Press 2001.

10 al-Biqāʿī, *Naẓm al-durar*, vol. 2, 16–17 (Indian edition: vol. 4, 227–229).

11 Ibid.

12 Biqāʿī, *Naẓm al-durar*, vol. 7, 464 (Indian edition: vol. 19, 311).

qad adkhaltu kalām baʿḍihim fī baʿḍ wa-jamaʿtu mā tafarraqa min al-maʿānī fī siyāqātihim bi-ḥaythu ṣāra al-kull ḥadīthan wāḥidan).[13] This was a formidable achievement, not least because it is certain that he produced this Diatessaron directly from the four Gospels. He had no knowledge of the Arabic or Syriac Diatessaron traditions. There is no indication that he got the idea from a Christian informant. It is most probably the result of his *ḥadīth* education in which harmonies of different versions of the same *ḥadīth* were fashioned when retold by later scholars. His harmony is intricate in its sophistication, betraying an encyclopaedic knowledge of the four Gospels – even when we do not know the way he went about collating his Diatessaron (there were no writing desks to allow easy comparison of the four copies of the Gospels). His Diatessaron anticipated the modern European harmonies that would be done in the wake of the Reformation and the printing revolution.

In the following tables we have tried to be exhaustive in the presentation of al-Biqāʿī's citations and the manner of their order. This will hopefully make it much easier for scholars of Christian Arabic to give us insights into al-Biqāʿī's method. Moreover, the tabulation of the citations will make it clear that this was indeed a harmony, and not just a crude attempt at harmonisation. The main point to emphasise here is that in the annals of the Islamic religious tradition al-Biqāʿī's was an unprecedented usage of the Gospels, both in form and intention. Never was such positive attention given to the Gospels with the intention of making them available to a Muslim audience.

The tables below are self-explanatory. Al-Biqāʿī presents his Diatessaron at intervals in his commentary in block form. Each block of citations is presented here, with a breakdown of the verses and any anomalies. Al-Biqāʿī has cited almost all the major events and sayings of Jesus except for the Transfiguration. The page references are to the pages in the pirated Lebanese print (since it is the most widely available) as well as to the Qurʾān verse under which the Gospel block is cited – thus any copy of *al-Naẓm* may be consulted. References to the Indian edition are given in the notes at the beginning of each block. Note that the number of quotations is not an indication of the number of verses quoted. Rather it refers to the discrete units of verse(s) that are cited from a certain Gospel before al-Biqāʿī moves on to another Gospel.

13 Ibid., vol. 2, 102. (Indian edition: vol. 4, 430).

Appendix

The Four Gospels' Harmony

Table 1: Biqāʿī, Ibrāhim b. ʿUmar al-, *Naẓm al-durar fī tanāsub al-āyāt wa-l-suwar*, Bairūt: Dār al-Kutub al-ʿIlmīyah 1995, vol. 1.

Quote #	*Matthew*	*Mark*	*Luke*	*John*	*Page # from al-Biqāʿī*	*Notes*
1	**4:12–17**				vol. 1, 185 sub Q. 2:87	Arabic name of Naphtali is transcribed incorrectly–بغتاليم instead of نفتاليم. Error of this edition or of manuscript? Indian Edition vol. 2, 21–29.
2		**1:14–15**			186	
3	**4:18–22**				187	Al-Biqāʿī quotes name of father (زبدي) in verse 22, while both Greek and Syriac omit name in this verse.
4				**1:28–51**	187–188	Omits ان هذا هو ابن الله from verse 34 and ابن الله from verse 49.
5				**2:1–13**	188	Omits section of verse 9 "though the servants who had drawn the water knew. "
6				**4:1–54**	188	Reproduces whole of chp. 4 with minor variations. Omits half of verse 14, "the water that I shall give him will become in him a spring of water welling up to eternal life". Omits from verse 22, "For salvation is from the Jews". Consitently renders πάτρί and ܐܒܐ as رب.
7		**1:21–22**			188–189	Omits "not like the scribes".
8	**4:23–25**				189	
9	**5:1–12**				vol. 1, 487 sub Q. 2:253	Indian Edition vol. 4, 7–19.
10		**6:23**			487	Inserts gloss–المتنبئين يعنى–in verse 26.
11	**5:13**				487	
12			**14:34–35**		487	
13	**5:14–19**				487	
14	**6:5–13**				487	**Lord's Prayer**
15		**11:25**			487–488	
16	**6:14–15**				488	

Quote #	*Matthew*	*Mark*	*Luke*	*John*	*Page # from al-Biqāʿī*	*Notes*
17			**11:1–10**		488	
18	**6:16–18**				488	
19			**17:7–10**		488	
20			**12:13–21**		488	
21	**6:19–20**				488	
22			**12:3**		488	
23	**6:21–25**				488	Ends quotation halfway through verse 25.
24			**12:23–24**		488–89	
25	**6:26–28**				489	This is a loose rendering of verse 26.
26			**12:27**		489	Quotes only half the verse.
27	**6:29–34**				489	
28			**12:35–37**		489	Repeats العبيد لأولئك توبى at end of verse.
29			**12:41–48**		489	
30			**16:10–12**		489	
31			**12:49–53**		489	
32	**7:1–2**				489	
33			**6:37–39**		489–90	
34	**7:3–12**				490	
35			**16:17**		490	
36			**18:2–8**		490	الله تعالى, رب سبحانه.
37	**7:13–18**				490	
38			**6:44–45**		490	
39	**7:19–23**				490–91	
40			**13:23–28**		491	Omits from verse 26: "And you taught in our streets".
41	**7:24**				491	
42			**6:48–49**		491	
43	**7:28–29**				491	Not seperated from previous quotation from Lk.
44	**8:28**				vol. 1, 532 sub Q. 2:275	First half of verse, Indian Edition vol. 4, 114–122.
45			**8:26–27**		532	Interjects passage from Lk which refers to only one possessed person.

Quote #	*Matthew*	*Mark*	*Luke*	*John*	*Page # from al-Biqāʿī*	*Notes*
46	**8:28–29**				532–33	Continues from Quote 44. Replaces "Son of God" of Mt 8:29 with يسوع.
47			**8:29–30**		533	
48		**5:8–12**			533	The last part of this quotation "اذهبوا لهم فقال" is actually from Mt 8:32.
49	**8:32**				533	
49		**5:13**			533	
50	**8:32–34**				533	First half of 34 only.
51		**5:15; 5:17**			533	Skips Mk 5:16.
52			**8:37**		533	Part only.
53		**5:18–20**			533	
54			**8:39**		533	Second half only.
55	**9:32–34**				533	
56	**12:22–24**				533	
57	**17:14**				533	
58			**9:38**		533	Points out that Lk has "teacher" instead of "Lord".
59	**17:15**				533	
60		**9:17–18**			533	
61			**9:38–40**		533	
62	**17:16–17**				533–34	
63			**9:42**		534	
64		**9:20–27**			534	Skips section of verse 22.
65	**17:18–21**				534	وهذا الجنس لا يخرج الا بصلاة وصوم. This textual varient appearently is only attested in ancient sources.
65		**9:29**			534	Most sources do not mention fasting.
66	**1:23–26**				534	
67			**4:35–37**		534	
68		**7:24–30**			534	This quotation is from Mk, but he does not cite it as so.
69		**16:9**			534	
70			**8:1–3**		534-5	
71			**13:10–17**		535	

Table 2: Biqāʿī, Ibrāhim b. ʿUmar al-, *Naẓm al-durar fī tanāsub al-āyāt wa-l-suwar*, Bairūt: Dār al-Kutub al-ʿIlmīyah 1995, vol. 2.

Quote #	*Matthew*	*Mark*	*Luke*	*John*	*Page # from al-Biqāʿī*	*Notes*
72			**1:30–33**		vol. 2, 16 sub Q. 3:7	Al-Biqā'ī sets the stage with a brief introduction, then begins at verse 30. In 31, has passive يدعى not active, "you will name him". In 32, substitutes عذاء ابن for Son of God. Indian Edition vol. 4, 227–233.
73	**4:7 and 10**				17	Al-Biqā'ī quotes only the words of Jesus, and gives a paraphrase of the context. Incidentally, all the words quoted come from the OT, Deut. 6:16 and 6:13.
74			**4:17–20**		17	Second Half of verse 18 is omited, and I cannot account for: الهنا أعطانا التى الايام. This does not appear in Lk, though if one returns to Is., immediately following section quoted by Jesus is found: "and a day of vengeance from our God." Is. 61:1–2.
75	**10:33 and 40; 18:5**	**9:37**	**9:48; 10:16; 12:9**	**13:2 and 20**	17	He seems to be paraphrasing similar verses from several gospels. He is continuing from Lk, but makes no mention of the child which is the center of the first verse. He comments that this saying occurs similarly in the others, references are given. His quoting of the last verse is odd, inserting: الناس قدام أنكرته
76				**3:34**	17	
77				**4:34**	17	He misconstrues the context a bit.
78				**5:24 and 30**	17	Only quotes first half of 24.
79		**7:8**			17	
80	**16:23**	**8:33**			17	Follows Mk here.
81	**6:9–13**		**11:1–4**		17	Combines elements of Mt and Lk Our Father.

Quote #	*Matthew*	*Mark*	*Luke*	*John*	*Page # from al-Biqāʿī*	*Notes*
82	**21:12–13**	**11:15 and 17**	**19:45–46**		17	Follows Mt most closely omits second half of 21:12.
83	**6:9**				18	
84	**5:16**				18	
85	**5:44–45**		**6:27–28**		18	Combines these two sections from Mt and Lk.
86	**6:1–4**				18	
87	**6:6**				18	Quotes only the second half.
88			**8:19–21**		18	Mentions that this story occurs in the other Gospels as well.
89			**1:5–80**		vol. 2, 82 sub Q. 3:43	Skips first half of verse 20. Skips half of verse 53, 54 and 55. Indian Edition vol. 4, 380–393.
90			**3:1–6**		83	
91	**3:1–3**				84	
92	**3:3–6**				85	Introduced with phrase: وقال مرقس, though this quotation is actually from Mt.
93		**1:4–5**			85	Mk version of John story. Introduced with: وفي مرقس, the section from فقال to الافاعى ثمرة does not appear in the common text of Mk.
94	**3:7–10**				85	Mentions that this passage also occurs in Lk.
95			**3:10–16**		85	He continues here without noting that he has switched to Lk.
96	**3:11**				85	Part
97		**1:7–8**			85	Mk does not have "and fire", this only occurs in Mt and Lk.
98	**3:12**		**3:17–18**		85	Though he continues as if quoting Mk from above, this section comes from Mt and Lk only.

Quote #	*Matthew*	*Mark*	*Luke*	*John*	*Page # from al-Biqāʿī*	*Notes*
99				**1:6–7a and 9 and 11–12a and 14–18**	85	Quotes sections from the Prologue, omits "Children of God" and "only Son of the Father". Interesting version of last verse of Prologue.
100				**1:19–28**	86	Condensed a bit.
101			**3:19–20**		86	
102		**6:14–16**			86	Herod is not the speaker of the first statement in the common Mk.
103	**14:1–3a**				86	
104		**6:17–39**			86	
105	**14:12–14**				87	
106				**7:18**	vol. 2, 94 sub Q. 3:51	Indian Edition vol. 4, 410.
107	**1:17–25**				vol. 2, 102 sub Q. 3:60	Indian Edition vol. 4, 430–441
108			**2:1–34a**		102	
109			**2:36–41**		103	
110	**2:1–23**				104	
111			**2:42–51a and 52**		104	
112	**3:1**				105	
113	**3:13–16**				105	
114		**1:9–13**			105	Omits "and he was tempted by Satan".
115	**4:2a**				105	
116			**3:21–22a**		105	
117			**3:23**		105	
118			**4:1–2**		105	Again, omits "tempted by the devil".

Quote #	*Matthew*	*Mark*	*Luke*	*John*	*Page # from al-Biqāʿī*	*Notes*
119			**4:14–21**		105	Quotation from Isaiah seems to follow LXX here.
120				**5:31–47**	105	Very interesting that he quotes this passage. He takes many liberties, omitting language of "Father and Son", etc. Skips parts of verses, edits others. Why does he choose to include this passage if it is only marginally related to the narrative from above and he takes such liberties with the text?
121	**23:39; 24:1–3a**				vol. 2, 351 sub Q. 4:158	He introduces this passage by setting the scene of Jesus preaching and debating in the Temple. Indian Edition vol. 5, 467–495.
122		**13:3b–5**			351	13:3 appears to be paraphrased.
123		**13:6–8a**	**21:8b–11a**		351	He states that this appears both in Mk and Lk. Seems to follow Mk here.
124			**21:11b**		352	Attributes this to Lk, thought the last phrase about the birthpangs occurs only in Mt and Mk.
125		**13:8b–9a**			352	
126			**21:12**		352	
127		**13:9b–11**			352	He does not signify that he returns to Mk here.
128			**21:15**		352	
129		**13:12**			352	And back to Mk again.
130	**24:9–14a**				352	Omits "in my name".
131	**24:15–17 and 19**				352	Cites Mk, but this text closer to Mt, it appears.
132			**21:21–22 and 23b–25a and 26a**		352	
133	**24:21a–22**				352	He interjects that Mk has "those days".

Quote #	*Matthew*	*Mark*	*Luke*	*John*	*Page # from al-Biqāʿī*	*Notes*
134		**13:20a**			352	Another short injection from Mk.
135	**24:23–31**				352	
136		**13:27b**			353	
137	**24:32a**				353	
138			**21:29b**		353	Lk has "all the trees".
139	**24:32b–36**				353	
140			**17:20–24**		353	
141	**24:37–39**				353	
142			**17:28–34a**		353	
143	**24:40–41**				353	
144		**13:33 and 35–37**			353	This version of Mk also adds "pray" to the commands in 13:33.
145			**21:36**		353	
146	**24:42–25:46**				353	Mentions slight variations which occur in Lk.
147	**26:1–2a**				355	Skips 26:2b:"and the Son of Man will be delivered up to be crucified".
148		**14:1**			355	
149	**26:3–5**				355	
150		**14:2b**			355	
151				**11:47–55 and 57**	355	
152				**12:1–2a and 9–11**	355	Skips Story of the Anointing.
153				**12:17**	355	
154				**12:12 and 13b–15:**	355	
155				**12:23–25**	356	

Quote #	*Matthew*	*Mark*	*Luke*	*John*	*Page # from al-Biqāʿī*	*Notes*
156				**12:28–32**	356	
157				**12:34–36**	356	
158				**13, 33**	356	
159				**8:21–22a and 23–24a and 25**	356	
160				**8:39–41a**	356	
161				**8:44–46a**	356	
162				**13:34–35**	356	Paraphrased
163				**12:44–49a**	356	**Farewell Discourses**
164				**14:12a**	357	
165				**14:15–18**	357	
166				**14:23a and 24–31a**	357	
167				**15:1–8 and 10a and 12 and 18–19**	357	
168				**15:22 and 24a and 25–27**	357	
169				**16:1–2a**	358	
170				**16:4b–5a and 7–8a**	358	
171				**16:12–14**	358	
172				**16:16b–17a**	358	

Quote #	*Matthew*	*Mark*	*Luke*	*John*	*Page # from al-Biqāʿī*	*Notes*
173				**16:20–21**	358	
174				**17:1–5a and 6a**	358	
175				**17:7 and 8b**	358	
176				**17:11–12a**	358	
177				**17:15–18**	358	
178				**17:20–21**	358	
179				**18:1–3**	358	
180				**13:1a**	358	**Washing of the feet**
181				**13:2–10a**	358	
182				**13:12–15**	359	
183				**13:16**	359	
184				**13:21b**	359	
185	**26:6–7**				359	**Anointing at Bethany**
186	**26:14–19**	**14:12a**			359	Notes that Mk adds "when they sacraficed the passover lamb".
187			**21:37–38**		359	
188			**22:1–8**		359	
189			**22:14–16**		359	Omits "before I suffer".
190	**14:18–19**				359	
191				**13:21b–26**	359	
192	**26:23–25 and 30**				360	
193			**22:25–30**		360	
194			**22:39–41**		360	**Gethsemane**

Quote #	*Matthew*	*Mark*	*Luke*	*John*	*Page # from al-Biqāʿī*	*Notes*
195	**26:31 and 33–34**				360	
196				**13:38**	360	
197				**14:1**	360	
198	**26:35**				360	
199		**14:31–32 and 34b and 37a**			360	Condenses Gethsemane story.
200		**14:37b–38a**			360	Not sure what to make of مستبشرة .
201		**14:38b–39a and 40a**			360	Again, condenses the story and summarizes Mk.
202			**22:43–44**		360	
203	**26:45a and 47–50 and 55–56a**				360	**Arrest**
204				**18:3–6 and 8–9**	361	
205	**26:56b–58**				361	
206		**14:54b**			361	
207				**18:15–18**	361	
208	**26:63b–64a and 67–68**				361	
209		**14:66–67**			361	
210	**26:69b**				361	
211			**22:56–57**		361	
212	**26:70–73**				361	

Quote #	*Matthew*	*Mark*	*Luke*	*John*	*Page # from al-Biqāʿī*	*Notes*
213		**14:70b–72**			361	Seems to incorporate some words from Lk.
214	**27:1–11a and 19b and 22b–23 and 24–25**				362	**Trial** Adds some commentary.
215			**23:4 and 7–13 and 14b–15a and 21b**		362	His quotations here seem paraphrased and condensed.
216				**19:13**	362	
217		**15:33–34 and 38**	**27:51b–53**		362	The second half of this passage is obviously from Lk, though the MS does not separate it from the previous passage from Mk.
218	**27:55–56**				363	This passage obviously from Mt, though ms does not separate it from previous passage.
219				**19:25b**	363	
220		**15:42b**			363	
221				**19:31**	363	This passage is heavily paraphrased.
222	**28:6b–18**				363	A quick abbreviation of these verse is given, introduced with: وأقامه، ثلاث بعد جاء الملك ان للنسوة وقال, which does not occur in Mt, or any of the Gospels.
223			**24:36–43 and 50–52**		363	Some interesting variants.
224				**20:17b**	363	
225	**28:18–19a**				363	**End of Passion Narrative**

Quote #	*Matthew*	*Mark*	*Luke*	*John*	*Page # from al-Biqāʿī*	*Notes*
226	**10:1**				vol. 2, 413 sub Q. 5:12	Indian Edition vol. 6, 53–45.
227		**3:13–15**			414	
228			**9:1–2; 6:14a**		414	Provides only partial list of the apostle's names.
229		**3:17b–18**			414	
230			**6:16**		414	
231			**13:1–9**		vol. 2, 468 sub Q. 5:46	Indian Edition vol. 6, 161–180
232	**8:1–4**	**1:44b**			468	Notes different wording in Mk.
233			**5:15b–16**		468	
234	**8:5–13**		**13:29b: 28b**		468	Notes that Lk adds "north and south", and "all the prohpets will be in the kingdom of heaven and you will be outside. The first will be last and the last will be first". However this quotation from Lk is from an entirely different context than the Story of the Centurion in Mk.
235			**7:1–17**		468	
236	**8:14**				469	
237		**1:29b–31a**			469	
238	**8:15**		**4:39b**		469	
239		**1:32a and 33–34**			469	
240	**8:16b**				469	
241		**1:35–39**			469	This passage is from Mk and has no parallel in Mt.
242			**4:42–44; 5:1–11**		469	

Quote #	*Matthew*	*Mark*	*Luke*	*John*	*Page # from al-Biqāʿī*	*Notes*
243	**8:18–20**				470	
244			**9:59–60a and 61–62**		470	
245	**8:23**				470	
246			**8:22–25**		470	
247		**4:37–38**			470	
248	**8:25b–26**				470	This passage is not seperated from the previous, though the wording strongly suggests it belongs to Mt.
249	**9:1–2**				470	While this appears to continue the narrative from the previous passages, it in fact jumps to another chapter and skips the story of the demonics, which he dealt with, anyways, in vol. 1.
250		**2:3–4 and 11–12**	**5:18–19 and 24b–25a and 26a**		470	Condensed version drawing on both Mt and Lk.
251				**5:1–14**	470	This section is paraphrased and expanded with some explanatory comments.
252				**7:22–24**	470	
253				**9:1–14 and 16–18 and 20 and 34**	470	Condensed version of this story.
254	**9:9**				471	
255			**5:27–29**		471	
256		**2:13–15a**			472	
257	**9:10–13**				472	
258			**7:36–47b and 50**		472	
259			**8:1–3**		472	
260	**9:14–16**				472	

Quote #	*Matthew*	*Mark*	*Luke*	*John*	*Page # from al-Biqāʿī*	*Notes*
261		**2:21**			472	
262	**9:17**				472	
263			**5:39**		472	
264	**9:18–20a**				472	
265		**5:26**			473	
266	**9:20b–23a**				473	
267		**5:37**			473	
268	**9:23b–25**				473	
269		**5:40b–43**			473	
270	**9:26**				473	
271	**5:21 and 22b–25**				474	
272			**12:54–58**		474	
273	**5:26–29 and 31–41**				474	
274			**6:30–31**		475	
275	**5:43–47**				475	He seems to mix up Mt and Lk here, لاعنيكم باركوا occurs only in Lk.
276			**6:32–35a and 36**		475	Skips "sonship" language in 35b.
277	**5:48**				475	
278	**12:1**				475	
279			**6:10**		475	Notes different wording in Lk.
280	**12:2**				475	
281			**6:20**		475	Again shows different wording in Lk.
282	**12:3–4**				475	
283		**2:26b–27**			476	Notes that Mk adds this to story.
284	**12:5–7**		**14:1–6**		476	This version is condensed.
285	**19:3–6**				476	

Quote #	*Matthew*	*Mark*	*Luke*	*John*	*Page # from al-Biqāʿī*	*Notes*
286		**10:9b**			476	Notes different wording in Mk.
287	**19:7–8a**				476	
288		**10:3–5**			476	
289	**19:9**				476	Does not say that this is from Mt, though it obviously is.
290		**10:10–12**			476	Mk's version
291			**16:18**		476	Lk's version
292	**19:10–12**				476	
293	**12:22–30**				vol. 2, 513 sub Q. 5:73	Indian Edition vol. 6, 250–253.
294		**3:22–30**			513	
295	**12:30–37**				513	
296			**11:27–28**		514	
297	**12:38–39**				514	
298			**11:30**		514	
299	**12:41a**				514	
300			**11:32b**		514	
301	**12:41b–45**				514	
302	**15:29–32**				vol. 2, 519 sub Q. 5:78	Indian Edition vol. 6, 262–265.
303		**8:3**			520	Mk adds this.
304	**15:33–38**				520	
305	**16:1–5**				520	His quoting of 16:3a is condensed.
306		**8:14b**			520	
307	**16:6**				520	
308		**8:15b**			520	
309	**16:7–12**				520	

Quote #	*Matthew*	*Mark*	*Luke*	*John*	*Page # from al-Biqāʿī*	*Notes*
310			**12:1a–12:5a**		520	
311	**9:53**				vol. 2, 564 sub Q. 5:11	Indian Edition: vol. 6, 343–353.
312	**11:2–3**				564	
313			**7:21**		564	
314	**11:4–7**				564	
315			**7:24b**		564	
316	**11:8**				564	
317			**7:25b**		564	
318	**11:9–11**				564	
319			**7:29–29**		564	Difficult to separate passages of M and Lk in previous section.
320	**11:15–24**				565	
321	**12:9–10a**				565	
322			**6:6b**		565	Notes that Lk says "right hand".
323	**12:10b–12**				565	
324			**6:8b–9**		565	"But they were silent" occurs only in Mk–in fact this whole passage probably belongs in Mk.
325	**12:13–14a**				565	
326		**3:6b**			565	
327	**12:14b–21**				565	He skips the rest of Mt 12 as he quoted it in a previous section.
328	**13:1–4**				565	**Parable of the Sower**
329			**8:5b**		565	
330	**13:5–7**				565	
331		**4:7b**			565	Small addition in Mk.
332	**13:8**				566	
333			**8:8b**		566	

Quote #	*Matthew*	*Mark*	*Luke*	*John*	*Page # from al-Biqāʿī*	*Notes*
334	13:9–11a				566	
335			8:10a		566	
336	13:11b–12				566	
337			8:18b		566	
338	13:13–16				566	
339			8:11b		566	
340	13:19–21				566	
341		4:17b			566	
342			8:13b		566	
343	13:22a				566	
344			8:14b		566	
345		4:19			566	
346	13:22b–23a				566	
347			8:15		566	
348	13:23b–32a				566	Parable of the Mustard Seed
349		4:31b			566	
350	13:32b				566	
351		4:32b			567	
352			13:19b		567	
353	13:33				567	Parable of the Leaven
354		4:21			567	Parable of the Lamp
355			8:16		567	
356		4:22			567	
357			11:34–36		567	
358		4:23–29			567	Parable of the Seed Growing Secretly
359	13:34a and 35–50 and 53–53				567	
360		6:2b			568	

Quote #	*Matthew*	*Mark*	*Luke*	*John*	*Page # from al-Biqāʿī*	*Notes*
361			**4:22b**		568	
362	**13:55b–59**				568	
363		**6:4**			568	
364			**4:23–32**		568	
365			**13:31–55a**		568	
366			**9:7–9a**		568	
367	**14:1–2**				568	
368	**10:1**				vol. 2, 603 sub Q. 6:19	**Commissioning of the Twelve.** Indian Edition vol. 7, 48–57.
369		**3:13–15**			603	
370			**6:12–13**		603	
371		**9:1–2**			603	
372	**10:2**				603	
373		**3:17b**			603	
374	**10:3–4**				603	Notes that Lk moits Thaddaeus in favor of Judas, son of James.
375		**6:7**			603	
376	**10:5–10**				603	
377		**6:8**			604	
378			**9:3**		604	
379	**10:11–14**				604	
380		**6:1**			604	
381	**10:15–18**				604	
382		**13:10?**			604	
383	**10:19–20**				604	
384		**13:11b**			604	
385	**10:21–42; 11:1**				604	
386		**6:12–13**			605	
387			**10:1–2**		605	

Quote #	*Matthew*	*Mark*	*Luke*	*John*	*Page # from al-Biqāʿī*	*Notes*
388	**9:36**				605	Astutely notes that the previous verse from Lk appear in Mt, though addressed to the Twelve.
389			**10:3–24**		605	
390	**28:16–19b**				606	
391		**16:15–20a**			606	
392			**24:36–53**		606	

Table 3: Biqāʿī, Ibrāhīm b. ʿUmar al-, *Naẓm al-durar fī tanāsub al-āyāt wa-l-suwar*, Bairūt: Dār al-Kutub al-ʿIlmīyah 1995, vol. 3.

Quote #	*Matthew*	*Mark*	*Luke*	*John*	*Page # from al-Biqāʿī*	*Notes*
393	**19:30; 20:1–16**				vol. 3, 127 sub Q. 7:157	Indian Edition: vol. 8, 112–117.
394	**22:14**				127	
395	**21:23–26a**				127	
396			**20:6b**		127	
397	**21:26b**				127	
398		**11:32b**			127	
399	**21:27**				127	
400		**12:10**			127	
401	**21:28–33**				128	
402			**20:9b**		128	Notes that Lk has "for a long time".
403	**21:34–22:14**				128	
404			**14:16b–21 and 23–24**		128	Lk's version
405				**10:1–3 and 11b–13 and 16 and 19–21a**	129	

Table 4: Biqāʿī, Ibrāhim b. ʿUmar al-, *Naẓm al-durar fī tanāsub al-āyāt wa-l-suwar*, Bairūt: Dār al-Kutub al-ʿIlmīyah 1995, vol. 5.

Quote #	*Matthew*	*Mark*	*Luke*	*John*	*Page # from al-Biqāʿī*	*Notes*
406	**14:13–14**				vol. 5, 109 sub Q. 21:91	Indian Edition vol. 12, 473–476.
407		**6:34–35**			109	
408	**14:15–16; 19a**				109	
409		**6:39–40**			109	
410				**6:5b–6a and 7a and 8–9a and 10a**	109	
411	**14:19b**				109	
412		**6:41–44**			109	
413	**14:21b**				109	
414				**6:14b–15**	109	
415	**14, 22**				109	
416				**6:17b**	109	
417	**14:23a**				109	
418		**6:45–46**			109	
419	**14:23b–24**				109	
420				**6:19a**	109	
421	**14:25–32**				109	
422				**6:21b–27a and 38b and 45; 47: 28–29**	110	
423	**14:34**				110	
424		**6:53b**			110	
425				**7:2–5 and 7–8a and 14–19 and 37–38 and 40–43**	vol. 5, 205 sub Q. 23:50	Indian Edition vol. 13, 150–154.

Quote #	*Matthew*	*Mark*	*Luke*	*John*	*Page # from al-Biqāʿī*	*Notes*
426		**7:1–3a and 4–5**			205	
427	**15:3–6**				206	
428		**7:6–7 and 13b and 14–15**			206	
429	**15:12–20**				206	This is listed as coming from Mk, but obviously comes from Mt.
430		**7:18b–23**			206	

Table 5: Biqāʿī, Ibrāhim b. ʿUmar al-, *Naẓm al-durar fī tanāsub al-āyāt wa-l-suwar*, Bairūt: Dār al-Kutub al-ʿIlmīyah 1995, vol. 7.

Quote #	*Matthew*	*Mark*	*Luke*	*John*	*Page # from al-Biqāʿī*	*Notes*
431	**15:21–28**				vol. 7, 45 sub Q. 43:64	Indian Edition vol.17, 465–474.
432		**7:29–30 and 32–37**			45	
433		**8:22–25**			45	
434	**16:13–16a and 17a and 18b–19 and 21a and 25–26**				46	This passage clearly from Mt, though not quoted as such. Heavily edits Peter's confession, removing reference to Son of God and the cross and resurrection.
435			**14:25–26 and 27b–29 and 31–33**		46	
436			**14:8 and 10b–15**		46	This passage paraphrased.
437	**18:1–5**				46	
438		9:37b			47	
439			**9:48b**		47	
440	**18:6–8**				47	
441		**9:49–50**			47	
442			**18:9–11 and 13–17**		47	
443	**18:10a:11–12**				47	
444			**15:4b**		47	Notes that Lk has "until he finds it".
445	**18:13–14**				47	
446			**15:1–32**		47	
447			**16:19–31; 17:1–2**		47–49	Edition has جيرانك قتلت in Lk 16:25 but should probably be خيارك قبلت?

Quote #	*Matthew*	*Mark*	*Luke*	*John*	*Page # from al-Biqāʿī*	*Notes*
448	**18:15–18a**				vol. 7, 464 sub Q. 57:27	Indian Edition vol. 19, 311–323
449			**17:3–4**		464	
450	**18:21–35; 19:1–2**				465	
451			**9:51–53a and 54–56**		465	Includes extended passage from ancient authorities.
452	**19:13–15**				465	
453		**10:15–16**			465	
454	**19:15b–16a**				465	
455		**10:17b**			465	
456	**19:16b–18**				465	
457		**10:19b**			465	
458	**19:19b–21a**				465	
459		**10:21**			465	
460	**19:22–29**				465	Should الجبل in 19:28 read العالم instead?
461			**18:29b–30**		446	
462	**19:30; 20:1–2a**				466	
463	**19:30; 20:1–16**				466	
464	**20:17a and 20–21 and 23b–24**				467	
465		**10:41b**			467	
466	**20:25–27**				467	Mentions that Mk has servant "of all" and slave "of all".
467	**20:28–30 and 32–34**				467	
468		**10:46**			467	

Quote #	*Matthew*	*Mark*	*Luke*	*John*	*Page # from al-Biqāʿī*	*Notes*
469			**18:35b–37**		467	
470		**10:47–52**			467	
471			**18:43b**		467	
472			**17:11–19**		468	
473	**21:1a**				468	**Entry into Jerusalem**
474		**11:1a**			468	
475	**21:1b–8**				468	
476		**11:2b–8**			468	
477	**21:9a**				468	
478		**11:9b–10**			468	
479			**19:37–44a**		468	
480	**21:10–13**				469	
481				**2:13b–15**	469	
482	**21:14–21**				469	
483		**11:22b–24**			469	
484	**21:22**				469	
485		**9:38–41**			469	
486				**11:1; 3:6b–8 and 11–12 and 14 and 17–24 and 30b–32a and 33a and 34–41 and 42b–49a and 50b**	vol. 7, 578 sub Q. 61:6	**Raising of Lazarus.** Indian Edition vol. 20, 18–28.
487	**22:15–22**				579	
488				**7:33–35**	579	
489	**22:23**				579	
490		**12:26**			579	
491			**20:37**		579	

Quote #	*Matthew*	*Mark*	*Luke*	*John*	*Page # from al-Biqāʿī*	*Notes*
492	22:33–37a				579	
493		12:29–30a			579	
494	22:37b–39				579	
495		12:31b			579	
496	22:40				579	
497		12:32–34a			579	
498			10:29b–37		579	The Good Samaritan
499		12:34b and 37b			580	
500				2:23	580	
501				3:1–2	580	
502	23:1–23a				580	
503			11:42		581	
504	23:24–26				581	
505			11:41		581	
506	23:27				581	
507			11:44		581	
508	23:28				581	
509			11:46 and 52		581	
510	23:29a				581	
511			11:47b		581	
512	23:29b–35a				581	
513			11:48–50		581	
514	23:35b–39				581	
515		12:41–44; 13:1a			581	

List of Plates / Plates

Plate 1: T-S Ar. 28.144r, an early Judaeo-Arabic copy of Saadiah's *tafsīr* on parchment. Courtesy Cambridge University Library.

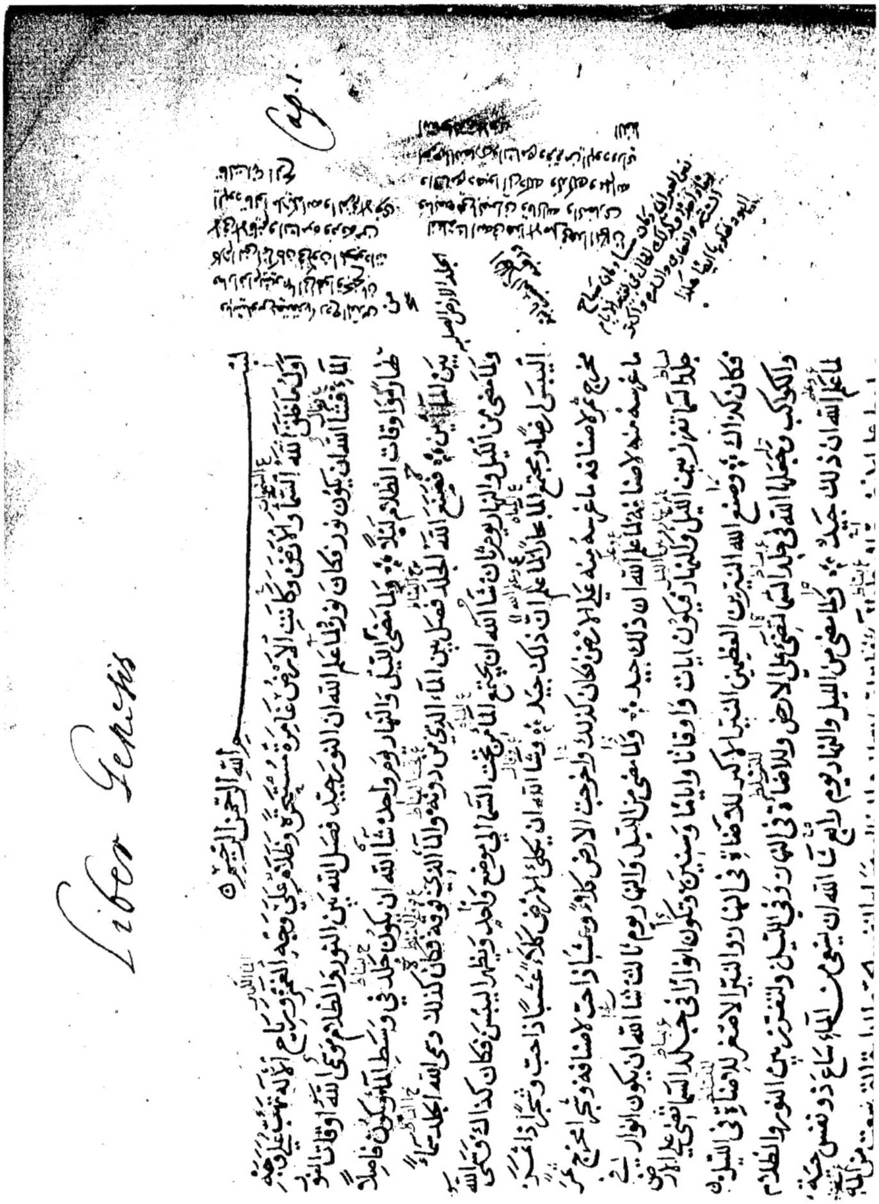

Liber Genesis

Plate 2: MS Paris BNF Ar. 1 fol. 4r.

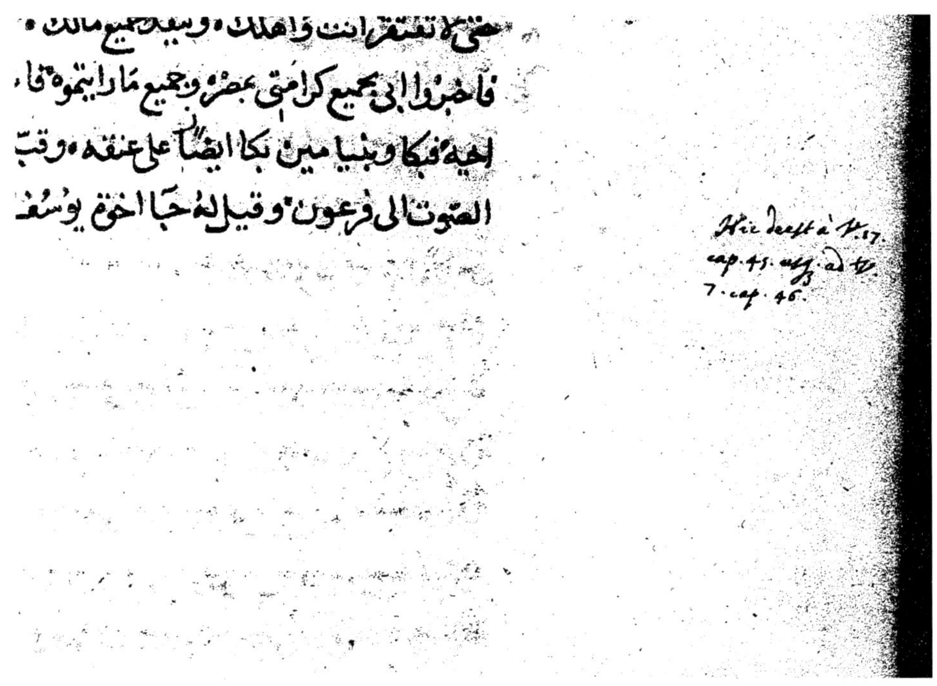

Plate 3: MS Paris BNF Ar. 1, detail showing Sionita's editorial notes.

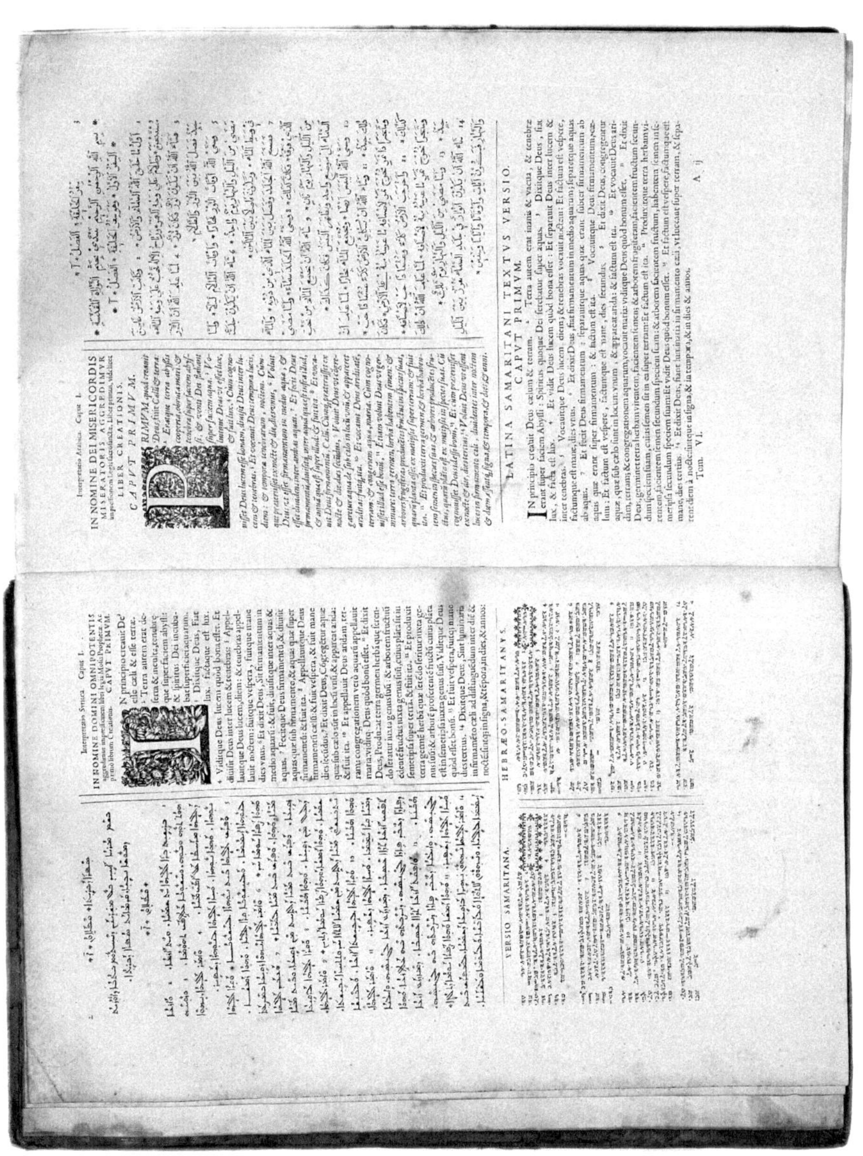

Plate 4: Paris Polyglot, vol. VI. Courtesy Cambridge University Library.

Interpretatio Arabica. Caput I.

IN NOMINE DEI MISERICORDIS
MISERATORIS AGGREDIMVR
impressionem Legis sacrosanctæ. Liber primus, videlicet
LIBER CREATIONIS.

CAPVT PRIMVM.

RIMVM quod creauit
*Deus,*fuit *Cælũ & terra:*
[2] *Eratque terra abyssis*
cooperta, obruta mari: &
tenebræ super faciem abys-
si, & venti Dei flabant
super faciem aquæ. [3] *Vo-*
luitque Deus vt esset lux,
& fuit lux. [4] *Cùm cogno-*
uisset Deus lucem esse bonam, diuisit Deus inter lu-
cem & tenebras. [5] *Et vocauit Deus tempora lucis,*
diem : & tempora tenebrarum , noctem. Cúm-
que præteriisset ex nocte & die, dies vnus, [6] *Voluit*
Deus vt esset firmamentum in medio aquæ , &
esset diuidens inter ambas aquas. [7] *Et fecit Deus*
firmamentũ, diuisitq; inter aquã quæ est infra illud,
& aquã quæ est super illud: & fuit ita. [8] *Et voca-*
uit Deus firmamentũ , Cælũ. Cùmq; præteriisset ex
nocte & die, dies secũdus, [9] *Voluit Deus vt cõgre-*
garetur aqua de sub cælo in locũ vnũ, & appareret
ariditas: fuitq; ita. [10] *Et vocauit Deus ariditatẽ,*
terram: & congeriem aquæ , maria. Cùm cogno-
uisset illud esse bonũ, [11] *Etiam voluit Deus vt ger-*
minaret terra germen, herbã habentem semen: &
arbores frugiferas producẽtes fructus in species suas,
quarũ planta esset ex metipsis super terram: & fuit
ita. [12] *Et produxit terra germen, & herbã haben-*
tem semen in species suas, & arbores producẽtes fru-
ctus, quarũ plãta est ex metipsis in species suas. Cũ
cognouisset Deus id esse bonũ, [13] *Et cùm præteriisset*
ex nocte & die, dies tertius, [14] *Voluit Deus vt essent*
luces in firmamento cæli , diuidentes inter noctem
& diem, essentq; signa, & tempora, & dies, & anni.

سفر الخليقة * الفصل * آ * 3
* بسم الله الرحمن الرحيم نبتدي بختم التوراة المقدسة *
* السفر الاول * وهو سفر الخليقة * الفصل * آ *
1 اول ما خلق الله السماء والارض * 2 وكانت الارض غامرة
مستبحرة * وظلام علي وجه الغمر * ورياح الاله تهب علي وجه الماء *
3 فشاء الله ان يكون نور فكان نور * 4 لما علم الله ان النور
جيد فصل الله بين النور والظلام *
5 وسمي الله اوقات النور نهارا * واوقات الظلام ليلا * ولما
مضي من الليل والنهار يوم واحد * 6 شاء الله ان يكون جلد
في وسط الماء * ويكون فاصلا بين الماءين *
7 فصنع الله الجلد وفصل بين الماء الذي من دونه * والماء
الذي فوقه * فكان كذلك * 8 وسمي الله الجلد سماء * ولما مضي
من الليل والنهار يوم ثان * 9 شاء الله ان يجمع الماء من تحت
السماء الي موضع واحد ويظهر اليبس فكان كذاك *
10 وسمي الله اليبس ارضا * ومجتمع الماء بحارا * لما علم ان
ذلك جيد * 11 وشاء الله ان يكسي الارض كلاء عشبا ذا حب *
وشجرا ذا ثمر يخرج ثمرا لاصنافه ما غرسه منه علي الارض * فكان
كذلك * 12 واخرجت الارض كلاء وعشبا ذا حب لاصنافه *
وشجرا يخرج ثمرا ما غرسه منه لاصنافه * لما علم الله ان ذلك
جيد * 13 ولما مضي من الليل والنهار يوم ثالث *
14 شاء الله ان يكون انوار في جلد السماء تفرز بين الليل
والنهار فيكون ايات واوقاتا واياما وسنين *

Plate 5: Paris Polyglot, vol. VI, detail of the Arabic portion. Courtesy Cambridge University Library.

سفر كون الدنيا

ويقال له بالعبراني براشيت

في البدء خلق الله السما والارض ، وكانت الارض خاليه غير متقنه ،
وكانت الظلمه على وجه الغمر ، وكان روح الله يطفوا على المياه ،
وقال الله ليكن الضو فكان الضو ، وراء الله الضو انه حسنا ، وافصل
بين الضو والظلمه ، وسما الضو نهارا ، والظلمه ليلا ، وكان
مسا وكان صباح يوما واحدا ، وقال الله ليكن جلد متواسط بين المياه
وليفصل بين ما وما ، وصنع الله الجلد وافصل فيما بين المياه التي تحت
الجلد ، وفيما بين المياه التي فوق الجلد ، وكان كذلك ، وسما الله
الجلد سما ، وكان مسا وكان صباح يوما ثانيا ، وقال الله تجتمع
المياه التي تحت السما الى موضع واحد ، ولتظهر اليابسه وكان كذلك
وسما الله اليابسه ارضا ، ودعا مجامع المياه بحارا ، وراء الله ذلك
حسنا ، وقال الله لتنبت الارض نبات حشيش بازرا بزرا ، وعودا
مثمرا عاملا ثمرا على حد وجنسه ، بزره فيه على الارض وكان كذلك
واخرجت الارض نبات حشيش بازرا بزرا على حد وجنسه ، وعودا مثمرا
وكل عود زرعه فيه على حد وجنسه ، وراء الله ذلك حسنا ، وكان مسا
وكان صباح يوما ثالثا ، وقال الله لتكن مصابيح في جلد السما لتفصل
بين النهار والليل ، ولتكن للعلامات والازمان والايام والسنين
للضيا في جلد السما ، وللاشراق على الارض وكان كذلك ، وصنع الله
النيرين العظيمين ، النير الاعظم لرياسة النهار ، والنير الاصغر لرياسة

الليل

Plate 6: *SOCG* (= *Scritture Originali riferite nelle Congregazione Generali, Archives of the Congregation De Propaganda Fide*), vol. 180 (*Lettere di Lingua straniera dall'Anno 1631 sino al 1645*), fol. 67. Courtesy Archivo storico della Congregazione per l'Evangelizzazione dei Popoli.

فلنصنعن له معينًا نظيره • وجبل الرب الاله من الارض كل دبابات الصحره
وكل طاير السماء • واوردها الى ادم لينظر ماذا يسميها • وكل نفس
حيه سماها ادم فهو اسمها • وسما ادم الدبابات باسمايها • ولكل
طيور السما • ولكل وحوش الارض • واما ادم فلن يجد له معينًا
شبيهًا له • فالقا الرب الاله على ادم سباتًا فنام • واخذ واحدة
من اضلاعه وملا موضعها لحمًا • وبنا الرب الاله الضلع التى اخذها
من ادم امراه وقادها الى ادم • فقال ادم هذه الان عضمًا من اعظامي •
ولحمًا من لحمي • هذه تدعى امراه • لانها اخذت من امرئ • من اجل
هذا يترك الانسان اباه وامه ويلصق بامراته • ويكونا الاثنان
جسد واحد • وكانا كلاهما ادم وامراته عريانان وما كانا يخجلان •

الفصل الثالث

واما الحيه فكانت اكثر مكرًا من كل دباب الارض الذي صنعه
الرب الاله • فقالت الحيه للامراه لماذا اوصاكما الله ان لا تاكلا من كل
شجرة في الفردوس • فاجابتها الامراه من ثمرة كل عود في الفردوس
ناكل • واما من ثمرة العود الذي في وسط الفردوس اوصانا الله ان لا
ناكل منها • ولا نلمسها لئلا نموت • فقالت الحيه للامراه لم تموتا
موتًا • وان الله عالم في اي يوم تاكلان منها تنفتح اعينكما وتكونا
كالهة عارفين الخير والشر • فرات الامراه ان الشجرة طيبة للماكل
وشهية للنظر ومطربة للبصر • فتناولت من ثمرتها واكلت •
واعطت لرجلها فاكل • فانفتحت اعينهما فاعرفا انهما عريانان • خيطا

04

Plate 7: *SOCG* (= *Scritture Originali riferite nelle Congregazione Generali, Archives of the Congregation De Propaganda Fide*), vol. 180 (*Lettere di Lingua straniera dall'Anno 1631 sino al 1645*), fol. 70. Courtesy Archivo storico della Congregazione per l'Evangelizzazione dei Popoli.

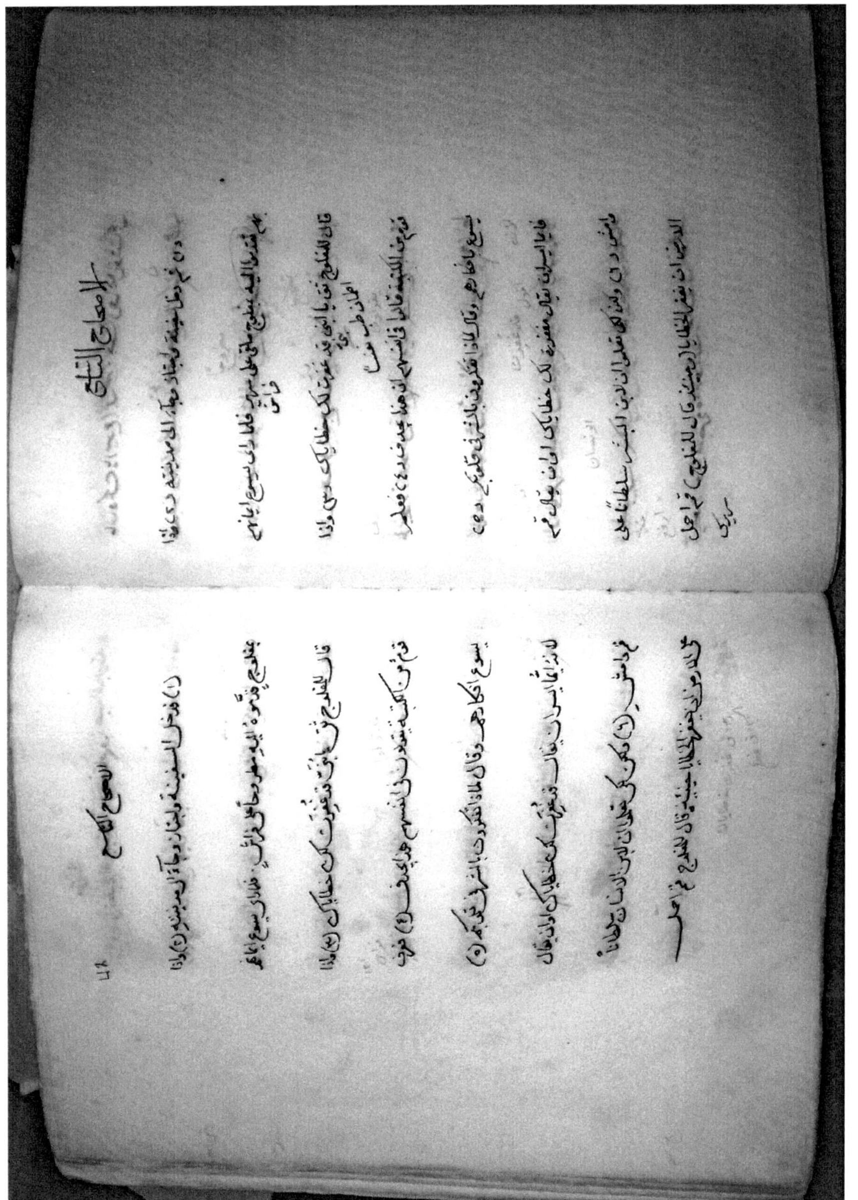

Plate 8: Near East School of Theology, Bible MS., Box No. III, Booklet 1, Matth. 9:1–6. Courtesy Near East School of Theology Beirut.

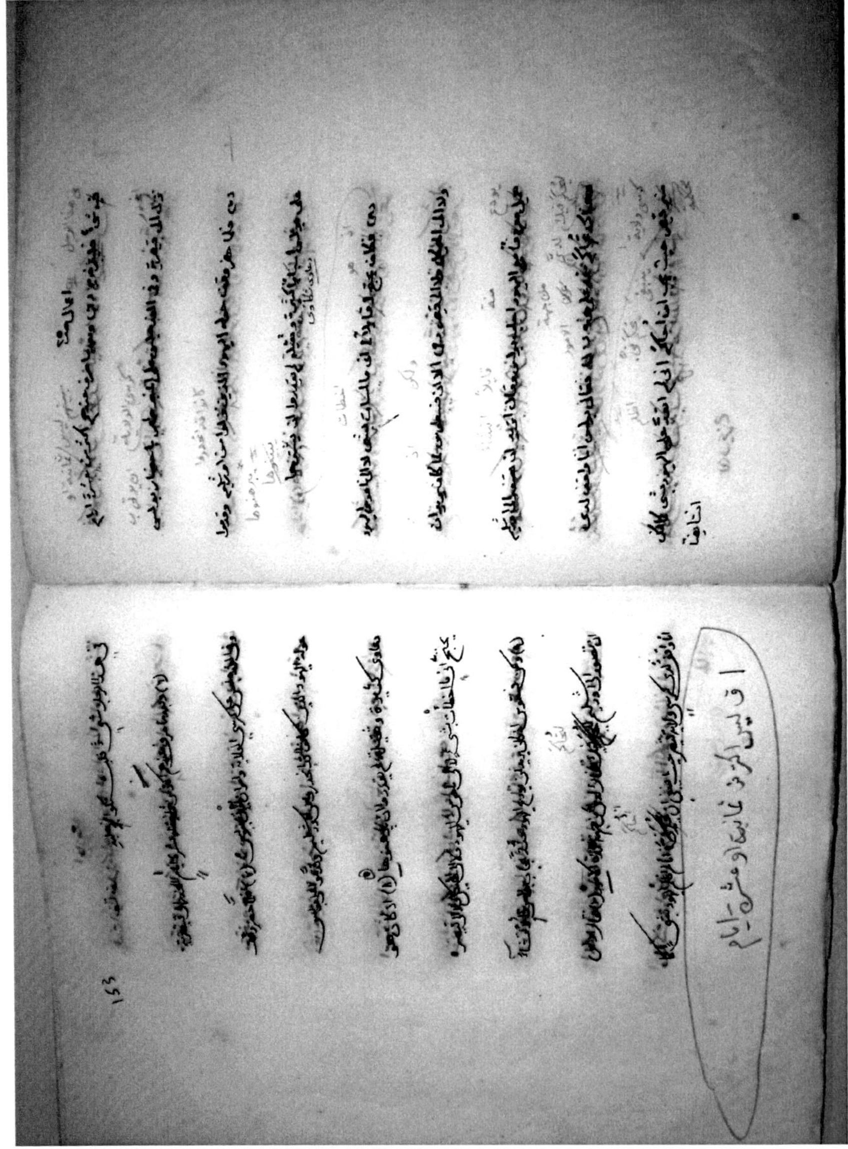

Plate 9: Near East School of Theology, Bible MS., Box No. III, Booklet 5, Acts 25:6–10. Courtesy Near East School of Theology Beirut.

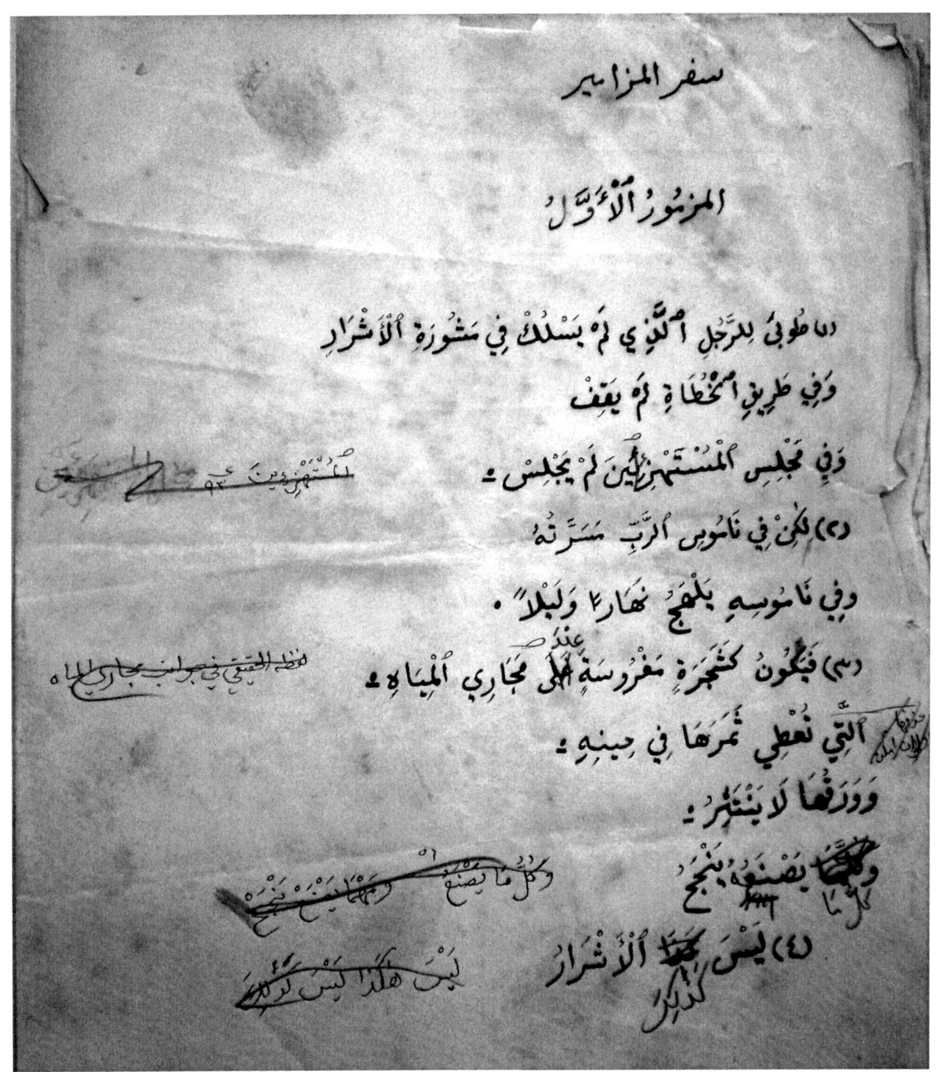

Plate 10:Near East School of Theology, Bible MS., Box No. IV, Booklet 1, Psalms 1:1–4. Courtesy Near East School of Theology Beirut.

" setting up Feb. 4th 1868

التكوين

الأصحاح الأول

١ في البدء خلق الله السموات والأرض. ٢ وكانت الأرض خربة وخالية وعلى وجه ١
الغمر ظلمة وروح الله يرف على وجه المياه. ٣ وقال الله ليكن نور فكان نور. ٤ ورأى الله ٣
النور أنه حسن. وفصل الله بين النور والظلمة. ٥ ودعا الله النور نهارا والظلمة دعاها ليلا. ٥
وكان مساء وكان صباح يوما واحدا
٦ وقال الله ليكن جلد في وسط المياه. وليكن فاصلا بين مياه ومياه. ٧ فعمل الله الجلد ٦
وفصل بين المياه التي تحت الجلد والمياه التي فوق الجلد. وكان كذلك. ٨ ودعا الله الجلد ٨
سماء. وكان مساء وكان صباح يوما ثانيا
٩ وقال الله لتجتمع المياه تحت السماء إلى مكان واحد ولتظهر اليابسة. وكان كذلك. ٩
١٠ ودعا الله اليابسة أرضا. ومجتمع المياه دعاه بحارا. ورأى الله ذلك أنه حسن. ١١ وقال الله ١٠
لتنبت الأرض عشبا وبقلا يبزر بزرا وشجرا ذا ثمر يعمل ثمرا كجنسه بزره فيه على الأرض. وكان
كذلك. ١٢ فأخرجت الأرض عشبا وبقلا يبزر بزرا كجنسه وشجرا يعمل ثمرا بزره فيه كجنسه. ١٢
ورأى الله ذلك أنه حسن. ١٣ وكان مساء وكان صباح يوما ثالثا ١٣
١٤ وقال الله لتكن أنوار في جلد السماء لتفصل بين النهار والليل. وتكون لآيات ١٤
وأوقات وأيام وسنين. ١٥ وتكون أنوارا في جلد السماء لتنير على الأرض. وكان كذلك. ١٥
١٦ فعمل الله النورين العظيمين. النور الأكبر لحكم النهار والنور الأصغر لحكم الليل. والنجوم. ١٦
١٧ وجعلها الله في جلد السماء لتنير على الأرض ١٨ ولتحكم على النهار والليل ولتفصل بين النور ١٧

٢

Plate 11: Near East School of Theology, Bible MS., Box No. V, Old Testament, undated, vowelled by hand, Gen. 1, with commentary by Van Dyck: "Commenced vowelling this Bible Jan 7 1868 CVD/ setting up Feb. 4·, 1868". Courtesy Near East School of Theology Beirut.

Bibliography

Primary Sources, published

Altmann, Alexander, ed., *The Book of Doctrines and Beliefs* (Philosophia Judaica). Oxford: East and West Library, 1946.

Augustinus Ciasca, ed., *Tatiani Evangeliorum harmoniae arabicae.* Romae: Typ. Polyglotta S.C. de Propaganda Fide, 1888.

Biblia Hebraica, Samaritana, Chaldaica, Graeca, Syriaca, Latina, Arabica, quibus textus originales totius [Paris Polyglot] Le Jay, Guy Michel, ed., 10 vols. Paris: A. Vitré 1629-45.

Biblia polyglotta, Walton, Brian, ed., 6 vols., London 1653-57.

Biblia Sacra Arabica Sacrae Congregationis de Propagande Fide Iussu Edita. Al-Kutub al-muqaddasah bi-l-lisān al-ʿarabī, Rome: Typis Sacrae Congretionis de Propaganda Fide, 1671-73. Reprint: *Kitāb al-muqaddas*, printed by Richard Watts, London, 1831.

Biqāʿī, Ibrāhim b. ʿUmar al-, *Naẓm al-Durar fī tanāsub al-āyāt wa-l-suwar*, Bairūt: Dār al-Kutub al-ʿIlmīyah, 1995.

Idem, *Naẓm al-Durar fī tanāsub al-āyāt wa-l-suwar*, Ḥaidarābād: Dār al-Maʿārif al-ʿUthmānīyah, 1976–1982.

Idem, *In defense of the Bible. A critical edition and introduction of al-Biqāʿīs Bible treatise*, Saleh, Walid, ed., Leiden: Brill, 2008.

Dabbās, Athanasius al-, ed., *Kitāb al-injīl al-sharīf al-ṭāhir wa-l-miṣbāḥ al-munīr al-zāhir*, Ḥalab 1706.

Derenbourg, Joseph, Derenbourg, Hartwig and Lambert, Mayer, eds., *Saadia Ben Joseph: Œuvres Complètes de R. Saadia ben Iosef al-Fayyoûmî*, Paris: E. Leroux, 1893–1899.

Erpenius, ed., *Pentateuchus Mosis Arabicè*, Lugduni Batavorum: Maire, 1622.

Fākhūrī, Jūrj, ed., *al-Kitāb al-Muqaddas, al-ʿahd al-jadīd,* Jūnyah: al-Maṭbaʿa al-Būlusiyyah, 1953.

Gall, August Freiherr von, ed., *Der Hebräische Pentateuch der Samaritaner*, Giessen: Verlag von Alfred Töpelmann, 1914.

Geographia Nubiensis, id Est Accuratissima Totius Orbis in Septem Climata Divisi Descriptio, Continens Præsertim Exactam Universæ Asiæ Et Africæ Explicationem. Recens Ex Arabico in Latinum Versa a Gabriele Sionita et Joanne Hesronita, Paris: H. Blageart, 1619.

Giustiniani, Agostina, ed., *Psalterium Octaplum: Hebreum, Grecum, Arabicum, & Chaldeum: Cum Tribus Latinus Interpretationibus & Glossis*, Genuæ: Petrus Paulus Porrus, 1516.

Injīl al-sharīf, al-, Bairūt: Dār al-Kitāb al-Sharīf, 1990.

Jabbūr, Makāriyūs and al-Khūrī, Ziyād Tawfīq, eds., *Wathā'iq hāmmah fī khidmat kanīsatinā al-anṭākīyah. Man ṣanaᶜ al-infiṣāl sanat 1724?*, Bairūt: Manshūrāt al-Nūr, 2000.

Khalīl, Samīr, ed., *Anājīl ᶜAbd-Yashūᶜ al-Ṣūbāwī al-musajjaᶜah*, 2 vols., Bairūt: al-Maktabah al-Bulūsīyah, 2007.

Kitāb al-Ḥayāh: New International Version [Bible in English and Arabic], [S.l.]: International Bible Society, 1984.

Kitāb al-Muqaddas, al-, aiy kutub al-ᶜahd al-qadīm wa-'l-ᶜahd al-jadīd, Bairūt: al-Maṭbaᶜa al-Amrīkāniyyah, 1864.

Kitāb al-Muqaddas, al-, aiy kutub al-ᶜahd al-qadīm wa-'l-ᶜahd al-jadīd, Bairūt: Maṭbaᶜat al-Mursilīn al- Yasūᶜiyīn, 1882.

Kitāb al-Muqaddas, al-, aiy kutub al-ᶜahd al-qadīm wa-'l- ᶜahd al-jadīd, at-tarjama al-ᶜarabiyyah al-mushtaraka min al-lughāt al-aṣliyyah, [Bairūt:] Dār al-Kitāb al-Muqaddas fī-'l-Sharq al-Awsaṭ 1993.

Kitāb al-Muqaddas, al-, ar-Rahbana al-Dūminīkāniyyah fī-'l-ᶜIrāq, ed., al-Mauṣil 1878, reprint Bairūt: Jamᶜiyyat al-Kitāb al-Muqaddas, 2000.

Kitāb al-Muqaddas, al-, ar-Rahbana al-Yasūᶜiyyah, Bairūt: Dār al-Mashriq, 1989.

Kitāb al-Ṣalāh al-ᶜāmmah wa-ijrā' al-sirrīn wa-al-rusūm wa-al-ṭughūs al-kanā'isīyah ᶜalā mūjib istiᶜmāl kanīsat inkiltarah wa-irlandah al-muttaḥidah maᶜa Kitāb Mazāmīr Dāwūd, London: William Watts, 1850.

Lambeck, Petrus, ed., *Commentariorum de Augustissima Bibliotheca Caesarea Vindobonensi*, Vienna: Typis Joannis Christophori Cosmerovii, 1665–1679.

Lambert, Mayer, ed., *Saadia ben Joseph: Commentaire sur le Séfer Yesira, ou Livre de la Création*, Paris: É. Bouillon, 1891.

Macarius b. al-Zaᶜīm, *Kitāb al-Naḥla*, in: Ḥabīb al-Zayyāt, ed., *Khazā'in al-kutub fī Dimashq wa-ḍawāḥīha*, al-Fajjāla: Maṭbaᶜat al-Maᶜārif, 1902.

Maizeaux, Pierre des, ed., *Scaligerana, Thuana, Perroniana, Pithoenana, et Colomesiana*, Amsterdam: Covens & Mortier, 1740.

Masᶜūdī, al-, *Kitāb at-tanbīh wa-l-ishrāf*, De Goeje, M. J., ed., (Bibliotheca Geographorum Arabicorum VIII), Lugduni Batavorum, 1894.

Qāfiḥ, Yosef, ed., *Saadia ben Joseph: sefer ha-nivhar ba-emunot va-de'ot*,Kiryat Ono: mekhkon mishnat ha-rambam, 1998.

Raimundi, Giovan Battista, ed., *Liber Tasriphi Compositio Est Senis Alemami*, Romae: Ex Typographia Medicæ linguarum externarum, 1610.

Idem, ed., *al-Injīl al-muqaddas li-Rabbinā Yasūᶜ al-Masīḥ al-maktūb min arbaᶜ al-injīlīyīn al-muqaddasīn aᶜnī Mattā wa-Marqus wa-Lūqā wa-Yūḥannā = Evangelium sanctum Domini nostri Iesu Christi conscriptum a quatuor evangelistis santis, idest Matthaeo, Marco, Luca et Iohanne*, Roma: Typographia Medecea, 1591.

Ryer, André du, *Rudimenta Grammatices Linguæ Turcicæ*, Paris, 1630.

Salabi, Kamal and Khoury, Yusuf K., eds., *The Missionary Herald. Reports from Ottoman Syria. 1819–1870*, 5 vols., Amman: The Royal Institute for Interfaith Studies, 1995.

Savary de Brèves, François, *Relation Des Voyages De M. De Brèves, Tant en Grece, Terre-Saincte, et Ægypte, qu'aux Royaumes de Tunis & Arger. Ensemble un Traicte Faict l'an 1604, entre le Roy Henry le Grand & l'empereur des Turcs et Trois Discours du dit Sieur. Le tout Recueilly par le S[Ieur] D[u] C[astel]*, Paris: N. Gasse, 1628.

Scialac Acurrensis, Vittorio, *Introductio ad Grammaticam Arabicam*, Romae: Excudebat Stephanus Paulinus, 1622.

Idem, *Totum Arabicum Alphabetum, ad unam Tabellam cum suis Vocalibus et Signis, Facilitatis Causa, Reductum*, Romae: Apud Stephanum Paulinum, 1624.

Scialac, Vittorio and Sionita, Gabriel, eds., *Dauidis Regis et Prophetae Psalmi*, Romae: Ex Typographia Savariana. Excudebat Stephanus Paulinus, 1619.

Shidyāq, Aḥmad Fāris al-, ed., [Psalter in Arabic], London: Society for Promoting Christian Knowledge, 1850.

Idem, ed., *Kitāb al-ʿahd jadīd*, London: Society for Promoting Christian Knowledge, 1851.

Sionita, Gabriel and Hesronita, Jean, *Grammatica Arabica Maronitarum*, 1 vol., Paris: Ex Typographia Savariana, Excudebat Hieronymus Blageart, 1616.

Sionita, Gabriel and Scialac, Vittorio, eds., *Doctrina Christiana: Illustrissimi & Reuerendiss. D.D. Roberti S.R.E. Card. Bellarmini, Nunc Primùm ex Italico Idiomate in Arabicum, Iussu S.D.N. Pauli V. Pont. Max. Translata per Victorium Scialat Accurensem, & Gabrielem Sionitam Edeniensem, Maronitas e Monte Libano, Philosophiae, ac Sacra Theologiae Professores*, Romae: Ex Typographia Savariana: Excudebat Stephanus Paulinus, 1619.

Sionita, Gabriel, ed., *Liber Psalmorum Dauidis Regis et Prophetæ ex Idiomate Syro in Latinum translates*, Paris: Antoine Vitré, 1625.

Idem, ed., *Veteris Philosophi Syri de Sapientia Divina Poëma Aenigmaticum*, Paris: Antoine Vitré, 1628.

Smith, Eli, "Report of E. Smith, in March 16th 1844, on the existing Arabic Versions of the Scriptures", in: *Brief documentary history of the translation of the Scriptures into the Arabic Language by Rev. Eli Smith, D.D., and Rev. C.V.A. Van Dyck, D.D.*, Presbyterian Church in the U.S.A, Syrian Mission, ed., Beirut: American Presbyterian Mission Press 1900, 1–4.

Idem, "Dr. Smith's Report on the translation of the Scriptures, April 1854", in: *Brief documentary history of the translation of the Scriptures into the Arabic Language by Rev. Eli Smith, D.D., and Rev. C.V.A. Van Dyck, D.D.*, Presbyterian Church in the U.S.A, Syrian Mission, ed., Beirut: American Presbyterian Mission Press 1900, 4–13.

Soncino, Eliezer, ed., *Judaeo-Arabic Pentateuch*, Istanbul: privately printed, 1546.

Staal, Harvey, ed., *Mt Sinaï Arabic Codex 151. I, Pauline Epistles* (CSCO 452–453), Louvain, 1983.

Van Dyck, Cornelius, "Dr. C.V.A. Van Dyck's Report on the translation, April 29th, 1863", in: *Brief documentary history of the translation of the Scriptures into the Arabic Language by Rev. Eli Smith, D.D., and Rev. C.V.A. Van Dyck, D.D.*, Presbyterian Church in the U.S.A, Syrian Mission, ed., Beirut: American Presbyterian Mission Press, 1900, 14–18.

Idem, "Dr. Van Dyck's History of the Arabic translation of the Scriptures, March 7th, 1885", in: *Brief documentary history of the translation of the Scriptures into the Arabic Language by Rev. Eli Smith, D.D., and Rev. C.V.A. Van Dyck, D.D.*, Presbyterian Church in the U.S.A, Syrian Mission, ed., Beirut: American Presbyterian Mission Press, 1900, 22–31.

Zucker, Moses, ed., *Saadia ben Joseph: perushe rav Se'adyah Gaon li-ve-reshit*, New York: Jewish Theological Seminary, 1984.

Primary Sources (unpublished)

MS. Bodl. Ar. Hunt. 424

MS. Borg. syr. 49

MS. Florence BML or. 112 (olim 21)

MS. Homs, Greek Orthodox Metropolitanate 27, fols. 23b-27b, fol. 30b, fol. 33a, fols. 51a–51b

MS. Leiden Warner 377

MS. London, British Museum, ar. chr. 28 [Add. 9965], fols. 158a–158b, fols.161a–161b, fols. 239b–240b

MS. Paris BNF Ar. 1 (fol. 1v)

MS. Ṣarbā, Dayr al-Mukhalliṣ, Collection Dayr al-Šīr 600, p. 488

MS. St Petersburg, Institute of Oriental Studies, B 1227, fols. 40a–50a, fols. 122a–126b

MS. Vat. Ar. 13

MS. Vat. Ar. 419

MS. Vat. Ar. 468

MS. Vat. Ar. 489

MS. Vat. Ar. 490

MS. Vat. Ar. 606 (1344)

MS. Vat. Casanatense arabe. Carsh 2 (no. 2108)

Near East School of Theology, Bible MS. (Smith/Van Dyck), Boxes I-V

Sinai Arabic Codex 1

Sinai Arabic Codex 72

Sinai Arabic Codex 151

Sinai Arabic Codex 589

SOCG (= Scritture Originali riferite nelle Congregazione Generali, Archives of the Congregation *De Propaganda Fide*), vol. 180 (*Lettere di Lingua straniera dall'Anno 1631 sino al 1645*)

SOCG vol 181 (*Lettere in Diverse Lingue dall'anno 1622 a 1629*)

Van Dyck, C.V.A., "Reminiscences of the Syrian Mission from 1839 to 1850", Beirut: Office of the Commission Representative, (unpublished typeset manuscript).

Secondary Sources in Western Languages

Aboussouan, Camille, *Exposition Le Livre et le Liban jusqu'à 1900*, Paris: Unesco: AGECOOP, 1982.

Abramson, Shraga, "On Isaac Ibn Ghayyat's Commentary to Kohelet", *Kiryat Sefer* 52 (1977), 156–172.

Abraṣ, Mīkhāʾīl, "Makhṭūṭat *majmūʿ laṭīf* li-l-baṭriyark Makāriyūs al-thālith Zaʿīm", *al-Mashriq* 68 (1994), 421–448. (Cf. Secondary Sources in Arabic)

Abū al-Rūs Slīm, Suʿād, "Makhṭūṭ *majmūʿ mubārak* li-l-baṭriyark Makāriyūs al-thālith al-Zaʿīm", *al-Mashriq* 68 (1994), 175–196. (Cf. Secondary Sources in Arabic)

Abullif, Wadi, "La Traduction des Quatre Evangiles d'al-Asʿad Ibn al-ʿAssāl (XIIIe Siècle)", *Studia Orientalia Christiana,* 24 (1991), 216–224.

Idem, "al-Asʿad Ibn al-ʿAssal, Introduzioni alla Traduzione dei Quattro Vangeli", *Studia Orientalia Christiana,* 33 (2000), 227–249.

Adams, Sarah Flower, *Nearer My God to Thee*, Whitefish (Montana): Kessinger Publishing [reprint], 2005.

Addas, C., "Baḥīrā", in: *Dictionnaire du Coran*, Robert Laffont, ed., 2007, 105.

Adler, J. G. C., *Kurze Übersicht seiner Biblisch-Kritischen Reise*, Altona: Eckardt, 1783–4.

Alexandre, Monique, *Le commencement du livre Genèse I–V. La version grecque de la Septante et sa reception*, Paris: Beauchesne, 1988.

Almalgia, R., "Giovan Battista Britti e Gerolamo Vecchietti Viaggiatori in Oriente", *Rendiconti dell'Academia Nazionale dei Lincei* 11 (1956), 313–350.

Idem, "Giovan Battista Britti Cosentino Viaggiatore in Oriente", *Archivio storico per la Calabria e la Lucania,* 25 (1957), 75–101.

Anderson, Rufus, *History of the Missions of the American Board of Commissioners for Foreign Missions to the Oriental Churches*, Boston: Congregational Publ. Soc., 1872.

Arbache, Samir, "Bible et liturgie chez les Arabes chretiens (VIe–IXe siècle)", in: *The Bible in Arab Christianity*, Thomas, David, ed., Leiden/Boston: Brill, 2007, 37–48.

Argyriou, Astérios, "La Bible dans le monde orthodoxe au XVIe siècle", in: *Le temps des Réformes et la Bible*, Guy Bedouelle, Bernard Roussel, eds., (Bible de tous les temps, vol. V), Paris: Beauchesne 1989, 385–400.

Atiya, A.S., *The Arabic Manuscripts of Mount Sinaï. A hand-list of the Arabic manuscripts and scrolls microfilmed at the Library of the Monastery of St Catherine Mount Sinaï*, vol. 1, Baltimore: John Hopkins 1955.

Auvray, Paul, "Jean Morin (1591–1659)", *Revue Biblique*, 66 (1959), 397–414.

Bacher, Wilhelm, "Il Manoscritto Fiorentino della Traduzione del Pentateucho di Saadja", *Rivista Israelitica*, 2 (1905), 45–49.

Bachmann-Medick, Doris, ed., *Übersetzung als Repräsentation fremder Kulturen*, Berlin: E. Schmidt, 1997.

Baghdadi, Nadia al-, "The Cultural Function of Fiction: From the Bible to Libertine Literature. Historical Criticism and social critique in Aḥmad Fāris al-Šidyāq", in: *Arabica* 46 (1999), 375–401.

Bailey, Kenneth E., "Hibat Allah Ibn al-ʿĀssāl and his Arabic thirteenth century critical edition of the Gospels (With special attention to Luke 16:16 and 17:10)", in: *Theological Review (NEST)*, I,1 (1978), 11–26.

Bakhtine, Mikhaïl, *Esthétique de la création verbale,* traduit du Russe par Alfreda Aucouturter, préface de Tzvetan Todorov, Paris: Gallimard, 1982.

Balagna Coustou, Josée, *L'imprimerie Arabe En Occident : XVIe, XVIIe et XVIIIe Siècles*, Paris: Editions Maisonneuve & Larose, 1984.

Baptist Hymnal, Nashville (Tennessee): Convention Press, 1975.

Ben Shammai, Haggai, "An 'East Wind' from the South", in: *Studies in the History of Eretz Israel Presented to Yehuda ben Porat*, Yehoshua Ben-Arieh and Elchanan Reiner, eds., Jerusalem: Yad ben Zvi, 2003, 288–307.

Idem, "Extra-Textual Considerations in Medieval Judaeo-Arabic Bible Translations: The Case of Saadya Gaon", *Materia Guidaica* 8/1 (2003), 53–66.

Bengtsson, Per A., *Translation Techniques in two Syro-Arabic Versions of Ruth*, Stockholm: Almkvist & Wiksell International, 2003.

Bennett, Sanford Fillmore, *Sweet By and By*, Boston (Massachusetts): E. P. Dutton, 1885.

Benveniste, Emile, "Le jeu comme structure", *Cahiers de philosophie* 2 (1947), 161–167.

Bernard, Auguste Joseph, *Antoine Vitré et les Caractères Orientaux de la Bible Polyglotte de Paris. Origines et Vicissitudes des Premiers Caractères Orientaux Introduits en France avec un Specimen de ces Caractères*, Paris: Dumoulin, 1857.

Blau, Joshua, *A Grammar of Christian Arabic 9*, (CSCO, vols. 267, 276, 279), Louvain: CSCO 1966–1967.

Idem, "Saadya Gaon's Pentateuch Translation in the Light of an Early-Eleventh-Century Egyptian Manuscript", *Leshonenu,* 61 (1998), 111–130.

Bloom, Harold, *American Religious Poems: An anthology*, New York: Library of America, 2006.

Bobzin, Hartmut, "Agostino Giustiniani (1470–1536) und seine Bedeutung für die Geschichte der Arabistik", in: *XXIV. Deutscher Orientalistentag vom 26. bis 30. Sep-*

tember 1988 in Köln. Ausgewählte Vorträge, W. Diem and A. Falaturi, eds., Stuttgart: Steiner, 1990, 131–139.

Idem, "Vom Sinn des Arabischstudiums im Sprachkanon der Philologia Sacra", *Hallesche Beiträge zur Orientwissenschaft*, 24 (1998), 21–32.

Bottini, Giovanni-Claudio, "Tommaso Obicini (1585–1632) Custos of the Holy Land and Orientalist", in: *The Christian Heritage in the Holy Land*, Anthony O'Mahony with Göran Gunner and Kevork Hintlian, eds., London: Scorpion Cavendish 1995, 97–101.

Brock, Sebastian, "A neglected Witness to the East Syriac New Testament Commentary Tradition; Sinaî, Arabic MS. 151" in: *Studies on the Christian Arabic Heritage* (Eastern Christian Studies 5), R. Ebied, H. Teule, eds., Leuven: Peeters, 2004, 205–215.

Idem, *The Bible in the Syria tradition*, Piscataway, N.Y.: Gorgias Press, 2006.

Brody, Robert, *The Geonim of Babylonia and the Shaping of Medieval Jewish Culture*, New Haven; London: Yale University Press, 1998.

Idem, *Rav Se'adyah Gaon*, Jerusalem: Merkaz Zalman Shazar le-Toldot Yisra'el, 2006.

Caillois, Roger, *Babel, orgueil, confusion et ruine de la littérature*, Paris: Gallimard, 1948.

Idem, *L'homme et le sacré*, Paris: Gallimard, 1948.

Cannuyer, Christian, "Langues usuelles et liturgiques des Melkites au XIIIe s.", *Oriens Christianus* 70 (1986), 110–117.

Cantemir, Dimitrie, *The Salvation of the Wise Man and The Ruin of the Sinful World / Ṣalāḥ al-ḥakīm wa-fasād al-ʿālam al-dhamīm*, Ioana Feodorov, ed., Bucharest: Acad. Romane, 2006.

Cattan, Basilio, "La Chiesa Copta nel Secolo XVII: Documenti Inediti", *Bessarione*, 34 (1918), 133–161.

Charon, Cyrille, *Histoire des Patriarcats Melkites (Alexandrie, Antioche, Jérusalem) depuis le schisme monophysite du sixième siècle jusqu'à nos jours*, Rome/Paris: Forzani, 1909.

Cheikho, Louis, *Catalogue raisonné des manuscrits de la Bibliothèque Orientale*, vol. 4: *Philosophie et Écriture Sainte*, (*Mélanges de l'Université Saint Joseph*, 10,5), Beyrouth: Impr. Catholique, 1925 (Kraus Reprint 1973).

Chiesa, Bruno, "Un Testimone della Traduzione Araba del Pentateucho di Saadia", in: *Manoscritti, Frammenti e Libri Ebraici nell'italia dei Secoli XV–XVI*, G. Tamani and A. Vivian, eds., Rome: Carucci, 1991.

Cohen, Jean, *Le haut langage, théorie de la poéticité*, Paris: Flammarion, 1979.

Compagnon, Antoine, *La seconde main ou le travail de citation*, Paris: Seuil, 1979.

Cooley, Carolyn Lindsay, *The Music of Emily Dickinson's Poems and Letters*, Jefferson (North Carolina): McFarland, 2003.

Dabbās, Anṭuwān Qayṣar, Rashshū, Nakhla, *Tārīkh al-ṭibāᶜa al-ᶜarabīya fī al-mashriq. Al-baṭriyark Athanāsiyūs al-thālith Dabbās (1685–1724)*, Bayrūt: Dār al-Nahār, 2008. (Cf. Secondary Sources in Arabic)

De Certeau, Michel, "La lecture un braconnage", in: idem, *L'invention du quotidien*, Paris: Éd. 10/18, 1980.

Den Heijer, Johannes, "Relations between Copts and Syrians in the Light of Recent Discoveries at Dayr as-Suryān", in: *Coptic Studies on the Threshold of a New Millennium: Proceedings of the Seventh International Congress of Coptic Studie*, Mat Immerzeel and Jacques Van Der Vliet, eds., Leuven: Uitgeverij Peeters en Dep. Oosterse Studies, 2004, 924–938.

Denzinger, Heinrich, *Enchiridion Symbolorum, Definitionum et Declarationum de rebus fidei et morum,* Freiburg i. Br.: Herder 1991.

Dib, P., *Etude sur la liturgie maronite,* Paris: Lethielleux 1919.

Dictionnaire historique de l'Islam, Paris: Presses universitaires de France, 2004.

Dimaras, C. Th., *Histoire de la littérature néo-hellénique des origines à nos jours,* Athènes: Institut Français d'Athènes, 1965–1966.

Dorn, Bernhard, "Ein Nachtrag zu Schnurrer's Bibliotheca Arabica aus den Schätzen der Kaiserlichen öffentl. Bibliothek zu St. Petersburg", *Zeitschrift der Deutschen Morgenländischen Gesellschaft*, 8 (1854), 386–389.

Dozy, R., *Supplément aux dictionnaires arabes*, [1881], repr. Beyrouth: Libraire du Liban, 1968.

Drint, Adriana, "The Mount Sinaï Arabic Version of IV Ezra. Characteristics and Relevance of an Early Arabic Translation of the Syriac Text", *Orientalia Christiana Periodica* 58 (1992), 401–422.

Idem, *The Mount Sinaï Arabic Version of 4 Ezra* (CSCO 563, 564), Louvain: Peeters, 1997.

Duverdier, Gerald, "Les Caractères de Savary de Brèves, Les Débuts de la Typographie Orientale et la Présence Francaise au Levant au 17e Siècle", *L'art du Livre à L'imprimerie Nationale*, Paris: Impr. Nationale, 1973.

Idem, "Les Impressions Orientales en Europe et le Liban", in: Camille Aboussouan ed., *Exposition le Livre et le Liban jusqu'à 1900*, Paris: Unesco, 1982, 157–73.

Féghaly, Paul, "Les épîtres de saint Paul dans une des premières traductions en arabe", *Parole de l'Orient* 30 (2005), 103–129.

Idem, "Versions arabes de Ben Sira", *Parole de l'Orient* 30 (2005), 65–78.

Garland, A.G., "An Arabic Translation of the Gospel According to Mark", unpublished thesis (1979).

Gdoura, Wahid, *Le début de l'imprimerie arabe à Istanbul et en Syrie: evolution de l'environnement culturel (1706–1787)*, (Publications de l'Institut Supérieur de Documentation, 8), Tunis: Institut Supérieur de Documentation, 1985.

Gemayel, Nasser, *Les Échanges Culturels Entre les Maronites et l'Europe: Du Collège Maronite de Rome (1584) au Collège de Ayn-Warqa (1789)*, 2 vols., Beyrouth: Impr. Y. et Ph. Gemayel, 1984.

Gil, Moshe, *A History of Palestine, 634–1099*, Cambridge: Cambridge University Press, 1992.

Glass, Dagmar, *Malta, Beirut, Leipzig, and Beirut again. Eli Smith, the American Mission and the Spread of Arabic Typography*, Beirut: Orient-Institut Beirut, 1998.

Golden Bells, London: Scripture Union (no date).

Graf, Georg, "Die koptische Gelehrtenfamilie der Aulād al-ʿAssāl und ihr Schriftum", *Orientalia* 1 (1932), 34–56, 129–148, 93–204.

Idem, *Geschichte der christlichen arabischen Literatur*, Città del Vaticano: Biblioteca Apostolica Vaticana, vol.1–5, 1944–1953.

Idem, *Verzeichnis arabischer kirchlicher Termini*, Louvain: Durbecq, 1954.

Griffith, S., "Stephen of Ramleh and the kerygma in Arabic in 9th-century Palestine", *Journal of Ecclesiastical History* 36 (1985), 23–45.

Idem, *Arabic Christianity in the Monasteries of Ninth-Century Palestine*, Aldershot: Variorum, 1992.

Idem, "Les premières versions arabes de la Bible. Les liens avec la langue syriaque", in: *L'ancien Testament en syriaque* (Études Syriaques, 5), Paris: Geuthner, 2008, 221–245.

Guidi, I., *Le traduzioni degli Evangelii in arabo e in etiopico* (Atti della R. Accademia dei Lincei, anno 295 [1888], Series Quarta Classe di Scienze morali, storiche e filologiche, Vol IV, Parte I, Memorie, 32).

Hainthaller, T., *Christliche Araber vor dem Islam* (Eastern Christian Studies, 7/2007), Leuven: Peeters, 2007.

Hedaya, Marcel, "Germanos Farhat, Bishop of Aleppo and Arabist (1670–1732)", *Melto* 2 (1966), 115–129.

Homerin, Th. Emil, *From Arab Poet to Muslim Saint: Ibn al-Fāriḍ, His Verse, and His Shrine*, Cairo: American University, 2001 (reprint of 1994 edition).

Hopkins, S. A., *Studies in the Grammar of Early Arabic. Based upon Papyri Datable to before 300 AH/ AD 912,* Oxford: Oxford University Press 1984.

Hourani, Albert, *Arabic Thought in the Liberal Age 1798 – 1939*, Oxford: Oxford University Press, 1962.

Idlibī, Nāwifitūs (Neophytos Edelby), *Asāqifat al-Rūm al-Malakīyīn bi-Ḥalab fī l-ʿaṣr al-ḥadīth*, Ḥalab: Maṭbaʿat al-Iḥsān, 1983. (Cf. Secondary Sources in Arabic)

Jauss, Hans Robert, *Pour une herméneutique littéraire,* Paris: Gallimard, 1982.

Jessup, Henry Harris, *Fifty Three Years in Syria*, New York and Chicago: Fleming H. Revell Company, 1910.

Idem, *The Women of the Arabs*, New York: Dodd and Mead, 1873.

Jones, John Robert, *The Arabic and Persian Studies of Giovan Battista Raimondi (C. 1536–1614)*, London: University of London, 1981.

Idem, *Learning Arabic in Renaissance Europe (1505–1624)*, London: University of London, 1988.

Idem, "The Medici Oriental Press (Rome 1584–1614) and the Impact of Its Arabic Publications on Northern Europe", in: *The "Arabick" Interest of the Natural Philosophers in Seventeenth-Century England*, G. A. Russell, ed., Leiden/New York: E.J. Brill, 1994, 88–108.

Kachouh, Hikmat, "The Arabic Versions of the Gospels: A Case Study of John 1.1 and 1.18", in: *The Bible in Arab Christianity*, David Thomas, ed., (The History of Christian-Muslim Relations, 6), Leiden/Boston: Brill, 2007, 9–36.

Idem, "Sinai Ar.N.F. Parchment 8 and 28, its contribution to textual criticism of the Gospel of Luke, *Novum Testamentum* 50 (2008), 28–57.

Idem, *The Arabic Version of the Gospel: the manuscripts and their families*, 3 Vols., Birmingham: University of Birmingham, 2008.

Kades, Tharwat, *Die arabischen Bibelübersetzungen im 19. Jahrhundert*, Frankfurt/M. u.a.: Lang 1997.

Kahle, Paul, *Die Arabischen Bibelübersetzungen: Texte mit Glossar und Literaturübersicht*, Leipzig: J.C. Hinrichs, 1904.

Khalidi, Tarif, *The Muslim Jesus: Sayings and Stories in Islamic Literature*, Cambridge: Harvard University Press, 2001.

Khūrī, Sāmī al-, "Al-Shaykh Ibrāhīm al-Yāzijī wa-l-maṭbaʿa al-kāthūlīkiyyah, baina 1872 wa 1881", *Al-Mashriq* 65 (1991), 127ff. (Cf. Secondary Sources in Arabic)

Knysh, Alexander D., *Ibn ʿArabi in the Later Islamic Tradition: The Making of a Polemical Image in Medieval Islam*, New York: State University of New York, 1999.

Kowalsky, Nikolaus, "Zur Vorgeschichte der arabischen Bibelübersetzung der Propaganda von 1671", *Neue Zeitschrift für Missionswissenschaft* XVI (1960), 268–274.

Lassithiotakis, Michel, "Le role du livre imprimé dans la formation et le développement de la littérature en grec vulgaire (XVIe–XVIIe siècles)", *Revue des Mondes Musulmans et de la Méditerranée* 58/59 (1999), 187–208.

Leavy, Margaret R., *Eli Smith and the Arabic Bible*, New Haven, CT: Yale Divinity School Library, 1993.

Lelong, Jacques, *Discours Historique sur les Principales Editions des Bibles Polyglottes*, Paris: Pralard, 1713.

Lentin, Jérôme, *Recherches sur l'histoire de la langue arabe au Proche-Orient à l'époque moderne*, unpublished Thèse de Doctorat d'état, Université de Paris III, 1997.

Lobrichon, G., "Versions anciennes de la Bible, B. La Vulgate", in: *Dictionnaire Encyclopédique de la Bible*, Turnhout: Brepols, 1982, 1322–1323.

Löfgren, Oscar, *Studien zu den arabischen Danielübersetzungen, mit besonderer Berücksichtigung der christlichen Texte; nebst einem Beitrag zur Kritik des Peschittatextes*, Uppsala: Almqvist & Wiksell, 1936.

Macdonald, Duncan B., "Ibn al-ᶜAssāl's Arabic Version of the Gospels", in: *Homenaje á D. Francisco Codera en su Julibilación del Profesorado*; Eduardo Saavedra, ed., Zaragoza: M. Escart, 1904, 375–392.

Makdisi, Ussama, *Artillery of Heaven. American Missionaries and the failed conversion of the Middle East*, Ithaca: Cornell University Press, 2008.

Malter, Henry: *Saadia Gaon : His Life and Works*, Philadelphia: The Jewish Publication Society of America, 1921.

Mieses, J., "Textkritische Bemerkungen zu R. Saadja Gaons arabischer Pentateuchübersetzung", *Monatsschrift für die Geschichte und Wissenschaft des Judentums* 63 (1919), 269–290.

Monferre Sala, Juan Pedro, "Liber Job detractus apud Sin. Ar. 1: Notas en torno a la *Vorlage* siriaca de un manuscrito arabe cristianeo (s. IXe)", *Collectanea Christiana Orientalia* 1 (2006), 119–142.

Montgomery, J.E., "The Empty Hijaz", in: *Arabic Theology, Arabic Philosophy: From the Many to the One. Essays in Celebration of Richard M. Frank*, J.E. Montgomery, ed., (Orientalia Lovaniensia Analecta, 152), Leuven: Peeters, 2006, 37–97.

Moreh, Shmuel, Modern Arabic Poetry 1800 – 1970: *The Development of Its Forms and Themes under the Influence of Western Literature*, Leiden: Brill, 1976.

Morozov, D. A., "Arabskoje Evangelije Daniila Apostola (K istorii pervoj arabskoj tipografii na Vostoke)", in *Archiv russkoj istorii*, vyp. 2, Moscow 1992, 193–203.

Nasrallah, Joseph, *Histoire du mouvement littéraire dans l'église melchite du Ve au XXe siècle*, vol. 4, 1 : *Période ottomane 1516–1724*, Louvain: Peeters, 1979.

Idem, "La liturgie des Patriarcats melchites de 969 à 1300", *Oriens Christianus* 71 (1987), 156–181.

Newby, G.D., *A History of the Jews of Arabia. From ancient Times to their Eclipse under Islam*, Columbia (SC): University of South Carolina, 1988.

Nida, Eugene A. and Taber, Charles R., *The Theory and practice of translation*, Leiden: Brill, 2003 (4th ed.).

Omont, H., "Projet D'un Collège Oriental a Paris Au Début Du Règne De Louis Xiii", *Bulletin de la Société de l'histoire de Paris et de l'Île de France*, 22 (1895), 123–27.

Onasch, Konrad, arts. "Evangelium"; "Lesebücher"; "Lesungen", in: idem, *Lexikon Liturgie und Kunst der Ostkirche*, Berlin: Buchverlag Union, 1993.

Ormsby, Eric L., *Theodicy in Islamic Thought: The Dispute over al-Ghazālī's "Best of All Possible World"*, Princeton: Princeton University Press, 1984.

Padwick, C.E., "Al-Ghazali and the Arabic Versions of the Gospels", *Moslem World* 29, 2 (1939), 130–140.

Pančenko, K. A., Fonkič, B. L., "Gramota 1594 g. antiochijskogo Patriarcha Ioakima VI Zarju Fedoru Ivanoviču", in: *Monfokon. Issledovanija po paleografii, kodikologii i diplomatike / Montfaucon. Etudes de paléographie, de codicologie et de diplomatique*, Rossijskaja Akademija Nauk, Institut vseobščej istorii, Zentr "Paleografija, Kodikologija, Diplomatika", ed., vol. 1, Moscow and St Petersburg: Al'jans Archeo 2007, 166–184.

Papaconstantinou, A., "'They Shall Speak the Arabic Language and Take Pride in It': Reconsidering the Fate of Coptic after the Arab Conquest", *Le Muséon*, 120 (2007), 273–299.

Peters, Melvin K. H., *A Critical Edition of the Coptic (Bohairic) Pentateuch* (Septuagint and Cognate Studies Series; 15) Chicago: Scholars Press, 1983.

Picard, Michel, *La lecture comme jeu*, Paris: Minuit, 1986.

Podskalsky, Gerhard, *Griechische Theologie in der Zeit der Türkenherrschaft (1453–1821). Die Orthodoxie im Spannungsfeld der nachreformatorischen Konfessionen des Westens.* München: C.H. Beck, 1988.

Polliack, Meira, *The Karaite Tradition of Arabic Bible Translation: A Linguistic and Exegetical Study of Karaite Translations of the Pentateuch from the Tenth and Eleventh Centuries C.E* (Etudes sur le Judaïsme Médiéval), Leiden; New York: E.J. Brill, 1997.

Presbyterian Church in the U.S.A., *The Church at Home and Abroad*, Philadelphia (Pennsylvania): Presbyterian Church in the USA, 1.1887–24.1898.

Qāshā, Suhayl, "al-Kitāb al-Muqaddas wa-l-lugha al-ʿarabiyya", in: *Tarjamāt al-Kitāb al-Muqaddas fī l-Sharq. Buḥūth bībliyya muhadāt ilā Lūsyān ʿAqqād*, Ayyūb Shahwān, ed., Bayrūt: al-Rābiṭa al-Kitābiyya 2006 (Dirāsāt bībliyya 30), 79–96. (Cf. Secondary Sources in Arabic)

Reformed Church in America, *The Church Hymnary: A Collection of Hymns and Tunes for Public Worship*, compiled by Edwin A. Bedell, New York: Maynard Merrill, 1892.

Reichmuth, Stephan and Schwarz, Florian, eds., *Zwischen Alltag und Schriftkultur: Horizonte des Indivduellen in der arabischen Literatur des 17. und 18. Jahrhunderts*, Beirut/Würzburg: Ergon Verlag, 2008.

Reverdin, Olivier, "Livres grecs imprimés à Genève au XVIe et au XVIIe siècle", in: *Cinq siècles d'imprimerie genevoise. Actes du Colloque internationale sur l'histoire de l'imprimerie et du livre à Genève*, Jean-Daniel Candaux and Bernard Lascaze, eds., Geneva: Société d'histoire et d'archéologie, 1980, 209–238.

Rhode, Joseph Francis, *The Arabic Versions of the Pentateuch in the Church of Egypt: A Study from Eighteen Arabic and Copto-Arabic Mss. (IX–XVII Century) in the National Library at Paris, the Vatican and Bodleian Libraries and the British Museum*, Leipzig: W. Drugulin, 1921.

Richard, Francis, "Les Manuscrits Persans Repportés par les Frères Vecchietti et Conservés aujourd'hui à la Bibliothèque Nationale", *Studia Iranica* 9 (1980), 291–300.

Idem, "Les Frères Vecchietti, Diplomates, Érudites et Aventuries", in: *The Republic of Letters and the Levant*, Alastair Hamilton, Maurits Van Den Boogert, and Bart Westerweel, eds., Leiden/ Boston: Brill, 2005, 11–26.

Richter, T. S., "O. Crum Ad. 15 and the Emergence of Arabic Words in Coptic Legal Documents", in: *Papyrology and the History of Early Islamic Egypt*, Petra Sijpesteijn and Lennart Sundelin, eds., Leiden/Boston: Brill, 2004.

Rilliet, F., "Georges des Arabes", in: *Dictionnaire Encyclopédique du Christianisme Ancien*, Paris: Cerf, 1990.

Rubenson, Samuel, "Translating the Tradition: Some Remarks on the Arabization of the Patristic Heritage in Egypt", *Medieval Encounters*, 2/1 (1996), 4–14.

Saleh, Walid A., "A Fifteenth-Century Muslim Hebraist: Al-Biqāʿī and His Defense of Using the Bible to Interpret the Qurʾān," *Speculum* 83 (2008), 629–654.

Idem, "Sublime in Its Style, Exquisite in Its Tenderness: The Hebrew Bible Quotations in al-Biqāʿī's Qurʾān Commentary," in: *Adaptations and Innovations*, Tzvi Langermann and Josef Stern, eds., Paris: Peeters, 2007, 331–347.

Saltini, G.E., "Della Stamperia Orientale Medicea e di Giovan Battista Raimondi", *Giornale Storico degli Archivi Toscani* 4 (1860), 257–308.

Idem, "La Bibbia Poliglotta Medicea secondo il Disegno e gli Apparecchi di Gio. Battista Raimondi", *Bollettino italiano degli studii orientali*, 22 (1882), 490–495.

Samir, Samir Khalil, "Trois Versions Arabes du Livre des Juges. Réflexions Critiques sur un Livre Récent", *Oriens Christianus*, 65 (1981), 87–101.

Idem, "La Version Arabe des Évangiles d'al-Asʿad Ibn al-ʿAssāl. Étude des Manuscrits et Spécimens", *Actes du 4e Congrès International d'études Arabes Chrétiennes (Cambridge, Septembre 1992)*, Samir, Samir Khalil, ed., Kaslik: Université Saint-Esprit, 1994, 441–551.

Sankey, Ira D., *My Life and the Story of the Gospel Hymns*, Philadelphia (Pennsylvania): The Sunday School Times Company, 1906.

Sarrazin, Bernard, *Le rire et le sacret*, Paris: Gallimard, 1991.

Shahid, Irfan, *Rome and the Arabs: A Prolegomenon to the Study of Byzantium and the Arabs*, Washington (DC), Dumbarton Oaks, 1984.

Simaika, Marcus, *Catalogue of the Coptic and Arabic Manuscripts in the Coptic Museum, the Patriarchate, the Principal Churches of Cairo and Alexandria and the Monasteries of Egypt*, Cairo: Government Press, Būlâq, 1939.

Staikos, Konstantinos Sp. and Sklavenitis, Triantaphyllos E., *The Publishing Centres of the Greeks. From the Renaissance to the Neo-Hellenic Enlightenment*, Athens: National Book Centre of Greece, 2001.

Stone, E., "A New Manuscript of the Syro-Arabic version of the Fourth Book of Ezra", *Journal for the Study of Judaism* 8 (1976/77), 183–184.

Takla, Hany N., "Copto (Bohairic)-Arabic Manuscripts: Their Role in the Tradition of the Coptic Church", in: *Coptic Studies on the Threshold of a New Millennium: Proceedings of the Seventh International Congress of Coptic Studie*, Mat Immerzeel and Jacques Van Der Vliet, eds., Leuven: Uitgeverij Peeters en Dep. Oosterse Studies, 2004, 639–646.

Thomas, David ed., *The Bible in Arab Christianity*, Leiden/Boston: Brill, 2007.

Thompson, John Alexander, *The Major Arabic Bibles: Their Origin and Nature*, New York: American Bible Society, 1956.

Tibawi, A.L., *American Interests in Syria 1800–1901. A Study of Educational, Literary and Religious Work*, Oxford: Clarendon, 1966.

Idem, "The American Missionaries in Beirut und Buṭrus al-Bustānī", in *Middle Eastern Affairs* 3 (1963), 137–182.

Tinto, Alberto, *La Tipografia Medicea Orientale* (Studi e Ricerche di Storia del Libro e delle Biblioteche, 1) Lucca: M. Pacini Fazzi, 1987.

Idem, "Un Diario di Giovanni Battista Raimondi (22 Giungo 1592–12 Dicembre 1596)", *Archivo Storico,* 151 (1993), 671–684.

Trivedi, Harish, "Translating Culture versus Cultural Translation", in: *91st Meridian*, vol. 4, no. 1, University of Iowa, 2005.

Troupeau, Gérard, *Catalogue Des Manuscrits Arabes: Première Partie: Manuscrits Chrétiens Nos. 1–6933*, Paris: Bibliothèque Nationale, 1972.

Tymoczko, Maria and Edwin Gentzler, eds., *Translation and Power*, Amherst/Boston: University of Massachusetts Press, 2002.

Vaccari, Alberto, "Le Versioni Arabe Dei Profeti", *Biblica* 2 (1921), 401–423.

Idem, "I Caratteri Arabi della 'Typographia Savariana'", *Rivista degli Studi Orientali* 10 (1923–25), 37–47.

Idem, "Un codice carsciunice della Casanatense e la Bibbia araba del 1671", *Biblica* IV (1923), 96–107.

Idem, "Una Bibbia Araba Per Il Primo Gesuita Venuto Al Libano", *Mélanges de l'Université Saint-Joseph de Beyrouth* 10/4 (1925), 79–104.

Van Esbroeck, Michel, "Les versions orientales de la Bible: une orientation bibliographique", in: *The Interpretation of the Bible. The International Symposium in Slovenia*, Jože Kražovac, ed., Ljublana/Sheffield: Slovenska akademija znanosti in umetnosti/Sheffield Academic Press, 1998, 399–507.

Vaporis, N.M., "Patriarch Kyrillos Loukaris and the translation of the Scriptures into Modern Greek", *Ekklēsiastikos Pharos* 59 (1977), 227–241.

Vercellin, Giorgio, *Venezia e l'origine della Stampa in Caratteri Arabi*, Padova: Il Poligrafo, 2001.

Violet, B., *Ein zweisprachiges Psalmfragment aus Damaskus*, (Berichtigter Sonderabzug aus der Orientalischen Literaturzeitung), 1901.

Vollandt, Ronny, "Some Observations on Genizah Fragments of Saadiah's Tafsīr in Arabic Letters", *Ginzey Qedem: Genizah Research Annual,* 6 (2009), 9–44.

Idem, "From the working desks of a Coptic-Muslim workshop: MS Paris–BNF Arabic 1 and the mass production of Arabic deluxe Bibles in early Ottoman Cairo", in: *Patronage and the Sacred Book*, E. Alfonso and J. Decter, eds., Turnhout: Brepols, 2012 (forthcoming).

von Kremer, A., "Nâṣîf aljâziǵî", *ZDMG* 25 (1871), 244–45.

Vööbus, Arthur, *Early versions of the New Testament. Manuscript studies*, (Estonian Theological Studies in Exile, 6) Stockholm 1954.

Walbiner, Carsten-Michael, *Die Mitteilungen des griechisch-orthodoxen Patriarchen Makarius b. az-Zaʿīm von Antiochia (1647–1672) über Georgien nach dem arabischen Autograph von St. Petersburg*, Ph.D. thesis, Leipzig, 1995.

Idem, "*Kitāb al-injīl al-sharīf al-ṭāhir wa-l-miṣbāḥ al-munīr al-zāhir* (The Book of the honourable pure Gospel and the illuminative lamp)", in: *The Beginnings of Printing in the Near and Middle East: Jews, Christians, Muslims*, Klaus Kreiser, ed., Wiesbaden: Harrassowitz, 2001, 24–25.

Idem, "'Und um Jesu Willen, schickt sie nicht ungebunden!' Die Bemühungen des Meletius Karma (1572–1635) um den Druck arabischer Bücher in Rom", in: *Studies on the Christian Arabic Heritage in Honour of Father Prof. Dr. Samir Khalil Samir S.I. at the Occasion of his Sixty-Fifth Birthday*, Rifaat Ebeid and Herman Teule, eds., Leuven: Peeters, 2004, 163–175.

Idem, "Some Observations on the Perception and Understanding of Printing amongst the Arab Greek Orthodox [Melkites] in the Seventeenth Century", in: *Printing and Publishing in the Middle East. Papers from the Second Symposium on the History of Printing and Publishing in the Languages and Countries of the Middle East, Bibliothèque nationale de France, Paris 2–4 November 2005*, Philip Sadgrove, ed., Oxford: University Press 2008, 65–76.

Idem, "Preserving the past and enlightening the present. Macarius b. al-Zaʿīm and Medieval Melkite literature", *Parole d'Orient*, 24 (2009), 433–441, here 437–438,440–441.

Watts, Isaac, *The Psalms of David, Imitated in the Language of the New Testament* (different editions).

Wörterbuch der klassischen arabischen Sprache, Bd. I: *Kāʾ*, Wiesbaden: Harrassowitz, 1970.

Zaborowski, J. R., "From Coptic to Arabic in Medieval Egypt", *Medieval Encounters,* 14 (2008), 15–40.

Zachs, Fruma, *The Making of a Syrian Identity. Intellectuals and Merchants in Nineteenth Century Beirut*, Leiden: Brill, 2005.

Secondary Sources in Arabic

أبرص، ميخائل، "مخطوطات مجموع لطيف للبطريرك مكاريوس الثالث زعيم"، *المشرق* ٦٨، ١٩٩٤، ٤٢١-٤٤٨.

ابن الخطيب، لسان الدين، جيش *التوشيح*، تحقيق هلال ناجي، تونس: مطبعة المنار، ١٩٦٧. نسخة أخرى: تصحيح ألن جونز، جامعة كامبريدج: سلسلة جب التذكارية، ١٩٩٧.

أبو شبكة، إلياس، *روابط الفكر والروح بين العرب والفرنجة*، طبعة ٢، بيروت: منشورات دار المكشوف، ١٨٤٥.

أبو الروس سليم، سعاد، "مخطوطات مجموع لطيف للبطريك مكاريوس الثالث زعيم"، *المشرق* ٦٨، ١٩٩٤، ١٩٦-١٧٥.

الإدلبي، ناوفيتوس، أساقفت الروم الملكيين بحلب في العصر الحادث، حلب: مطبعة الإحسان، ١٩٨٣.

أدونيس، *قصائد أُولى*، طبعة ٢، بيروت: دار مجلّة شعر والمكتبة العصرية، ١٩٦٣.

– ، علي أحمد سعيد، *ديوان الشعرالعربي*، ثلاثة أجزاء، صيدا ـ بيروت: المكتبة العصرية، ١٩٦٤.

إسماعيل، عزّ الدين، *الشعر العربي المعاصر، قضاياه وظواهره الفنّية والمعنوية*، بيروت:دار العودة، ١٩٨٨.

باكثير، علي أحمد، *روميو وجوليت* (مسرحية مترجمة عن شكسبير عام ١٩٣٦)، القاهرة: الفجالة، ١٩٤٦.

البطل، علي، *شبح قايين بين إيديث سيتول وبدر شاكر السياب (قراءة تحليلية مقارنة)*، طبعة ١، بيروت: دار الأندلس، ١٩٨٤.

تقيّ الدين، أمين، *ديوان أمين تقيّ الدين*، جمعه وحقّقه وقدّم له د. سامي مكارم، بيروت: دار صادر، ١٩٩٦.

الدجيلي، عبد الكريم، *البند في الأدب العربي: تاريخه، نصوصه*، بغداد: مطبعة المعارف، ١٩٥٩.

دباس، انطوان قيصر ،رشو، نخلة، تاريخ الطباعة العربية في المشرق: البطريرك اثناسيوس الثالث دباس (١٦٨٥-١٧٢٤)، بيروت: دارالنهار ٢٠٠٨.

جاسبر، دايفيد، *مقدّمة في الهرمينوطيقا*، ترجمة وجيه قانصو، بيروت: الدار العربية للعلوم، منشورات الإختلاف،٢٠٠٧.

جب، هاملتون، *دراسات في حضارة الإسلام*، ترجمة إحسان عباس ومحمد نجم ومحمود زايد، بيروت: دار العلم للملايين، ١٩٦٤.

جبر، جميل، *إلياس أبو شبكة شاعر الحب*، طبعة ١، بيروت: دار الجيل، ١٩٩٤.

جبران، جبران خليل، *المجموعة العربية الكاملة*، دمشق: دار ومؤسسة الرسلان ٢٠٠٨.

حاوي، إيليا، *مع خليل حاوي في مسيرة حياته وشعره*، بيروت: مؤسسة خليفة للطباعة، ١٩٨٦.

حاوي، خليل، *نهر الرماد*، طبعة ٣، بيروت: دار الطليعة، ١٩٦٢.

– ، *فلسفة الشعر والحضارة*، تحرير ريتا عوَض، بيروت: دار النهار، ٢٠٠٢.

الحدّاد، أمين واليازجي، ابراهيم، "ترجمة المرحوم الشيخ ناصيف اليازجي"، في: *ديوان الشيخ ناصيف اليازجي*، بيروت: دار مارون عبّود، ١٩٨٣.

حوراني، ألبرت، *الفكر العربي في عصر النهضة ١٧٩٨-١٩٣٩*، بيروت: دار النهار، ١٩٧٧.

الخال، يوسف، *قصائد في الأربعين*، بيروت: دار مجلّة شعر، ١٩٦٠.

– ، *الأعمال الشعرية الكاملة*، بيروت: دار العودة ، ١٩٧٩.

– ، *قصائد مختارة*، جمعها مع مقدّمة علي أحمد سعيد (أدونيس)، بيروت: دار مجلّة شعر (لا تاريخ).

الخوري، سامي، "الشيخ إبراهيم اليازجي والمطبعة الكاثوليكية بين ١٨٧٢ و ١٨٨١"، المشرق ٦٥، ١٩٩١، ١٢٧ff.

الرافعي، مصطفى صادق، *تحت راية القرآن*، طبعة ٣، القاهرة: مكتبة الإستقامة، ١٩٥٣.

روّاد لبنانيون، المجلّد ١، زوق مكايل: منشورات جامعة سيّدة اللويزة، ٢٠٠٦.

سعادة، جبرائيل، "الياس صالح اللاذقي"، مجلّة *التراث العربي* (فصلية تصدر عن اتّحاد الكتّاب العرب في دمشق)، العدد ٤١، تشرين الأول/أوكتوبر ١٩٩٠.

سعيد، خالدة، *حركيّة الإبداع، دراسات في الأدب العربي الحديث*، طبعة ١، بيروت: دار العودة، ١٩٧٩.

سقال، ديزيره، "الأرض الخراب والشعر العربي المعاصر"، مجلة *الفكر العربي المعاصر*، عدد ١٠، شباط/فبراير ١٩٨١.

سيل، سيكل (Morris S. Seale) ، "الترجمات وقيمتها"، في *المرشد إلى الكتاب المقدّس*، بيروت: مكتبة المشعل الإنجيلية، ١٩٥٨.

السيّاب، بدر شاكر، *أساطير*، النجف: مطبعة الغزّي الحديثة، منشورات دار البيان، ١٩٥٠.

– ، "تعليقات"، مجلّة *الآداب*، العدد ٦، حزيران/يونيو ١٩٥٦.

– ، *أنشودة المطر*، بيروت: دار مجلّة شعر، ١٩٦٠.

– ، *المعبد الغريق*، بيروت: دار العلم للملايين، ١٩٦٢.

– ، *الأعمال الشعرية الكاملة*، المجلّد الأول، ديوان أنشودة المطر، طبعة ١، بيروت: طبعة دار العودة، ١٩٨٩.

الشّابي، *رسائل أبو القاسم الشّابي*، إعداد محمد الحليوي، طبعة خاصة لوزارة الثقافة، تونس: دار المغرب العربي، ١٩٩٤.

شهوان، أيوب (الناشر)، *ترجمات الكتاب المقدس في الشرق: بحوث بيبلية مهدات إلى لسيان عقاد*، (دراسات بيبلية رقم ٣٠)، جونية: الرابطة الكتابية، ٢٠٠٦.

– ، "الترجمات العربية المتلاحقة للكتاب المقدّس شهادة على همّ علمي وكنسي متواصل" في أيوب شهوان (الناشر)، *ترجمات الكتاب المقدس في الشرق*، (دراسات بيبلية رقم ٣٠)، جونية: الرابطة الكتابية، ٢٠٠٦، ٢٥٧-٢٨٨ .

شوقي، أحمد، *الأعمال الشعرية الكاملة*، المجلّد الأول، الجزء الثاني، بيروت: دار العودة، ١٩٨٨.

شيبوب، خليل، قصيدة "الشراع"، مجلّة *حلقة أبولو*، السنة الأولى، العدد ٣، ١٩٣٢.

شيخو، لويس، *تاريخ الآداب العربية في الربع الأول من القرن العشرين*، المجلّد ١، بيروت: مطبعة الآباء اليسوعيين، ١٩٢٦.

صعب، أديب، "أثر المؤسسات الأنكلوسكسونيّة في وعي الأرثوذكس وخطابهم"، في: *الأرثوذكس والإنجيليّون في المشرق العربي - قراءة تاريخية وآفاق مستقبليّة*، البلمند: منشورات جامعة البلمند، ٢٠٠٤.

–، *هموم حضاريّة*، بيروت: دار النهار، ٢٠٠٦.

–، "الأثر الإنجيلي والأنكلوسكسوني لدى نخبة من المفكرين العرب"، في: *هموم حضاريّة*، بيروت: دار النهار، ٢٠٠٦.

الصليبي، كمال، *تاريخ لبنان الحديث*، طبعة ٦، بيروت: دار النهار، ١٩٨٤.

العظمة، نذير، "بدر شاكر السيّاب والمسيح"، مجلة *الفكر العربي*، عدد ٢٦، آذار/مارس ١٩٨٢.

عكولة، باسيل، "المراجعة العربية للكتاب المقدّس في طبعته الموصلية، دراسة وتحليل" في أيوب شهوان (الناشر)، *ترجمات الكتاب المقدس في الشرق*، (دراسات بيبلية رقم ٣٠)، جونية: الرابطة الكتابية، ٢٠٠٦، ٥٣-٧٨.

الفغالي، بولس، "الكتاب المقدّس، الترجمة الكاثوليكية الحديثة" في أيوب شهوان (الناشر)، *ترجمات الكتاب المقدس في الشرق*، (دراسات بيبلية رقم ٣٠)، جونية: الرابطة الكتابية، ٢٠٠٦، ٢٧-٤٢.

قاشا، سهيل، "الكتاب المقدّس واللغة العربية" في أيوب شهوان (الناشر)، *ترجمات الكتاب المقدس في الشرق*، (دراسات بيبلية رقم ٣٠)، جونية: الرابطة الكتابية، ٢٠٠٦، ٧٩-٩٦.

قبّاني، نزار، *الرسم بالكلمات*، بيروت: منشورات نزار قباني، ١٩٦٧.

–، *يوميّات امرأة لامبالية*، بيروت: منشورات نزار قباني، ١٩٦٨.

كتاب الترانيم الروحية للكنائس الإنجيلية، بيروت: مكتبة المشعل، ١٩٦٥.

لؤلؤة، عبد الواحد، *الأرض اليباب (الشاعر والقصيدة)*، طبعة ١، بيروت: المؤسّسة العربية للدراسات والنشر، ١٩٨٠.

المقدسي الخوري ، أنيس، مقدّمة الطبعة الجديدة لكتاب *الترانيم الروحية للكنائس الإنجيلية*، بيروت: مكتبة المشعل، ١٩٦٥.

–، *الإتجاهات الأدبية في العالم العربي الحديث*، طبعة ٣، بيروت: دار العلم للملايين، ١٩٦٦.

الملائكة، نازك، *قضايا الشعر المعاصر*، بغداد: مكتبة النهضة، ١٩٦٥.

من قضايا الشعر العربي المعاصر (دراسات وشهادات)، تقديم عزّ الدين إسماعيل، إعداد ريتا عوض، تونس: المنظمة العربية للتربية والثقافة، ١٩٨٨.

موريه، شموئيل (Schmuel Moreh)، *الشعر العربي الحديث (١٨٠٠/١٩٧٠) تطوّر أشكاله وموضوعاته بتأثير الأدب الغربي*، ترجمه وعلّق عليه شفيع السيّد وسعيد مصلوح، القاهرة: دار الفكر العربي، ١٩٨٦.

نعيمة، ميخائيل، *همس الجفون*، طبعة ٤، بيروت: دار صادر، ١٩٦٢.

–، *الغربال*، طبعة ٧، بيروت: دار صادر، ١٩٦٤.

النواجي، شمس الدين محمد بن حسن، *عقود اللآل في الموشحات والأزجال*، تحقيق عبد اللطيف الشهابي، بغداد: دار الرشيد للنشر، ١٩٨٢.

اليازجي، كمال، *الشيخ ابراهيم الحوراني: عصره، حياته، أدبه، ومختارات من شعره وأبحاثه*، بيروت: مكتبة رأس بيروت، ١٩٦٣.

يوسف، سعدي، *قصائد مرئية*، صيدا - بيروت: المكتبة العصرية، ١٩٦٥.

About the authors

Hedi Ayadi, Professor of Modern Arabic Literature at Tunis University, completed a PhD on the literary style of Khalil Gibran in 1997. Other publications include “Les symboles bibliques dans la poésie moderne” and “Le pacte lyrique dans la poésie moderne”.

Sara Binay studied Arabic Language and History. From 2005 to 2008 she was a research associate at the Orient-Institut Beirut. Her research interests include the Bedouin in classical Arabic literature (PhD thesis 2005), political humour in Lebanon and intercultural studies in Germany.

Kevin Casey is a PhD graduate at the University of Toronto. His dissertation was on early Islamic mysticism and Syriac mysticism.

Issa Diab is a professor of Semitic and Interfaith Studies at various universities in Lebanon. He is a Doctor of Theology, History and Cultural Studies with a special interest in the historical origins of the monotheistic religions.

Paul Féghali holds a PhD in History of religions from the Sorbonne University and a doctorate in Theology. He has edited numerous works on philological and other aspects of the Biblical Scriptures.

Ghassan Khalaf holds a doctorate in Theology from the Evangelical Theological Faculty of Leuven, Belgium. He teaches as a professor of Theology and was president of the Arab Baptist Theological Seminary in Lebanon from 1993 to 2008. He has published books on a range of topics, .e.g. “Lebanon in the Bible”.

Hilary Kilpatrick is an independent scholar living in Lausanne. She has published on Modern and Classical Arabic Literature. Her current research is on Arabic literature by Muslims and Christians in the early Ottoman period.

Stefan Leder is professor of Arabic and Islamic studies at the Martin-Luther-Universität at Halle (Germany) and director of the Orient-Institut Beirut. He has extensively studied medieval Arabic literature, Islamic scholarship and history.

Adib Saab graduated from the American University of Beirut and the University of London. Doctor of Philosophy and Religious Studies, he is a professor of Philosophy and of Arabic Poetics in Lebanon. He is the author of numerous books in philosophy and cultural criticism, as well as of collections of poetry.

Walid Saleh is Associate Professor at the Department of Near and Middle Eastern Civilizations, University of Toronto. He holds a PhD from Yale University (2001) and has frequently published in the field of Quranic studies. He is a specialist on the reception of the Bible in Islam.

Ronny Vollandt holds a PhD (2011) from the Faculty of Middle Eastern Studies, University of Cambridge. He has studied at Berlin and Jerusalem and held visiting fellowships at Rome and Oxford. His research interests include Semitic languages, Judaeo-Arabic, medieval Jewish literature and, in particular, Arabic versions of the Bible.

Carsten Walbiner studied Arabic Language and Economics and received a PhD from Leipzig University in 1995. From 1995 to 2001 he was a research associate at the Orient-Institut Beirut. His research interests include Arab Christianity in the Ottoman period.

ترجمة الكتاب المقدّس إلى العربيّة:
قضايا تاريخيّة، روائيّة وأدبيّة

نصُوصٌ وَ دِرَاسَات بَيْروتيَّة

سِلسِلة يُصدرُها

المَعهد الألمانيّ للأبحاث الشرقيّة في بَيروت

١٣١

ترجمة الكتاب المقدّس إلى العربيّة:
قضايا تاريخيّة، روائيّة وأدبيّة

هيئة التحرير

سارة بيناي

ستيفان ليدر

بيروت ٢٠١٢

يُطلبْ من دَار النَشر

«إرغون فرلاغ» ڤورتسْبورغ

تصميم الغلاف:
Taline Yozgatian

صورة الغلاف:
Near East School of Theology Beirut, Bible MS., Box No. III, Booklet 1, Matth. 9:1–6.

المعهد الألماني للأبحاث الشرقية

الطبعة الأولى

٢٠١٢

طُبع على نفقة وزارة الثقافة والأبحاث العلميّة
التابعة لجمهوريّة ألمانيا الاتّحاديّة
بإشراف المعهد الألماني للأبحاث الشرقيّة في بيروت
في مطبعة إرغون، ڤورتسبورغ – ألمانيا

المحتويات

ترجمة الكتاب المقدّس إلى العربية والمؤثرات

غسان خلف

إن العام ٢٠٠٨ تاريخ موعد هذه الندوة حول ترجمة الكتاب المقدّس في الشرق العربي يصادف مرور خمسين ومائة سنة على بدء «المرحلة الحديثة» لترجمة الكتاب المقدّس إلى العربية التي ابتدأت عام ١٨٥٧ بصدور ترجمة الشدياق- واطس، وكان آخر ما صدر من ترجمات، هو «العهد القديم العبري: ترجمة بين السطور»، عام ٢٠٠٧.

يمكن تسمية هذه المرحلة «المرحلة الحديثة» بحق للأسباب التالية:

أولاً: الإنطلاقة المميّزة لترجمات هذه المرحلة علميًا ولغويًا، وكذلك من جهة نوعية الطباعة.

ثانيًا: تعدد الترجمات وتكاثرها، حيث بلغت ترجمات الكتاب المقدّس بعهديه القديم والجديد كاملاً تسع ترجمات، أَضف إليها عشر ترجمات للعهد الجديد مستقلّة، يُضاف إليها تلك الصادرة مع العهد القديم، وست ترجمات للأناجيل الأَربعة، وثلاث ترجمات لكتاب المزامير. وترجمة العهد القديم بين السطور. وبين هذه الترجمات التي ذُكرت ما صدر بالعامّية تتراوح بين الكتاب المقدّس بكامله، أَو العهد الجديد، أَو الأَناجيل الأَربعة، أَو كتاب واحد كإنجيل يوحنا، قام بترجمته كمال الشرابي بالحرف اللاتيني وباللهجة اللبنانية وقدّم له وأَصدره الشاعر سعيد عقل.

وثالث هذه الأَسباب تعدّدُ الكنائس والإرساليات والمؤسسات المشتركة في إقرار هذه الترجمات وإنجازها خلال هذه المرحلة، وهي على التوالي: الأَنكليكانية، الإنجيلية المشيخية، الكاثوليكية الكلدانية (الدومنيكان)، الكاثوليكية (اليسوعيون)، الأرثوذكسية الأَنطاكية، الروم الكاثوليك الملكية، الأرثوذكسية القبطية، الإنجيلية الحرّة، المارونية، وجمعية الكتاب المقدّس.

ورابع الأَسباب المكوِّنة لهذه «المرحلة الحديثة» هو العمق الزمني الحديث الذي امتد «مسافة قرن ونصف» المنصرمة، ونحن بالفعل امتداد لها. وبالتالي فإن جميع الترجمات العربية للكتاب المقدّس الصادرة في هذه المرحلة لا تزال قيد التداول، يتم تنقيحها أَو إعادة طبعها، وهي في متناول الأَيدي، في حين نجد أن ما سبق هذه المرحلة من ترجمات قد استقرّ في المتاحف.

وخامس هذه الأَسباب التوافق الزمني بين هذه «المرحلة الحديثة» و«عصر النهضة الأَدبية والعلمية الحديثة»، وقد بدأَ مع مطلع القرن التاسع عشر، بل كان العاملون في ترجمات الكتاب المقدّس إلى العربية هم أَنفسهم روّاد عصر النهضة الأَدبية (فارس الشدياق، بطرس البستاني، ناصيف وإبراهيم اليازجيان).

وحيث إن هذه «المرحلة الحديثة» للكتاب المقدّس في العربية صار لها مدىً تاريخيٌّ يبلغ القرنَ والنصف، وميدان من التنوّع والتعدّد في إصداراتها، فقد غدا بالإمكان القيام بسبر المؤثرات التي طبعت هذه الترجمات المتعدّدة بطابعها، سواء كانت هذه المؤثرات دينية أَم طائفية أَم لغوية أَم سياسية، والتوصّل إلى استنتاجات بشأنها عن طريق العمل النقدي التقويمي والمقارنة.

المؤثرات الفاعلة في عملية الترجمة

تأثر نقل الكتاب المقدّس بالنصوص العبرية واليونانية التي يُنقل عنها

يُنقل الكتاب المقدّس إلى العربية عن لغتين أساسيتين هما: العبرية لغة العهد القديم، واليونانية لغة العهد الجديد. وتوجد لكل من العهدين مخطوطاتُه القديمة، وقام علماء تحقيق النصوص بإصدار طبعات علمية تحمل حصيلة عملهم النقدي في تحقيق أسلم القراءات لكل من العهدين.

وقد صدرت للعهد القديم طبعة كاملة نقدية محقّقة عام ١٩٧٧ دُعيت بـ (Biblia Hebraica Stuttgartensia)، كما صدرت للعهد الجديد طبعتان تحملان النص ذاته هما: العهد الجديد اليوناني (The Greek New Testament) إصدار جمعيات

الكتاب المقدّس عام ١٩٧٥، و(Novum Testamentum Graece) إصدار نستله-ألاند عام ١٩٧٩.

وحيث أن إشكاليات تعدّد القراءات بين مخطوطات العهد القديم هي قليلة بالمقارنة مع العهد الجديد، فقد تركز الخلاف حول أية أُسرة من أُسر المخطوطات اليونانية يعتمد المترجمون في نقلهم العهد الجديد إلى العربية. فهناك الأسرة الإسكندرية والأسرة الغربية، ويفضّلها الكاثوليك بسبب النسخة الفاتيكانية ورمزها B، وهناك النسخة الغربية ورمزها D، عدا الترجمات اللاتينية القديمة، فظهر ذلك في ترجماتهم إلى العربية. وهناك أسرة المخطوطات البيزنطية الممثلة في العهد الجديد اليوناني المُسمَّى «النص المقبول» (Textus Receptus) الذي نشره إيراسمُس عام ١٥١٦.

إن نص إيراسمس هو أساس ترجمة الملك جايمس الإنكليزية الشهيرة، وعن «النص المقبول» نقل فاندايك العهد الجديد إلى العربية. فأضحت ترجمة فاندايك البروتستانتية، حاملةُ النص البيزنطي، هي المفضّلة عند أقباط مصر الأرثوذكس وعند معظم أرثوذكس بلاد الشام.

من الضروري في عصرنا الحاضر أن لا تشدّنا تقاليدنا المتنوّعة نحو تفضيل أية أسرة من المخطوطات اليونانية لذاتها، بل يجدر بنا أن نتّبع حصيلة علم تحقيق النصوص الحديث الممثل في الطبعتين النقديتين السالفتي الذكر، وقد اشترك في تحقيق نصهما الموحد علماء إنجيليون وأرثوذكس وكاثوليك، كما يظهر في مطلع الطبعة الرابعة المنقّحة الصادرة عام ١٩٩٣.

ويجدر بنا هنا، تأييدًا لدعوتنا لتبنّي «النص المحقّق» في ترجماتنا، أن نلقي نظرة على الفرق بين «النص المقبول» البيزنطي المنقول عن مخطوطات متأخرة، و«النص المحقّق» المعتمد بالإجمال على الأسرة الغربية، وهي أقدم تاريخًا وأنقى نصًا. حيث يبلغ حجم هذا الفرق بينهما نحو ثلاثة آلاف اختلاف تجدر ملاحظتها. وهذا الإحصاء مبنيٌّ على مسح قمت به شخصيًا مقارِنًا بين النصين.

وواقع الحال من جهة استعمال أسر المخطوطات اليونانية في الترجمة هي أن جميع الترجمات العربية للعهد الجديد في القرن العشرين هجرت استعمال المخطوطات

البيزنطية، واتجهت نحو «النصوص المحقّقة» التي تستند إلى الأصول الإسكندرية كالمخطوطة الفاتيكانية والسينائية والبرديات القديمة.

ومن جهة العهد القديم، فقد أصدر الأبوان بولس الفغالي وأنطوان عوكر ترجمة «بين السطور» للنص العبري، وقد استخدما فيها طبعة شتوتغارت النقدية كمادة أساسية، وكذلك فعلت ترجمات العهد القديم الحديثة مثل اليسوعية والمشتركة.

تأثر نقل الكتاب المقدّس بالترجمات الشهيرة قديمها وحديثها، وقد صارت جزءًا من التراث الكنسي

تُقسَم ترجمات الكتاب المقدّس عادة إلى قسمين: الترجمات القديمة، والترجمات الحديثة. أما الترجمات القديمة فعديدة نذكر منها: الترجمة السبعينية اليونانية، والترجمات اللاتينية والقبطية والسُريانية.

التأثر بالترجمات القديمة

تتأثر الترجمات العربية بالسبعينية عند تفضيل قراءاتها على نص عبراني مضطرب وغير واضح، وهذا النهج تعتمده معظم الترجمات في جميع أنحاء العالم وليس حصرًا في الترجمات العربية. وأكثر ما يكون التأثر عندما يتم النقل إلى العربية مباشرة من السبعينية اليونانية، كما فعل رزق الله عرمان في ترجمته «كتاب المزامير الشريف».

كذلك فعل الأقباط في مصر في ترجمتهم للأناجيل الأربعة، من إصدار دار المعارف. فقد عبّروا عن توجّههم للإفادة من مخطوطات الترجمات القبطية القديمة، وليس الإقتصار على المخطوطات اليونانية. وكان الأقباط قد نشروا في عام ١٩٣٥ ترجمةً للأناجيل الأربعة مباشرة عن المخطوطات القبطية في نص متقابل بين اللغتين.

ومثل الأقباط، فعل الأب يوسف عون، الماروني، عندما ترجم العهد الجديد إلى العربية عن النص السرياني المعروف بـ«الفشيطتو».

هذا من جهة الترجمة من أصول كاملة، وقد رأينا أمثلة عن النقل المباشر من السبعينية اليونانية ومن المخطوطات القبطية والسريانية.

أما من جهة التأثر بالترجمات القديمة وتبنّي بعض قراءاتها لأسباب عقيدية وليتورجية، فإن أوضح مثلٍ هو ما قامت به الترجمات العربية التي أصدرها الكاثوليك متأثّرين بالترجمات اللاتينية القديمة وعلى رأسها الفولغاتا، ابتداءً من الترجمة المعروفة بالبروباغاندا، ومروراً بالدومنيكانية عام ١٨٧٦، وباليسوعية القديمة عام ١٨٨١، وصولاً إلى اليسوعية الجديدة عام ١٩٦٩، والليتورجية عام ٢٠٠٣.

يمكن الإشارة في هذا المجال إلى «شاهد الثالوث» الوارد في (١يو ٥: ٧-٨)، وهو يقول: «الذين يشهدون في السماء هم ثلاثة: الآب، والكلمة، والروح القدس». فلقد تأثرت اليسوعية القديمة عام ١٨٨١ ببعض المخطوطات اللاتينية القديمة فتبنّتها، وكذلك فعلت الدومنيكانية عام ١٨٧٦، لكنها أدرجت «شاهد الثالوث» بين مزدوجين معقوفين، مع ملاحظة في الحاشية تنكر وجوده في المخطوطات اليونانية. وأحلّت الليتورجية عام ٢٠٠٣ «شاهد الثالوث» محلّه في نصها.

أما ما سواها من الترجمات الكاثوليكية، فقد أغفلت «شاهد الثالوث» ولم تذكره، وهي: الترجمة اليسوعية الجديدة عام ١٩٦٩ وما لحقها من طبعات منقّحة، والبولسية عام ١٩٥٣، والبولسية المجدّدة عام ٢٠٠٠، وترجمة الكسليك عام ١٩٩٢. ولا يرد «شاهد الثالوث» في نص الفشيطتو السرياني حسب ترجمة الأَب يوسف عون.

إن «شاهد الثالوث» هو إضافة مُقحمة لغرض عقيدي نشأ في الكنيسة الغربية في القرن الخامس، ثم وجد طريقه إلى «النص المقبول» الذي نشره إراسموس عام ١٥١٦، فذاع صيته. وهذا الشاهد لا يوجد إلا في ثلاث أو أربع مخطوطات يونانية نُسخت بعد القرن الحادي عشر المسيحي، وقد نُقل إليها مترجمًا عن اللاتينية.

التأثر بالترجمات الحديثة

وتتأثر الترجمات العربية بالترجمات الأجنبية الحديثة، وذلك طبيعي، بسبب رغبة المترجمين في الإطلاع على ما قام به غيرهم أو من سبقهم في هذا المجال، وبخاصة من اللغات العالمية التي يتقنونها، مثل الفرنسية والإنكليزية والألمانية.

ونذكر في هذا الإطار مثلاً لتأثر بعض الترجمات الكاثوليكية العربية بالترجمات الفرنسية الشهيرة.

فقد صدرت الترجمة الفرنسية الشهيرة (La Bible de Jerusalem) عام ١٩٥٣، وشكّلت نهجًا جديدًا لعلم ترجمة الكتاب المقدّس لدقّتها العلمية، وقد قام بوضعها علماء كاثوليك كبار. لكن هذه الترجمة خرجت عن النص اليوناني الذي يقول: «الذين وُلدوا من الله» في إشارة إلى المؤمنين في يوحنا (١: ١٣)، وفضّلت إدراج القراءة التي تقول: «الذي وُلد من الله» في إشارة إلى يسوع المسيح. وهذه القراءة الأخيرة مدعومة من آباء الكنيسة، مثل ترتليانس، وإيريناوس، وبعض المخطوطات اللاتينية.

بعد ذلك وفي العام ١٩٧٥ صدرت ترجمة الطبعة المسكونية للكتاب المقدّس باللغة الفرنسية (Traduction Oecuménique de la Bible)، واشترك في وضعها علماء ينتمون إلى الكنائس الكاثوليكية والبروتستانتية والأرثوذكسية. في هذه الترجمة وردت عبارة (يو ١: ١٣) بصيغة الجمع في إشارة إلى المؤمنين، لا بالمفرد إشارة إلى المسيح.

وقد تأثرت الترجمة اليسوعية الجديدة عندنا في الشرق بهذا التحوّل. فبعد أن كانت سابقتها اليسوعية القديمة الصادرة عام ١٨٨١، تقرأ (يو ١: ١٣) بصيغة الجمع، تبنّت اليسوعية الجديدة الصادرة عام ١٩٦٩ قراءة الترجمة الأورشليمية بصيغة المفرد، لتعود فتتبنّى في الطبعة الثامنة الصادرة عام ١٩٨٢ صيغة الجمع الواردة في الترجمة الفرنسية المسكونية الصادرة عام ١٩٧٥. وقد أشار إلى هذا التوجّه المسكوني الأبوان صبحي حموي ويوسف قوشاقجي في مقدمة الطبعة الثامنة، حيث اعتمدا الترجمة والتفسير المتوافق عليها بين جميع الكنائس المسيحية.

ورغم إجماع المخطوطات اليونانية القديمة بأسرها على قراءة (يو ١: ١٣) بصيغة الجمع، وتراجع اليسوعية الجديدة عن موقفها السابق بقراءتها (يو ١: ١٣) بالمفرد، فإننا نرى أن ترجمة الكسليك المارونية الصادرة عام ١٩٩٢ التي تتبنّى صيغة المفرد في (يو ١: ١٣) معتبرةً الدليل الداخلي أقوى.

وكما يتأثر الكاثوليك بترجمات لهم فرنسية، يتأثر البروتستانت بترجمتهم الشهيرة، ترجمة الملك جايمس (The King James Bible, or The Authorized Version). فعندما قام عالي سميث وبعده كورنيليوس فانديك بالعمل على نقل الكتاب المقدّس إلى العربية، اعتمدا النص اليوناني ذاته، أي: Textus Receptus، المعتمد في طبعة الملك جايمس، وليس ذلك فحسب، بل يُلاحظ تأثير أسلوب النقل الحرفي، كما في العبارة: «حَاسِبِينَ بَعْضُكُمُ الْبَعْضَ أَفْضَلَ مِنْ أَنْفُسِهِمْ» (let each esteem other better than themselves) (في ٢: ٣). وصحيحها ينبغي أن يكون: «ليحسب الواحد منكم غيرَه أفضل منه» (let each esteem others better than himself) ، ومثل هذا كثير. وبعض التعابير اللاهوتية، مثل: «أبواب الجحيم» (The gates of hell) (مت ١٦: ١٨)، وفي العادة «أبواب الهاوية» عند فانديك، وعبارة «أيام تطهيرها (مريم) » (The days of her purification)، وفي «النص المقبول» اليوناني كما في «النص المحقّق»: «أيام طهورهما (مريم ويسوع) ».

تأثر نقل الكتاب المقدّس في شرقنا بالتقاليد الكنسية والمصطلحات الليتورجية

يتطلّب نقل الكتاب المقدّس إلى العربية استعمال ألفاظ وكلمات وعبارات لاهوتية وعلمية، تاريخية وتقنية، تتعلّق بمكان وزمان استعمالها في سياقها الأساسي. ويحدث من الناحية الأخرى على الصعيد الكنسي أن يحدث تطوّر في استعمال هذه الألفاظ والعبارات على مدى مئات السنين، تحت تأثير الأدب الشعبي والغلو الديني، اللذين يحرفانها عن معناها الأصلي ويباعدان بينها وبين مدلولاتها الحقيقية. يظهر هذا بكل وضوح عندما يجلس علماء الكنائس في هذا الشرق ليترجموا الكتاب المقدّس،

فيصدمهم هذا الواقع، ويعانون من حالة تمزّق بين ما يجب أن يقرّوه من ترجمة وبين التمسّك بالتقليد الكنسي والشعبي.

هذا الواقع يمكن أن نطلق عليه عبارة: «المعاناة من ثقل التاريخ»، فليس من السهل على الكنائس، من مختلف الطوائف، القيام بتغيير العبارات والمصطلحات العقيدية والليتورجية في نص الترجمات التي تقوم بها لتوافق نص العهد الجديد اليوناني، وقد اعتادت على ذلك بسبب ممارستها على امتداد المئات من السنين.

الترجمة الليتورجية في مقابل ترجمة الكسليك

لنأخذ مثلاً عما يجري تداوله من أحاديث حول واقعة القيام بوضع ترجمة «الكسليك» الشهيرة بواقعيتها العلمية. لقد رغب واضعوها في أن يكون لطلاب اللاهوت، في كلية اللاهوت بجامعة الكسليك، للعهد الجديد نصًا علميًا يوازي ما يوجد في الغرب من ترجمات علمية، ليتمكنوا من القيام بأبحاثهم اللاهوتية باللغة العربية معتمدين على أدقّ المراجع[١].

إن المنهجية التي اعتمدها المترجمون في وضع ترجمة علمية خاصة لطلاب كلية اللاهوت، تمسك بالمعاني الأساسية لنص الإنجيل ولا تراعي المصطلحات الدينية التاريخية لتقاليد الكنيسة، في حين توضع ترجمة أخرى لبقية الرعايا خارج الجامعة تراعي ما اعتاد عليه الناس من تعابير ليتورجية، يترتب على هذه المنهجية أضرار كبيرة تلحق بالرعيّة التي تتبع الكنيسة، حيث يضطرب الناس في ما يعتقدون. كما ترسل إشارات تثير الشك في عقول ونفوس من هم خارج الكنيسة.

---

(١) *ترجمات الكتاب المقدّس*، الناشر: أيوب شهوان، دراسات بيبلية رقم ٣٠، بيروت، الرابطة الكتابية ٢٠٠٦، ١٧٤.

فليس للكتاب المقدّس لغتان واحدة للخاصة وواحدة للعامة، بل لغة واحدة. هذه اللغة الواحدة يجب أن توضع في النص، وليكن للحاشية دورها في شرح ما يجب شرحه في ضوء تعاليم الكنائس.

ويبدو أن هذا الصراع غير الصحّي تمثّل أخيرًا بظهور «الترجمة الليتورجية» عام ٢٠٠٣. يمكن لعين المراقب أن تلاحظ أن صدورها كان ردة فعل إعتراضية واضحة على الترجمتين اليسوعية الجديدة (١٩٨٨)، والكسليك (١٩٩٢)، اللتين سبقتاها لخلوّهما من لفظة «كاهن»، ولاستعمالهما لفظة «شيخ» في كل المواضع التي ترد فيها اللفظة اليونانية (presbuteros) بمعنى رعاة الكنيسة. فأعادت «الترجمة الليتورجية» لفظة «الكاهن» و«الكهنة» إلى جميع المواضع التي ترد فيها كلمة «شيخ» و«شيوخ» لرعاة الكنيسة.

شيخ أم كاهن

ترد كلمة (presbuteros) تسع عشرة مرة في العهد الجديد بمعنى يدل على الرعاة والمتقدّمين في الكنيسة، عشر مرات في أعمال الرسل، وتسع مرات في الرسائل. وتعني كلمة (presbuteros) «الشيخ» ومدلولها «الراعي»، ولكنها لا تعني «الكاهن» في استخدامها الكنسي في العهد الجديد. وتوجد كلمة يونانية خاصة تعني «الكاهن» هي (hiereus)، وقد وردت ٣١ مرة في العهد الجديد، ولم تطلق مرةً على أحد بمعنى الراعي المسيحي، عدا يسوع المسيح، وذلك في الرسالة إلى العبرانيين.

أقباط مصر وشيوخ الرؤيا

ويلاحظ المراقب أن نهج إرجاع كلمة «كاهن» إلى نص العهد الجديد المترجم الذي تستعمله بعض الكنائس، لم يقتصر على الموارنة والروم الكاثوليك في لبنان، فلقد قامت المطرانية القبطية الأرثوذكسية في بور سعيد في مصر بإصدار طبعة خاصة

للعهد الجديد عام ٢٠٠٥، لنص ترجمة البستاني- فانديك، حيث غيّرت فيه كلمة «شيخ» أو «قسّ» في كل المواضع التي ترد فيها إلى كلمة «كاهن»، وذلك في سبعة عشر موضعًا ما عدا رسالتي يوحنا الثانية والثالثة. وقد ظهر في هذا النص تغيير إضافي غير مسبوق، لم يلاحَظ في أية ترجمة أخرى في «المرحلة الحديثة» إلى العربية، هو استعمال لفظة «قسيس» و«قسوس» في سفر الرؤيا، بدلاً من «شيخ» و«شيوخ»، وصفًا للشيوخ الأَربعة والعشرين.

مُنعَم عليها أم ممتلئة نعمة

وهناك تعبير ليتورجي يظهر من خلاله الصراع بين ترجمة النص اليوناني بكامل مضامينه، وبين الإبقاء على الصيغة التقليدية التي أَلِفها العامة من الشعب. وهذا التعبير هو تحيّة الملاك لمريم العذراء مبشّرًا إياها بولادة المخلِّص منها، وصياغته في الترجمة اليسوعية القديمة: السلام عليك يا ممتلئةً نعمة (لو ١: ٢٨). إن معنى العبارة في النص اليوناني هو «أيتها المُنعَم عليها» (ترجمة البستاني-فانديك، والبولسية المُجَدّدة)، تمامًا كما وردت في ترجمة الكسليك المارونية: «يا مُنعَمًا عليكِ». غير أن اليسوعية الجديدة أبقت الصياغة القديمة: «أَيتها الممتلئةُ نعمة»، وكذلك الترجمة القبطية (١٩٧٨). وأعتقد أن الترجمة الليتورجية (٢٠٠٣) أنصفت المعنى دون أن تجافي التقليد بترجمة العبارة على النحو التالي: «يا مملوءةً نعمةً».

تقاليد أم تعاليم

وكما هي الحال عند الكاثوليك والأرثوذكس كذلك عند البروتستانت. إذ ترد الكلمة اليونانية (paradosis)، وهي تعني «التقليد»، ثلاث عشرة مرة في العهد الجديد، مثل: «تقليد الشيوخ» (مر ٧: ٣)، و«تقليد الناس» (كو ٢: ٨)، و«تقليدات آبائي» (غل ١: ١٤). واستعملت ترجمة «البستاني- فانديك» كلمة «التقليد» في

كل مرة ترد فيها الكلمة اليونانية (paradosis)، ما عدا ثلاثة أَماكن في رسائل بولس: (١ كو ١١: ٢) «وتحفظون التعاليم (التقاليد) كما سلّمتها إليكم»؛ و(٢ تس ٢: ١٥) «وتمسّكوا بالتعاليم (التقاليد) التي تعلّمتموها سواء كان بالكلام أَم برسالتنا»؛ و(٢ تس ٣: ٦) «وليس حسب التعليم (التقليد) الذي أَخذه منا».

والسؤال: لماذا غيّر واضعو ترجمة «البستاني- فانדايك» كلمة «التقليد» إلى كلمة «التعليم» في هذه الأماكن الثلاثة التي أشرنا إليها؟

يبدو أن واضعي ترجمة «البستاني – فانديك»، وهم إنجيليون، وذلك قبل ١٤٠ سنة، قد رغبوا في تجنّب الإحراج، في وقت كانوا هم يعترضون على تقاليد الكنائس الشرقية، فغيّروا كلمة «تقليد» إلى «تعليم» في نص رسائل بولس لئلا تكون حجةً عليهم.

تأثر نقل الكتاب المقدّس إلى العربية بالمستوى اللغوي وتنوّع اللهجات الإقليمية

حضر الأديب المصري طه حسين في أواسط القرن العشرين مناسبة دينية في كنيسة للأقباط الأرثوذكس، فهاله المستوى المتدنّي لنصوص اللغة العربية التي تُتلى خلال العبادة سواء من الإنجيل أو من الصلوات، وعبّر للصحف عن ذلك. وجدت كلمات طه حسين صدى لها في بيروت، فصدرت ترجمة للعهد الجديد عام ١٩٦٩ عمل عليها الأبوان اليسوعيان صبحي حموي ويوسف قوشاقجي، وهذّب عبارتها الأستاذ بطرس البستاني. وعلى أثر صدور هذه الترجمة، أدلى الأستاذ فؤاد أفرام البستاني بتعليق جاء فيه: لأول مرة في التاريخ يتكلم الرسول بولس اللغة العربية بفصاحة.

وفيما يلي نص لبولس الرسول مقتبَس من هذه الترجمة يعبّر عن بلاغتها:

«قد سمعتم بسيرتي الماضية في ملة اليهود وكيف كنت أَضطهد كنيسة الله غاية الإضطهاد، وأحاول تدميرها وأَتقدّم أَكثر أَترابي من بني قومي في ملة اليهود وأَفوقهم حميَّة على سُنَن آبائي.

ولكن لمَّا شاء ذاك الذي اصطفاني مذ كنت في بطن أمي، فدعاني بنعمته وكشف ابنه فيَّ لأبشّر به بين الوثنيين، لم أَستشر اللحم والدم، ولا صعدت إلى أورشليم لألقى من تقدّمني من الرسل، بل ذهبت من ساعتي إلى ديار العرب، ثم عدت إلى دمشق» (غل ١: ١٣-١٧).

ثم عاد الإنجيل ينطق بلغة على مستوى رفيع من الفصاحة مع الأب يوحنا قمير في ترجمة الكسليك، وفي ما يلي أُنموذج منها منغَّم:

«يسِّر لنا خبز يومنا
واعفُ عنَّا ذنوبَنا عفوَنا عمن أذنب إلينا،
وفي محنة لا تُدخلنا
بل من الشرير نجّنا» (مت ٦: ١١-١٣).

وأَيضًا:

«فأَتوا إلى يوحنا وقالوا له: أَيها المعلّم، إن من كان معك في عبر الأُردن،
وله شهدتَ، شرع يعمد، وكل الناس يأْتون إليه.
قال يوحنا: لا يسعُ إنسانًا نيلُ أَيّ شيء ما لم تَجُد به عليه السماء.
قلتُ: أَنا لست المسيح، بل أَنا مرسل قدامه، وأَنتم على ما قلتُ شهود.
ذو العروسِ عروس. أَما صديقُه، الواقفُ يُصغي إليه، فيطرَب فرَحًا لصوته.
هذا الفرحُ فرحي قد اكتمل.
عليه هو أَن يعظُم، وعليَّ أَنا أَن أَصغُر» (يو ٣: ٢٦-٣٠).

وتراجعت الترجمة اليسوعية الجديدة عن موقفها من إصدار الإنجيل بلغة عالية الفصاحة، إذ وجد واضعوها أنها نأت عن عامة الناس بسموّ عبارتها، فبسّطوا عبارة الترجمة في طبعاتها اللاحقة. وكذلك فعل الذين أعدّوا الترجمة الليتورجية، في مقابل لغة يوحنا قمير في ترجمة الكسليك في البشائر والأعمال.

أما الترجمة القدسيّة للبشائر الأربع الصادرة عام ١٩٩١، فرغبت أن تقلّد لغة القرآن وأسلوبه المسجَّع، وهنا أُنموذج عنها:

« يا أَبانا في السماء،
ليُوقِّر اسمَكَ القدوسَ خالقُك
ومن الآنَ ليَحكُم ملكوتُك،
وعلى الأَرض ليُعمل ما تشاء
مثلما في السماء» (الترجمة القدسية ١٩٩١).

السهل الممتنع

في مقابل هذه المحاولات لوضع الإنجيل في ترجمات ترنو إلى لغة عربية عالية الفصاحة، كان همّ جمعية الكتاب المقدّس إصدار ترجمة للعهدين بلغة عامة الناس بأسلوب «السهل الممتنِع». وقع الإختيار على الشاعر يوسف الخال، فهو أفضل من يقوم بهذا المشروع. قام الشاعر يوسف الخال بتهذيب عبارة الترجمة، وكان مثاله في أسلوب الكتابة العربية ابن المُقفَّع في كتاب كليلة ودمنة. وطبّق يوسف الخال كذلك على لغة «الترجمة المشتركة» مبادئ دعوته إلى جعل اللغة العربية المكتوبة قريبة إلى المحكية، التي سمّاها «الولادة الجديدة». وفي مقدمة هذه المبادئ إسقاط كل لفظة من لغة الكتابة ما عادت تنطقها العامة، وهكذا سقطت من «الترجمة المشتركة» التي عمل عليها يوسف الخال الأَدوات التالية: ليس، ولم، وقد، وكل الألفاظ الجافّة والمقعَّرة، وما تجاورت حروفه وعَسُرَ لفظه، مثل: جَثْسَيْماني – جَتْسيماني. فجاءت ترجمته آية في السلاسة والجذالة، يستطيبها المتضلّع والعامي.

لغة كنسية أم لغة عربية عامة يفهمها الجميع

ومن الأمور التي يواجهها واضعو ترجمات الكتاب المقدّس إلى العربية مسألة: أية تعابير يتم اختيارها للتحدث عن قضايا الإنجيل، أيختارون تعابير متداولة بين شعب الكنائس أم يستعملون التعابير العامة التي يفهمها كل العرب؟

لنأخذ مثلاً كلمة: يكرز، وكرازة، وكارز، المشتقّة من اليونانية «كِريسو» ومعناها «ينادي بـ». هذه الكلمة لا نجد معناها المسيحي، أي: «ينادى بالتوبة» أو «ينادى برسالة الإنجيل» في القواميس التي يصدرها علماء مسلمون، مثل: «المعجم العربي الأساسي»، إصدار لاروس، أو «المعجم الوسيط»، إصدار مجمع اللغة العربية في مصر، رغم ارتباط لفظة «الكرازة» باسم الكنيسة القبطية الأرثوذكسية، إذ تسمّي نفسها «كنيسة الكرازة المرقسية»، وهي من أكبر الكنائس المسيحية في مصر والعالم العربي. بينما نجد المعنى المسيحي لكلمة «يكرز» يرد في قاموس «محيط المحيط» لبطرس البستاني، وفي «البستان» لعبد الله البستاني، و«المنجد» لدار المشرق، و«الرائد» لجبران مسعود. وكذلك يرد الجذر «كرز» بمعناه المسيحي في القواميس العربية-الإنكليزية، مثل قاموس «هانز فير»، وقاموس «المورد» لروحي البعلبكي.

استعملت لفظة «يكرز» ترجماتُ القرن التاسع عشر: الإنجيلية، والدومنيكانية، واليسوعية، ولم يستعملها فارس الشدياق. ولا ترد لفظة «يكرز» في اليسوعية الجديدة، والمشتركة، والكسليك، وكتاب الحياة، واستُعمل بدلاً منها إما «ينادي» أو «يبشّر».

لغة وادي النيل أم لغة بلاد الشام

مسألة أخرى تواجه نقل الكتاب المقدّس إلى العربية هي التغيير الطفيف الذي يسبّبه التباعد الإقليمي في العالم الناطق باللغة العربية. وهذا الشأن يثيره عادة أهل مصر، لأنهم يستعملون ترجمات للكتاب المقدّس وُضعت في لبنان. ومن الفوارق ما يخص المعنى، كاستعمال الجزّار واللحّام، وما يخص أسلوب الكتابة، مثل مسئولية ومسؤولية.

هذا، ولقد نشأ شأن جديد في هذا العصر، عصر الكومبيوتر، هو استعمال الأرقام العربية بدل الهندية، وهذه المسألة آخذة في الإنتشار. كان استعمال الأَرقام

العربية محدودًا بمنطقة المغرب العربي، غير أنه امتدّ هذه الأيام ليشمل منطقة الخليج والجزيرة العربية وكثيرًا من مجالات النشر في مصر وبلاد الشام.

تأثر نقل الكتاب المقدّس إلى العربية بالصراع على المصطلحات الدينية بين المسيحية والإسلام

إن اللغة العربية التي يستعملها المسلمون والمسيحيون هي لغة واحدة. ومن جهة ثانية، ثمة تشابه كبير في المصطلحات الدينية بين اللغة العربية واللغة العبرانية في العهد القديم لأن اللغتين ساميتان وشقيقتان، الأمر الذي يجعل المسلمين العرب والمسيحيين العرب يستعملون مفردات مشتركة في الكثير من التعابير الدينية.

رغم ذلك، تبقى هناك مفاهيم غير متطابقة وحساسيات دينية، ترافق بعض المصطلحات بحيث تجعل من الصعب، بل أحيانًا من المستحيل، استعمال المرادفات ذاتها في الحقل الديني بين المسيحية والإسلام، وبخاصة في الكتاب المقدّس.

من هذه العبارات والمصطلحات أورد النماذج التالية:

يسوع أم عيسى

لا يرد اسم «عيسى» المستعمل في القرآن ليسوع المسيح في ترجمات الكتاب المقدّس إلى العربية إلا في بضع مخطوطات قديمة لم تنتشر. فيما عدا ذلك، لا توجد ترجمة تحوي الإسم «عيسى»، حتى تلك التي صدرت في المغرب العربي، في الجزائر والمغرب، في أواسط القرن العشرين، حيث لا تأثير مسيحي يُذكر. هناك ترجمة واحدة فقط استعملت الأسماء القرآنية هي «الكتاب الشريف» التي صدر منها «الإنجيل الشريف» عام ١٩٩٠، والكتاب الكامل بعهديه عام ٢٠٠٠. هذه الترجمة استعملت اسم «عيسى» ليسوع، و«يحيى» ليوحنا المعمدان، و«إلياس» لإيليا، و«يونس» ليونان، الخ. وهذه الترجمة ترغب في تقريب لغة الكتاب المقدّس إلى المسلمين، وخاصة في شمال أفريقيا الغربي.

الزواج أم النكاح

يروي الأديب الشعبي سلام الراسي نقلاً عن الشيخ إبراهيم الحوراني الذي عاصر فانديك كيف عارض ناصيف اليازجي اقتراح الشيخ يوسف الأسير استعمال لفظة «نكاح» بدلاً من «زواج»، بسبب طابعها الديني وتجنّب المسيحيين استعمالها في أحوالهم الشخصية.

تأثر نقل الكتاب المقدّس إلى العربية بالأوضاع السياسية وتقلّباتها في الوطن العربي

ولا يكتمل عرض الأساسي من المؤثرات على نقل الكتاب المقدّس إلى اللغة العربية إن أغفلنا ذكر المؤثر السياسي. إن هذا المؤثر لا يظهر بشكل واضح لأن المسيحيين لا يلعبون دورًا سياسيًا بارزًا في دنيا العرب، ولأن الكتاب المقدّس هو كتاب ديني لا علاقة له بالسياسة، وخاصة في العهد الجديد. لكن الإهتمام بالعهد القديم ازداد، وبالتالي العهد الجديد، بسبب مشكلة الشرق الأوسط وظهور دولة إسرائيل. لقد سبّب قيام دولة إسرائيل الكثير من سوء الفهم لمضامين الكتاب المقدّس، بسبب الخلفية الدينية والجغرافية الواحدة قديمًا للشعب الفلسطيني وللشعب اليهودي، والتالي بسبب تسييس معاني نبوءات العهد القديم في خدمة غايات عنصرية.

ملكوت روحي أم مملكة سياسية

لهذا السبب وغيره من الأسباب، يتمسّك المسيحيون، ومنهم مترجمو الكتاب المقدّس، باستعمال المصطلح «ملكوت الله» ولا يترجمونه عن الأصل كما هو «مملكة الله». هذه الكلمة السُريانية «ملكوت» صارت عربية وتبنّى القرآن استعمالها، لكن هذا ليس السبب الأساسي لاستعمال المسيحيين لها في كتبهم المقدّسة، إنما خوفهم من أن تُسيَّس كلمة «المملكة» وتُتَّهم كتبهم بما لا تعنيه. فالمسيح لم يأتِ ليؤسس مملكة سياسية في هذا العالم.

القدس لمن؟

ومن الأمور التي تسبّب سوء الفهم ويكون لها تداعيات سياسية تشابهُ الألفاظ، وبخاصة عندما يكون المعني بذلك عاصمة تاريخية ودينية شهيرة كمدينة القدس. فقد أوردت ترجمات القرن التاسع عشر: «لا تُعطوا القُدس للكلاب، ولا تطرحوا درركم قدام الخنازير» (مت ٧: ٦). هكذا جاءت العبارة في ترجمة «البستاني- فانديك» وفي الترجمة «الدومنيكانية» وفي الترجمة «اليسوعية القديمة».

وذكر أمامي الأستاذ فؤاد عقاد، المدير الأسبق لجمعية الكتاب المقدّس في لبنان، أنه كان يتلقى بشكل متواصل رسائل من قرّاء الكتاب المقدّس في العالم العربي يسألون فيها: لماذا قال يسوع: لا تعطوا مدينة القدس للكلاب، ومن المقصود بالكلاب؟

وبدأ التغيير في هذه العبارة يظهر في ترجمات القرن العشرين مع الأب جورج فاخوري «البولسية» عام ١٩٥٣ بعد النكبة عام ١٩٤٨، فقال: «لا تعطوا الأقداس للكلاب». وقالت الترجمة «اليسوعية الجديدة» عام ١٩٦٩: «لا تعطوا الكلاب ما هو مقدّس»، و«كتاب الحياة» عام ١٩٨٨، وكذلك الترجمة «المشتركة» عام ١٩٩٣. وقالت ترجمة «الكسليك» عام ١٩٩٢: «لا تعطوا الكلاب المقدّسات»، وكذلك قالت الترجمة «الليتورجية» عام ٢٠٠٣.

لا يريد أَحد من واضعي الترجمات العربية، بعد قيام دولة إسرائيل واستيلاء اليهود على مدينة القدس والصراع القائم حاليًا حولها، أن يبقي النص غامضًا في هذا الموقع في (مت ٧: ٦). وللأمانة العلمية ينبغي ذكر فارس الشدياق الذي سبق كل هذه الترجمات بترجمته النص: «لا تعطوا ما هو قُدس للكلاب»، وذلك عام ١٨٥٩.

فلسطين أم فلسطيا

وثمة مصطلح جديد يعالج سوء الفهم واستغلال روايات الكتاب المقدّس في التداخلات السياسية والحروب المعاصرة بين الفلسطينيين والإسرائيليين في الزمن

الحاضر، وهذا المصطلح هو مصطلح تاريخي علمي يسمي «فِلَسْطين» باسم «فِلِسْطيا»، و«الفِلَسْطينيين» باسم «الفِلِسْطيين». لقد تبنّت «الترجمة المشتركة» التي تصدرها جمعية الكتاب المقدّس هذين المصطلحين، وكذلك «العهد القديم العبري» (ترجمة بين السطور). فيما عدا الفائدة العلمية، يساعد هذا المصطلح على تجنّب قراءة العهد القديم وكأن أحداث رواياته تجري حاليًا.

الخاتمة

بعد استعراض هذه المؤثرات على ترجمة الكتاب المقدّس إلى العربية، تتبيّن بجلاء خطورة العمل الذي يقوم به المشرفون على مناهج الترجمة في هذا الحقل.

فمن جهة، تكون المؤثرات سلبية، كمثل طغيان التقليد الكنسي على النص الكتابي، أو أسر معنى كلمات النص ضمن مفاهيم مسبقة عقيدية، أو تحميل النص ما يريد المترجم له أن يحمل.

ومن جهة أخرى، تكون المؤثرات إيجابية، كمثل تنوّع استخدام الأساليب اللغوية ومستوياتها، وتحاشي وقوع الترجمة أَسيرة أسلوب واحد يحدّ من انتشارها، وأخذ الأذواق الإقليمية في استعمال اللغة العربية بعين الاعتبار. كذلك ضرورة التنبّه لئلا ترد في الترجمة عبارات مسيئة للقضايا المذهبية والدينية والسياسية.

والحقّ يقال إن القيام بترجمة الكتاب المقدّس إلى العربية ليس بالقضية السهلة، بل دونها الكثير من المصاعب والكثير من الإشكاليات، غير أن هذا الواقع يجب ألا يثْني عزائمنا عن محاولة تعريب الكتاب المقدّس والقيام بالعمل الجادّ ليكون لنا في عالمنا العربي ترجمة علمية دقيقة للكتاب المقدّس تليق بكرامة كلمة الله، وبكرامة اللغة العربية، وبكرامة الإنسان الذي يطالعه.

أفكار لاهوتية وراء اختيار بعض الكلمات في بعض ترجمات الكتاب المقدّس العربية

عيسى دياب

الأطروحة التي نريد أن نبرهنها في هذه المقالة هي أن العقيدة الدينية هي التي وجّهت الترجمة في ترجمات الكتاب المقدّس العربية. لقد اخترنا لهذه الدراسة الترجمات التالية: من الجهة البروتستانتية، ترجمة سميث- فانديك؛ ومن الناحية الكاثوليكية، الترجمة الدومنيكانية واليسوعية في طبعتها الأولى. ثم نتفحّص الموضوع في الطبعات اللاحقة لهذه الترجمات لنرى نوعية تطوّره. ويقتصر التدقيق على الترجمة اليسوعية في الطبعة المراجعة، إذ إنه لا توجد مراجعة لترجمة سميث - فانديك. مرجعنا في هذه المقارنة هو النص الماسوراتي العبري، ونص السبعينية اليوناني للعهد القديم، ثم نص نستله ألاند اليوناني للعهد الجديد في طبعته الأخيرة.

لا يخفى على أحد مدى التوتر الذي كان سائداً بين المرسلين الكاثوليك والمرسلين البروتستانت في القرن التاسع عشر، وروح المنافسة التي سادت عمل الفريقين. وعلى الرغم من أن حِدّة المنافسة، خاصة في العمل الديني، غير مستحبة، إلا أن ذلك حفّز الفريقين على وفرة الإنتاج وتحسينه.

أولاً: تنظير في الإشكالية: النص أولاً أم التفسير؟

لقد كانت نظرة كل من الكاثوليك والبروتستانت إلى النص الكتابي قد تكوّنت في وعيهم عبر خبرات ثقافية انبثقت مع بدايات عصر النهضة ومن قبل ذلك بالنسبة للكاثوليك. إننا نوافق ديفيد جاسبر في قوله عن هذا الموضوع:

«في الواقع فإن التحوّل من الكلمة المكتوبة باليد إلى الكلمة المطبوعة (...) غيّر بالكامل الطريقة التي كان يدرك ويُفهم فيها العالم، حيث انتقل التواصل من الاعتماد على النصوص المدوّنة باليد، مع حتمية الخطأ فيها، إلى نصوص متناسقة وقابلة لإعادة الطبع بلا نهاية طبقاً لنموذج موحّد».[١]

حتى بداية عصر النهضة، كانت نظرة الكاثوليك إلى الكتاب المقدّس مطبوعة بنظرة آباء الكنيسة إليه ثم بنظرة توما الأكويني، وهي أن تقليد الكنيسة يأتي أولاً ثم يليه الكتاب المقدّس؛ وما الكتاب المقدّس إلا تقليد من ضمن التقاليد الآبائية، إنه التقليد الذي أجمع عليه آباء الكنيسة. لكن ما حدث في عصر النهضة جعل الكثيرين، وأهمهم مارتن لوثر، يغيّر نظرته. ما لا شك فيه أن هذه النقلة من الصفحة المخطوطة إلى الصفحة المطبوعة قد أثّرت في وعي مارتن لوثر وشكّلت نظرته المستحدثة إلى الكتاب المقدّس، فأراه الله نفسه يتكلّم بالمقارنة مع البابا الذي كان أيضاً يتكلّم.

كما الإصلاح البروتستانتي، كذلك الإصلاح الكاثوليكي المضاد، كلاهما شحذا الوعيين المتميّزين في نظرتيهما المختلفتين إلى الكتاب المقدّس. وبعد الإصلاح، وحتى عصر النقد التاريخي، لم يطرأ برأينا أي عامل كان قادراً على جعل الفريقين يعدّلان نظرتيهما. فبقي الفريق الكاثوليكي يقيس الكتاب المقدّس بالتقليد، وبقي الفريق البروتستانتي يعتبر النص الكتابي المرجع الأخير لكل ما يتعلّق بالعقيدة والأخلاق.

يصف جاسبر طريقة الكنيسة المبكرة في قراءة الكتاب المقدّس على أنها نظرة تاريخية، أي أن الكتاب رواية تاريخية والأحداث المذكورة فيه حدثت بالفعل ولو لمرة واحدة؛ وأن الله نفسه كان وراء هذه الأحداث التاريخية، ثم يعلّق قائلاً :

«إن كل التوصيفات أو التحديدات التي ذكرناها أو ذُكرت عن الكتاب المقدّس ليست صحيحة بالضرورة. بل هي نتيجة لطريقة قراءة وفهم خاصّين في كيفية عمل النص. بإيجاز، هي نتاج لاستراتيجية هرمينوطيقية خاصة، هي بدورها أيضاً نتاج تصوّر لاهوتي معيّن ومولِّدة لرؤية

---

(١) دايفيد جاسبر، *مقدّمة في الهرمينوطيقا*، ترجمة وجيه قانصو، بيروت، الدار العربية للعلوم، منشورات الإختلاف ٢٠٠٧، ٣٤.

لاهوتية في آن بطريقة تشبه الحركة الدائرية. فاعتقاد معيّن يفرض علينا طريقة خاصة في قراءة الإنجيل [الكتاب المقدّس] وتلك الطريقة الخاصة تقوم بدورها في تثبيت صحة الإعتقاد ومشروعيته.»(٢)

إن ما يطرحه جاسبر يدعم أطروحتي، وهي أن العقيدة أتت أولاً في ترجمات الكتاب المقدّس العربية ثم تلاها النص المقدّس مفسّراً عن طريق الترجمة لتثبيت العقيدة كما قال جاسبر. ودعا هذه العملية «الدائرة الهرمينوطيقية»: التفسير – النص – دعم التفسير.

إن الكتاب المقدّس بنظر المسيحيين كلهم هو مصدر العقيدة المسيحية الرئيس ومرجع المعتقدات الكنسية. إلا أن كلاً من الكاثوليك والبروتستانت يفسّرون هذه النظرة كل على طريقته الخاصة. ففي العرف الكاثوليكي، إن المعتقد المعروف بـ«التقليد الرسولي» هو «معيار الحقيقة» الذي ينظّم قراءتنا المناسبة والصحيحة للنص الكتابي. أما المصلح مارتن لوثر فكان يعتقد بأن النص الكتابي هو الذي يقدّم المبادئ التي نفحص بها تفسير النص الكتابي: الكتاب المقدّس يفسّر نفسه بنفسه. أما تفسير النص الإنجيلي عند الكاثوليك فيخضع لمعيار التفسير الذي هو التقليد الرسولي، وهذا بدوره يشكّل لسان حال المؤسسة الكنسية.

فريديريك شلايرماخر (١٧٦٨-١٨٣٤) أعطى رأياً في الموضوع، فقال واصفاً ما يحدث في معظم الأحيان:

«من أجل تحصيل رؤية شاملة عن النص بكلّيته، لا بد أن نعير اهتماماً مناسباً للتفاصيل والخصوصيات. إلا أنه لا يمكن معرفة ميزة هذه التفاصيل والخصوصيات من دون وجود رؤية واضحة عن النص بأكلمه. أي أننا نبدأ بالفكرة الكبيرة، ثم نقرأ تفاصيل النص بوضوح على ضوء هذه الفكرة، ثم نستعين بالنص لتثبيتها».(٣)

---

(٢) المرجع نفسه، ٣٦.

(٣) شلايرماخر، مقتبسة عن دايفد جاسبر، المرجع نفسه، ٣٩. الخط الثخين للكاتب.

يُثبت مارتن هايدغر (١٨٨٩-١٩٧٦) ما سبقه إليه مواطنه شلايرماخر مع إعطاء بعض التفاصيل التوضيحية، فيرى أن الأهمية لا تكمن في الخروج من دائرة التأويل (العقيدة أو التفسير السابق للقراءة - قراءة النص - تثبيت العقيدة) لأن ذلك أمر مستحيل، ولكنها تكمن في كيفية الدخول إليها من البداية. شلايرماخر يحصر التفسير المسبق للقراءة، ليس بالتقليد الرسولي أو بالتقليد الكتابي، بل بالإيمان أو الشك. فيوجد من يقارب الكتاب على خلفية إيمان مطلق بحقيقة تاريخية وحرفية للأحداث، ويوجد من يقرأ النص على خلفية الشك في كل شيء. يقول شلايرماخر مخاطباً قارئه: «بعبارة أخرى، بأية فكرة تبدأ عملية القراءة، بالإستناد إلى الإيمان أم إلى الشك أم إلى مزيج من الإثنين؟ وما هي مسبقاتك وفرضيّاتك الأولى وترجيحاتك؟ التي لا تكون بالضرورة جيدة أو سيئة، ولكننا نحملها جميعاً لتشكّل بمجموعها كيفية القراءة والتفسير».(٤)

لقد انعكس هذا التوتّر السائد بين الكاثوليك والبروتستانت في نظرة كل منهما إلى الكتاب المقدّس على تعريبهما للكتاب المقدّس، انطلاقاً من المبدأ المعروف أن كل ترجمة للنص هي بالحقيقة تفسير له. وهذا ما سنراه في الأمثلة التي سنطرحها في سياق هذه الدراسة.

ثانياً: الظروف التي أُعدّت فيها الترجمات التي نتناولها في هذه الدراسة

قبل أن نتناول الأمثلة من الترجمات نفسها، نودّ أن نبرهن هنا أن الظروف التي أُعدّت فيها الترجمات تدعم أيضاً أطروحتنا. فكل من الفريقين البروتسانتي والكاثوليكي نفّذ مشروعه للترجمة على خلفية العقيدة، وكل منهما أراد أن تكون ترجمته رافعةً لعقيدته. وإليكم البراهين على ما نقول من مقدّمات الترجمات نفسها.

(٤) دايفيد جاسبر، المرجع نفسه، ٣٨.

تختلف المراجع في تعداد الترجمات العربية للكتاب المقدّس[٥]. وعلى الرغم من صعوبة الموضوع فقد أوردت دائرة المعارف الكاثوليكية (www.catholic.org) ما يلي:

«أُعدّت، في القرن العاشر الميلادي ترجمة عربية للكتاب المقدّس العبري بواسطة سعديا هاغون. ولم يبقَ منها إلا الأسفار الخمسة والأنبياء الصغار وإشعيا والمزامير وأيوب. وفي سنة ١٦٧١، نشر الكتاب المقدّس باللغة العربية في روما بعناية [المطران] سركيس الرزي، رئيس أساقفة دمشق. وظهر هذا العمل في طبعات عديدة بعد ذلك. ثم إن طبعة محرّفة عنها وُزِّعت بواسطة جمعية الكتاب المقدّس (لندن ١٨٢٢). وللحدّ من هذا التأثير البروتستانتي، أصدر الآباء الدومنيكان في الموصل (١٨٧٥-١٨٧٨) والآباء اليسوعيون في بيروت (١٨٧٦-١٨٧٨) ترجمتيهما العربيتين من الكتاب المقدّس كاملاً». [٦]

لا أدري ماذا يكمن وراء تجاهل ترجمتَي فارس الشدياق (بمساعدة صموئيل لي وطوماس جاريت) سنة ١٨٥٧ (العهد الجديد سنة ١٨٥١)، وسميث- فانديك البروتستانتيتين كلياً، على الرغم من أننا أصبحنا في زمان ينشط فيه العمل المسكوني.

وإليكم نبذة مختصرة عن الترجمات العربية التي سنشير إليها:

(٥) أنظر باسيل عكولة، «المراجعة العربية للكتاب المقدّس في طبعته الموصلية، دراسة وتحليل»؛ وسهيل قاشا، «الكتاب المقدّس واللغة العربية»؛ وأيوب شهوان، «الترجمات العربية المتلاحقة للكتاب المقدّس شهادة على همّ علمي وكنسي متواصل» أيوب شهوان، *ترجمات الكتاب المقدس في الشرق*، جونية: جامعة الروح القدس، الرابطة الكتابية ٢٠٠٦، ٦٥-٦٧ ، ٧٩-٩٦، ٢٥٧-٢٧٧.

(٦) www.catholic.org/encyclopedia/view.php?id=11999.
An Arabic version of the Hebrew Bible was made in the tenth century by Saadia ha Gaon. Only its Pentateuch, Minor Prophets, Isaias, Psalms, and Job have been preserved. In 1671 an Arabic Bible was published at Rome under the direction of Sergius Risi, Archbishop of Damascus. It appeared in numerous later editions. A mutilated reprint of it (London, 1822) was circulated by the Bible Society. To offset this Protestant influence, complete Arabic versions were issued both by the Dominicans at Mossul (1875-8) and the Jesuits at Beirut (1876-8).

١. ترجمة فاندايك

يفيد القسّ سيكل سيل بأنه لما رأى الرعيل الأول من المرسلين البروتستانت «أن الترجمات العربية الموجودة في تلك الفترة للكتاب المقدّس غير مرضية، وغير خليقة بأن تجاري نهضة اللغة في ذلك العصر، قرّروا وضع ترجمة عربية صحيحة عن الأصل العبراني واليوناني».[٧] إذا تذكّرنا أن المرسلين وصلوا إلى لبنان سنة ١٨٢٣، نرى أنهم أدركوا أنه كانت توجد ترجمات عربية آنذاك، لكنهم حكموا بأنها «غير مرضية» ولا تفي بالحاجة. ماهي الترجمات العربية التي كانت متداولة في ذلك الوقت؟ دون شك هناك ترجمة الشدياق (١٨٥٧)، وما تبقّى من ترجمة سركيس الرزي اللتان أشرنا إليهما أعلاه، وربما بعض المقاطع البيبلية في الكتب الليتورجية الشرقية المتداولة كنصوص أُعدت للإحتفالات الليتورجية باللغة العربية. وسرعان ما عني الأميركي عالي سميث باختيار الخط العربي المطلوب وسبك الأحرف وإنشاء مطبعة وجمع مكتبة متخصّصة تساعده في هذا العمل. استعان سميث بإثنين من جهابذة اللغة العربية آنذاك، أعني بطرس البستاني الذي اعتنق البروتستانتية، وناصيف اليازجي الذي حافظ على مذهبه (روم كاثوليك). كان سميث يأخذ أيضاً برأي المرسلين البروتستانت في الدول العربية الأخرى وخاصة برأي العلماء الألمان، واحتفظ لنفسه بإعداد المخطوط النهائي المعدّ للطبع. لم يتمكّن سميث من إنجاز عمله، إذ إن المنية قد وافته سنة ١٨٥٨، وكان قد أنجز بشكل نهائي أسفار التوراة والعهد الجديد وأجزاء مختلفة من الأنبياء. ثم أخذ المرسل كرنيليوس فانديك على عاتقه إكمال المهمة، فاستعان بالشيخ يوسف بن عقل الأسير الحسيني، الذي كُلِّف قبل كل شيء بمراجعة ما أعدّه سميث، ثم العمل إلى جانب فاندايك. وصدر العهد الجديد سنة ١٨٦٠، ثم العهد القديم سنة ١٨٦٥.

---

(٧) سيكل سيل، «الترجمات وقيمتها»، في *المرشد إلى الكتاب المقدّس*، بيروت، مكتبة المشعل الإنجيلية ١٩٥٨، ٥٨.

يقوِّم سيكل سيل العمل كالتالي:«كانت طريقة سميث في الترجمة أن يستعمل اللغة الفصحى، إنما كان ينتقي المفردات القريبة المنال. بيد أن فانديك رأى أن ينوّع أسلوبه في الكتابة بحسب تنوّع الأسلوب في النص العبري. فكان أسلوبه في كتابة الأسفار التاريخية مثلاً بسيطاً وواضحاً، في حين أن أسفار الشريعة كتبها بأسلوب أرفع كما هو الأمر في الأصل».(٨)

أما الأمر الذي لم تشر إليه المصادر البروتستانتية فهو محاولة تقريب الترجمة العربية من الترجمة الرسمية في العالم الأنكلوساكسوني البروتستانتي (ترجمة الملك جيمس المسماة «الترجمة المجازة»). ولو أننا لم نجد أثراً للتعبير عن نيّة في هذا العمل أو خطة لتحقيقه، إلا أن مجرد قراءة ترجمة فانديك وترجمة الملك جيمس تظهر مدى التطابق في الخيارات.

٢. الترجمة الدومنيكانية

جاءت الترجمة العربية التي أُعدِّتها و نشرتها الرهبنة الدومنيكانية (١٨٧٥-١٨٧٨) كردّة فعل على ترجمة سميث - فانديك، بحسب اعتراف دائرة المعارف الكاثوليكية أعلاه. وهذا ما أكّدته مقدمة الترجمة نفسها أيضاً. فقد جاء في «شهادة المدقق الأول»، المطران الكلداني جرجس عبد يشوع، من مقدمة الطبعة الأولى: «ويا حبذا أنه من اليوم النصارى بل الخارجون أيضاً حيثما نطق بلغتنا هذه الحسيبة سيحصلون بأمان على الأسفار القدسية بأسرها تامة مصحّحة غير ملعوب بها أو محذوف منها بيد الرَّفَضَة المستجدين (وهم البروتستنت) ».(٩) وجاء أيضاً في التقرير نفسه:

> «لأنه كما أنه من سوء أميال الناس صار مجيء المسيح بعينه أي كلام الله الجوهري باعثاً إلى الهلاك لكثيرين (لو ٢: ٣٤ و٣٥) كذلك كلام الله المسطور يسقط في سببه كثيرون. كما هو حال

---

(٨) سيكل، المرجع نفسه، ٥٩.

(٩) الرهبنة الدومنيكانية في العراق، *الكتاب المقدّس*، الموصل، ١٨٧٨، أعيد طبعه في بيروت، جمعية الكتاب المقدّس ٢٠٠٠، (شهادة المدقق الأول) دون ترقيم الصفحات.

الهراطقة وشرذمات البروتستنت، لتأويلهم إياه برأي نفوسهم مبتدعين الضلال حسب أهوائهم، فيجعلون الدواء الشافي في نفسه سمًّا لنفوسهم ناقعاً لرداء باطنهم». [١٠] وفي الوقت نفسه، تفيد المقدمة بأن الرهبنة الدومنيكانية استعانت بالأحرف العربية التي سبكها المرسلون البروتستانت في بيروت من أجل طبع الكتاب.

وجاء في شهادة المدقق الثاني، الراهب يوحنا المعمدان لاوي، ما يلي:

«وأشهد أنني ما وجدت فيها غلطاً ولا شيئاً مخترعاً ولا مما يخالف الإيمان الكاثوليكي المقدّس أو قوانين المجمع التريدنتيني الطاهرة، لا بل أقرّر بأن صاحب هذا التحرير النفيس قد تتبّع بكل وسعه الترجمة اللاتينية الفولغاتا في حرفيتها ومعناها مقتدياً بالنسخة الفاتيكانية المشهورة، وذلك بما يجلّ ويعظّم من الدقة والحذاقة، وحاذياً حذو الترجمات القديمة الخالصة المستعملة دون غيرها في الكنائس الشرقية». [١١]

لكن باسيل عكولة يقدّم البراهين المقبولة على أن الطبعة الدومنيكانية الموصلية للكتاب المقدّس ليست ترجمة بالمعنى الصحيح للكلمة بل مراجعة لترجمة الرزي (١٦٧١) لـ«دوزنتها على الترجمات المرجعية الكاثوليكية وأهمها الفولغاتا». ويفيد عكولة مشيراً إلى المقدمة الدومنيكانية: «فهو [يوسف داود] يقول بصراحة ... «قرّرت ألا أقوم بترجمة جديدة». وانطلاقاً من هذه النقطة، يشرح لنا الطريقة التي اتّبعها لتهيئة النص العربي المعدّ للطبع، ويمكن تلخيصها كالتالي:

أ- اعتماد النص العربي المطبوع في روما سنة ١٧٠٣ للأناجيل والعهد الجديد...

ب- اعتماد النص العربي المطبوع في روما سنة ١٦٧١ للعهد القديم، الذي يسميه «الترجمة الشرقية» لأنها الأقدم ولأنها أساس الترجمات اللاحقة، ومن بينها نص الرزي المتداول في الكنائس الكاثوليكية الحديثة في الشرق...

---

(١٠) الرهبنة الدومنيكانية في العراق، المرجع نفسه.

(١١) المرجع نفسه.

ج- الإقدام على تصحيح النص العربي بمقارنته بالأصول أي النص العبراني والترجمات اليونانية والبسيطة والسريانية واللاتينية، خصوصاً في ما يتعلّق بالأسفار المنحولة».

ويفيد عكولة أيضاً بأن الطبعات العربية السابقة «شكّلت أرضية واسعة وثابتة لعمل يوسف داود من الناحيتين اللغوية العربية والأمانة الكاثوليكية، ولم يستطع أن يتجاهل بعضها أو ألا يتأثّر بها، لا سيما تلك المطبوعة في روما من جهة تطابقها مع الفولغاتا اللاتينية التي اعتُبرت في أعقاب المجمع التريدنتيني أمّ الكتاب بالنسبة إلى الكنيسة الكاثوليكية في صراعها مع الإصلاح البروتستانتي».[١٢]

٣. الترجمة اليسوعية الأولى

في سنة ١٨٨١، أنهت الرهبانية اليسوعية إصدار نص الكتاب المقدّس بكامله في ترجمة عربية. وقد أسهم الشيخ إبراهيم اليازجي في صياغة كتابة نصّ العهد القديم، «فاتّسمت، إلى جانب ميزاتها الكتابية العلمية، بفصاحة اللفظ وجمال السبك».[١٣] أقتبس عن الفغالي ما جاء في مجلة المشرق حول الإعداد لهذه الترجمة: «في غرة ١٨٧٢، أقرّ اليسوعيون في بيروت المباشرة بترجمة عربية جديدة للعهد القديم... وأجمع الرأي على الإستعانة بالشيخ إبراهيم اليازجي لصياغة هذا النص الجديد، تهيّئ اللجنة ترجمة حرفية تبرز دقائق الأصول بأمانة كلية فيضفي الشيخ عليها ديباجته العربية الفخمة».[١٤]

يتكلم الفغالي في مقالته التي اقتبسنا منها عن خلافات بين أعضاء الفريق أدّت إلى بطء في العمل، حتى صدر أخيراً سنة ١٨٨١.

---

(١٢) باسيل عكولة، المرجع نفسه، ٦٧.

(١٣) الرهبانية اليسوعية، «المقدّمة»، *الكتاب المقدّس*، بيروت، المكتبة الشرقية ١٩٩٠، ٧.

(١٤) الأب سامي خوري اليسوعي، *المشرق* ٦٥ (١٩٩١)، الجزآن الأول والثاني، ١٢٨- ١٢٩، مقتبسة عن بولس الفغالي، «الكتاب المقدس، الترجمة الكاثوليكية الحديثة» في كتاب أيوب شهوان (الناشر)، *ترجمات الكتاب المقدس في الشرق*، بيروت، الرابطة الكتابية ٣٧.

إننا لا نجد أي أثر لتعاون يمكن أن يكون قد حصل بين الرهبان اليسوعيين والرهبان الدومنيكان على صعيد ترجمة الكتاب المقدّس، خاصة وأن الترجمتين أُعدّتا في الفترة الزمنية نفسها: الترجمة اليسوعية (١٨٧٢-١٨٨١)، والترجمة الدومنيكانية (١٨٧٥-١٨٧٨). ومع أننا نعرف الدوافع التي دفعت الرهبنة الدومنيكانية إلى إعداد ترجمتها، إلا أننا لا ننتظر أن تكون دوافع اليسوعيين مختلفة ألا وهي: الردّ على ترجمتي البروتستانت، وخاصة ترجمة سميث-فانديك. ويلزمنا أن نذهب إلى الأرشيف المتعلق بهذه الترجمة لنتمكّن من الحصول على برهان يقيني على ما نقول. إلا أن ما نقوله ليس ببعيد عن المنطق.

في مقالة للقسّ سيكل سيل، كتبها سنة ١٩٥٨ وأُلحقت بتنقيح لكتاب «مرشد الطالبين»، قال فيها متكلّماً عن الترجمة المسماة «اليسوعية»:

«وقد أخذت الترجمة اليسوعية عن الأصل العبري والآرامي واللاتيني، غير أن واضعيها كانوا يرجعون كما ذُكر في مقدمة الكتاب إلى الترجمة اللاتينية في ما يتعلّق بعقائد الكنيسة ووصاياها. وهي أقوى من ترجمة سميث- فانديك لغة وأسلوباً، بيد أنها أقل دقّة من حيث الترجمة. أما أسلوب الكتابة في هذه الترجمة فيسير، كما يقول البعض، على نمط واحد، في حين أن هناك اختلافاً في الأصل بين أسلوب الأسفار التاريخية وأسلوب الأسفار النبوية.»[١٥]

٤. الترجمة اليسوعية الثانية

في سنة ١٩٤٩، أخذت الرهبانية اليسوعية تعيد النظر في ترجمتها للكتاب المقدّس لإثرائها بما وصلت إليه الدراسات الكتابية وأساليب الترجمة وفنون الإخراج والطباعة. فصدرت في سنة ١٩٦٩ ترجمة العهد الجديد. وفي سنة ١٩٨٠، بدأ العمل على العهد القديم، ونُشر الكتاب المقدّس كاملاً سنة ١٩٨٩.

---

(١٥) سيكل سيل، «الترجمات وقيمتها»، *المرشد إلى الكتاب المقدّس*، بيروت، مكتبة المشعل الإنجيلية ١٩٥٨، ص ٦٠

سار العمل، كما تقول مقدمة الطبعة الأخيرة، على المبادئ التالية: «الأمانة للأصل العبري واليوناني ولنص الترجمة القديمة قدر المستطاع، لا سيما من ناحية استعمال المفردات الكتابية المسيحية المألوفة، والبساطة في اختيار الألفاظ، والمحافظة على أسلوب إبراهيم اليازجي، وعلى الإنشاء العربي التقليدي»[١٦]. إذاً ما زلنا في إطار الإستناد إلى نقاط عقيدية كاثوليكية مفصلية: الفولغاتا وترجمة بيبليا أورشليم الفرنسية. وهذا ما يؤكّده بولس الفغالي حيث كتب عن هذه الترجمة في طبعتها الأخيرة: «عادت بكلّيتها تقريباً إلى الترجمة المسكونية للكتاب المقدّس. فأخذت المداخل والحواشي ونقلتها كما هي، فجاءت للأسف غريبة عن عالمنا الشرقي مع ترجمات يمكن أن نقول إنها ليست دقيقة».[١٧] ويضيف الفغالي: «ومن زيارة إلى العاملين في الترجمة الجديدة، كان نص بيبليا أورشليم هو المنارة، ولا سيما في نصوص العهد القديم».[١٨] إذا كان هذا الأمر صحيحاً، فنكون قد عدنا، أيضاً في الترجمة الحديثة، إلى المبدأ نفسه الذي اتُّبع في الترجمة القديمة، أي العقيدة ثم الترجمة، أو العقيدة توجّه الترجمة.

الخلاصة

أردنا من هذه المقدمات للترجمات العربية، توضيح أن الخلفية العقائدية التي نشأت فيها كل من الترجمات كان العامل المسيطر على عمل الترجمة. الأمر الذي يعتبر مخالفة لأصول الترجمة العلمية. وفي هذا السياق، يقول باسيل عكولة: «لذا نظن أن كافة النصوص العربية للكتاب المقدّس الكاثوليكية التي نشرت في القرنين الثامن عشر والتاسع عشر لا تنطبق عليها تسمية «الترجمات»؛ بسبب التزامها المطلق

---

(١٦) الرهبانية اليسوعية، «المقدّمة»، *الكتاب المقدّس*، بيروت، المكتبة الشرقية ١٩٩٠، ٧.

(١٧) بولس الفغالي، «الكتاب المقدّس، الترجمة الكاثوليكية الحديثة»، *ترجمات الكتاب المقدّس في الشرق*، دراسات بيبلية رقم ٣٠، أيوب شهوان (ناشر)، بيروت، الرابطة الكتابية ٢٠٠٦، ٢٩.

(١٨) بولس الفغالي، المرجع نفسه، ٣٠.

بـنص الفولغـاتا الـتي بـنيَت عليهـا النسخة الـشرقية الـتي نـقلها ميخائيـل الـرزي[١٩] مطران دمشق الماروني إلى روما. وعمل بعض تـلامذة المدرسة المارونيـة هنـاك عـلى تـهذيبها جزئياً لتأتي مطابقة للنص اللاتيني الرسمي، لأن العملية كانت تـفوق طـاقتهم، ولأن الضغوط الكنسيـة الفائقة الحساسية في هـذا المـوضوع كانت تـمنع أي خـروج عن المألوف. فاقتصر الأمـر عـلى اسـتبدال كلمـة بـكلمة أو عبـارة بـعبارة لتـأتي أكثر تـطابقاً مع الفولغاتا، مستعينين بـالأصول والترجمات العبرية واليونانيـة والبـسيطة أي الفشيطتا / الفشيـطتو واللاتينية».[٢٠]

كذلك الأمر، فقد حرص البروتـستانت عـلى ملاءمـة تـرجمتهم لعقيـدتهم وللترجمـة البروتستانتية الرسمية في الغرب البروتستانتي.

وسنعرض لهذا الضعف في أمثلة مختارة من النصوص الأصلية والترجمات.

ثالثاً: نـصوص نـموذجية

حيث أنه من الصعب مقارنة نـص الكتاب المقدّس كاملاً وتحليل الفروقات، رأينـا أن نـنتقي بعض النـصوص الدقيقـة التي تـبرز فيهـا الفروقـات العقائديـة: (أنظـر اللائحـة المرفقة)

---

(١٩) يرد اسمه في بعض المراجع «سركيس» الرزي.

(٢٠) باسيل عكولة، المرجع نفسه، ٦٧.

مقارنة نصوص منتقاة في عدد من الترجمات العربية

المقطع البيبلي	النص في سميث فانديك	النص في الدومنيكانية	النص في اليسوعية الأولى	النص في اليسوعية الثانية	النص في الماسوراتية (ع ق) أو في اليونانية (ع ج)	النص في السبعينية
تكوين ٣: ١٤-١٥	فقال الرب الإله للحية .... وأضع عداوة بينَكِ وبين المرأة وبين نسلِكِ ونسلِها. هو يسحق رأسكِ، وأنتِ تسحقين عقبه	فقال الرب الإله للحية: ... وأضع عداوة بينك وبين المرأة وبين نسلك ونسلها. هو يسحق رأسك وأنت ترصدين عقبه.	فقال الرب الإله للحية: ... وأجعل عداوة بينك وبين المرأة، وبين نسلك ونسلها، فهو يسحق رأسك وأنت ترصدين عقبه	فقال الرب الإله للحية: ... وأجعل عداوة بينك وبين المرأة، وبين نسلك ونسلها، فهو يسحق رأسك وأنت تصيبين عقبه	וַיֹּאמֶר יְהוָה אֱלֹהִים ׀ אֶל־הַנָּחָשׁ ... : וְאֵיבָה ׀ אָשִׁית בֵּינְךָ וּבֵין הָאִשָּׁה וּבֵין זַרְעֲךָ וּבֵין זַרְעָהּ הוּא יְשׁוּפְךָ רֹאשׁ וְאַתָּה תְּשׁוּפֶנּוּ עָקֵב׃	καὶ εἶπεν κύριος ὁ θεὸς τῷ ὄφει ...καὶ ἔχθραν θήσω ἀνὰ μέσον σου καὶ ἀνὰ μέσον τῆς γυναικὸς καὶ ἀνὰ μέσον τοῦ σπέρματός σου καὶ ἀνὰ μέσον τοῦ σπέρματος αὐτῆς· αὐτός σου τηρήσει κεφαλήν, καὶ σὺ τηρήσεις αὐτοῦ πτέρναν.
متى ١: ٢٥	وَلَمْ يَعْرِفْهَا حَتَّى وَلَدَتِ **ٱبْنَهَا ٱلْبِكْرَ**. وَدَعَا ٱسْمَهُ يَسُوعَ.	ولم يعرفها حتى ولدت **ابنها البكر**. فدعا اسمه يسوع.	ولم يعرفها حتى ولدت ابنها **البكر** وسماه يسوع.	على أنه لم يعرفها حتى ولدت **ابناً** فسماه يسوع.	٢٥ καὶ οὐκ ἐγίνωσκεν αὐτὴν ἕως οὗ ἔτεκεν **υἱόν**· καὶ ἐκάλεσεν τὸ ὄνομα αὐτοῦ Ἰησοῦν.	
متى ١٦: ١٨-١٩	وَأَنَا أَقُولُ لَكَ أَيْضًا: **أَنْتَ بُطْرُسُ، وَعَلَى هَذِهِ ٱلصَّخْرَةِ أَبْنِي كَنِيسَتِي**، وَأَبْوَابُ ٱلْجَحِيمِ لَنْ تَقْوَى عَلَيْهَا. ١٩ وَأُعْطِيكَ مَفَاتِيحَ مَلَكُوتِ	وأنا أيضاً أقول لك: **إنك أنت الصخرة. وعلى هذه الصخرة أبني بيعتي**. وأبواب الجحيم لن تقوى عليها. وأعطيك مفاتيح	وأنا أقول لك **أنت الصفاة وعلى هذه الصفاة سأبني كنيستي** وأبواب الجحيم لن تقوى عليها. وسأعطيك مفاتيح	وأنا أقول **لك أنت صخر، وعلى الصخر هذا سأبني كنيستي،** فلن يقوى عليها سلطان الموت. وسأعطيك مفاتيح	κἀγὼ δέ σοι λέγω **ὅτι σὺ εἶ Πέτρος, καὶ ἐπὶ ταύτῃ τῇ πέτρᾳ οἰκοδομήσω μου τὴν ἐκκλησίαν** καὶ πύλαι ᾅδου οὐ κατισχύσουσιν αὐτῆς. ١٩ δώσω σοι τὰς κλεῖδας τῆς βασιλείας τῶν οὐρανῶν, **καὶ ὃ ἐὰν δήσῃς ἐπὶ τῆς γῆς ἔσται δεδεμένον ἐν**	

المقطع البيبلي	النص في سميث فانديك	النص في الدومنيكانية	النص في اليسوعية الأولى	النص في اليسوعية الثانية	النص في الماسوراتية (ع ق) أو في اليونانية (ع ج)	النص في السبعينية
	ٱلسَّمَاوَاتِ، **فَكُلُّ مَا تَرْبِطُهُ عَلَى ٱلْأَرْضِ يَكُونُ مَرْبُوطًا فِي ٱلسَّمَاوَاتِ. وَكُلُّ مَا تَحُلُّهُ عَلَى ٱلْأَرْضِ يَكُونُ مَحْلُولاً فِي ٱلسَّمَاوَاتِ».**	ملكوت السموات. **وما ربطته على الأرض. يكون مربوطاً في السموات. وما حللته على الأرض يكون محلولاً في السموات.**	ملكوت السموات **فكل ما ربطته على الأرض يكون مربوطاً في السماوات وكل ما حللته على الأرض يكون محلولاً في السماوات.**	ملكوت السموات. **فما ربطته في الأرض رُبط في السموات. وما حللته في الأرض حُلّ في السموات.**	**τοῖς οὐρανοῖς, καὶ ὃ ἐὰν λύσῃς ἐπὶ τῆς γῆς ἔσται λελυμένον ἐν τοῖς οὐρανοῖς**	
تي ١: ٥	مِنْ أَجْلِ هٰذَا تَرَكْتُكَ فِي كِرِيتَ لِكَيْ تُكَمِّلَ تَرْتِيبَ ٱلْأُمُورِ ٱلنَّاقِصَةِ، وَتُقِيمَ فِي كُلِّ مَدِينَةٍ **شُيُوخًا** كَمَا أَوْصَيْتُكَ.	إنما أنا خلفتك في اقريطش لهذا السبب. أي لتصلح الأمور الناقصة، وتقيم **قسوساً** في مدينة مدينة كما أوصيتك	إني إنما تركتك في كريت لترتب الناقص وتقيم **كهنة** في كل مدينة كما عينت لك	إنما تركتك في كريت لتتم فيها تنظيم ما بقي من الأمور وتقيم **شيوخاً** في كل بلدة كما أوصيتك.	Τούτου χάριν ἀπέλιπόν σε ἐν Κρήτῃ, ἵνα τὰ λείποντα ἐπιδιορθώσῃ καὶ καταστήσῃς κατὰ πόλιν **πρεσβυτέρους**, ὡς ἐγώ σοι διεταξάμην	
١ بط٥: ١-٢	أَطْلُبُ إِلَى ٱلشُّيُوخِ ٱلَّذِينَ بَيْنَكُمْ، أَنَا ٱلشَّيْخَ رَفِيقَهُمْ، وَٱلشَّاهِدَ لِآلَامِ ٱلْمَسِيحِ، وَشَرِيكَ ٱلْمَجْدِ ٱلْعَتِيدِ أَنْ يُعْلَنَ، ٢ اِرْعَوْا رَعِيَّةَ ٱللهِ ٱلَّتِي بَيْنَكُمْ **نُظَّارًا**،...				Πρεσβυτέρους οὖν ἐν ὑμῖν παρακαλῶ ὁ συμπρεσβύτερος καὶ μάρτυς τῶν τοῦ Χριστοῦ παθημάτων, ὁ καὶ τῆς μελλούσης ἀποκαλύπτεσθαι δόξης κοινωνός· ٢ ποιμάνατε τὸ ἐν ὑμῖν ποίμνιον τοῦ θεοῦ **[ἐπισκοποῦντες]**	

تكوين ٣: ١٤-١٥

ورد في هامش الترجمة اليسوعية الحديثة حول هذا النص: « يـنبئ النص العبري بقيام عداوة بين نسل الحية ونسل حواء، أي بين الإنسان والشيطان، ويُلمح إلى انتصار الإنسان في النهاية، وفي ذلك أول بصيص للخلاص قبل الإنجيل. وفي الترجمة اليونانية تبتدئ الجملة الأخيرة بضمير المذكر فنسب ذلك الإنتصار، لا إلى نسل المرأة بوجه عام، بل إلى أحد أبناء تلك المرأة، ومن هنا انطلق التفسير المشيحي الذي أوضحه فيما بعد كثير من آباء الكنيسة. ومن قال المشيح قال أمه. فالتفسير المريمي للترجمة اللاتينية («هي تسحق») أصبح تقليدياً في الكنيسة الكاثوليكية. »

وورد في هامش الترجمة الدومنيكانية ما يلي: «لا يخفى ما في هذه الكلمات من المعنى الروحاني كما فهم جميع معلمي الكنيسة. وذلك أن الله بعدما جزم بالقصاص على الحية أي على الشيطان لإسقاط آدم وحواء في الخطأ، وقبل أن يوبّخ آدم وحواء على كسرهما وصيته ويحتّم عليهما بالعقاب المستوجب، سلّاهما بوعد الخلاص الذي سيكون لهما ولأولادهما على يد إنسان هو من نسل حواء يعادي الشيطان وأجناده ويسحق رأسه وهو المسيح».

متى ١: ٢٥

نلاحظ أن ترجمات فانديك والدومنيكانية واليسوعية الأولى تتطابق في هذا النص. وأعتقد أن الترجمة الدومنيكانية والترجمة اليسوعية الأولى تبنّتا نص فانديك الذي أضاف كلمة «البكر» إلى النص في الترجمة. لكن اليسوعية الثانية أحدثت تغييراً كبيراً بعدم إيرادها كلمة «البكر»، وهذا برأيي أصحّ بالنسبة إلى اليونانية. واضح أن إضافة «البكر» في الترجمات الأخرى كانت قد أتت كتدبير وقائي ضد التيارات البروتستانتية الليبرالية التي تعود إلى إشعياء (٧: ١٤) بحسب الماسوراتية وليس بحسب السبعينية، فيخفّفون من دوغماتية الولادة العذراوية. وكانت هذه المسألة محتدمة في الوقت الذي كانت تعدّ فيه الترجمات العربية.

متى ١٦: ١٨-١٩

توجد في هذا المقطع إشكاليتان: بطرس والخلافة الرسولية، والربط والحلّ. بخصوص **الإشكالية الأولى**، نلاحظ أن فاندايك ترجم «Πέτρος» « **بطرس**»، طبعاً تماشياً مع العقيدة البروتستانتية الداحضة للخلافة البطرسية، وانسجاماً مع ترجمة الملك جيمس الرسمية في العالم البروتستانتي الأنكلوساكسوني، بينما عمدت الترجمات الكاثوليكية القديمة إلى ترجمتها بـ« الصخرة» و« الصفاة». لكن اليسوعية الثانية ترجمتها « صخر». ونحن نعتقد أن هذا التفسير الأخير هو الصحيح، وكل ما سبقه يحمل تفسيراً مسبقاً للنص المترجم.

الإشكالية الثانية، وهي مسألة الربط والحلّ؛ فقد ترجم فاندايك الفعلين: ربط وحلّ في المضارع، وهذا برأيي هو الصحيح بحسب النص اليوناني؛ بينما استعملت الترجمات الكاثوليكية صيغة الماضي لتعليق هذه المهمة الموكلة إلى بطرس بمسألة الإعتراف العقيدي الذي تفوّه به، فيصبح هو من يرسم العقائد. والتفاسير في الهوامش تشير بالطبع إلى هذا الأمر.

تي ١: ٥

كلمة πρεσβυτέρους التي ترجمت بلفظة « كهنة» في الترجمة اليسوعية الأولى، ترجمت بلفظة « شيوخ» في اليسوعية الثانية، وقد جاء في هامش الترجمة اليسوعية الثانية: « عن « الشيوخ» و« الأساقفة» راجع: (١طي ٣ :١) »، إضافة إلى أن عنوان الفقرة هو « الشيوخ». يوجد إذن إصرار على الانتقال من « كهنة» إلى « شيوخ».

إليكم لائحة بالمواضع حيث أتت كلمة πρεσβυτέρους في العهد الجديد وترجمتها في اليسوعية الأولى والثانية:

المرجع	الترجمة في اليسوعية الأولى	الترجمة في اليسوعية الثانية
LUK ٧:٣	**شيوخ** اليهود	أعيان اليهود (هامش: الترجمة اللفظية: شيوخ)
LUK ٢٢:٥٢	رؤساء الكهنة وولاة الهيكل و**الشيوخ**	عظماء الكهنة وقادة حرس الهيكل والشيوخ
ACT ٤:٥	...رؤساؤهم و**الشيوخ** والكتبة	...رؤساؤهم والشيوخ والكتبة
ACT ٦:١٢	...الشعب والشيوخ والكتبة	...الشعب والشيوخ والكتبة
ACT ١١:٣٠	...وبعثوا إلى الشيوخ	فأرسلوا معونتهم إلى الشيوخ
ACT ١٤:٢٣	ولما رسمنا لهم كهنة. (أع ١٤: ٢٢)	فعيّنا شيوخاً في كل كنيسة
ACT ١٥:٢	...إلى الرسل والكهنة...	...حيث الرسل والشيوخ
ACT ٢٠:١٧	فاستدعى كهنة الكنيسة	يستدعي شيوخ الكنيسة
TIT ١:٥	أن تقيم في كل مدينة كهنة	...وتقيم شيوخاً في كل بلدة
JAS ٥:١٤	...فليدعُ كهنة الكنيسة	...فليدعُ شيوخ الكنيسة
١PE ٥:١	أسألُ الكهنة الذين فيكم أنا الكاهن معهم...	فالشيوخ الذين بينكم، أعظهم أنا الشيخ مثلهم...
REV ٤:٤	أربعة وعشرون شيخاً	أربعة وعشرون شيخاً

على الرغم من أن اليسوعية الثانية أبدلت ترجمة «كهنة» بترجمة «شيوخ» في كثير من المواضع، إلا أن ذلك ليس تراجعاً عقائدياً بل تبدّلاً في التفسير. فبعد أن كان مترجمو اليسوعية الأولى يرون في «البريسبيتيروس» «كهنة»، أصبحوا يرون فيهم «مجلس شيوخ» في الكنيسة المسيحية ملحقاً بالرسل [ربما الكرادلة اليوم]، على غرار مجلس الشيوخ عند اليهود الذي كان ملحقاً برؤساء الكهنة.[٢١]

يبدو أننا انتقلنا، في العصر الحديث، من دعم العقيدة بالنص البيبلي مباشرة إلى دعمها بعلم الهرمينوطيقا.

---

(٢١) راجع الرهبنة اليسوعية، *الكتاب المقدّس*، بيروت، دار المشرق ١٩٨٩، ٤٠٦. التعليق في الهامش على أع ١١:٣٠، ملاحظة رقم ٢٢.

خلاصة المقارنة

لقد قدّمنا براهين نظرية على أن مبدأ الحياد في الترجمة لم يكن مطبَّقاً في الترجمات العربية، وأن الأفكار اللاهوتية المسبقة هي التي وجّهت اختيار المفردات العربية؛ ثم دعمنا البراهين بأمثلة عملية من النصوص الأصلية وترجماتها. وكانت الخلاصة أن الإصدارات الأولى للترجمات العربية كانت مقيّدة بالعقائد الدينية، وأن مراجعات هذه الترجمات الصادرة في العصر الحديث لم تتحرّر نهائياً من هذه القيود، فالحركة المسكونية، وربما أيضاً العلوم الكتابية ساهمت في تخفيف القيود والإقتراب أكثر من الموضوعية المتوخّاة في كل ترجمة.

حتى وإن كان الحياد الخالص مستحيلاً في مسألة فهم النص ومن ثم ترجمته، فإن دراسات الترجمة، بما تحتوي عليه من علوم الحضارات والإناسة والألسنية والتدرب على التقنيات العلمية لنقل النص من لغة وحضارتها إلى لغة أخرى وحضارتها بأمانة، جديرة بتدريب الدارس على أن يكون من الحياد على بعد قاب قوسين أو أدنى.

لا أقول إن الترجمات الغربية هي الأكثر تحرّراً، فعلى الرغم من تقدّم العلوم البيبلية ونشاط الحركة المسكونية وتقدّم الفكر العلماني في كل مكان، فما زالت أسماء العلم، خاصة المتعلقة بالألوهة وأسماء الأماكن والمصطلحات الدينية القديمة، تترجم ولا تنقل بشكلها. فاسم العلم واسم المكان والمصطلح لا يجب أن يترجم حتى يتمكن القارئ من تتبّع الظاهرة الدينية وتطورها عبر تاريخ أسفار الكتاب المقدّس.

إنه لأمر طبيعي أن يقارب كل مؤمن وكل مسؤول في المؤسسة الدينية النصَّ المقدّس بإيمان متوخياً أن يكون تفسيره أو ترجمته داعماً لهذا الإيمان. وأنا لا أعترض على ذلك مطلقاً، ولو كنت في أي موقع ديني لقمت بالعمل نفسه.

لكنني كباحث في الدراسات السامية القديمة وكمؤرّخ أديان، وكون الكتاب المقدّس مرجعاً مهمًّا في هذه الحقول المعرفية، أرى بأننا نحتاج إلى ترجمة عربية علمية خالصة للكتاب المقدّس، على غرار ما حصل في بعض اللغات الغربية، ومنها الفرنسية بالتأكيد وربما في الإنكليزية والألمانية، ترجمةٍ، كما قلت أعلاه، تحافظ على

أسماء الأشخاص والأماكن وخاصة الإله أو الآلهة والمصطلحات الدينية القديمة بلفظها في اللغات الأصلية، كي يتمكن العلماء من دراسة تطور الفكر الديني عند الشعوب السامية. لقد سبق وفتح ولهاوزن الباب بتطبيقه النظرية التطورية في الفكر الديني، ونحن اليوم نحتاج إلى مثل هذه الدراسة في اللغة العربية لتخليص القارئ من القيود الميثولوجية للنص الديني في كثير من الأحيان. أنا المؤمن أقول ذلك إيماناً مني بأنه عندما تزول هذه القيود سيبقى الجوهر الديني الصافي هو القاعدة المهمة التي ينطلق منها كل حوار بين الأديان أو الحضارات.

الشاهد الإنجيلي عند يوسف الخال
اللعب مع القداسة و ضدّها

الهادي العيّادي

الشعراء العرب والكتاب المقدّس

تجربة الوصول

تعود صلة الشعراء العرب بالكتاب المقدّس إلى القرن التاسع عشر، حين تم نشره سنة ١٨١٤ م، بعد أن أمر القنصل الروسي بوضع ترجمة له.[١] وقد سبقت هذه الترجمة محاولات لتعريب المزامير ونشيد الإنشاد وترانيم الأناجيل، إذ قام إبراهيم سركيس بنقلها إلى اللغة العربية.[٢]

فحدث المجيء إلى الكتاب المقدّس مثّل لحظة اكتشاف له، والاكتشاف مقدّمة لامتلاك معاجمه وإيقاعه ورموزه. نلاحظ أن حدث المجيء كان مختلفاً من شاعر إلى آخر، ولعلنا نتبيّن ثلاثة مسالك سلكها الشعراء إليه:

أولها مسلك موصول بالبيئة الدينية والفكرية التي عاش فيها الشعراء، إذ كان الكتاب المقدّس عنصراً من عناصر تكوينهم، ونذكر من هؤلاء جبران خليل جبران وميخائيل نعيمة وإلياس أبا شبكة وخليل حاوي.

---

(١) شموئيل موريه (Schmuel Moreh)، *الشعر العربي الحديث (١٩٧٠/١٨٠٠) تطوّر أشكاله وموضوعاته بتأثير الأدب الغربي*، ترجمه وعلّق عليه شفيع السيّد و سعيد مصلوح، القاهرة، دار الفكر العربي ١٩٨٦، ٢٥.

(٢) المرجع نفسه، ٦٢-١٢٩.

وثانيها مسلك الانتماء المدرسي، وقد تبلور هذا المسلك مع لحظة التحديث الرومنطيقي. وفيها تعرّف شعراء عاشوا في بيئة إسلامية إلى رموز هذا الكتاب انطلاقاً من أعمال المهجريين أو من الأدب الأوروبي.

وثالثها مسلك موصول بلحظة الحداثة الثانية وبتجربة الشعر الحرّ، إذ جاء الاطّلاع على الكتاب المقدّس ضمن الاطّلاع على مادّة ثقافية وإنسانية تلقّفها الشعراء. وطبيعي أن يستثمر الشعراء هذه المادّة أو يحوّلوها إلى نصوصهم المنجزة، « فالشعر العربي الحديث يمثّل حلقة من التراث الإنساني.»(٣)

هكذا نصنّف الشعراء العرب الذين تفتّحوا على الكتاب المقدّس إلى صنفين:

صنف وصل إليه عن طريق وسائط ثقافية وأدبية، فقرأ رموزه وحوّلها أو قام بزرعها في أشعاره.

وصنف قرأ الكتاب المقدّس من داخل منظومته الدينية فاستوعب رموزه وتغلغلت فيه بعد أن تشبّع بها.

ونلاحظ أن هذه العودة إلى الكتاب المقدّس تجاوبت مع تيّار الحداثة بصفة عامة، إذ من كشوفات الرومنطيقية مثلاً وصل الشعر بالمقدّس.(٤)

فهذه العودة لم تخلُ من مخاطر ومزالق، إذ جوبهت بالرفض والاستنكار، فوقف قدّامها المحافظون وعارضوها وسعوا إلى محاصرتها وتحقير أصحابها، رافعين بذلك سيف المقدّس الديني (الإسلامي هذه المرة). ولكن تجربة الوصول إلى الكتاب المقدّس تمت رغم الممانعة والاحتراز والتشكيك في عقيدة أصحابها ووطنيتهم .

ولقد لفت عزّ الدين إسماعيل الانتباه إلى هذه المسالة في كتابه المذكور سالفاً فقال: «أثار هذا الموقف شبهات لدى من يرفضون تجربة الشعر المعاصرة. فقد اتهموا شعراء هذه التجربة في قوميتهم العربية، وذلك عندما وجدوهم يستخدمون في أشعارهم أساطير قديمة من التراث الإغريقي أو الروماني أو البابلي أو الفرعوني، كما

---

(٣) عزّ الدين إسماعيل، *الشعر العربي المعاصر، قضاياه وظواهره الفنيّة والمعنوية*، بيروت، دار العودة ١٩٨٨، ٤٠.

(٤) Cohen, Jean, *Le haut langage, théorie de la poéticité*, Paris : Flammarion, 1979, 270.

اتهموهم في إسلامهم حين وجدوهم يعرضون لأفكار من التراث الوثني والمسيحي وبخاصة فكرة صلب المسيح أو فكرة الخلاص.»[٥]

وأشار الناقد محمود أمين العالم إلى موقف المفكّر المصري زكي نجيب محمود، وهو موقف لا يخلو من تحامل وتحريض. يقول: «صاغ زكي نجيب محمود بياناً تاريخياً وجّه فيه تهمة إيديولوجية تتمثّل في خروج هذا الشعر على القيم الدينية الإسلامية الثابتة باستخدامه مصطلحات تنتسب إلى ديانات أخرى غير الديانة الإسلامية كالخطيئة والصلب والخلاص.»[٦]

كما استهجنت خالدة سعيد موقف إحسان عبّاس من حضور رمز المسيح في شعر السيّاب، إذ أرجعه إلى رغبة في دخل إضافي من أصحاب مجلة شعر. تقول: «استغرب رأي ناقد بارز كالدكتور إحسان عبّاس في رمز المسيح عند السيّاب... فعودة السيّاب إلى هذا الرمز كان نتيجة اتصاله بمجلة شعر، بل هو وليد رغبة في دخل إضافي (هكذا)... ونرى أن الدكتور إحسان عبّاس لم يؤيّد هذا التفسير بأي دليل بل اكتفى بالشائعات.»[٧]

المسلك الأول:
مسلك النشأة والبيئة الدينية

استهوى الكتاب المقدّس طائفة من الأدباء والشعراء اللّبنانيّين، فأقبلوا على قراءته ووجدوا فيه مادّة لغوية وروحية. ولعل البداية الحقيقية كانت مع جبران خليل جبران. فصلته بالكتاب المقدّس جليّة، وقد عثرنا في مجموعته العربية على إشارات تشي

(٥) عزّ الدين إسماعيل، المرجع السابق، ٣٦.

(٦) أنظر كتاب: *من قضايا الشعر العربي المعاصر (دراسات وشهادات)*، تقديم عزّ الدين إسماعيل، إعداد ريتا عوض، تونس، المنظمة العربية للتربية والثقافة والعلوم ١٩٨٨، ٣٣.

(٧) خالدة سعيد، *حركيّة الإبداع، دراسات في الأدب العربي الحديث*، الطبعة الأولى، بيروت، دار العودة ١٩٧٩، ١٣٦.

باطّلاعه على نواحي مهمة من الأناجيل، ونسوق هذه الأمثلة لندلّل على هذه القراءة، فهناك قرائن جاءت على لسان أبطاله في نصوصه القصصية الأولى:

النص	المجموعة	الصفحة	المثال
يوحنّا المجنون	عرائس المروج	٦٩	« ثم يفتح الخزانة الخشبية ويأتي بكتاب العهد الجديد ويقرأ منه سرّاً على نور مسرجة ضعيفة. »
خليل الكافر	الأرواح المتمرّدة	١٣١	« وأخذت أبيّن لهم أفكاري وأتلو على مسامعهم آيات الكتاب التي تبيّن ضلالهم وكفرهم. »
خليل الكافر	الأرواح المتمرّدة	١٣٤	« فتحت الإنجيل، وقرأت منه بصوت عال هذه الآية: يا أولاد الأفاعي من أراكم أن تهربوا من الغضب الآتي، فاصنعوا أثماراً تليق بالتوبة»
على ملعب الدهر	دمعة وابتسامة	٣٠٩	« تلك الدقيقة كانت مهد نشيد سليمان وموعظة الجبل»
مناجاة أرواح	دمعة وابتسامة	٣٢٧	وردّدت على مسامعي نشيد سليمان ورنّات قيثارة داود.

إن جبران، لم يكتفِ بالإشارة إلى قراءته للكتاب المقدّس، بل وظّفه في طرق الأداء في اختيار الأطر المكانية لنصوصه القصصية، وفي صياغته لتراكيب جمله وفي بنائه لصوره.

فقد نزّل أحداث قصصه في إطار طقوسي (تواتر أمكنة محفوفة بالقداسة كالهيكل والمعبد). ثم إنه حاكى التركيب التوراتي في بناء الجمل، إذ نجد في بداية الجملة ونهايتها ترديداً لما ورد في نشيد الإنشاد أو في المزامير.

أما بالنسبة إلى الصورة الشعرية فيكون المشبّه أو المشبّه به ضارباً في نصوص العهد القديم. وهذه الأمثلة تجلي ما ذكرناه، إذا عقدنا الصلة بين الكتابتين، الكتابة الجبرانية والكتابة التوراتية أو الإنجيلية:

الكتابة الجبرانية	الكتابة التوراتية أو الإنجيلية
- ودخل هيكل عشتروت وأوقد المباخر فتصاعدت روائح المرّ واللُّبان.(٨)	- من هذه الصاعدة من القفر كأعمدة من دخان معطَّرة بالمرّ واللُّبان.(٩)
- باطلة الأباطيل، وكلّ شيء تحت الشمس باطل(١٠)	باطلاً يتعب البنّاؤون... وباطلاً يسهر الحادث الحارس، باطلاً تكدّون من الفجر المبكّر إلى وقت متأخّر من الليل.(١١)
- فجثا على ركبتيه مثلما فعل موسى عندما رأى العلّيقة مشتعلة.(١٢)	- أما موسى فكان يرعى غنم حميه يثرون كاهن مديان... وهناك تجلّى له ملاك الربّ بلهيب نار وسط علّيقة.(١٣)

إن هذا التقليد الجبراني في قراءة الكتاب المقدّس وفي توظيفه في عملية الكتابة، نجد امتداداً له عند شاعر لبناني آخر هو إلياس أبو شبكة. يقول أحد دارسيه: أقبل أبو شبكة على الكتاب المقدّس في عهديه بفعل المدارس التي تعلّم فيها، ثم أدمن قراءته للأدب الرومانسي والجبراني، فإذا رموزه وحكمه وحتى تعابيره تتسم بطابع توراتي إنجيلي.(١٤)

على أن إلياس أبا شبكة تحدّث عن مرجعياته وحدّد الروافد الشعرية والثقافية التي تعامل معها فقال: «ففي أساطير الدهور لفيكتور هيغو عرق طيّب من التّوراة، وفي الفردوس المفقود لملتون وحي مستمد من سفر التكوين، وفي قصيدة لامرتين «سقوط ملاك» المتضمّنة اثني عشر ألفاً من الأبيات وثبات متأثّرة ببعض

---

(٨) جبران خليل جبران، *المجموعة العربية الكاملة*، تقديم و إشراف ميخائيل نعيمة، بيروت، دار صادر ١٩٤٩، ١٣.

(٩) الكتاب المقدّس، نشيد الإنشاد، الإصحاح ٣، الآية ٦.

(١٠) جبران خليل جبران، المرجع نفسه ١٥٣.

(١١) الكتاب المقدّس، المزمور١٢٧، الآيتان ١-٢.

(١٢) جبران خليل جبران، المرجع نفسه ٥٤١.

(١٣) الكتاب المقدس، سفر الخروج، الإصحاح ٣، الآيتان ١- ٢.

(١٤) جميل جبر، *إلياس أبو شبكة شاعر الحب*، الطبعة الأولى ، بيروت، دار الجيل ١٩٩٤، ١٥٠.

فصول من ثنية الاشتراع وسفر الملوك الثالث وبعض فصول من سفر التكوين، وفي مطلع قصيدة «فاوست» لغوته شبه قريب بمطلع سفر أيّوب.»[١٥]

أما الشاعر خليل حاوي، فقد كان تعليمه الديني وملازمته للكتاب المقدّس منذ صباه ولتراتيل الكنيسة جزءاً من تكوينه الأول، وهذا ما وجّه ممارسته الشعرية فيما بعد. يقول إيليّا حاوي: «كانت المعلّمتان تستلاّن الكتاب المقدّس وتأخذان في تلاوة أسفار منه، قصصاً وأناشيد ومزامير... ومعظم المزامير التي حفظها خليل ترجع إلى ذلك العهد الباكر من عمره... كان يحفظها ويتلوها عن ظهر قلب دون فهم لها، إلا أنه حين شبّ كانت تلك المزامير قد ولجت إلى نفسه... وكانت التراتيل تبلغ مسمعه قرب الكنيسة فتسمعها أذناه، وكان يقتبس منها طقوسها وأساليبها.»[١٦]

المسلك الثاني: مسلك التعرّف إلى الكتاب المقدّس أبو القاسم الشابي أُنموذجاً

في رسالة من رسائل محمد الحليوي إلى أبي القاسم الشابي، نجد بداية الاكتشاف للكتاب المقدّس، ونكتشف لذّة التعرّف إلى هذا الكنز الروحي والشعري. ولعل الرسالة وجدت هوى في نفس شاعر تونس الكبير، وهو الباحث عن مسالك جديدة في الكتابة الشعرية، الرافض للمدرسة القديمة في الشعر، نقرأ رسالة الحليوي فنكتشف بهجة من وجد لقيا سعيدة، يقول مخاطباً صديقه: «اشتريت روايات شكسبير كلها مترجمة للغة الفرنسية، وقد طالعت منها لحدّ الآن عطيل وهملت ومكبث، فللّه أي متعة. واشتريت كذلك الكتاب المقدّس وقد جمعت فيه التوراة والأناجيل، ومن كتب التوراة مزامير داود وسفر أيّوب ونشيد الإنشاد لسليمان، وكذلك سفر الجامعة. وكل هاته الأسفار اشتملت على أروع الشعر وأعمق الحكمة،

---

(١٥) إلياس أبو شبكة، *روابط الفكر والروح بين العرب والفرنجة*، الطبعة الثانية ، بيروت، منشورات دار المكشوف ١٨٤٥، ١٠٤.

(١٦) إيليّا حاوي، *مع خليل حاوي في مسيرة حياته وشعره*، لبنان، مؤسسة خليفة للطباعة ١٩٨٦، ٧٢ و١٣٢.

ويكفيك أن تعرف أن كثيراً من الأدب الأوروبي والشعر خاصة مستوحى من هاته الأسفار. ولا شك عندي أن جبران وجماعة المهجر يتغذّون من تلك الكتب. وها إني أنقل لك بعض الكلمات من الإصحاح الأول من سفر الجامعة، ومنه تدرك مقدار العمق في هذا الكتاب... كلام الجامعة ابن داود الملك في أورشليم: باطل الأباطيل قال الجامعة، باطل الأباطيل، الكل باطل.»[١٧]

لا تخلو رسالة محمد الحليوي إلى صفّيه أبي القاسم الشابي من الخصائص التالية:

أنها جاءت حاملة للهجة انبهار وإعجاب بالقيمة الفنية للكتاب المقدّس، فهو اشتمل على أروع الشعر وأعمق الحكمة، وهو كذلك كتاب خيال، خيال افتقده الشابي في نصوص الشعرية العربية القديمة، فوجده الحليوي في نص مقدّس لا ينتسب إلى بيئته الدينية والفكرية.

لقد انتبه إلى الوشائج التي تشدّ الشعر الأوروبي والشعر العربي في المهجر ومن أقطابه جبران إلى الكتاب المقدّس، فهو مفتاح من مفاتيح الشعرية الحديثة، ولا ضير من التفتّح عليه. إنه ردّ صامت على موقف مصطفى صادق الرافعي، أحد ممثّلي التيار المحافظ في الأدب العربي الحديث، إذ هاجم الرافعي جبران فحقّره واستهجن تجربته الإبداعية واتهمها بالانسلاخ عن التراث. معركة ضارية أقطابها المجدّدون ودعاة القدامة، استُخدم فيها الدين سلاحاً عاتياً لإسكات الخصوم أو للنيل منهم. يقول الرافعي: «فإن هذه العربية لغة دين قائم على أصل خالد هو القرآن الكريم، وقد أجمع الأوّلون والآخرون على إعجازه بفصاحته... فانك واجد في أهل سنة ١٩٢٣[١٨] من يقول في هذه اللغة بعينها : لك مذهبك ولي مذهبي... ولك لغتك ولي لغتي... فمتى

---

(١٧) *رسائل أبو القاسم الشّابي*، إعداد محمد الحليوي، طبعة خاصة لوزارة الثقافة، تونس، دار المغرب العربي ١٩٩٤، ٩٠-١٠٦، ورسالة مؤرخة في ١٩٣٢/١٢/١٦.

(١٨) سنة ١٩٢٣ هي تاريخ تصريح جبران لمجلة الهلال المصرية و حديثه عن ضرورة تطوير أساليب اللغة العربية وترك قاموسها القديم الذي فقد كل طاقة إيحائية و شعرية، و هذا الحديث الذي أدلى به جبران لمجلة الهلال صدر بعد ذلك في مقال عنوانه : «مستقبل اللغة العربية» و هذا المقال موجود في كتابه «البدائع و الطرائف» ص ٥٥٤ و ما بعدها.

كنت يا فتى صاحب اللغة وواضعها، ومنزّل أصولها ومخرج فروعها وضابط قواعدها؟». ثم يواصل الرافعي تعريضه بجبران ويصل به الأمر إلى التشكيك في انتمائه الوطني أو القومي: «فهؤلاء المجدّدون وهبوا طبعاً زائفاً في انتحال المدنيّة الأوروبية إلى ما يتخطّى العلل والمقادير...أجازوا إلى فرنسا وإنكلترا. فأقاموا بها مدة، ثم رجعوا إلى بلادهم ومنبتهم ينكرون الميراث العربي بجملته، في لغته وعلومه وآدابه، ويقولون: ما هذا الدين القديم؟ وما هذه اللغة القديمة؟»[١٩]

فهذا الشاهد على طوله – يختزل مرحلة الصراع في أدبنا العربي الحديث، صراع مداره تحديث الخطاب الأدبي وخلفياته مقام اللغة فيه – وجوهرها ديني وتنزيلي عند الرافعي- ومحوره الكبير الموقف من تفتّح شعراء العربية على مرجعيات غير مألوفة، فكان لزاماً تعطيل حركية هذا النسق المرجعي الجديد.

المسلك الثالث:
لحظة الحداثة الثانية أو التفتح على الكتاب المقدّس مع تجربة الشعر الحر.

وقد اخترنا الشاعر العراقي بدر شاكر السيّاب ممثّلاً لهذا المسلك الثالث، فهو الذي ارتبطت تجربته الشعرية بالتحوّل في طرق صياغة القصيدة، وبالتحوّل في مضامينها، وهو الذي وصل إلى رموز الكتاب المقدّس «ومن أهم رموزه المسيح وقايين ولعازر وأيّوب، وستكون لنا معه وقفة طويلة». وقبل ذلك الوصول كان السيّاب قد جاء إلى تجربة إليوت الإبداعية، فتلقّف قصيدته الذائعة الصيت «الأرض الخراب ،»قصيدة عدّها النقد معلماً من معالم الشعر الأوروبي الحديث.[٢٠]

---

(١٩) مصطفى صادق الرافعي، *تحت راية القرآن*، الطبعة الثالثة ، القاهرة، مكتبة الإستقامة ١٩٥٣، ٩ و١٠ و ١٦ و١٩.

(٢٠) من المراجع النقدية التي توقفت عند علاقة شعر السيّاب بالرموز ذات الأصل التوراتي والإنجيلي نذكر:

ا - علي البطل، شبح *قايين بين إيديث سيتول وبدر شاكر السياب (قراءة تحليلية مقارنة)*، الطبعة الأولى ، بيروت، دار الأندلس ١٩٨٤.

كان إليوت (Eliot) قد التفت في قصيدته تلك إلى الأبعاد الدينية والإنسانية التي افتقدها في الحضارة الغربية، فجاء نصه مثقلاً بالرموز الإنجيلية، مشيرا إلى الخطيئة والخلاص وإلى الموعظة على الجبل.(٢١)

لقد اتّحد عند السيّاب عالم الشر القاييني برمز يهوذا الإسخريوطي، التلميذ الذي خان معلّمه وسلّمه إلى الخطاة، وبعجل سيناء في التوراة، كل ذلك ليؤسس لرؤية شعرية ترى العالم ينهض على قيم زائفة. يقول السيّاب في قصيدته «المسيح بعد الصلب» من ديوانه «أنشودة المطر»:

هكذا عدت، فاصفرّ لما رآني يهوذا...
فقد كنت سرّه.
كان ظلاًّ، قد اسودّ مني، وتمثال فكره.
جمّدت فيه، واستلّت الروح منها،
خاف أن تفضح الموت في ماء عينيه.(٢٢)

ففي ديوان أنشودة المطر للسيّاب، لا تنحصر رموز الكتاب المقدّس في النسيج اللغوي للخطاب، وإنما تكون العلامة الأولى في الديوان، فتستقبل قارئها وتثير

ب - نذير العظمة، «بدر شاكر السيّاب والمسيح»، مجلة *الفكر العربي*، (آذار/مارس ١٩٨٢)، عدد ٢٦.

ج - ديزيره سقال، «الأرض الخراب والشعر العربي المعاصر»، مجلة *الفكر العربي المعاصر* (شباط/فبراير ١٩٨١)، عدد ١٠.

(٢١) عبد الواحد لؤلؤة، *الأرض اليباب (الشاعر والقصيدة)*، الطبعة الأولى، بيروت، المؤسّسة العربية للدراسات والنشر ١٩٨٠. وإشارة إليوت إلى الموعظة على الجبل جاء في القسم الثالث من قصيدة «الأرض اليباب»، وهي استحضار لما ورد في إنجيل متى: «وإذ رأى جموع الناس، صعد إلى الجبل، وما إن جلس حتى اقترب إليه تلاميذه، فتكلّم وأخذ يعلمهم» إنجيل متى، الإصحاح ج ٥، الآيتان ١-٢.

(٢٢) بدر شاكر السيّاب، *الأعمال الشعرية الكاملة*، المجلّد الأول، ديوان أنشودة المطر، الطبعة الأولى، بيروت، دار العودة ١٩٨٩، ٤٥٩.

اهتمامه وتوجّه أفق انتظاره منذ العنوان. ولنا قصيدتان على سبيل التمثيل واحدة من ديوان أنشودة المطر وردت تحت عنوان «المسيح بعد الصلب»، والأخرى من ديوان «منزل الأقنان» وردت تحت عنوان «سفر أيّوب». ثم يعود رمز أيّوب، في قصيدة ثالثة بنفس الديوان، عنوانها: «قالوا لأيّوب». فهي عتبة من عتبات القصيدة تصاحبها وتستدرج المتلقي إلى مرجعيات جديدة، قلما تم التفكير فيها.

وقد نجد الإحالة إلى الكتاب المقدّس في الهوامش النثرية التي يثبتها الشاعر في أسفل الصفحات، ودليلنا عل ذلك قصيدة «العودة لجيكور» من ديوان أنشودة المطر:

الشاهد الشعري	الإحالة في الهامش إلى الكتاب المقدّس
على جواد الحلم الأشهب أسريت عبر التلالْ أهرب منها، من ذراها الطوال من سوقها المكتظّ بالبائعين من صبحها المتعب من ليلها النابح والعابرين، من نورها الغيهب، من ربّها المغسول بالخمر، من عارها المخبوء بالزهر، من موتها الساري على النهر	١) كان المسيح في عهده هو الذي مشى على الماء
على جواد الحلم الأشهب وتحت شمس المشرق الأخضر في صيف جيكور السّخي الثري أسريت أطوي دربي النائي بين الندى والزهر والماء أبحث في الآفاق عن كوكب[١]	١) ... وبزغ كوكب عرف منه المجوس أن المخلّص قد وُلد
من الذي يحمل عبء الصليب في ذلك الليل الطويل الرهيب؟	١) وألبسوا المسيح تاجا من الشوك... سخريّة به.

الشاهد الشعري	الإحالة في الهامش إلى الكتاب المقدّس
من الذي يبكي ومن يستجيب للجائع العاري؟ من ينزل المصلوب عن لوحه؟ من يطرد العقبان عن جرحه؟ من يرفع الظلماء عن صبحه؟ ويبدّل الأشواك بالغار؟	

إن هذه الهوامش والمناطق الحافّة بالنصوص لا تخلو من التباس. فهي تقع خارج القصائد، جيء بها لإبراز الذاكرة النصية للمبدع، أو في إطار التباهي بتلك الذاكرة (قدرة الذات الشاعرة على الإلمام بنصوص من خارج ثقافتها أو ديانتها). كما وقع استقدامها في إطار الحوارية مع نص غائب هو نص الأناجيل. ولعل الناقد ميخائيل باختين (Mikhaïl Bakhthine) هو أول من انتبه إلى مبدأ مهم تنبنى عليه النصوص الشعرية والنثرية هو مبدأ الحوارية (le principe dialogique et non pas le principe de dialogique.) إذ يرى أن كل مبدع ينشئ إبداعه في عالم مليء بكتابات الآخرين. ووسط هذا العالم المقدود من كلمات غيره، يريد أن يشقّ طريق التفرّد والابتكار. لكن كل كلمة من كلمات نصوصه لها ذاكرة، إذ تسكنها أصوات من كتابات أخرى تظهر على أديم الخطاب، وقد تتوارى فيتم التكتّم عنها. وقد تستفزّ القارئ فيسعى إلى أن يسدّ النقص، أو هذا البتر الماثل في القصيدة، فتردّه تلك الإحالات في الهوامش إلى النص الغائب أي إلى الأناجيل. وهو ما قمنا به، فوضعنا أمام كل هامش ما يناسبه من موطن نصي في الأناجيل:

الهامش في قصيدة السيّاب	ما يناسبه في الأناجيل
١) كان المسيح في عهده هو الذي مشى على الماء	« وهبّت عاصفة قويّة، فاضطربت البحيرة وبعدما جذّف التلاميذ نحو ثلاثة أميال أو أربعة، رأوا يسوع يقترب من القارب ماشياً على ماء البحيرة فاستولى عليهم الخوف. » إنجيل يوحنّا، إ ٦ آ ١٨ و١٩.
٢) وبزغ كوكب عرف منه المجوس أن المخلّص قد وُلد	« وبعد ما وُلد يسوع في بيت لحم الواقعة في منطقة اليهوديّة، على عهد الملك هيرودوس، جاء إلى أورشليم بعض المجوس القادمين من الشرق، يسألون: أين هو المولود ملك اليهود؟ فقد رأينا نجمه طالعاً في الشرق، فجئنا لنسجد له. » إنجيل متّى، إ ٢ آ ١و٢.
وألبسوا المسيح تاجاً من الشوك سخريّة به	فاقتاد جنود الحاكم يسوع إلى دار الحكومة وجمعوا عليه جنود الكتيبة كلها فجرّدوه من ثيابه وألبسوه رداءاً قرمزياً، وجدلوا إكليلاً من الشوك وضعوه على رأسه. ووضعوا قصبة في يده اليمنى، وركعوا أمامه يسخرون منه، وهم يقولون: « سلام يا ملك اليهود» إنجيل متّى إ ٢٧ آ ٢٧-٢٨-٢٩

أ – في تعريف مصطلح اللعب

ذهب ميشال بيكار (Michel Picard) إلى أن اللعب (le jeu) مثّل الجانب المكبوت في الدراسات الأدبية الحديثة ، إذ لم ينتبه أقطاب النّقد البنيوي والنقد الجديد إلى قيمة اللعب، فظلّ المصطلح مهملاً لا يؤبه به ولم ينل قيمة تذكر.

إن اللعب نسق جديد ينضاف إلى الأنساق الكبرى الرائجة في الغرب : النسق التأويلي والنسق البنيوي والنسق المعرفي.[٢٣] على أن مصطلح اللعب ظلّ ملتبساً وغائماً تتنازعه حقول معرفية شتى. فهو ينتمي إلى حقل التحليل النفسي (فرويد

---

(٢٣) Picard, Michel, *La lecture comme jeu*, Paris: Minuit, 1986, 153.

وبرغسون)، وانكبّ عليه عالم لساني هو إيميل بنفنيست (Emile Benveniste)[٢٤] ثم إنه شاع في أعمال دارسين اشتغلوا على النص الديني.[٢٥] لقد قرأ هؤلاء الباحثون الحداثة قراءة نقدية، فرأوا فيها جهداً صناعياً مادياً ينهض على سطوة المؤسسات ويميل الى التقنين ونشر قيم الإستهلاك التي تعطّل الأبعاد الأخرى في الإنسان، فتعمد الى طمسها و تلاشيها و ضياعها.

ولعل أهم ضياع تمثّل في ضياع هويّة الإنسان الأول هويّته ككائن لاعب. ولا يكون اللعب نقيضاً للجدّ، وإنما هو بعد آخر قد يتعارض والواقع أو قد يؤسس قواعد لواقع بديل. وتقترب مقولة اللعب من الشعر: فالنص الشعري وليد لعبة فنية أجاد الشاعر حبك قوانينها وصياغة موضوعاتها، لعبة تنوس بين الخفاء والتجلي، فلا قراءة جادّة دون فهم قوانين تلك اللعبة.

ب - مصطلح اللعب ومنعطف ما بعد الحداثة

رام ميشال بيكار وهو يحلّل ظاهرة اللعب تنزيلَ هذه الظاهرة في أعمال فرويد (Freud) ونيتشه (Nietzsche) وكافكا (Kafka) وبريتون (Breton). لقد أبرز فرويد قيمة اللعب (le jeu, le ludique) وأضاف إليها نيتشه قيمة الضحك (le rire). فكانت النصوص الإبداعية اللاعبة و الضاحكة فاتحة للون أدبي جديد، أدب يكتب خارج المؤسسات، ويتمرّد على كل الأنساق والأعراف، فهو كيان مارق ومتمرّد. كتابة خارج مؤسسة الأدب، كتابة تحتفي بالمكبوت والممنوع والمحظور، تفلت من كل رقابة وتستبيح الموانع. إن التاريخ الأدبي المعاصر جاء خالياً من اللعب، وحتى القراءات البنيويّة العالمة وهي تتصنّع الموضوعية في مقاربة النصوص لم تنسق الى ممارسة

(٢٤) Benveniste, Emile, « Le jeu comme structure », *Cahiers de philosophie* (1947), n° 2,

(٢٥) Sarrazin, Bernard, *Le rire et le secret*, Paris : Gallimard, 1991; Caillois, Roger, *L'homme et le sacré*, Paris : Gallimard, 1948; De Certeau, Michel, « La lecture un braconnage » in: idem, *L'invention du quotidien*, Paris : Éd. 10/18, 1980.

اللعب، لهذا أدخلت الضيم على تلك النصوص فحوّلتها إلى جثث هامدة يتم تشريحها بطريقة آلية، دون متعة أو رغبة. فتلك القراءات العالمة والجافّة حرمتنا من ضربين من اللعب :

- اللعب الفنّي مع النصوص، وهو الذي يستفز العاطفة والذوق والفكر والوجدان.
- اللعب الجسدي، إذ إننا نوظّف حواسّنا للوقوف عند الشواهد ، نقرأ الشاهد الذي يستوقف أولاً حاسّة البصر، نرصد الكلام المؤطّر بين قرائن طباعية، وما تلك القرائن المادية إلاّ إيقاعات بصرية موصولة بلعبة الكتابة وقادحة للعبة القراءة.(٢٦)

هكذا يضحي اللعب في القصيدة ضرباً من ضروب الجدّ، عزم على التشكيل الفني للنص الشعري، وقدرة على إخراجه إخراجاً بصريا، واستدراج للقارئ حتى يمارس لعبة التفكيك والتهشيم قبل أن يدرك مرتبة التأليف والتركيب والبناء للمتشظّي.

ج – اللعب والنظرية الجديدة للنص

لقد ميّز ميشال بيكار في مصنّفه «القراءة باعتبارها لعباً» (La lecture comme jeu) بين صنفين من النصوص :

I. النصوص المتجهّمة التي تروّج لمعنى واحد ويتيم، فهي نصوص فقيرة مجالها الدلالة (la signification)، تجيء طاقتها الإبداعية ضامرة ومحدودة، وهذا النوع من النصوص أفرزته المؤسسات (مثّل على ذلك بالنص الديني الذي تحتكره المؤسسة فتحتكر فهمه وتفسيره وتأويله وتراقب طرق تلقّيه)، ولا تقدّم المؤسسة لهذا النوع من النصوص سوى جواب واحد يختزل الكثرة ويرجعها إلى الواحد.

---

(٢٦) Compagnon, Antoine, *La seconde main ou le travail de citation*, Paris : Seuil 1979, 106.

II. النصوص الشبكية وهي نصوص التدلال (la signifiance). يعود الفضل في بلورة هذا المصطلح إلى جوليا كريستيفا (Julia Kristeva)، إذ النص لم يعد منتوجاً (un produit) بل هو إنتاجية (une productivité)، فهو مقدود من الكثرة، مليء بالدلالة، وطافح بأبعاد المعنى. إن لعبة إنتاج المعنى لا تتوقّف ولا يدركها فتور، وكذلك لعبة تلقّيه. فالنص الشعري بين شدّ وجذب، دلالة غزيرة ينوء بها نسيج الخطاب، وقابلية لشتى القراءات يحقّقها مطلق القرّاء دون أن يحدث ذلك نزيفاً دلالياً. لقد انتهت القراءة التقليدية الى مأزق عندما بحثت عن أحادية الدلالة فإذا بها تنخرط في لعبة قدرية (un jeu fataliste) يرغَم فيها القارئ على استهلاك ما يراد له، فيكون مسلوب الإرادة لا يضيف و لا يتعاطى تعاطياً إيجابياً مع النصوص.

أما القراءة التي تمارس اللعب، فهي صيد محظور للمعنى (lire c'est braconner le sens) كما يرى ميشال دوسرتو (Michel de Certeau). والقارئ اللاعب هو الذي يقوم بتكميل الخطاب الشعري المليء بالثقوب والثغرات، يترجم مواطن البياض والصمت إلى دلالة حيّة، فإذا بقراءته لعبة هادفة تبتعد عن البراءة، تحوّل فراغ القصيدة الى مناطق آهلة بالدلالة (des zones textuelles signifiantes). فإدراج مقولة اللعب في عملية القراءة أمر لا يخلو من رمزية الردّ على حداثة فقدت إنسانيتها، حداثة قنّنت الإنسان وشدّته إلى أنساق نمطية جامدة. فلا خلاص إلا بتكسير صلابة تلك الأنساق، وبتخطّي طابعها الإلزامي والإكراهي (سيّما الأنساق المنغلقة التي تروّج لمعنى واحد أو لفكر واحد).

د – اللعب من جهة القارئ

كانت غاية ميشال بيكار رسم صورة جديدة للقارئ، قارئ مستقلّ (un lecteur autonome) يتحرّر من جبروت السلطة النقدية، يلعب بالمطلقات والنواميس

الجافّة والمسطّرة، ينظر إلى الخطاب الشعري بعيني طفل. لأن الشعر نظر إلى العالم بعيني البراءة الأولى، قبل ظهور الفكر المفسّر، وهو أمر لم يغب عن أقطاب المدرسة الرومنطيقية، فعدّت الشعر خطاب بدايات انبثق منذ فجر الوجود حتى كأن الإنسان الأول ولد مزوّداً بغريزة الشعر.

إن هذا القارئ كما أسلفنا يسعى إلى ضربين من اللعب:

I. اللعب المادّي: وفيه أو به يكتشف لعب الشاعر بالكلمات (le jeu de mots)، لعبه بالإيقاع ثم لعبه بالصورة. هذا اللعب يجعل الصورة الشعرية متجدّدة لا تجاعيد فيها (une image sans rides). لذا كانت المباشرة الأولى للنص مباشرة حسّية تفتن بملموس العلامة اللغوية، و تصغي إلى وقع الأصوات وجرسها، إلى الشعر الذي يقرع الأسماع قبل الأفهام. وإن هذا الضرب من التلقّي/اللعب، فضلاً عن بعده عن التجريد يحدث عقداً ضمنياً بين سلطتين، سلطة النص في صلابتها وانغلاقها وتأبّيها على القارئ، وسلطة القارئ اللاعب الذي يخلخل أركان الكيانات النصية ويجعلها تلين فتُستدرج بدورها الى لعبة القراءة.

II. اللعب الفكري: وهو لعب يحرّرنا من الخوف، فلا يخشى الشاعر مرجعية الشواهد الدينية، بل يخضعها إلى رهانه الجمالي، يجرّدها من قداستها، ويخرجها من السياجات ليدفعها دفعاً إلى عالم القصيدة، كأنه يعيد كتابتها من جديد. هذا اللعب بالشواهد ذات الأصول التوراتية والإنجيلية عند يوسف الخال مؤشّر على نزع القداسة عن تلك الشواهد، إنه ضرب من البلبلة وسعي إلى التخليط والمزج بين نصوص غائبة تستدعى ويُعاد تشغيل مقاطع منها، وأخرى حاضرة تحتضن تلك الشواهد وتعمد إلى تحويلها والعدول بها. إن اللعب تأسيس لزمن شعري جديد، زمن يجرّد النصوص من القداسة.(٢٧)

و يمكن أن نعدّ النص الشعري الذي كُتب في سياق الحداثة نصاً شيطانياً (un texte diabolique)، يستعير من سفر التكوين قصة بابل القديمة، بابل التي عوقبت

---

(٢٧) Picard, Michel, « Le jeu est une opération désacralisante », *La lecture comme jeu*, 28.

بـبلبلة الألـسن. والبلـبلة لم تـعد عقـاباً وإنما هي سمـة فنيـة، تـجعل القـصيدة (أو للقصيدة) مستويات لغوية متداخلة، وضروباً إيقاعيـة شـتى تـجمع بـين إيقـاع وزني تـقليدي وإيقاع صوتي وإيقاع بـصري، وتنشئ صورة لا تـمنحك النظر إلى المعنى (l'image qui ne donne pas à voir)، وإنما صورة محفوفـة بـالغموض واللبس، ممهورة بالأضداد والمناقضات.(٢٨)

هـ – اللعب و الموقف من المعنى في الشعر الحديث

لاحظ أحد مؤسـسي نـظرية جماليـة التلقّي أن مـسألة المعنى في الخطـاب الـشعري الحديث تـرتبط بـمقوّم الغمـوض. ذلك أن الـنص الـشعري الحديث بـسيط العبـارة معقّـد الدلالة، وكأن مـن غـايات القـصيدة تـخييب انتظـار القـارئ ومفاجأتـه ثـم مباغتته.(٢٩)

فالغموض كثافة في الدلالة، وهو تـرك للوضوح والشفافية وملء القصيدة بـالإيحاء والإحتمال. لقـد نـعت الـشاعر الفرنـسي سـتيفان مـالارمي (Stéphane Mallarmé) بـالـشاعر الغـامض والـصعب، لأن فـضاء القـصيدة عنـده فـضاء إمـكانات دلاليـة لا تـتوقّف عـن بـثّ المعنى، فصُنّفت تـلك القـصيدة ضمن النـصوص المختلةأو الغير المنتظمة من منظور الجمالية الكلاسيكية.

إن المعنى الـشعري الغـامض يكـسب اللعبـة الفنيـة أبعـاداً أخـرى، إذ إن عمليـة تـأويل الدلالة تـعطيها فـضاءً يـحقّق فيه المؤول ذاتـه ويفـرض «أناه» رغم استعصاء النص وتمنّعه.(٣٠)

---

(٢٨) Caillois, Roger, *Babel, orgueil, confusion et ruine de la littérature,* Paris : Gallimard, 1948, 186.

(٢٩) Jauss, Hans Robert, *Pour une herméneutique littéraire,* Paris : Gallimard, 1982.

(٣٠) أحدث ميشال بيكار تـناغماً صوتياً بين كلمتي: le jeu et le je، و كان هذا اللعب اللفظي موحياً بوظيفة تـأويل النصوص : امتلاك المعنى وفهمه قصد فرض الذات القارئة، فتكون بـذلك سلطة ثـانية موازية لسلطة المبدع (انظر الصفحة ٢٤ من كتابه).

إن ممارسة اللعب مع النصوص الصعبة والعصيّة تتضمّن سعياً الى إزالة الإغتراب، إغتراب شخصية القارئ عن اللغة والمعنى. ويلي ذلك سعي ثان إلى تجميع المعاني المشتّتة (les sens disséminés)، وهذا التشرّد الدلالي صنو لتشرّد الشواهد في النص الشعري الحديث. فهي شذرات نصية و بقايا من خطابات قديمة انفصلت عن سياقاتها وحلّت في سياقات جديدة، فمرّت من الغياب إلى الحضور ومن التشتّت إلى التجمع. فإذا بالمعاني المتشظّية والشواهد المتفرّقة تصهر في رؤية جديدة، فيتحوّل اللعب بها من مجرد لهو ومتعة إلى ظاهرة جادّة تقطع مع النظريات التي استسهلت أمر اللعب فعدّته ظاهرة مجانية لا تستحق البحث والدراسة.

و – اللعب بالشاهد الإنجيلي عند يوسف الخال

يرتبط مفهوم الشاهد الأدبي بالممارسة النصية وبعملية الكتابة، ذلك أنه لا يحضر إلا في حيّز نصي فيتخذ قرائن شكلية، و يجيء محفوفاً بمؤشّرات طباعية دالّة عليه (لعبة الظفرين ولعبة الأقواس في الخطاب الشعري الحديث).[٣١]

ولقد أدرج انطوان كمبنيون للشاهد الأدبي ضربين من الاستعارة:

- إستعارة اللعب (La métaphore du jeu).
- إستعارة الجراحة (La métaphore de la chirurgie).

فالشاعر الذي يشغّل في قصيدته شواهد هو في الأصل طفل لاعب يمارس عملية القصّ والاقتطاع، ويقوم بإلصاق تلك الفسيفساء من الشواهد. وهذا الإلصاق (collage) زرع (une greffe) لملفوظات قديمة في نص جديد، زرع ينمّ عن تمثّل لنصوص الثقافة السابقة وعن تعامل خلاق معها. بل إن الشاهد في النص الأدبي أعاد إحياء مؤسسة المؤلّف بعد أن أعلنت البنيوية موته، فمجرد الاستشهاد بأقوال، ينطوي على اعتراف ضمني أو صريح بصاحب تلك الأقوال وبمنتجها، رغم

---

(٣١) Compagnon , Antoine, *La seconde main ou le travail de citation*, Paris : Seuil, 1979, 10.

سعي الكتابة الشعرية الحديثة إلى تقنية المحو والتكتّم، إذ هي تعمّي في الغالب على مرجعياتها، فتزيل آثار (les traces) النصوص القديمة من فضائها في إطار الإيهام بلعبة التفرّد والنبوغ والاختصاص بالإضافة والتجديد. ولقد عدل الناقد السوفياتي ميخائيل باختين عن هذا التوهّم والإيهام، فنزل الشاهد الأدبي ضمن التبادل اللفظي بين النصوص. فالشاهد الأدبي كلام الآخرين (la parole d'autrui) وقد حلّ في النصوص المنجزة، فهو أمارة على الغيرية في العملية الإبداعية برمتها، ذلك أن الكاتب أو الشاعر يكتب في عالم مقدود من كلام الآخرين، يتمثل ذلك الكلام ويحوّله إلى نصوصه. وهذا الكلام المحوَّل والمستحلب يحمل سمتين فنيتين مختلفتين:

أ - وفاؤه لرؤية الخطاب الأول الأصلي.

ب - قابليته لاحتضان رؤية جديدة يرغمه المؤلف على حملها، فهو كيان لفظي مطواع ومرن ينصهر في السياق النصي الجديد الذي يستضيفه.(٣٢)

لعل اللعب بالشواهد في نصوص الحداثة الشعرية مردّه إلى جعل تلك الشواهد تقبل الإنخراط في لعبة نصية جديدة، بعد أن استُهلكت في لعبة نصية قديمة، وهذا يكسبها حركية و مقدرة على الترحال والتشرّد، فتهاجر من كيان نصي الى كيان آخر، وفي مسار هجرتها تخضع إلى تحويل وتبديل. ها هنا تتقلّص ظاهرة الغيرية، فإزالة القرائن الطباعية وحذف المؤشرات الدالّة على الأخذ والإكتفاء بالتلميح، هو ضرب من تقليص المسافة بين النصوص. إذ الشاهد المؤطّر بين ظفرين والمحفوف بالمؤشرات الطباعية يتمسّك باستقلاليته عن النص الذي يحضر فيه، يعلن نقاوة أصله وجذره قبل أن يعمد الخطاب الشعري الحديث إلى عملية المزج والتداخل محدثاً تهجيناً لغوياً (un métissage linguistique) أقرب الى بلبلة الألسن واختلاطها.

---

(٣٢) Bakhtine, Mikhaïl, *Esthétique de la création verbale,* traduit du Russe par Alfreda Aucouturter, préface de Tzvetan Todorov, Paris : Gallimard, 1982, 300.

ز – يوسف الخال و إفساد اللعب

إن أقوال المسيح في قصائد يوسف الخال[٣٣] جملة ملفوظات وشواهد ترتسم على أديم القصيدة وسطحها، شواهد اقتطعها الشاعر من الأناجيل ثم قام بإلصاقها وزرعها من جديد. والقارئ المتمعّن للمتن الشعري عند يوسف الخال يقف على درجة التواتر لتلك الشواهد. إذ شاعت في مجموعتيه «البئر المهجورة» و« قصائد في الأربعين»، فخضعت إلى المعاودة و الترديد، ترديد يشي بكفاءة الشاعر في تمثيل تلك الشواهد وبحذقه لقانون اللعبة النصية، وبمقدرته على تطبيق قواعدها والالتزام بشروطها.[٣٤]

و لقد استبان لنا ضربان من اللعب مارسهما يوسف الخال وهو يعيد تنشيط شواهده الإنجيلية :

أ - اللعب مع تلك الشواهد (jouer avec les citations)، إذ يقوم النص الشعري بترديد تلك الشواهد. وعندها يتخلّى الشاعر عن صوته ليفسح المجال لصوت المسيح، فلا يدّعي امتلاك هذا الصوت الذي يحافظ على نقاوة جذوره، ولا يلتبس في الظاهر بجوهر القصيدة، ولا يقدر الشاعر على تدجينه وسلب ملامحه. فإذا بصوت المسيح المتكلّم سلطة ثانية في القصيدة توازي سلطة الشاعر المتلفّظ. ولنا مثالان شعريان يدلاّن على ذلك:

---

(٣٣) اعتمادنا هنا على قصائد يوسف الخال الواردة بأعماله الشعرية الكاملة، طبعة دار العودة، بيروت ١٩٩٧.

(٣٤) Picard, Michel, *La lecture comme jeu*, 246.

القصيدة	المجموعة الشعرية و الصفحة	الشاهد الشعري	الصلابة الطباعية	المرجع النص من الأناجيل
الدارة السوداء	البئر المهجورة ص ٢٠١	أتراني أهجر الدار وأمضي ؛ « يدفن الأموات موتاهم » وأمضي ؟	استخدام الظفرين	و قال له آخر من تلاميذه اسمح لي أولاً فأدفن أبي. فأجابه يسوع: دع الموتى يدفنون موتاهم(٣٥)
Mémento more	البئر المهجورة ص ٢١٥	خلني أمشي على الماء قليلا«، » مدّ لي يا ربّ شطآن خلاصي	استخدام الظفرين	و في الربع الأخير من الليل جاء يسوع الى التلاميذ ماشياً على ماء البحيرة، فلما رآه التلاميذ ماشياً على الماء، اضطربوا قائلين « إنه شبح».(٣٦)

إن اللعب مع الشاهد الإنجيلي في نصوص يوسف الخال الشعرية قد حقّق جملة من الوظائف:

I. وظيفة التناصّ التي تشير الى اللقاء الصريح و المعلن بين يوسف الخال، أحد مؤسسي الحداثة الشعرية، ومرجعية إنجيلية تنتسب إلى فضاء القداسة. ويكون رهان اللعبة الشعرية ممثلاً في الوفاء للنسق المرجعي والسعي إلى تحويله في آن.

II. تحقيق عودة المسيح ورجعته، فهو الرمز الجامع عند يوسف الخال، يحدث بالقصيدة كوّة نصية يطل منها ويرتفع صوته، صوت النبوّة عند شعراء الحداثة، فيصنع في رؤية الخال فرح الكيان، ويحصّن نص القصيدة عن الجدب والقحط ، إذ يجيء محمّلاً بالعطايا المادية والروحية :

(٣٥) إنجيل متى، إصحاح ٨، الآيتان ٢١-٢٢.

(٣٦) إنجيل متى، إصحاح ١٤، الآيتان ٢٥-٢٦.

غداً يعود سيدي.
محمّلا بالذهب،
بفضّة تصاغ للهياكل
محمّلا يعود سيدي
بالعاج صولجان ملك، سريره
محمّلا يعود سيدي
بالشوق لي والأمل.(٣٧)

III. التجاوب بين أطراف العملية التواصلية أو بين أطراف اللعبة الفنية: الشاعر باعتباره منتج الخطاب وصاحبه، والمسيح الرمز الجامع والناطق في قصائد يوسف الخال، والقارئ باعتباره سلطة تفهم قوانين اللعبة الفنية فتمارسها أثناء عملية التفكيك و التأويل.

ب- اللعب ضد الشواهد (jouer contre les citations) ونعني به مقدرة الشاعر على طمس ملامح الصوت المستدعى، فتذوب الفواصل بين صوت الشاعر وصوت المسيح وتزول الحدود بينهما، فيندمج الصوتان ويتوحّدان. عندها تجيء أقوال المسيح عارية من القرائن الطباعية. يمحي مؤشر الظفرين وتتلاشى الأقواس. ولعل ظهور الكتابة الشعرية الجديدة في مجلّة «شعر» أسهم في بلورة تجربة التخوم (l'expérience des limites)، فإذا بالنص الشعري فضاء تحضر في تلاوينه ملفوظات من نصوص أخرى، يتكتّم الشاعر عن مرجعيتها فيعوّل على كفاءة القارئ. ونسوق ثلاثة أمثلة شعرية للاستدلال على ذلك:

(٣٧) يوسف الخال، *الأعمال الشعرية الكاملة*، مجموعة البئر المهجورة، قصيدة العودة ٢٣٦-٢٣٧.

القصيدة	المجموعة الشعرية والصفحة	الشاهد الشعري	المؤشّر الطباعي	المرجع النص في الأناجيل
العشاء الأخير	قصائد في الأربعين ص ٢٨٠	وعند صياح الديك، قليلون سيشهدون لملكوت الأرض	غياب الظفرين	« و لكن بطرس قال: ولو شكّ الجميع فأنا لن أشكّ. فقال له يسوع : إنك اليوم في هذه الليلة قبل أن يصيح الديك مرّتين تكون قد أنكرتني ثلاث مرات.(٣٨)
القصيدة الطويلة	قصائد في الأربعين ص ٢٨٨	وهاهم الباعة ملأوا رحاب الهيكل	دون مؤشّر طباعي	وقال لبائعي الحمام « أخرجوا هذه من هنا. لا تجعلوا بيت أبي بيتا للتجارة».(٣٩)
التوبة	قصائد في الأربعين ص ٢٩٦	متى يا أبي ستعبر كأسي متى يا أبي سأهبط دربي	دون مؤشّر طباعي	« ثم ابتعد قليلاً وخرّ على الأرض وأخذ يصلّي لكي تعبر عنه الساعة إن كان ممكناً وقال: « يا أبي كل شئ مستطاع لديك فأبعد عني هذه الكأس».(٤٠)

إن هذا الضرب من اللعب ينشئ في قصائد الخال حوارية الأصوات والنصوص، مما يكسب القصيدة طابعها المتعدد. فالمتلفّظ في النص الشعري ذو صوت مركّب. إذ يصغي القارئ إلى صوت المسيح من خلال صوت الشاعر. وبذلك لا يغيب الرمز

---

(٣٨) إنجيل مرقس، إصحاح ١٤، الآيتان٢٩ و٣٠.

(٣٩) إنجيل يوحنا، إصحاح ٢٢، آية ١٦.

(٤٠) إنجيل مرقس، إصحاح ١٩، الآيتان ٣٥ و ٣٦.

غياباً كلياً، فهو منخرط في لعبة الغياب والحضور، صوت نبوي قديم يسكن خطاب قصيدة حاملة سمة الحداثة. إن هذا الصوت/الشاهد الذي لا تحفّ به قرائن طباعية، يقدح فينا لذة التعرّف ومتعة الاكتشاف. فيمسك بمآتيه ومنابته، ويقدر حضوره النصي وفاعليته في صنع شعرية القصيدة.

و لعل فحص القواميس الشعرية في قصائد يوسف الخال يقودنا إلى ظاهرة التنوّع فيها. ففي قصيدة «العشاء الأخير» من مجموعة «قصائد في الأربعين»، يقترح علينا العنوان سجلاً لغوياً مشتركاً سرعان ما نتخلّى عنه لننخرط في السجل اللّغوي للأناجيل.

يقول يوسف الخال :

لنا الخمر و الخبز
و ليس معنا المعلم
جراحنا نهر من الفضة(٤١)

إذا ما اكتفينا بالدلالة الأولى لألفاظ العشاء والخمر والخبز، نتلف جمالية الخطاب الشعري ونعصف بطاقته الإيحائية. فهذا القاموس الشعري يسلمنا الى مشهد بدئي رسمته الأناجيل الأربعة، مشهد العشاء الربّاني: ولما جاءت الساعة اتّكأ ومعه الرسل، وقال لهم :«اشتهيت أن آكل الفصح معكم ، قبل أن أتألّم. فإني أقول لكم: لن آكل منه بعد حتى يتحقّق في ملكوت الله... ».(٤٢)

فشواهد المسيح المستدعاة جملة من الألفاظ والمقاطع قيلت في سياق ديني (العشاء الربّاني الذي يلتقي فيه المسيح بخاصّته و يودعهم تعاليمه الأخيرة). إلا أن الشاعر قام بإبدال ذلك السجل، فالخبز لم يعد طعاماً مادياً بل هو تعاليم روحية

---

(٤١) أنظر قصيدة «العشاء الأخير» المأخوذة من مجموعته الشعرية «قصائد في الأربعين» من *الأعمال الشعرية الكاملة* ليوسف الخال ، ٢٧٩.

(٤٢) إنجيل لوقا، إصحاح ٢٢، الآيات ١٤-٢٠.

يلتهمها التلاميذ، والخمر دم المسيح المسفوك على الصليب وهو الحقيقة المصلوبة في دلالة ثانية، والعشاء إطار مادي وفضاء روحي فيه يفرغ المسيح ذاته ويجعل أقواله تنفصل عنه ليمتلئ به الحواريون.

إن قصيدة «العشاء الأخير» ليوسف الخال نسخة معدّلة من العشاء الربّاني في الأناجيل، فيها تمارَس لعبة التحوير والتبديل والانتهاك، فيحدث حوار صامت بين نص القداسة و نص الحداثة الشعرية.

وتنهض الظاهرة الإيقاعية في قصيدة «التوبة» بوظائف متكثّرة تمارس علينا لعبة الإيهام .فالقصيدة في مجموعة شعرية كتب فيها يوسف الخال قصيدة النثر، إلا أن الناظر في نظامها الإيقاعي يكتشف خضوعها للقالب الوزني، فتفعيلاتها جاءت على بحر المتقارب:

على جبل الصمت ، في موعدي
مع التآئبين ، رفعت جبيني
(ذراعاي مشدودتان الى صخرة)
متى يا أبي ستعبر كأسي(٤٣)

وينهض الإيقاع البصري على مخاتلة ثانية، إذ تغيب قرائن الاستفهام لينشئ الأسلوب الإنشائي سياقاً ابتهالياً يستعيد الشاعر فيه وبه ترانيم المسيح الأخيرة وهو يدخل في التجربة، تجربة ضيق يعيشها النبي المتألّم. إن هذا الضرب من الإيقاع والترنيم والتنغيم يشبع الخطاب الشعري بنغمة حزينة ومتكسّرة، هو إيقاع التجربة الإنسانية، تجربة العذاب والألم الهاجعة في الأناجيل والممتدّة إلى حاضر الحداثة. وهكذا يختار يوسف الخال من سيرة المسيح نهايتها فلا يتولّى سرد فصول وشذرات منها لنمذجة الرمز وللارتقاء به، بل يجعل من شخصية المسيح معادلاً موضوعياً

---

(٤٣) أنظر قصيدة «التوبة» ضمن *الأعمال الشعرية الكاملة* ليوسف الخال ، مجموعة قصائد في الأربعين ٢٩٦.

للشاعر الحديث، فيتوحّد الذاتي بالموضوعي والكوني. فإذا بالتجربة، تجربة الصلب وهي ملموسة وحيّة وقعت أحداثها قبل كتابة القصيدة، تزخر بالرموز فتحوز طابعاً شمولياً و كونياً يحقّق لها الخلود.

الترانيم الإنجيلية والأشكال الحديثة في الشعر العربي

أديب صعب

I. أشكال الشعر العربي

إن بحثنا هذا يتناول الشكل الموسيقي أو النغمي للشعر العربي. لذلك هو يشمل الشعر الموزون الذي تضيف القافية، في حال وجودها، إلى نغمه. لكنه يَستثني على الفور أي كتابة قد تصنَّف في عداد الشعر وهي خارج الوزن. ومن هذا القبيل ما يسمى «الشعر المنثور» أو «قصيدة النثر». ويقع الشعر العربي الموزون تحت ثلاثة أشكال رئيسية تنتمي إلى تطوّره الزمني، من غير أن يلغي الشكلُ الطارئُ ما سبقه أو يحل محلّه. هذه الأشكال هي: (١) الشعر العمودي، (٢) الموشَّح، (٣) شعر التفعيلة.

الشعر العمودي أو شعر البيت هو أقدم الأشكال المعروفة. وهو عمودي نسبةً إلى ما اصطلح النقاد الأوائل على تسميته «عمود الشعر» أو عماده أو شروطه أو معاييره، وأبرزها وحدة الوزن. فالقصيدة العربية التقليدية، منذ الجاهلية حتى اليوم، تجري كلها على وزن واحد في أحد أشكاله الرئيسية أو مجزوءاته. وما فعله الخليل بن أحمد (ت. ٧٨٦)[١]، واضع علم العروض، أي أوزان الشعر، كان تصنيف الأوزان وضبط مصطلح لعلمها وتحرّي مقاييس الصحة والخطأ فيها وتجزيء بيت الشعر في كل وزن إلى وحداته الموسيقية أو تفاعيله. فالوزن أو البحر البسيط، مثلاً، في أحد أشكاله الرئيسية، مؤلف من: مستفعلن فاعلن مستفعلن فَعِلن، مكرَّرةً في شطرَي البيت، أي صدره وعجزه. والطويل، في أحد أشكاله الرئيسية، مؤلف من: فعولن مفاعيلن فعولن مفاعلن. والمتقارِب من: فعولن فعولن فعولن فعولن. والسريع

---

(١) التاريخ المذكور بعد أسماء الأشخاص في هذه الدراسة هو سنة الوفاة، إلا عندما يُشار إلى تاريخَي الولادة والوفاة. والتواريخ كلها ميلادية.

من: مستفعلن مستفعلن فاعلن. والرمَل من: فاعلاتن فاعلاتن فاعلن. والكامل من: متفاعلن متفاعلن متفاعلن. وهكذا بالنسبة إلى كل الأوزان، وهي ستة عشر وزناً، في مختلف أشكالها التامّة ومجزوءاتها.

ومنذ أقدم عصور الشعر العربي، نقع على قصائد أو مقاطع رائعة من الشعر العمودي[٢]، ما يزال الكثير منها يتمتع بصفة المعاصَرة لتعبيره عن هموم الانسان واهتماماته الأزلية التي لا تتبدل بتبدل الزمان والمكان. ولا يتمالك القارئ المرهف إلا أن يقول حيال أي من هذه الروائع: «هذا هو الشعر». وفي كثير من الأحيان يكفي بيت واحد تعبيراً عن هذه الروعة، كما في قول المعرّي (على الكامل): أنا صائمٌ طولَ الحياةِ، وإنّما / فِطْري الحِمامُ، وبَعد ذاكَ أُعَيِّدُ. أو كما في قوله أيضاً (على معْتَلّ المديد): شَرُّ أشجارٍ علمْتُ بها / شَجَراتٌ أثمرتْ ناسا. أو كما في قول أبي نواس (على السريع): أُضْمِرُ في البعد عتاباً له، / فإنْ دَنا أُنْسيتُ من هَيْبَتِهْ. أو كما في قول الأخطل الصغير (على الخفيف): كلُّنا ناحلٌ: فأنتَ بَراكَ / اللهُ، لكنْ أنا بَراني السقامُ. أو كما في قول نزار قبّاني (على المتدارَك): فأنا لا أملكُ في الدنيا / إلا عينيكِ وأحزاني. أو كما في قول المتنبّي (على البسيط): أتى الزمانَ بنوهُ في شبيبتهِ / فسَرَّهم، وأتيناهُ على الهَرَمِ. أو كما في قوله أيضاً (على الطويل): كفى بكَ داءً أن ترى الموتَ شافيا / وحَسْبُ المنايا أن يَكُنَّ أمانيا. أو كما في قول أحمد شوقي (على الوافر): وللحرّية الحمراء بابٌ / بكلّ يدٍ مضرَّجَةٍ يُدَقُّ.

لم يشذّ عن مفهوم البيت في الشعر التقليدي سوى الرجز في شكلين رئيسيين من أشكاله، تسقط في أحدهما وحدة القافية ليحل مكانها البيت المصرَّع، حيث لكل بيت قافيته الخاصة في الصدر والعجز، على نسق المثاني (couplets) الذي يَحمل الكثيرَ من الشعر التعليمي والحكمي والتاريخي. ومن هذا القبيل ألفيّة ابن مالك (١٢٧٤)، وهي قواعد اللغة العربية منظومةً في ألف بيت، مع الشروح التي كُتبت

(٢) مختارات الشعر العمودي مأخوذة من دواوين الشعراء أو من مجموعات الشعر العربي. انظر، مثلاً، علي أحمد سعيد (أدونيس)، *ديوان الشعرالعربي* (ثلاثة أجزاء)، صيدا/ بيروت، المكتبة العصرية ١٩٦٤.

عليها. ومنه أُرجوزة تاريخية شهيرة لابن المعتزّ (٩٠٨)، سجّل فيها بعضاً من أحداث عصره، ومن أبياتها:

وكلَّ يومٍ ملكٌ مقتولُ أو خائفٌ مروَّعٌ ذليلُ
وكم أميرٍ كان رأسَ جيشِ قد نغَّصوا عليه كل عيشِ
وكل يومٍ شغَبٌ وغَصبُ وأنفسٌ مقتولةٌ وضرْبُ
ويَطلبون كل يوم رزْقا يرونه دَيناً لهم وحَقّا
كذاك حتى أفقروا الخلافَهْ وعَوّدوها الرعبَ والمخافَهْ

ولئن سقط نظام القافية في هذا الشكل من الرجز، ففي الشكل الآخر سقط نظام البيت، ولم يبقَ هناك صدر و عجز. وهناك أراجيز كثيرة على هذا النسق، منها الآتي:

ساريةٌ لم تَكتَحِلْ بغَمْضِ
كدراءُ ذاتُ هَطَلانٍ محضِ
مُوْقَرةٌ من خلّةٍ وحمضِ
تَمضي وتُبقي نِعَماً لا تمضي
قَضَت بها السماءُ حَقَّ الأرضِ

هذا الشكل الشعري الذي كسر نظام البيت، أي الشطرين، ليعتمد نظام الشطر أو نصف البيت، سُمّي «المشطور». وهو لم يكن بالنادر في الشعر العربي القديم. بل على العكس من ذلك، نُظمت عليه مقاطع لا تحصى منذ الجاهلية، الأمر الذي أكسبَ هذا الشكل من الرجز لقب «حمار الشعر»، إشارةً إلى كثرة ما حُمّل. إلا أن هذه الأراجيز، على كثرتها، لم تنل صيتاً ذائعاً. ولعل ذلك عائد إلى كسرها نظام البيت. لكنها، مع هذا، قد تُعَدّ التحول الأول في الشكل التقليدي للشعر العربي، وإن ظل هذا التحول محدوداً لارتباطه بوزن واحد من الأوزان الخليلية الستة عشر.

أما التحول الأول الملحوظ الذي طرأ على شكل القصيدة العربية فكان الموشَّح. وقد ارتبطت نشأته بالغناء، ونُظم في الأندلس بين القرنين العاشر والرابع عشر للميلاد. كما نُظم في المشرق على نطاق واسع، خصوصاً في مصر والشام. وإذا كان الشعر صناعة فنية تتجلّى في النظم والسبك وضروب البلاغة، وهذه كلها مما يميّز التعبير الفني عن التعبير العادي عن المشاعر، فقد بلغت هذه الصناعة ذروتها في الموشّح، الذي عُرف عموماً باسم «الموشّح الأندلسي» لازدهاره في الغرب العربي. وتجدر الإشارة إلى أن عبارة «شِعْر» في اللغات الأُوروبية مشتقّة من اللغة اليونانية من فعل ποιέω (poieo) ومعناه «أَصْنَع»، والاسم ποίησις (poises) ومعناه «الصناعة» أو «الشعر». وقد ألّف النقاد العرب الأوائل كتباً أعطوها عناوين مثل «صناعة الشعر» و«صناعة النثر» و«كتاب الصناعتين» (إشارة إلى الشعر والنثر معاً). إلا أن الصناعة الفنية في الموشح الأندلسي بلغت حد التصنع أحياناً. وهذا آتٍ على وجه الخصوص من مغالاة بعض الشعراء في تقليد أحد الموشحات الذائعة في الوزن والقافية، من غير أن تكون لديهم جميعاً موهبة الشاعر الأصلي أو مقدرته على النظم بحيث يأتي مصنوعهم كما لو كان مطبوعاً. في أي حال، تبقى للموشح الأندلسي حلاوته وتألّقه وشكله المسبوك في وحدات متماثلة، قد يلجأ صانعها إلى استعمال وزن ومجزوئه، أو حتى إلى استعمال وزنين أو أكثر في القصيدة الواحدة، مع تنويع في القوافي يغدو جزءاً لا يتجزأ من اتّساق مقاطع القصيدة[٣].

هذه الوحدات المتماثلة تقوم أولاً على كسر نظام البيت وتجزيئه إلى شطور كما في أحد أشكال الرجز، وثانياً على ما يسمَّى القِفْل والدَّور. وهنا مثل من موشح شهير للطبيب الوزير ابن زُهر الاشبيلي (١١٦٢)، على وزن الرمَل:

---

(٣) مختارات الموشّح الأندلسي مأخوذة من الكتابين الآتيين: لسان الدين ابن الخطيب، جيش *التوشيح*، تحقيق هلال ناجي، تونس، مطبعة المنار ١٩٦٧، نسخة أُخرى: تصحيح ألن جونز، جامعة كامبريدج: سلسلة جب التذكارية، ١٩٩٧؛ شمس الدين محمد بن حسن النواجي، عقود *اللآل في الموشحات والأزجال*، تحقيق عبد اللطيف الشهابي، بغداد، دار الرشيد للنشر ١٩٨٢.

قِفْل أيُّها الساقي، إليكَ المشْتكَى
قد دَعَوناكَ وإنْ لم تَسْمعِ

دَور ونديمٍ همتُ في غرَّتِهِ
وبشرْبِ الراحِ من راحَتِهِ
كلّما استيقَظ من سكرته

قِفْل جَذَبَ الزقَّ إليه واتَّكا
وسقاني أرْبَعاً في أرْبَعَ

مستهَلّ الموشح يسمّى القفل. وهو مؤلف عادةً من شطرين، لكل منهما قافية. بعد ذلك يأتي الدَّور. وهو مؤلف عادةً من ثلاثة شطور على قافية واحدة. ثم يليه القفل ذو الشطرين، مكرّراً قافيتَي القفل الأول. ويأتي الدور الثاني والثالث والرابع، حتى الدور الأخير، كلٌّ على قافية معينة، مع محافظة الأقفال التي تتخلّلها على قافيتَي القفل الأول. وينتهي الموشح بقفل أخير يسمّى الخَرْجَة. وهذه كانت تأتي أحياناً بالعربية المحكية، أو حتى بالبربرية أو بعض الكلمات الإسبانية. وهنا مقطع آخر من موشح ابن زهر، يوضح ما ذكرناه حول الدور والقفل:

ما لعَيني عَشِيَتْ بالنظَرِ
أنكرت بعدَكَ ضوءَ القمر
وإذا ما شئتَ فاسمع خبري

عَشِيَت عيناي من طُول البُكا
وبكى بعضي على بعضي معي

وهذا مطلع موشح لابن الزِّقاق البَلَنْسي (١١٣٤) على معتلّ المديد:

خُذْ حديثَ الشوق عن نَفَسي
وعن الدمع الذي هَمَعا

بأبي رِيمٌ إذا سَفَرا
أَطلعتْ أزرارُه قمرا
فاحذروه كلّما نَظَرا

فَبِألحاظ العيون قِسِي
أنا منها بعضُ مَن صُرِعا

وهنا مطلع من ابراهيم بن سهل الإشبيلي (١٢٥١) على السريع، يزاوج بين الوزن التام ومجزوئه، وهو ما سوف نراه بكثرة في شعر التفعيلة لاحقاً:

باكِرْ إلى اللذّة والإصطباحْ
بشرْبِ راحْ
فما على أهل الهوى من جُناحْ

إغنَمْ زمانَ الوصل قبل الذهابْ
فالروضُ قد روّاه دمعُ السحاب
وقد بدا في الروض سرٌّ عُجاب

وَردٌ ونسرينٌ وزَهرُ الأقاحْ
كالمسكِ فاحْ
والطيرُ تشدو في اختلاف النواح

وهنا بعض موشح على الوزن الوافر لابن سناء المُلْك (١٢١٢)، وهو من كبار الوشاحين المصريين. وفيه تفنُّن في القفل والدور كليهما، إذ يقع القفل في أربعة شطور والدور في أربعة، مع استعمال جزء من تفعيلة في الشطرين الثاني والرابع من القفل ليغدو: فعولن، تأتي بعد: مفاعلتن مفاعلتن فعولن:

يُريكَ إذا تَلَفَّتَ طَرْفَ شادِنْ　　　سَقيما
وعَمّا عنه تَبتسم المعادِن　　　نَظيما

جَفَتْني كلُّ لائمةٍ ولائمْ
عليه لأنّ قلبي فيه هائم
وريمٍ مائس العطفين ناعِمِ
نَعِمْتُ به وأنفُ الدهر راغم

كغصنٍ أجْتَني منه ولكنْ نَعيما
يحييّني بِهاتيك المحاسن نديما

وهنا مطلع موشح على المنسرح، وهو وزن جميل لكن غير مألوف كثيراً، يتفنّن ناظمه صلاح الدين الصفدي (١٣٦٢) من فلسطين في ابتكار مجزوء في القفل، هو عبارة عن جزء من التفعيلة الأُولى:

لا تَحْسَبِ القلبَ عن هَواكَ سَلا
وإنما حاسِدي الذي نَقَلا حَرَّفْ

أسلو ولا صَبْرَ لي ولا جَلَدُ
ونارُ شَوقي وَسْط الحشا تَقِدُ
وكلُّ وَجْدٍ دون الذي أجِدُ

سعى إلى فيه يَطلب القُبَلا
والنملُ ما زال إنْ رأى العَسَلا يَزحَفْ

وهذا مطلع موشح على وزن الدوبيت المحْدَث الذي ظهر في الأندلس، وهو مركّب من: فَعْلُن فَعِلُن مستفعلن (مفاعلن) مفتَعِلن (مفعولن). وقد تفنّن ناظمه أبو بكر ابن حجّة الحموي (١٤٣٠) في ابتكار مجزوء مشتقّ منه، هو تكرار للتفعيلتين الأُولَيَين:

تا اللهِ غَدا صبري عليكم فاني والوَجدُ بَقِي
واللهِ وما حَنَثْتُ في إيماني والعبدُ تَقِي

مَن متُّ به صَبابةً وا أسَفي لو كان يَفي
قاسوه بغصن بانةٍ منعطِفِ بادي الهَيَفِ
قلتُ اتَّئدوا قد زدتُمُ في السَّرَفِ ما الأمرُ خَفي...

والواقع أن الوشاحين تفنَّنوا في كثير من الأوزان العربية. واستمرّ نظم الموشح خلال ما يسمّى عصر الانحطاط. ثم ظهر في القرنين التاسع عشر والعشرين على أيدي شعراء نظموه من حين إلى آخر مع الشعر العمودي. ومن هؤلاء حافظ ابراهيم وأحمد شوقي وخليل مطران وبشارة الخوري وأمين تقيّ الدين، مع عدد من شعراء المهجر أمثال أمين مشرق ونسيب عريضة والياس فرحات. واتخذ الموشح مع بعضهم أشكالاً جديدة مثل المثلَّث والمربَّع والمخمَّس (نسبة إلى عدد الشطور). وهي قصائد تجري على الأوزان المعروفة، لكنها تنتمي إلى الموشح من ناحية سقوط نظام البيت فيها، أي الصدر والعجز، وقيامها على نصف البيت، أي نظام الشطور، مع وحدة الوزن وتنويع القوافي. وهذا مثل من أحمد شوقي على المربَّع، وهو من قصيدة في وصف البوسفور[٤]:

على أيّ الجِنانِ بنا تَمرُّ
وفي أيّ الحدائق تَستقرُّ
رُوَيداً أيها الفلك الأبَرُّ
بَلَغْتَ بنا الربوعَ وأنتَ حُرُّ

على شبهِ السهول من المياهِ
تحيط بك الجزائرُ كالشياهِ
وأنتَ لهنّ راعٍ ذو انتباهِ
تكرُّ مع الظلام ولا تَفرُّ...

---

(٤) أحمد شوقي، *الأعمال الشعرية الكاملة*، المجلّد الأول، الجزء الثاني، بيروت، دار العودة ١٩٨٨، ٤٠.

وهنا أبيات على نمط المخمَّس من أمين تقيّ الدين[٥]:

بَرزَ البدرُ في السماء طُلوعا
يتهادى والليل جاء سريعا
قلتُ والعين لا تودّ الهجوعا
أوحِ يا بدرُ منكَ لي موضوعا
إنّ فيكَ المعانيَ الشعريَّهْ...

الثورة الثانية في شكل الشعر العربي حصلت قبيل منتصف القرن العشرين مع ظهور شعر التفعيلة أو الشعر الحرّ، وأخذ نطاقها يتسع باطّراد حتى كسَف هذا الشكل ما عداه إلى حين. ولئن كان الموشح أسقط البيت الشعري ليحلّ مكانه نصف البيت أو الشطر، فإن شعر التفعيلة أسقط البيت والشطر معاً ليختفي الاتّساق في شكل القصيدة ويخلي مكانه للشكل الحرّ، مع المحافظة على الوزن وتنويع القوافي أو التخلّي عن القافية أحياناً.

تقوم قصيدة التفعيلة على مفتاح موسيقي معين: فاعلاتُن (الرمَل)، متفاعلن (الكامل)، فعولن (المتقارِب)، فَعِلن أو فاعلن (المتدارَك)، أو غير ذلك. ثم يتحرّر الشاعر من طول الأبيات ومن وحدة القافية، وأحياناً من وحدة الوزن أيضاً في محاولة اعتماد وزنين أو أكثر. هكذا قد يأتي سطر أو بيت على ثلاث تفعيلات، يليه ثانٍ على سَبع، وثالث على اثنتين، ورابع على خَمس، وخامس على أربَع، وهكذا حتى آخر القصيدة، دونما اتّساق في عدد التفعيلات. أما مفهوم البيت في شعر التفعيلة فيحدّده أحد عاملَين: الأول هو القافية، بحيث أن كل شطر ينتهي عند قافية يؤلف بيتاً شعرياً، والآخر هو جزء من تفعيلة. فإذا كانت القصيدة الحرّة على مفتاح فاعلاتن الموسيقي (الرمَل)، مثلاً، فالبيت ينتهي إما عند قافية وإما عند جزء من

(٥) أمين تقيّ الدين، *ديوان أمين تقيّ الدين*، جمعه وحقّقه وقدّم له د. سامي مكارم، بيروت، دار صادر ١٩٩٦، ١٤٠-١٤١.

فاعلاتن، مثل فاعلا (فاعلن) أو فاعلاتْ. وهناك عامل ثالث هو تسكين المتحرّك، وإن لم يكن قافية.

من شعراء القرن العشرين الذين كتبوا قصيدة التفعيلة: بدر شاكر السيّاب، عبد الوهّاب البيّاتي، نازك الملائكة، بلند الحيدري (العراق)؛ أدونيس، يوسف الخال، خليل حاوي (سورية ولبنان)؛ فدوى طوقان، محمود درويش (فلسطين)؛ صلاح عبد الصَّبور (مصر). وقد استُعملت معظم المفاتيح الموسيقية في هذا النوع من الشعر. وهنا نماذج على أكثر هذه المفاتيح شيوعاً في الشعر الحرّ، بدءاً بمقطع لأدونيس[٦] على مفتاح فاعلاتن (الرمَل):

للطفولهْ
تشرق الشمسُ خَجولهْ
هِيَ يَنبوعُ حياةٍ يتفجَّرْ
وَهْي دُنيا وَهْيَ أكثر
في خُطاها يَصْغر الكونُ الكبيرُ
ويَضيقُ الأبَدُ
فَلَها الأرضُ غطاءٌ سَرْمدُ
ولها الدنيا سَريرُ

الأبيات في هذه القطعة تقرّرها القوافي المنوّعة. وعدد تفعيلاتها كالآتي: ١، ٢، ٣، ٢، ٣، ٢، ٣، ٢. وتجدر الإشارة إلى أن كلاً من البيتين السادس والسابع يشكّل بيتاً قائماً في ذاته بغضّ النظر عن القافية (الدال المضمومة)، إذ ينتهيان عند جزء من فاعلاتن، هو فاعِلا (فاعلن).

وهنا مثل آخر على الرمَل من خليل حاوي[٧]:

---

(٦) أدونيس، *قصائد أُولى*، الطبعة الثانية، بيروت، دار مجلّة شعر والمكتبة العصرية ١٩٦٣، ١٥-١٦.

(٧) خليل حاوي، *نهر الرماد*، الطبعة الثالثة، بيروت، دار الطليعة ١٩٦٢، ١٣٥-١٣٨.

وكفاني أنّ لي أطفال أترابي ولي في حبّهم خمرٌ وزادْ
من حصاد الحقل عندي ما كفاني، وكفاني أنّ لي عيد الحصادْ
أنّ لي عيداً وعيدْ
كلّما ضَوَّأ في القرية مصباحٌ جديد...
يَعبرون الجسر في الصبح خفافاً، أضلُعي امتَدّت
لهم جسراً وطيدْ
من كهوف الشرق، من مستنقَع الشرق، إلى الشرق الجديد
أضلعي امتدّت لهم جسراً وطيدْ

طبعاً، يمكن كتابة البيت في سطرين أو أكثر تبعاً لوحداته المعنوية أو لما يستوعب السطر من كلمات. وعدد التفعيلات في أبيات حاوي أعلاه هو: ٦، ٦، ٢، ٤، ٦، ٥، ٣.

وهذا مثل من أدونيس[٨] على السريع:

يَحْلو لخَطْوي اللهَبُ الأحمرُ
يحلو له المجدُ
وكلما طال به البُعدُ
يعلو ويَستكبرُ
وكلما قلتُ لدربي، تُرى
إلى متى عبءُ السُّرى، والسُّرى
متى أرى المشْتَهى
وأبْلغ المنتهى
وأهدأُ
قالت ليَ الدربُ: هنا أبْدَأُ

(٨) أدونيس، (قصائد أولى)، ٣٩.

وقد استخدم الشاعر في هذه القطعة «مستفعلن مستفعلن فاعلن» (أو «فعْلن»)، مع التجزيء إلى «مستفعلن فاعلن» و«مستفعلن فعْلن»، كما إلى «مستفعلن». وجاء عدد التفعيلات كالآتي: ٣، ٢، ٣، ٢، ٣، ٣، ٢، ٢، ١، ٣.

وليس بعيداً عن السريع بحرُ الرجَز الذي نُظم عليه الكثير من شعر التفعيلة، خصوصاً في عهده الأول. والفرق بين الوزنين يكمن في التفعيلة الأخيرة (الضَّرْب)، وهي فاعلن أو فعْلن في السريع، لكنها فَعولن أو مَفْعولن في الرجز. وهنا مقطع على الرجز من نزار قبّاني[٩]:

عزيزتي، إذا رجعتُ لحظةً لنفسي
أشعر أنّ حُبَّنا جريمَهْ
وأنني مهرّجٌ عجوزٌ
يقْذفه الجمهورُ بالصفير والشتيمه
أشعر أني سارقٌ يسطو على لؤلؤةٍ كريمَهْ
أشعر في قرارتي أنّ العباراتِ التي ألفظها جريمه

عدد التفعيلات هنا هو: ٤، ٣، ٣، ٤، ٥، ٦. وعلى رغم أن السطر الأول المنتهي بعبارة «لنفسي» والسطر الثالث المنتهي بعبارة «عجوزٌ» لا يستقرّان عند قافية، إلا أن كلاً منهما يشكّل بيتاً لانتهائه بجزء من تفعيلة: فَعولُن.

ويحتلّ البحر المتقارب (فعولن) مكاناً مرموقاً في شعر التفعيلة. وهنا أبيات من بدر شاكر السيّاب[١٠]:

لأني غَريبْ
لأنّ العراق الحبيبْ
بعيدٌ، وأني هنا في اشتياقْ
إليه، إليها، أُنادي: عِراق

---

(٩) نزار قبّاني، *الرسم بالكلمات*، بيروت، منشورات نزار قباني ١٩٦٧، ٦٢-٦٣.

(١٠) بدر شاكر السيّاب، *المعبد الغريق*، بيروت، دار العلم للملايين ١٩٦٢، ١٢٢-١٢٣.

فَيَرجع لي من ندائي نَحيبْ
تَفجَّرَ عنه الصدى
أُحسّ بأني عَبرتُ المدى
إلى عالم من رَدى لا يُجيبْ

وعدد التفعيلات في هذه القطعة هو: ٢، ٣، ٤، ٤، ٤، ٣، ٤، ٤.

ويجاور المتقاربَ وزنُ المتدارك (فاعلن) الذي يمكن أن أُسمّيه، بكل ثقة، «حمار الشعر العربي الحديث» (الحرّ) لكثرة ما حُمّل من قصائد. وهناك مجموعات شعرية كاملة، تحمل بعضها أسماء كبيرة، تقتصر قصائدها على هذا الإيقاع الذي أوقع الشعر الحديث في رتابة موسيقية مملّة. وقد يتداخل المتدارك والمتقارب في القصيدة الواحدة من غير أن يدرك القارئ، أو ربما أن يقصد الشاعر، ذلك. والحقّ أن هذين المفتاحين الموسيقيين يولد أحدهما من الآخر. وما علينا سوى التنبه إلى أن «فَعولُن» تصبح «فاعلن» بمبادلة مقطعيها ليصيرا: «لُنْ فَعو»، كما تتحوّل «فاعلن» إلى «فعولن» بمبادلة مقطعيها ليصيرا «عِلُنْ فا». وهذه أبيات من السيّاب على المتدارك[١١]:

ما نَفَضْتُ الندى عن ذُرى العشب فيها
ما لثَمتُ الضبابَ الذي يحتويها
جئتُها والضحى يزرع الشمسَ في كل حقلٍ وسطحِ
مثلَ أعواد قَمحِ
فَرَّ قلبي إليها كطيرٍ إلى عشّه في الغُروبِ

كما نجد عدداً كبيراً من القصائد على الشكل الآخر من المتدارك، وهو الخَبَب (فَعِلُن / فعْلن). وفي قصيدته الشهيرة «المسيح بعد الصلب»[١٢]، زاوج السيّاب بين الشكلين. وبمقدار أقلّ نجد قصائد حرّة على الوافر (مفاعلتن). ومن هذا القبيل

---

(١١) المصدر نفسه، ١٣٧.

(١٢) بدر شاكر السيّاب، *أُنشودة المطر*، بيروت، دار مجلّة شعر ١٩٦٠، ١٤٥-١٤٩.

مجموعة شعرية كاملة لنزار قبّاني بعنوان *يوميّات امرأة لا مبالية*، هي بمثابة قصيدة واحدة. وهذا مقطع منها[١٣]:

أُسائلُ دائماً نفسي
لماذا لا يكون الحُبُّ في الدنيا
لكلّ الناس، كلِّ الناسِ، مثلَ أشعّةِ الفجرِ (البيت ١)
لماذا لا يكون الحُبُّ مثلَ الخبز والخمرِ (البيت ٢)
ومثلَ الماءِ في النهرِ (البيت ٣)
ومثلَ الغيم والأمطار والأعشاب والزهرِ (البيت ٤)

وعدد التفعيلات هنا كالآتي: ٩، ٤، ٢، ٤.

وقد اتسع تفنّن الشعراء المحْدَثين من ناظمي قصيدة التفعيلة ليشمل الأوزان الأكثر تركيباً كالبسيط والطويل. وهذا مثل من التصرف بالوزن البسيط، نسوقه من السيّاب[١٤]، ينتقل في بيته الأخير إلى السريع بعفوية:

من أيّما رئةٍ من أيّ قيثارِ
(مسْتفعلن فَعِلن مستفعلن فعْلن)
تَنْهَلّ أشعاري
(مستفعلن فعْلن)
من غابة النارِ
(مستفعلن فعْلن)
أم من عويل الصبايا بين أحجارِ
(مستفعلن فاعلن مستفعلن فعْلن)
منها تنزّ المياهُ السود واللبنُ المشويُّ كالقارِ
(مستفعلن فاعلن مستفعلن فَعِلن مستفعلن فعْلن)

---

(١٣) نزار قبّاني، *يوميّات امرأة لامبالية*، بيروت، منشورات نزار قباني ١٩٦٨، ٥٨-٥٩.

(١٤) بدر شاكر السيّاب، *أنشودة المطر*، ١٨٤.

من أيّا شرفةٍ من أيّا دارِ
(مستفعلن فاعلن مستفعلن فعْلن)
تنهلّ أشعاري
(مستفعلن فعْلن)
كالثارِ
(مستفعِلْ أو مَفعولن)
كالنُّور في راياتِ ثُوّارِ
(مستفعلن مستفعلن فعْلن)

أخيراً، هنا مقطع من سعدي يوسف[١٥] على الطويل:

صَديقَ الأغاني والبحارِ صَديقَنا
(فعولن مفاعيلن فَعولُ مفاعِلُن)
مضينا معاً حتى عَرَفنا طريقَنا
(فعولن مفاعيلن فَعولُ مفاعلن)
رَبيعاً وإيمانا
(فعولن مفاعيلن)
وحُبّاً ونيرانا
(فعولن مفاعيلن)

ذكرنا أن شعر التفعيلة بدأ يظهر قبيل خمسينات القرن الماضي. وقد عزا كل من نازك الملائكة وبدر شاكر السيّاب هذه البداية إلى نفسه. ففي مقدّمة ديوانه *أساطير*، كتب السيّاب: «أوّل تجربة لي من هذا القبيل كانت في قصيدة ‹هل كان حبّاً› من ديواني الأول *أزهار ذابلة*. وقد صادف هذا النوع من الموسيقى قبولاً عند كثير من شعرائنا الشباب، أذكر منهم الشاعرة المبدعة نازك الملائكة»[١٦]. من جهتها،

(١٥) سعدي يوسف، *قصائد مرئية*، صيدا / بيروت، المكتبة العصرية ١٩٦٥، ١٢٢.

(١٦) بدر شاكر السيّاب، *أساطير*، النجف، مطبعة الغرّي الحديثة، منشورات دار البيان ١٩٥٠، ٦.

كتبت الملائكة في دراستها *قضايا الشعر المعاصر* أن « بداية حركة الشعر الحرّ سنة ١٩٤٧ في العراق... وكانت أول قصيدة حرّة الوزن تُنشر قصيدتي المعنونة ‹الكوليرا›. وقد نُشرت في بيروت ووصلت نسخها بغداد في أول كانون الأول ١٩٤٧. وفي النصف الثاني من الشهر نفسه صدر في بغداد ديوان بدر شاكر السيّاب *أزهار ذابلة*، وفيه قصيدة حرّة الوزن له من الرمَل». وتوضح أنها كتبت «الكوليرا» تعبيراً عن مشاعرها تجاه مصر التي أصابها وباء الكوليرا آنذاك. « وقد حاولتُ فيها التعبير عن وضع أرجُل الخيل التي تجرّ عربات الموتى من ضحايا الوباء في ريف مصر. وقد ساقتني ضرورة التعبير إلى اكتشاف الشعر الحرّ »[١٧].

الواقع أن قصيدة الملائكة المذكورة، مع تنوّع عدد تفعيلاتها على الخبب، تتبع سياقاً منتظماً يتكرّر في كل من قطعها الأربع. وهذا يجعلها تنتمي شكلاً إلى الموشح أكثر من انتمائها إلى الشعر الحرّ، إلا إذا أُخذت كل قطعة بمفردها كقصيدة تامة. لكن تجدر الإشارة، للأمانة التاريخية، إلى أن ثمة محاولات في مجال هذا الشعر ظهرت قبل السيّاب والملائكة كليهما. ففي العام ١٩٣٦ أنجز الشاعر اليمني الأصل علي أحمد باكثير (١٩١٠- ١٩٦٩) ترجمةً لمسرحية شكسبير *روميو وجولييت* تجري على نسق التفعيلة، أتبعها عام ١٩٣٨ بمسرحية من تأليفه، *إخناتون ونفرتيتي*، على النسق نفسه. ويقرّ السيّاب بأن محاولة باكثير كانت باكورة الشعر الحرّ من غير أن يعزو فضل «اكتشافه» إلى نفسه كما فعلت الملائكة[١٨]. ولعل الاثنين لم يطّلعا على ما كتبه باكثير إلا بعد نشر قصيدتيهما المذكورتين. وهنا نموذج من *روميو وجولييت* على الرجز[١٩]:

---

(١٧) نازك الملائكة، *قضايا الشعر المعاصر*، بغداد، مكتبة النهضة ١٩٦٥، ٢١-٢٢.

(١٨) بدر شاكر السيّاب، «تعليقات»، مجلّة *الآداب* (حزيران/ يونيو ١٩٥٦)، العدد ٦، ٦٩. تجدر الإشارة إلى أن نازك الملائكة تنبّهت إلى أسبقيّة باكثير في الطبعات اللاحقة من كتابها.

(١٩) علي أحمد باكثير، *روميو وجولييت* (مسرحية مترجمة عن شكسبير عام ١٩٣٦)، القاهرة، الفجالة ١٩٤٦، ١٥.

ليس لديّ غيرُ ما قد قلتُ لكْ
ما بَلَغتْ جوليتُ عمرَ البدر من أعوامها
فلم تزل غريبةَ النفس على أيّامها
فدَعْ لها صَيفين يُنْضِجانها
عندئذٍ تَنظر في تَزويجِها

وهذا نموذج على الكامل[٢٠]:

زَوجي الذي تيبالتُ حاولَ قَتْلَهُ حَيٌّ يَعيشْ
من حيثُ تيبالتُ الذي قد كان يَنْوي
قَتْلَ زوجي قد هَلِكْ
في كلّ هذا ما يُعَزّيني
فَفيمَ إذاً بُكائي

إلى الرجَز والكامل، نجد في المسرحية مقاطع على الرمَل والمتقارب والمتدارك. ولم يعتمد بأكثير القافية في ترجمته هذه لأنها تحدّ من التعبير. وكتب في المقدّمة أن طريقة الشعر الحرّ «في النظم هي أصلح ما يترجَم به شكسبير، وأعوَنُه على الاحتفاظ بروحه... وهو - أعني النظم - حرّ كذلك لعدم التزام عدد معين من التفعيلات في البيت الواحد»[٢١].

وهناك محاولة سبقت باكثير في هذا المجال، نقع عليها في مجلة حلقة أبولو الشعرية المصرية التي أسّسها الطبيب الشاعر أحمد زكي أبو شادي بمعاونة خليل شيبوب. فقد نشر شيبوب في مجلة الحلقة لدى تأسيسها عام ١٩٣٢ قصيدة على الرمَل بعنوان «الشراع»[٢٢]، جاء فيها:

---

(٢٠) المصدر نفسه، ٨٠.

(٢١) المصدر نفسه، ٣.

(٢٢) خليل شيبوب، قصيدة «الشراع»، مجلّة *حلقة أبولو* (١٩٣٢)، السنة الأُولى، العدد ٣.

هَدأ البحرُ رحيباً يملأ العينَ جَلالا
وصَفا الأُفْقُ ومالت شَمسُه ترنو دَلالا
وبدا فيه شراعْ
كخَيالٍ من بَعيدٍ يتمشّى
في بساطٍ مائجٍ من نَسْجِ عشْبِ
أو حَمامٍ لم يجد في الروض عشّا
فَهْو في خوفٍ ورعبِ

وعدد تفعيلاتها كالآتي: ٤، ٤، ٢، ٣، ٣، ٣، ٢. وقدّم لها شيبوب بقطعة جاء فيها: «الشعر المنطلِق أو الشعر الحرّ غير الشعر المنثور، لأن نثر الشعر هو افتكاكه من قيود الوزن والقافية». وقال أحمد زكي أبو شادي تعليقاً على القصيدة في العدد نفسه: «وإنما يرجع تقديرنا للشعر الحرّ إلى سنوات مضت... وفي اعتقادي أن الشعر العربي أحوَج ما يكون الآن إلى الشعر الحرّ وإلى الشعر المرسَل، إذا أردنا أن ننهض به نهضة حقيقية».

وكان أبو شادي على حقّ في أن الشعر الحرّ ظهر قبل الثلاثينات، إذ كان أسبق إلى الظهور في المهجر الأميركي الشمالي مع شعراء الرابطة القلمية، مثل نسيب عريضة وميخائيل نعيمة. وإذ تحوي أعمال جبران ونعيمة الشعرية قصائد على نسق الموشح، ففي ديوان نعيمة *همس الجفون*، وهو كتابه الشعري الوحيد، استخدام لنحو ١٣ وزناً[٢٣]، عمدَ إلى التصرف في معظمها شكلاً وقافية. وأقرب قصائد المجموعة إلى الشعر الحرّ واحدة[٢٤] على مفتاح «فاعِلُن» تعود إلى العام ١٩٢٣، ومنها:

---

(٢٣) ميخائيل نعيمة، *همس الجفون*، الطبعة الرابعة، بيروت، دار صادر ١٩٦٢. الأوزان التي استعملها نعيمة في الديوان هي: المجتثّ، الكامل، الوافر، الرمَل، الخفيف، السريع، الرجز، الطويل، المتقارِب، المديد، البسيط، مخلَّع البسيط، المتدارَك (فَعِلن)، المتدارَك (فاعلن).

(٢٤) المصدر نفسه، ٨٧-٩٢.

هَلِّلي هلّلي يا رياحْ
وانسجي حول نَومي وشاح
من خَريرِ الغَديرْ
واهتزازِ الأثير
واختلاجِ العَبيرْ
في دُموعِ الصباحْ
هَلِّلي هَلِّلي يا رِياحْ

وعدد تفعيلاتها كالآتي: ٣، ٣، ٢، ٢، ٢، ٢، ٣. إلا أن هذا السياق نفسه يتكرّر في المقاطع العشرة التالية من القصيدة، مما يجعلها على نسق الموشح الأندلسي إذا أُخذت ككلّ.

لكن مهما يكن من أمر القرن العشرين، فقد بات معروفاً اليوم أن أقدم نماذج الشعر العربي على نسق التفعيلة إنما تعود إلى «شعر البَنْد» الديني الذي نُظم في العراق خلال القرنين السادس عشر والسابع عشر[٢٥]. والبند المعروف يجري على وزنين هما الهزْج والرمَل، أو على مزيج منهما في القصيدة الواحدة. وهذا مثل على الرمَل من قصيدة للسيّد علي باليل الحسيني في مدح النبي:

يا مَناطَ السعد والعزّ جَمالا
ومحطَّ المجد والفخر رِحالا
سِرْتَ كالشمس وما الشمسُ لمولاها مثالا
إنّها سوف تُلاقي دون عَلياكَ زَوالا

عدد التفعيلات هنا كالآتي: ٣، ٣، ٤، ٤. وهذا مثل على الهزج من قصيدة للسيّد عبد الرؤوف الجدّ حفصي في مدح الإمام علي:

---

(٢٥) بالنسبة إلى شعر البند، راجع: عبدالكريم الدجيلي، *البند في الأدب العربي: تاريخه، نصوصه*، بغداد، مطبعة المعارف ١٩٥٩.

وقلبي كلّما دَبَّ الصَّبا الكَرْخيُّ في البانِ
فحاكى الغصنَ منه العرقُ في النَّبْضْ
سَعى يَلتمس المَخرَجَ حتى كادَ
بالتزفارِ من صدريَ ينقَض
ولا بدْعَ إذا اشتاقَ إلى أرضْ
بها الكلُّ، وكلّ العالمِ البعض
فَمَن لي أن يُداني بيَ حظّي النجفَ الأشرَفَ
كي أقضي به من قبل أن أقضيَ
ما فاتَ مِنَ الفَرضْ
وأُفضي بِمَصُونِ السرّ للمولى
الذي آملهُ في موقف العَرضْ

وعدد التفعيلات هو الآتي: ٧، ٦، ٣، ٣، ٩، ٦.

هذا كله بات معروفاً ومعترفاً به. لكنه لا يعني أبداً أن شعراء التفعيلة في القرن العشرين استلهموا البند شكلاً لقصائدهم. والأرجح أنهم لم يسمعوا به قبل صدور الدراسات الأُولى عنه، وذلك بعد انتشار موجة الشعر الحرّ. كما لا يعني أن أعمال باكثير المسرحية هي التي دفعت هذا الشكل الشعري قدماً. ولئن لم يَعرف شعراء التفعيلة الأوائل الموشح الأندلسي إلا على نطاق محدود، فقد كان أثر شعراء المهجر كبيراً عليهم، سواء من حيث القصائد التي كان ينشرها شعراء الرابطة القلمية، ولا سيما جبران ونعيمة، في المجلات المصرية والشامية، أو من ناحية التنظير النقدي الذي أطلقه نعيمة في مقالات كتابه *الغربال*، داعياً فيها إلى الإقلاع عن «نقيق الضفادع»[٢٦] وكتابة الأدب الجديد الذي يعبّر عن طموحات وآمال جديدة سعياً إلى حياة أكثر حرية واكتمالاً وغنى تتجلّى في مجتمع وعالم جديدين.

---

(٢٦) ميخائيل نعيمة، *الغربال*، الطبعة السابعة، بيروت، دار صادر ١٩٦٤، ٩٠-١٠٦.

II. طليعة الترانيم الإنجيلية

ثمة ضَرْب من الشعر العربي نشأ وازدهر خلال النصف الثاني من القرن التاسع عشر، وكان أثره كبيراً في لبنان وسورية وفلسطين والأُردن ومصر والعراق عبر المؤسسات التربوية التابعة للإرساليات الإنجيلية. أقصد بذلك الشعر الترانيم الدينية المنظومة على غرار بعض الترانيم في اللغات الأُوروبية، خصوصاً الإنكليزية[٢٧]. وقد عهدَ المرسلون الأميركيون، الذين وفدوا إلى بلاد الشام بدءاً من ١٨٢٠ واتَّخذوا من بيروت أهم مركز لهم، إلى عدد من الشعراء المحلّيين نظم ترانيم على غرار ما في الإنكليزية لاستخدامها للعبادة في الكنائس التي كانوا يؤسسونها لا في المدن فحسب، وعلى الأخص بيروت، لكن في القرى أيضاً مثل عبيه وسوق الغرب وبحمدون وعين زحلتا ورأس المتن والشوير.

من أبرز ناظمي الترانيم ناصيف اليازجي (١٨٧١) وابراهيم سركيس (١٨٨٥) ويوسف الأسير (١٨٩٠) وأسعد الشدودي (١٩٠٦) وسليم كسّاب (١٩٠٧) ويواكيم الراسي (١٩١٦) وابراهيم الحوراني (١٩١٦) والأميركي جورج فورد (١٩٢٨). وإذ لا تشير كتب الترانيم إلى تاريخ نظم كل ترنيمة لأن أهداف هذه الكتب تقَويّة أكثر منها توثيقية، لكن ثمة إشارات إلى أن الكثير من تلك الترانيم نُظم قبل صدور الترجمة العربية الإنجيلية (فانذايك) للكتاب المقدّس عام ١٨٦٥، بعدما استخدم المرسلون إحدى الترجمات الكاثوليكية زمناً قبل إنجاز ترجمتهم الخاصّة التي حرصوا على أن تأتي في لغة عربية فصحى أقرب ما تكون إلى المحكيّة كيما يتسنّى لجميع الفئات فهمها. وهم توخّوا هذه البساطة عينها في الترانيم المنظومة لئلا يبقى الشعب المؤمن منعزلاً عن الخِدَم الكنسية.

---

(٢٧) الاستشهادات المرقّمة من الترانيم العربية هي من الكتاب الآتي: *كتاب الترانيم الروحية للكنائس الإنجيلية*، بيروت، مكتبة المشعل ١٩٦٥. والاستشهادات المرقّمة من الترانيم الإنكليزية هي من الكتاب الآتي: *Golden Bells*, London: Scripture Union (no date).

وينقل هنري جسب (Henry Jessup)[٢٨]، أهم مؤرّخ للإرسالية الأميركية، عن سارة سميث، زوجة عالي سميث الذي استهلّ وفانديك مشروع ترجمة الكتاب المقدَّس، في يومياتها (بتاريخ ١٤ كانون الأول / ديسمبر ١٨٣٥) عن مدرسة البنات التي أسستها في بيروت مطلع العام ١٨٣٤ أن الفتيات اجتمعن في المدرسة ذات سبت مع بداية تعليم الموسيقى وأنشدن مقطعاً من مزمور. لكن لم تكن هناك مزامير منظومة تلائم مستواهنّ. «فاللغة العربية»، تقول سميث، «غير قابلة للتبسيط كالإنكليزية... وهذا، على الأقل، هو الرأي السائد حالياً. لكن لا نستطيع التكهّن بالتغييرات التي يمكن إحداثها في هذه اللغة»[٢٩]. ويروي جسب عن زيارته الأُولى إلى بحمدون في شباط ١٨٥٦ بعيد وصوله إلى سوريا وحضوره اجتماعاً يوم سبت في مدرسة للبنات. وبين أُولئك فتاة ذات تسع سنوات هي كاترينا صبرا، ابنة الياس صبرا الذي كان قد اعتنق البروتستانتية حديثاً، راحت تنشد بالعربية ترنيمة «قوموا ورَتِّلوا»[٣٠] على لحن الترنيمة الإنكليزية "Awake and sing the song / of Moses and the lamb". هذا يعني أن الترانيم العربية كانت معروفة في منتصف القرن التاسع عشر. ويضيف جسب أنه لم يكن في تلك الآونة كتاب ترانيم للأحداث في اللغة العربية، فوعد السكان أن يعدّ لهم مجموعة ترانيم بعد إتقانه اللغة. ووفى بوعده إذ نَشر عام ١٨٦١ كتاب *دوزان القيثار*، وفيه ثمانون ترنيمة للأحداث، قبل أربع سنوات من طبع ترجمة فانديك للكتاب المقدّس[٣١]. وفي الوقت نفسه نُشرت بالعربية قصص كتابية مع مجلة شهرية للأولاد، كانوا يقرأونها بشغف لسهولة لغتها[٣٢]. ويشير جسب إلى أن العام ١٨٣٦ شهد بداية إعداد

(٢٨) انظر هذين الكتابين من هنري جسب:

Jessup, Henry Harris, *The Women of the Arabs*, New York: Dodd and Mead, 1873.
Jessup, Henry Harris, *Fifty Three Years in Syria*, New York and Chicago: Fleming H. Revell Company, 1910.

(٢٩) Jessup, Henry, *The Women of the Arabs*, 125–126.

(٣٠) Ibid., 93–94.

(٣١) Ibid., 94.

(٣٢) Ibid., 126–127.

الأدبيات الإنجيلية العربية من قصص ومقالات تعليمية وترانيم[٣٣]، وأن عالي سميث (١٨٠١ -١٨٥٧) كان الأميركي الأول الذي يكتب ترانيم بالعربية الفصحى لكن المبسَّطة، لتكون في متناول الجميع ولا سيما الصغار[٣٤]. ويصف جسب[٣٥] انتشار هذه الترانيم على نطاق واسع جداً خصوصاً عبر المدارس، مشيراً إلى أن آلاف النسخ بيعت من كتاب الترانيم الذي حرّره. ويقول إن المعلمين أخذوا يلقّنون تلاميذهم الموسيقى في كل مدارس الإرسالية مع انتشار آلة البيانو، وبينها مدرسة أُسبوعية للترتيل أسسها هو وضمّت ٣٥٠ حدثاً. ويضيف أن تلاميذ المدارس الأميركية من كل الطوائف طفقوا ينشدون هذه الترانيم «في الصفّ والشارع والبيت ومدرسة السبت واجتماعات العبادة»[٣٦].

لعل أكبر ناظمي الترانيم شاعريةً الشيخ ناصيف اليازجي (١٨٠٠ – ١٨٧١) الذي تعاون مع المرسلين عن كثب في التدقيق اللغوي في ترجمة الكتاب المقدّس. وهو لم يعرف من اللغات سوى العربية التي كان أحد أبرز أئمّتها، بعدما كانت عربية المسيحيين العرب ركيكة عموماً حتى زمن غير بعيد عن ولادة اليازجي. وقد يكون أحد المرسلين ممّن أجادوا العربية، أو أحد المتعاونين المحلّيين ممّن يعرفون الإنكليزية، نقل له أنغام الترانيم الأُوروبية وما يعادلها في العربية، حتى إذا حفظ ضروبها صار ينظم المزامير وسواها من التسابيح والقصص الإنجيلية دونما استعانة بالآخرين[٣٧]. وهذا مطلع ترنيمة له (١٨) ينظم فيها المزمور ٩٥:

---

(٣٣) Ibid., 127–128.

(٣٤) Jessup, Henry, *Fifty Three Years in Syria*, 56.

(٣٥) Ibid., 247–251.

(٣٦) Ibid., 251.

(٣٧) يروي كورنيليوس فاندايك في ذكرياته المتعلّقة بعمل الارسالية بين ١٨٣٩ و١٨٥٠ أن الترتيل في العربية ظهر للمرة الأُولى عام ١٨٤٥. ويقول إنه، لدى ملاحظته الشبه الموسيقي بين الأوزان الشعرية الإنكليزية والعربية، طلب إلى «الشيخ ناصيف اليازجي نظم هذا أو ذاك من المزامير على أوزان محددة. وبعد إنجاز العمل طُبع أول كتاب، وهو صغير، يجمع بعض المزامير المنظومة وسواها من الترانيم».

الربُّ ذو السلطانْ	والمالئُ الكلّ
فَلْنُهدِ حمداً كلَّ آنْ	له على الفضلِ

وفي كتاب الترانيم الإنكليزي أكثر من ترنيمة على هذا الوزن، منها هذه (٢٩):

We give Thee but Thine own
Whate' er the gift may be
For all we have is Thine alone
A trust, O Lord, from Thee

أما وزن القطعة العربية فهو كالآتي:

الربُّ ذو السلطانْ	(٦ مقاطع)
o o / o / o// o/ o/	مستفعلن مفعولْ
والمالئُ الكلّ	(٦ مقاطع)
o / o / o// o/ o/	مستفعلن فعْلن
فَلْنُهدِ حمداً كلَّ آنْ	(٨ مقاطع)
oo// o/ o/ o// o/ o/	مستفعلن مستفعلاتْ
لَهُ على الفضْلِ	(٦ مقاطع)
o/ o/ o// o//	مفاعلن فعْلن

We	give	Thee	but	Thine	own			
/o	/o	/o	/o	/o	/o			(٦)
What	e'er	the	gift	may	be			
/o	/o	/o	/o	/o	/o			(٦)
For	all	we	have	is	Thine	a	lone	
/o	/o	/o	/o	/o	/o	/o	/o	(٨)
A	trust	O	Lord	from	Thee			
/o	/o	/o	/o	/o	/o			(٦)

Van Dyck, C.V.A., *Reminiscences of the Syrian Mission from 1839 to 1850*, Beirut: Office of the Commission Representative, (unpublished typeset manuscript), 21.

الإيقاع في الشعر، مهما كانت لغته، قائم على المقاطع (syllables). ولئن كان كل الكلام، نثراً أم شعراً، مؤلّفاً من مقاطع، فالمقاطع الشعرية تجري على انسجام موسيقي معين يؤلف ما يُعرف بالأوزان. والمقطع في الإنكليزية (واللغات الأُوروبية) مؤلّف من متحرِّك وساكن كما هو مبيّن في الترنيمة أعلاه. أما في العربية فالمقطع مؤلّف إما من متحرّك وإما من متحرّك يليه ساكن. وتتدرّج مقاطع الشعر العربي، حسب ملاحظتي الشخصية، من مقطع واحد إلى أربعة، على النحو الآتي:

- مقطع: /o (فا).
- مقطعان: //o (عِلُنْ).
- ثلاثة مقاطع: ///o (فَعِلُنْ).
- أربعة مقاطع: ////o (فَعِلَتُنْ).

هذا كل ما يمكن أن تستوعبه موسيقية الشعر العربي من مقاطع، بحيث يستقرّ السلّم في أعلاه على أربعة متحرّكات يليها ساكن، علماً أنه يمكن إضافة ساكن إلى آخر كل من المقاطع الأربعة ليستقرّ على ساكنَين. ولا يلتقي ساكنان في العربية إلا في ضَرْب الشعر، أي التفعيلة الأخيرة من كل بيت. أما المتحرّكات من خمسة صعوداً فتنتمي إلى النثر فقط وتقع خارج الإيقاع الشعري. وإذا طبَّقنا قاعدة المقاطع هذه، كما عبّرنا عنها، على تفعيلات الشعر العربي، لحصلنا على أمثلة كالآتي:

- مستفعلن: فا فا عِلُنْ (٤ مقاطع).
- مُتَفاعِلُن: فَعِلُن عِلُنْ (٥ مقاطع).
- مَفاعِلُن: عِلُنْ عِلُنْ (٤ مقاطع).
- مُفْتَعِلُن: فا فَعِلُنْ (٤ مقاطع).
- مَفْعولن: فا فا فا (٣ مقاطع).
- مُتَفاعِلاتُن: فَعِلُنْ عِلُنْ فا (٦ مقاطع).
- فَعولن: عِلُنْ فا (٣ مقاطع).

- مَفاعيلن: عِلُنْ فا فا (٤ مقاطع).
- مُفاعَلَتُن: عِلُنْ فَعِلُنْ (٥ مقاطع).

ترنيمة اليازجي أعلاه مؤلّفة من ستة مقاطع في كل من الشطور الأول والثاني والرابع، ومن ثمانية مقاطع في الشطر الثالث، في انسجام تام مع عدد مقاطع الترنيمة الإنكليزية وإيقاعها. من هنا نجد في كتب الترانيم الإنجيلية، الأجنبية والعربية على السواء، ذكراً لعدد المقاطع عند بداية كل ترنيمة. وإذا كان المقطع الأُوروبي مؤلّفاً من متحرّك وساكن، في حين يعلو المقطع العربي فوق هذا النموذج إلى متحرّكين فثلاثة فأربعة، فإن وضع الشعر العربي في قالب موسيقي وإنشاده من شأنه توحيد كل المقاطع بتحويلها إلى متحرّك يليه ساكن. وهذا إنما يحصل بمدّ الحركة إلى حرف العلّة الذي يجاريها، فتصبح الفتحة أَلِفاً والضمّة واواً والكسرة ياءً:

الربُّ [و] ذو السلطانْ

o/ o/ o/ o/ o/ oo/

والمالـ [ي] ـِ الْكلّ [ي]

o/ o/ o/ o/ o/ o/

فَلْنُهْد [ي] حَمْداً كلَّ [ا] آنْ

o/ o/ o/ o/ o/ o/ o/ oo/

لـ [ا] هُـ [و] عـ [ا] لى الْفَضْل [ي]

o/ o/ o/ o/ o/ o/

قاعدة المقاطع هذه تنطبق على كل الترانيم الإنكليزية ومعادلاتها العربية. لذلك سنكتفي من الآن فصاعداً بإيراد الترنيمة مع ذكر عدد مقاطعها أحياناً. لكننا، قبل ذلك، سنجري جولة على عدد من الترانيم الإنكليزية وصولاً إلى معادلاتها الإيقاعية العربية. وهنا عدد من النماذج:

(٦٤)
What a friend we have in Jesus (٨)
All our sins and griefs to bear (٧)
What a privilege to carry (٨)
Everything to God in prayer [pray'r] (٧)

المعادل العربي لهذا الإيقاع هو: فاعلاتن فاعلاتن / فاعلاتن فاعلن (أو فاعلاتْ).

(٢٧٠)
I heard the voice of Jesus say (٨)
Come unto me and rest (٦)
Lay down, thou weary one, lay down (٨)
Thy head upon my breast (٦)

والمعادل العربي هو: مستفعلن مستفعلن (مستفعلاتْ) / مستفعلن فعولْ (مفعولْ - فَعَلْ).

(٨٧)
Each little flower [flow'r] that opens (٧)
Each little bird that sings (٦)
He made their glowing colours (٧)
He made their tiny wings (٦)

والمعادل العربي هو: مستفعلن فعولن (مفعولن) / مستفعلن فعولْ (مفعولْ - فَعَلْ).

(٥٠)
For all the glories of the earth and sky (١٠)
For night's soft voice and morning's silent haze (١٠)
For trees that whisper and for winds that sigh (١٠)
We give Thee praise (٤)

والمعادل العربي هو: مستفعلن مستفعلن فعولْ (مفعولْ - فَعَلْ) في الشطور الثلاثة الأُولى، و: مستفعلن (مستفعلاتْ) في الشطر الرابع.

(٥٢٨)
Gleaming in the sunshine (٦)
Floating in the air (٥)
See the banner waving (٦)
Beautiful and fair (٥)

والمعادل العربي هو: فاعلن فعولن (مفعولن) / فاعلن فعولْ (مفعولْ - فَعَلْ).

(٣٦)
To God be the glory, great things He hath done (١١)
So loved He the world that He gave us His Son (١١)
Who yielded His life an atonement for sin (١١)
And opened the life-gate that all may go in (١١)

والمعادل العربي هو: فعولن فعولن فعولن فعولْ (فَعَلْ) في كل من الشطور الأربعة.

(٥٣٩)
There's a fight to be fought and a race to be run (١٢)
There are dangers to meet by the way (٩)
But the Lord is my light, and the Lord is my life (١٢)
And the Lord is my strength and stay (٨)

والمعادل العربي هو: فاعلن فاعلن فاعلن فاعلن (فاعلاتْ) / فاعلن فاعلن فاعلن (فاعلات) / فاعلن فاعلن فاعلن فاعلن (فاعلات) / فاعلن فاعلن فعْلن (مفعولْ).

النماذج المذكورة أعلاه تبرهن بوضوح عن تَشابُه الإيقاع الشعري بين اللغات، من غير أن يعني هذا أن الإنكليزية أو سواها تستطيع استيعاب كل الأوزان الشعرية العربية، خصوصاً الأوزان المركّبة من تفاعيل مختلفة كالطويل والبسيط والمنسرح، أو تلك التي تقوم على تفاعيل تحوي ثلاثة متحرّكات متجاورة مثل الكامل والوافر.

بالعودة إلى ناصيف اليازجي، هنا ترنيمة أُخرى (٣٢) من نظمه:

إليكَ أُبَكّرُ يا سَيّدي (١١) لأنّ اعتمادي عَلَيْكْ (٨)
إلى وجهكَ النفسُ عطشانةٌ (١١) ويَشتاق جسمي إليكْ (٨)

هذه القطعة نظمٌ للمزمور ٦٣. وهي تجري على المتقارب التام مع مجزوء له: فَعولن فَعولن فعولن فَعَلْ / فَعولن فَعولن فَعولْ.

هنا مطلع ترنيمة لليازجي (٦٢) ينظم فيها المزمور ٤٢، مستخدماً الرمَل مع مجزوء له:

مثلما الأيّلُ يَشتاقُ إلى جدوَلٍ صافي المياهْ
هكذا تَشتاق نفسي دائماً لملاقاةِ الإلهْ

وفي نظمه للمزمور ٢٤ (الترنيمة ٥٦)، يستخدم اليازجي في الشطرين الأوّلين الرجز التام (على ثلاث تفعيلات)، وفي الشطرين اللاحقين مجزوء الرجز (على تفعيلتين):

الأرضُ للربّ وما فيها ومَنْ (١٢) يَسكنُ فيها من شعوب البَشَرِ (١٢)
على البحارِ أُسِّسَتْ (٨) منْه وفوقَ الأنْهُرِ (٨)

وهنا قطعة لليازجي (٢٢٩) تجري على ثلاثة أوزان مختلفة، هي الرمَل والسريع والرجز:

نفسِ قومي واطلبي نَصيبَكِ الفاضِلْ
فاعلاتن فاعلن (رمَل) مَفاعِلن فعْلن (سريع)
نحوَ مَنْشاكِ اهْربي مِنَ الفَنا الباطِلْ
فاعلاتن فاعلن (رمَل) مفاعلن فعْلن (سريع)

كلُّ نجمٍ يَضْمَحِلّ والأراضي سَتَزولْ
فاعلاتن فاعلاتْ (رمَل) فاعلاتن فَعِلات (رمَل)
فاقصدي حيثُ يَحِلّ مجدٌ ولا يَحُولْ
فاعلاتن فَعِلاتْ (رمَل) مستفعلن فَعولْ (رجِز)

وهذه قطعة أُخرى لليازجي (٣٥٠) تجري على إيقاع قصير جداً من الرجز:

أراكَ بالإيمانْ يا حَمَلَ الرحمنْ
مفاعلن مفعولْ مستفعلن مفعولْ
رَبّي يَسوعْ
مستفعلاتْ (مستفعلنْ نْ)

وتميّز ترانيم اليازجي بمتانة اللغة وبساطتها في آنٍ معاً، كما بسلاسة النظم وقوّة السبك. وهنا قطعة (٢٩٥) على الرمَل، ينظم فيها قصة إنجيلية:

صَرخَ الأعمى ابْنُ طيما يا يَسوعُ ارحَمْ فَتاكْ
نالَ غَيري منكَ بِرْءاً فأعِنْ ضعفي كذاكْ

الجموعُ انتهرتْه غَضَباً وَهْو يَزيدْ
فَدَعاه الربُّ، أقْبِلْ ثمّ سَلْني ما تريد...

لَيْتَما كلُّ ضريرٍ يَعرفُ الشافي الوَحيدْ
ويُوافيه ليُعْطى بَصَراً منه جديد

وهذه قطعة أُخرى (٢٥٣) على المتقارب، يَنظم فيها المزمور ١٨:

أُحبُّكَ يا رَبُّ يا قُوَّتي فإنَّكَ حصنٌ بهِ أحتَجِبْ
حبالُ الهَوايا قد احْتَطَنَ بي وفخُّ المنايا أمامي نُصِبْ

طريقُ إلهِ العُلى كاملٌ وقولُ الإله شَريفٌ نَقي
وليس إلهٌ لنا غَيْرُهُ سلاحٌ وتِرْسٌ بهِ نَتَّقي...

لذلكَ أَحْمَدُهُ، إنّهُ خَلاصُ يتيم عليه اعْتَمَدْ
خَلاصٌ لكلّ بني شَعْبِهِ ينالون رَحْمَتَه للأبَدْ

ومن كبار ناظمي الترانيم أسعد الشدودي (١٨٢٦-١٩٠٦) من عاليه، الذي كان يدرّس الرياضيات في الكلية السورية الإنجيلية منذ تأسيسها عام ١٨٦٦. وله شعر حكمي (وهزلي)، منه أُرجوزة[٣٨] نظم فيها أمثال سليمان الحكيم على نحو مبسّط:

مخافةُ القديرِ رأسُ الحكمةِ فَمَن حواها حازَ كلَّ نعمةِ
بالحكمة الجهّالُ تَستَهينُ لكنْ بها الحكيمُ يَستعينُ
يا ابْنِ إذا أغراكَ أهلُ الشرِّ للسير في طريقهم، لا تَجْرِ

وهنا مطلع ترنيمة (٥٧) لأسعد الشدودي:

يا رَبِّ أقْرَبُ (٦) فَأَقْرَبُ (٤)
إليكَ يا رَبِّي (٦) وأرْغَبُ (٤)

في الحزْنِ والبَلا (٦) إليكَ أقْرَبُ (٦)
إليك أقْرَبُ (٦) فأقْرَبُ (٤)

وإذا أُخذت كل قطعة منها على حدة، فهي لا تختلف شكلاً عن الشعر الحرّ، تبعاً لاختلاف عدد مقاطعها في كل بيت (شطر): ٦، ٤، ٦، ٤، ٦، ٦، ٦، ٤. وهي تنقل وزن ترنيمة نظمتها سارة آدامز[٣٩] عام ١٨٤١:

---

(٣٨) لويس شيخو، *تاريخ الآداب العربية في الربع الأول من القرن العشرين*، بيروت، مطبعة الآباء اليسوعيين ١٩٢٦، المجلّد ١، ٤١٦.

Nearer my God to Thee (٦)
Nearer to Thee (٤)
E'en though it be a cross (٦)
That raiseth me (٤)
Still all my song shall be (٦)
Nearer my God to Thee (٦)
Nearer my God to Thee (٦)
Nearer to Thee (٤)

وفي ترنيمة أُخرى (٨١)، يكتب الشدودي:

لي كتابٌ من إلهي ما له عندي نَظيرْ
فَهْوَ لي كنزٌ، وليلي من سناه يَستنير

هذا على الرمَل. لكن يأتي قرار هذه الترنيمة على وزن آخر هو الرجَز:

كتابُ رَبّنا الإلهْ دَليلُنا إلى الحياهْ
كتابُ ربّنا الأمينْ مَنارُنا في كل حينْ

وهنا ترنيمة للشدودي (٢٧٧) على الرمَل أيضاً، مع تفنّن محكَم في نقل الوزن الإنكليزي إلى ما يعادله عربياً:

لا تَغضَّ الطرْفَ عَنّي أيُّها الفادي
فاعلاتن فاعلاتن فاعلاتن فا

أعْطِني حين أُصلّي نُورَ إرشادِ
فاعلاتن فَعِلاتن فاعلاتن فا

يا مُنَجّي أنتَ سلْواني
فاعلاتن فاعلاتن فا

ثَغْرُكَ البسّام يَشْفي ضعْفَ إيماني
فاعلاتن فاعلاتن فاعلاتن فا

(٣٩) Adams, Sarah Flower, *Nearer My God to Thee*, Whitefish (Montana): Kessinger Publishing (reprint), 2005.

ويمكن النظر إلى هذه القطعة موسيقياً على أنها تدمج وزنين، باعتبار أن الشطور المنتهية بمقطع «فا» يمكن قراءتها على معتلّ المديد ومجزوئه (فاعلاتن فاعلن فعْلن / فاعلن فعْلن). هكذا تكون القطعة أعلاه من الرمَل والمديد.

وفي ترنيمة أُخرى للشدودي (٢٢٦)، دفعَه نقل الإيقاع الإنكليزي إلى ابتكار وزن عربي جديد كما حصل بالنسبة إلى الدوبيت في الأندلس:

فارِحاً فارِحاً أمضي إلى الْـ مسكن مستنير بالحَمَلْ
فاعلن فاعلن مستفعلن فاعلن فاعلن مَفاعلن

يا لَشَوقي إلى ذاك اللقا عندَ سَمْعي ترانيمَ السما
فاعلن فاعلن مستفعلن فاعلن فاعلن مستفعلن

يا نِبالَ المنايا لا أخافْ فِعْلَكِ المرَّ يومَ الإنصرافْ
فاعلن فاعلن مستفعلاتْ فاعلن فاعلن مستفعلاتْ

وبين ترانيم الشدودي اثنتان شهيرتان تُنشَدان في الدفن، وهما رائعتا السبك والإيقاع:

خَلِّني قربَ الصليبْ حيث سالَ المجرى (١٣٥)
فاعلاتن فاعلاتْ فاعلاتن فعْلن

من دم الفادي الحبيبْ داءُ نفسي يَبْرا
فاعلاتن فاعلات فاعلاتن فعْلن

في الصليبْ، في الصليبْ راحَتي بل فَخْري
فاعلاتْ فاعلات فاعلاتن فعْلن

في حياتي وكذا بَعْدَ دفن القبرِ
فاعلاتن فَعِلات فاعلاتن فعْلن

والأصل الإنكليزي من نظم فاني كروسبي عام ١٨٦٩[٤٠]:

Jesus, keep me near the cross
There's a precious fountain
Free to all, a healing stream
Flows from Calvary's mountain

In the cross, in the cross
Be my glory ever
Till my raptured soul shall find
Rest beyond the river

والثانية (٢٢٢) على مفتاح «فاعلن» الذائع في الشعر العربي الحديث:

لي مقامٌ بهيجٌ، سَنا مجدِهِ فاق نورَ النهارْ
فاعلن فاعلن فاعلن فاعلن فاعلن فاعلاتْ

في العُلى حيث فادي الوَرى وَجهُه مثلَ شمسٍ أنارْ
فاعلن فاعلن فاعلن فاعلن فاعلن فاعلات

نَلْتَقي عن قريبْ حولَ عَرش المجيد الحبيبْ
فاعلن فاعلاتْ فاعلن فاعلن فاعلات

(مكرَّرة)

وهنا الأصل الإنكليزي الذي ألّف كلماته سانفورد بينيت عام ١٨٦٨ ووضع لحنه جوزيف وِبْستر[٤١]:

There's a land that is fairer than day
And by faith we can see it afar
For the Father waits over the way
To prepare us a dwelling place there
In the sweet By and by
We shall meet on that beautiful shore

(٤٠) Bloom, Harold, *American Religious Poems: An anthology*, New York: Library of America, 2006, 149.

(٤١) Bennett, Sanford Fillmore, *Sweet By and By*, Boston (Massachusetts): E. P. Dutton, 1885. See also: Sankey, Ira D., *My Life and the Story of the Gospel Hymns*, Philadelphia (Pennsylvania): The Sunday School Times Company, 1906, 199–200.

إلى اليازجي والشدودي، برع في نظم الترانيم أشخاص بينهم: ابراهيم سركيس، سليم كسّاب، يواكيم الراسي، ابراهيم الحوراني، يوسف الأسير، جورج فورد.

ابراهيم سركيس (١٨٣٤- ١٨٨٥) من مواليد عبيه، وهو شقيق خليل سركيس منشئ جريدة *لسان الحال* ومجلة *المشكاة* وصاحب مطبعة الآداب. وقد تحوّل ابراهيم من المارونية إلى الإنجيلية، فصار من شيوخ الكنيسة وتولّى إدارة المطبعة الأميركية حتى وفاته[٤٢]. وهو شاعر مطبوع، نظم ترانيم كثيرة وجمعها في كتاب *الترانيم والتسابيح*. ومنها الآتي (٥٢):

ما أحسنَ الجموعْ — في موضع الصلاهْ
مستفعلن فعولْ — مستفعلن فعولْ

تَنفي عن العين الهُجوعْ — محبّةُ الإلهْ
مستفعلن مستفعلات — مَفاعِلُنْ فعول

وله ترنيمة (٨٥) في نظم المزمور ١٢٣:

سراجٌ منيرٌ لنا في السبيلْ — كتابُكَ يا رَبَّنا
فعولن فعولن فعولن فعولْ — فعولُ فعولن فَعَلْ

سلاحُ ضعيفٍ شفاءُ العليل — وبابُ خَلاصٍ لنا
فعولُ فعولن فعولن فعول — فعولُ فعولن فَعَلْ

وعلى المتقارب ومجزوئه، له أيضاً هذه الترنيمة (٢٢٤):

أحنُّ اشتياقاً لذاك الوطَنْ — لأنْظرَ ربّي يَسوعَ المجيدْ
وأبقى هنالك طولَ الزمنْ — وأرفعَ صوتي بأعلى النشيدْ

هناكَ الرَّحومْ
وصَوتُ الملائكِ تَنْفي الهُمومْ

---

(٤٢) لويس شيخو، المرجع المذكور، ١٣٣.

ولا يقلّ سليم كسّاب (١٨٤١- ١٩٠٧) عن سركيس شاعريةً وتفنُّناً في تطويع الأُصول الأجنبية للإيقاع العربي. وهو قَدِم من مسقط رأسه دمشق إلى بيروت في أعقاب حوادث ١٨٦٠ الطائفية الدامية، حيث اعتنق الإنجيلية وعمل مع المرسَلين الإنكليز والأميركيين في تأسيس المدارس ومتابعة الشؤون الأدبية(٤٣). وأتقن عدداً من اللغات، بينها الإنكليزية والفرنسية والإيطالية. وهنا ترنيمة (٢٩٨) من نظم كسّاب:

يا نَفْسِ قد وافى يَسوعْ	رَبُّ الفِدى القَديرُ
مستفعلن مستفعلات	مستفعلن فَعولُنْ
شافيكِ من سُقْمٍ يَرُوعْ	طَبيبُكِ الخبيرُ
مستفعلن مستفعلات	مَفاعِلُنْ فَعولن
أحلى نشيدٍ في العُلى	والأرضِ لاسْمِهِ حَلا
مستفعلن مستفعلن	مستفعلن مفاعلن
فَلْتُؤدِّهِ المَلا	أَبْهَجَ الثناءِ
فاعلن مفاعلن	فاعلن فَعولن

والأصل الإنكليزي لهذه الترنيمة من نظم وليم هنتر(٤٤) عام ١٨٥٩:

The great Physician now is near
The sympathizing Jesus
He speaks the drooping heart to cheer
Oh, hear the voice of Jesus

---

(٤٣) شارل كسّاب عن سليم كسّاب، في الموقع الإلكتروني الآتي: www.kassableague.org

(٤٤) ترنيمة وليم هنتر المذكورة تحمل الرقم ١٠٢ في الكتاب الآتي:

Baptist Hymnal, Nashville (Tennessee): Convention Press, 1975.

لن نشير إلى المصادر بالنسبة إلى الترانيم الإنكليزية اللاحقة، لأن الترنيمة الواحدة موجودة في مصادر متنوّعة. ويمكن العثور على مواقع إلكترونية كثيرة تحوي كلمات الترانيم وحتى ألحانها. ومن كتب الترانيم القديمة الكتاب الآتي:

Reformed Church in America, *The Church Hymnary: A Collection of Hymns and Tunes for Public Worship*, compiled by Edwin A. Bedell, New York: Maynard Merrill, 1892.

[O] Sweetest note in seraph song
[O] Sweetest name on mortal tongue
Sweetest carol ever sung
Jesus, blessed Jesus

وهنا ترنيمة أُخرى (٢٢٣) من كسّاب:

هل لقاءٌ نَجْتَنيهِ عند فادينا الحبيبْ
فاعلاتن فاعلاتن فاعلاتن فاعلاتْ

مَنْ حَياةُ النفسِ فيهِ وَهْوَ للقلب نِعْمَ النصيبْ
فاعلاتن فاعلاتن فاعلن فاعلن فاعلات

وقد حمله الإيقاع في الشطر الرابع على الانتقال من الرمَل إلى المتدارك.

وهذه ترنيمة ثالثة (١٧٩) له أيضاً، تنطوي على تفنُّن في النظم:

يا أيُّها الروحُ المعزّي المنيرْ أقْبِلْ إلينا من عُلاكا
مستفعلن مستفعلن فاعلاتْ مستفعلن مستفعلاتن
واسكبْ علينا رحمةً في الضمير كالغَيث تجري من غناكا

وممّن أجاد نظم الترانيم، بشاعرية مطبوعة وسبك متين سلِس، يواكيم الراسي (١٨٤٠-١٩١٦) من إبل السقي (قضاء مرجعيون) جنوب لبنان. وهو والد الكاتب سلام الراسي وجدّ الباحث ألبرت حوراني لأُمّه (سُمَيّا الراسي). وكان شماساً أُرثوذكسياً قبل اعتناقه المذهب الإنجيلي ومشاركته في تأسيس المدرسة الإنجيلية الأميركية في صيدا[٤٥]. ومن منظوماته الميلادية البديعة (٩٩):

رَنَّ صوتٌ في الأعالي يا تُرى ماذا الخَبَرْ
فاعلاتن فاعلاتن فاعلاتن فاعلن
ولَمِ الأملاكُ تَشْدو بتَرانيم الظفَرْ

(٤٥) راجع الفصل عن سلام الراسي في كتاب: *روّاد لبنانيون*، المجلّد ١، زوق مكايل (لبنان)، منشورات جامعة سيّدة اللويزة ٢٠٠٦.

كلّهم في المجد غنّى　　بِأناشيدِ السرورْ
قد بدا أمرٌ عجيبٌ　　رحمةُ الله الغفور

وهنا ترنيمة أُخرى للراسي (٣٦٧) على مجزوء الرجز، وفيها أيضاً تتجلّى قوّة نظمه:

ما أعظمَ الحُبَّ السَّني　　من خالقٍ لم يَنْسَني
صارَ الشريفُ كالدَّني　　مفْتَقِراً وَهْو الغني
يا مَن سَمعتُمُ النِّدا　　يا مَن أخَذْتُمُ الهُدى
يا من قَبِلْتُمُ الفِدى　　حُبُّوا كما أُحبِبْتُمُ
رُدّوا على الآبِ الصدى　　أَعطوا كما أُعطيتُمُ

ولا يقلّ شاعريةً ابراهيم الحوراني (١٨٤٤-١٩١٦)[٤٦] الحمصي الأصل، الذي نظم الشعر العامي إلى جانب المعْرَب، وعلّم في الكلية السورية الإنجيلية بعد دراسته هناك لدى قدومه إلى بيروت. وهنا إحدى ترانيمه (٣) التي تنطوي على ابتكار في الإيقاع:

سَبِّحوا الرَّبّا　　من سماء المجد في الأعالي
فاعلن فعْلن　　فاعلن مستفعلن فعولن
　　(فاعلاتن فاعلن فعولن)
سَبِّحوا حُبّا　　أيُّها الأملاكُ ذا الجَلالِ
يا جُنودَ اللّهْ　　مَجِّدوا تَمْجيدا
فاعلن مفعولْ　　فاعلن مفعولن
فالوَرى لولاهْ　　لم يكن موجودا

---

(٤٦) كمال اليازجي، *الشيخ ابراهيم الحوراني: عصره، حياته، أدبه، ومختارات من شعره وأبحاثه*، بيروت، مكتبة رأس بيروت ١٩٦٣.

وهذه ترنيمة أُخرى للحوراني (٣١٤)، حمله تقليدُ الإيقاع الأصلي فيها (Light of the World) إلى ابتكار وزن عربي جديد برهاناً على اتّساع الشعر العربي لما يتجاوز الأوزان المعروفة:

ضَلَّ الوَرى في ظُلُماتِ الخَطا يَسوعُ نورُ العالَمْ
مستفعلن مفتعلن فاعلن مفاعلن مفعولن
مَنْ مَجدُه كالشمس يجلو الدجى يَسوعُ نورُ العالم

سِرْ إليه، سَناهُ يُسْفِرْ لاحَ حَولي للحَقّ يُظهِرْ
كنتُ أعمى والآنَ أُبصِرْ يَسوعُ نورُ العالم

ولئن كان مطلع الترنيمة على السريع في الشطرين الأول والثالث (لأن الضرب «فاعلن») وعلى الرجز في الشطرين الثاني والرابع ثم في الشطر الرابع للقرار (لأن الضرب «مفعولن»)، فالجديد الوزني هو في القرار نفسه، في شطوره الثلاثة الأُولى. ويمكن سكب هذا الوزن في التفعيلات الآتية: فاعلن مفعولن (فاعلن) فعولن. وهو قريب جداً إلى مخلّع البسيط: مستفعلن مفعولن (فاعلن) فعولن، إذ ينقص عنه مقطعاً واحداً من متحرّك وساكن في مطلع كل شطر. ويمكن تحويل هذه الشطور الثلاثة من الوزن الجديد، الذي ابتكره الحوراني عن طريق المحاكاة، إلى مخلّع البسيط بإضافة المتحرّك والساكن (فا) إلى بداية كل شطر لنحصل على شيء كالآتي:

سِرْ، سِرْ إليهِ، سَناهُ يُسفِرْ
قَدْ لاحَ حَولي للحَقِ يُظهِرْ
قد كنتُ أعمى والآنَ أُبصِرْ

ومن كتّاب الترانيم الأوائل الشيخ السنّي يوسف الأسير (١٨١٧- ١٨٨٩)[٤٧]. وهو فقيه ولغوي وشاعر وأحد روّاد الصحافة. تخرّجَ في الأزهر ودرّس العربية في

[٤٧] كمال الصليبي، *تاريخ لبنان الحديث*، الطبعة السادسة، بيروت، دار النهار ١٩٨٤، ١٨٨- ١٨٩.

الكلية السورية الإنجيلية بعد انضمامه مع ناصيف اليازجي وبطرس البستاني إلى فريق فانديك لترجمة الكتاب المقدّس. وهنا بعض ترنيمة (٢٩٠) للأسير على مجزوء الرمَل:

يا مسيحَ الربِّ كُنْ لي سَنَداً في كلّ حينْ
واجْعلَنْ كلّ فِعالي كَفِعال الصالحين

مالئٌ حُبُّكَ قلبي فَهْوَ لا يَهْوى سِواكْ
لستُ أرجو غيرَ قُربي منكَ حُبّاً بِرِضاكْ...

بِكَ آمَنّا وسُدْنا وأمِنّا مِن خَطَرْ
ولكَ الشكرَ أعَدْنا أيُّها الفادي البشَر

والأصل الإنكليزي من نظم تشارلز وِسْلي عام ١٧٤٧:

Love divine, all loves excelling
Joy of heaven, to earth come down
Fix in us Thy humble dwelling
All Thy faithful mercies crown

وعلى الوزن نفسه كتب الأسير (٤٢١):

يا يَسوعُ اسمَعْ دُعائي أيها الراعي العَظيمْ
واحْرِسَنّي في مسائي ودُجى الليلِ البهيم

وهذا مطلع ترنيمة له (٣٦) على مجزوء الرجز:

للربِّ مجدٌ في المَسا من أجل أنوار النهارْ
فَلْيَكنِ اللهمَّ لي تَحتَ جَناحيكَ اسْتتار

وفي ترنيمة أُخرى (٤١٩)، ابتكر إيقاعاً لا عهد للشعر العربي به:

أعظمُ الجِبالِ أوْسَعُ البحارْ
فاعلن فعولن فاعلن فعولْ

صارَ من رِمالِ ومن القِطارْ
فاعلن فعولن فَعِلن فعول

من بُزورٍ هانَتْ كانت الأشجارْ
فاعلن مفعولن فاعلن مفعولْ

وثَوانٍ، كانت أطْوَلُ الأدهارْ
فَعِلن مفعولن فاعلن مفعول

والأصل الإنكليزي نظمته جوليا كارني عام ١٨٤٥:

Little drops of water
Little grains of sand
Make the mighty ocean
And the beauteous land

ولئن كان ما يهمّنا على وجه الخصوص في هذه الدراسة هو الجديد الذي أدخلته الترانيم الإنجيلية على إيقاع الشعر العربي، ففي طليعة ناظمي الترانيم يأتي المرسَل الأميركي جورج فورد (١٩٢٨)[٤٨] الذي أتقن العربية ونظم بها شعراً يكشف عن موهبة كبيرة. وهو مؤسس المدرسة الأُولى في صيدا التي تفتح أبوابها للبنات. وهنا مقطع من إحدى ترانيمه (٢٨٦):

بَهْجَتي ونوري مَلِكي الوَديعْ
فاعلن فعولن فَعِلن فعولْ

منتهى سُروري أنتَ لي الشفيع
فاعلن فعولن فاعلن فعولْ

واثقاً آتي إليكْ طارحاً حِمْلي لَدَيك
فاعلاتن فاعلات فاعلاتن فاعلات

---

(٤٨) Presbyterian Church in the USA, *Presbyterian Church at Home and Abroad*, Philadelphia (Pennsylvania), 1894.

فاسْتَلِمْ أُموري أيُّها السميعْ

فاعلن فعولن فاعلن فعولْ

وهذه ترنيمة أُخرى له (٢٣٧) تحمل إيقاعاً عربياً مبتكَراً:

حُبُّ السيّدِ فَخرُ السُّجَّدِ

فعْلن فاعلن فعْلن فاعلن

حُلْوٌ ثابتٌ سامٍ عجيبْ

فعْلن فاعلن فعْلن فَعولْ

حُبٌّ طاهِرُ حُبٌّ وافِرُ

قُوموا مَجِّدوا الابْنَ الحبيبْ

ثم يأتي القرار:

مُلْكٌ مَجْدٌ قُوَّةٌ للفادي

فعْلن فعْلن فاعلن مفعولن

نادوا بالغفرانِ للأثيمْ

فعْلن فعْلن فاعلن فَعولْ

حُبُّ الرَّبِّ الْـ مُنْعِشُ الفؤادِ

فعْلن فعْلن فاعلن فَعولن

بابٌ للحياةِ والنَّعيمْ

فعْلن فاعلاتُ فاعلاتْ

في هذه الترنيمة نقل فورد إيقاع ترنيمة إنكليزية من نظم وليم شيروين عام ١٨٦٩:

Sound the battle cry
See the foe is nigh
Raise the standard high
For the Lord…

وهنا ترنيمة ذائعة من فورد (١٩١) على مجزوء الرجز:

ما أبْهجَ اليومَ الذي آمنتُ فيه بالمسيحْ
أضحى سُروري كاملاً ورَنَّ صوتي بالمديحْ
حُبّي لِفاديَّ المجيدْ يوماً فيوماً سَيَزيدْ
عمرٌ جَديدْ، يومٌ سَعيدْ يَومُ اختصاصي بالوَحيدْ

وهنا ترنيمة له (٥٩) قصيرة الإيقاع:

إليكَ حاجتي (٦) في كلّ حينْ (٤)
مفاعلن فَعَلْ مُسْتَفعلاتْ
وفيكَ قُوَّتي (٦) رَبّي الأمينْ (٤)

وأصلها الإنكليزي من نظم آني هوكس (١٨٣٥-١٩١٨):

I need Thee every hour (٦)
Most gracious Lord (٤)
No tender voice like Thine (٦)
Can peace afford (٤)

ومن أعذب ما نُظم شعراً عربياً مسيحيّاً ترنيمة فورد «يا محبّاً ماتَ عن جنس البشر» (٢٦٦):

يا محبّاً مات عن جنس البشَرْ أُمحُ إثمي أنتَ أوْلى مَن غَفَرْ
كن مُعيناً فأنا ممَّن عَثَرْ بالخطايا يا حبيبي يا يَسوعْ

أنتَ حصْني وإليكَ الملْتَجا منكَ ألقى بالتجائي الفَرَجا
فأعِنْ ضعفي ووَلِّدْ بي الرَّجا بِخَلاصي يا حبيبي يا يَسوع

أنتَ تدعو الخاطئَ الغِرَّ الأثيمْ لِيَنالَ الخُلْدَ في دار النعيم
وأنا مهما يَكن ذَنْبي عظيم لكَ آتي يا حبيبي يا يسوع

لعل العارف بأوزان الشعر يتساءل للوهلة الأُولى عن الأصل الإنكليزي الذي نقل عنه فورد ترنيمته، وعمّا إذا كان في الإنكليزية معادل للرمَل التام الذي نُظمت الترنيمة عليه. وما علينا أولاً سوى استحضار الترنيمة الإنكليزية:

Jesus is our shepherd
Wiping every tear
Folded in His bosom
What have we to fear
Only let us follow
Whither He doth lead
To the thirsty desert
Or the dewy mead

لو قصَد فورد نقل الترنيمة كما وجد أبياتها منسّقة في صيغتها الأصلية، لجاءت على الوزن الآتي: فاعلن فعولن / فاعلن فعولْ (مفعولْ ـ فَعَلْ). لكنه توخّى الابتكار، فَجعل من كل بيتين بيتاً واحداً حتى جاءت ترنيمته على الرمَل التام: فاعلاتن فاعلاتن فاعلن (فاعلات)، وأُعطيت لحناً شرقياً ذائعاً منقولاً عن الموشح الأندلسي « جادَكَ الغَيث». لكنها، في الوقت نفسه، أُعطيت لحنها الغربي الأصلي انطلاقاً من تنسيق أبياتها الأساسي على غرار بعض الترانيم، ومنها الترنيمة المعروفة "Onward Christian soldiers". وإذ ليس ثمة مانع وزني من جمع البيتين في الأصل الانكليزي ليؤلّفا بيتاً واحداً، فالجواب عن تساؤلنا هو أن للرمَل التام معادله في الإنكليزية أيضاً.

هناك ناظمون آخرون من العهد الأول، تعكس ترانيمهم شاعرية أكيدة. وبين هؤلاء: أسعد الراسي (١٩١٥)، سليمان ضومط (١٩٠١)، متري الحدّاد (١٩١٠)، شاكر داغر (١٩٠٤). ولهذا الأخير ترنيمة ميلادية بديعة (٩٧) على مفتاح « مستفعلن» (الرجز) مع تنويع في طول الشطور كما في القوافي:

[في هذا العيدْ]

المجدُ قد تعالى (مستفعلن فعولن)

والنورُ قد تَلالا (مستفعلن فعولن)

جاءَ المسيحْ (مستفعلات)

هذا المسيحُ المنتظَرْ (مستفعلن مستفعلن)

مَنْ حُبُّه قد عَمَّ أفرادَ البَشَرْ (مستفعلن مستفعلن مستفعلن)
قد سَرَّنا هذا الخبَرْ (مستفعلن مستفعلن)
بُشْرى لنا فالقلبُ أضحى مستريحْ (مستفعلن مستفعلن مستفعلات)

هكذا يكون عدد التفعيلات في كل شطر كالآتي: ٢، ٢، ١، ٢، ٣، ٢، ٣. وتأتي المقاطع اللاحقة مكرِّرةً السياق نفسه على غرار الموشح الأندلسي. وإذا اكتفينا بمقطع واحد من الترنيمة، كما مرّ معنا في نماذج سابقة، لرأينا أنه يجري على نسق شعر التفعيلة. وهذا يصحّ على كثير من الموشحات أيضاً.

وهناك ناظمون آخرون للترانيم، لا نقع على ذكرهم أو على منظوماتهم في كتب الترانيم الإنجيلية المعتمدة. ولعل أبرز هؤلاء الياس صالح (١٨٣٩- ١٨٨٥)[٤٩]، الذي كان رئيس الجمعية الخيرية الأُرثوذكسية في اللاذقيّة. وهو درّس في مدرسة الذكور التي أسستها الإرسالية الأميركية في اللاذقيّة عام ١٨٦٠. وكلّفته هذه الإرسالية عام ١٨٦٩ نظم المزامير شعراً لإنشادها أثناء العبادة. وقصد مصر لطبع مزاميره المنظومة، فصدرت عن المطبعة الأميركية في الإسكندرية عام ١٨٧٥ تحت عنوان *بهجة الضمير في نظم المزامير*، ثم صدرت طبعتها الثانية (٨١٤ صفحة) في بيروت عام ١٨٨٣.

III. ثورة شعرية مجهولة

سبقت الإشارة إلى أن تقدير الكنيسة الإنجيلية نفسها لتلك الترانيم، التي يرجع إليها فضل الحَفْز على كتابتها، اقتصر على الناحية التقويّة. ولم يكن من شأنها، في أي حال، النظر إلى الترانيم من حيث إضافتها إلى أشكال الشعر العربي وأوزانه. حتى إن بعض الطبعات صدرت غفلاً من أسماء الناظمين. وفي مقدّمته لطبعة ١٩٦٥

---

(٤٩) جبرائيل سعادة، «الياس صالح اللاذقي»، مجلّة *التراث العربي* (تشرين الأول/أُكتوبر ١٩٩٠)، فصلية تصدر عن اتّحاد الكتّاب العرب في دمشق، العدد ٤١. في الإنكليزية، نظم إسحق واطس (١٦٧٤- ١٧٤٨) المزامير شعراً. وكان يضع للمزمور الواحد عدداً من الصيَغ.
Watts, Isaac, *The Psalms of David, Imitated in the Language of the New Testament* (different editions).

من كتاب *الترانيم الروحية للكنائس الإنجيلية*، الصادر عن مكتبة المشعل التابعة للمطبعة الإنجيلية الوطنية في بيروت، أشار أنيس الخوري المقدسي[٥٠]، رئيس اللجنة التي عُهِد إليها إخراج الطبعة المذكورة، إلى أن «للكنيسة الإنجيلية في بلاد الغرب روائع عالمية من الأناشيد الروحية التي تُرجمت إلى عدة لغات، فكانت من أفعل العوامل في رفع القلوب وتوجيهها في سبل الخير والنبل والجمال. وإنه لمن دواعي غبطتنا أن يكون كتابنا هذا حاوياً عدداً كبيراً من هذه الروائع في ترجمات أصبحت من صميم حياتنا الإنجيلية». ويضيف المقدسي أن هذه الترانيم، سواء أكانت مترجَمة أم موضوعة أصلاً بالعربية، «على درجات متفاوتة من حيث النظم والإلهام الشعري». لكنه لا يلاحظ، حتى في كتابه حول الاتجاهات الأدبية العربية الحديثة[٥١]، أثرَ هذه الترانيم، وكذلك أثر الترجمة الإنجيلية للكتاب المقدّس في نهضة الأدب والشعر العربيَّين. وقد يكون هو الآخر قصَرَ النظر إلى هذه الترانيم على ناحيتها الدينية وأجلَّها عن المقارنة بآداب دنيوية غير روحية. وتتوزع الترانيم الإنجيلية على موضوعات كالآتي: عبادة الله، الخدمات الكنسية، ملكوت الله، مواضيع عامة، ترانيم للأحداث. وعن كل موضوع يتفرّع عدد من العناوين. فتحْت حياة المسيح تقع عناوين مثل ميلاده وتعليمه وصلبه وقيامته. وعن عبادة الله تتفرّع عناوين مثل التسبيح والشكر والابتهالات الصباحية والمسائية...

من ناحية أُخرى، ليس لدينا دليل على أن ناظمي الترانيم أنفسهم قدّروها لجهة إضافتها جديداً إلى الشعر العربي، لا في محتواه المسيحي فحسب بل في إيقاعاته المبتكرة وعفوية لغته وبساطة تعبيره. الشيخ ناصيف اليازجي، وهو في رأينا أعظم ناظمي الترانيم، لم يضمّن دواوينه أو أيّاً من كتبه شيئاً من ترانيمه المنظومة. ولا نقع على إشارة إليها في المقدمة التي وضعها حفيده أمين الحدّاد، منشئ صحيفة *البصير* في

(٥٠) أنيس الخوري المقدسي، مقدّمة الطبعة الجديدة لكتاب *الترانيم الروحية للكنائس الإنجيلية*، بيروت، مكتبة المشعل ١٩٦٥.

(٥١) أنيس الخوري المقدسي، *الاتجاهات الأدبية في العالم العربي الحديث*، الطبعة الثالثة، بيروت، دار العلم للملايين ١٩٦٦.

الإسكندرية، هو وخاله ابراهيم ناصيف اليازجي، بمثابة «ترجمة» أو سيرة للشيخ ناصيف في مقدمة ديوانه المجموع. ونقرأ في تلك الترجمة[٥٢] عن ولادته في قرية كفرشيما عام ١٨٠٠ وتلقّيه مبادئ القراءة على راهب من بيت شباب ثم انكبابه على مطالعة كتب اللغة والشعر وتأليفه كتباً تعليمية بينها مقامات لغوية وأراجيز وشرح لديوان المتنبّي، إضافة إلى دواوين «تُعَدّ من عيون الشعر»، كما جاء في الترجمة، «كثيرٌ منها محفوظ على الألسنة ولا سيما الأبيات الحكمية منها، وهي في شعره أكثر من أن تُحصى»[٥٣]. وتشير الترجمة إلى عمله كاتباً لدى الأمير بشير الشهابي حتى ١٨٤٠، ثم انتقاله وعائلته إلى بيروت «منقطعاً للمطالعة والتأليف والتدريس، فاشتهر ذكره في جميع البلاد العربية، وراسلَتْه أكابر الشعراء من العراق ومصر وغيرهما»[٥٤]. ولا تشير هذه الترجمة إلى المعاهد التي علّم فيها الشيخ ناصيف ولا إلى علاقته مع المرسَلين الأميركيين وارتباطه بترجمة الكتاب المقدّس، كما لا تشير من قريب أو من بعيد إلى الترانيم التي نظمها والتي، كما قلنا، لا أثر لها في دواوينه وكتبه. ولعله تخيَّر ربط اسمه بشعره العمودي الفخم اقتناعاً منه بأن ترانيمه المنظومة لا ترقى إلى ذلك الشعر، بل تنتمي إلى الشعر «الخفيف» وربما تقع خارج نطاق الشعر. وقد يكون الشيخ ناصيف أسقط عمداً ذكر كتاباته المسيحية حفاظاً على صداقاته الإسلامية المتينة في الشام والعراق ومصر، ومنها صداقة الشيخ عبد الهادي نجا الأبياري، مفتي المنوفية والغربية في الديار المصرية، الذي لم يتمالك نفسه عن وصف اليازجي في أبيات قرّظ بها براعته اللغوية[٥٥]:

ما سَمِعْنا بمِثْله عيسويّاً يتحدّى بمثل مُعْجِزِ أحمَدْ...
ألْمَعيٌّ... لكنه عيسويٌّ كان أوْلى بِفَضْلِ دِينِ مُحمَّدْ

---

(٥٢) أمين الحدّاد وابراهيم اليازجي، «ترجمة المرحوم الشيخ ناصيف اليازجي»، في: *ديوان الشيخ ناصيف اليازجي*، بيروت، دار مارون عبّود ١٩٨٣، ١٧-٣٩.

(٥٣) المصدر نفسه، ١٩.

(٥٤) المصدر نفسه، ٢٨.

(٥٥) المصدر نفسه، ١٣٣-١٣٤.

وتسبق سيرةَ اليازجي في ديوانه «مقدّمةٌ تحليلية» كتبها مارون عبّود، مأخوذة من كتابه *روّاد النهضة الحديثة* للطبعة الجديدة من الديوان. وجاء فيها أن اليازجي، بين الشعراء الذين دخلوا قصر الأمير بشير الشهابي، «أفْيَضهم قريحةً وأنقاهم ديباجةً»[٥٦]. إلا أنه، كما يرى عبّود، «في كل ما نظم وكتب زعيم المقلِّدين في عصره»[٥٧]، لكنه لم يبلغ مراتب الأوّلين، بل لبث «يظلع في سيره خلف القدماء»[٥٨]. ويختم عبّود كلامه بقوله إن اليازجي «كان خير شعراء زمانه تقليداً. فالتجديد في ذلك الزمان لم يكن في الحساب»[٥٩]. هكذا لم يلاحظ مارون عبّود، هو الآخر، التجديد الأكيد الذي انطوت عليه ترانيم اليازجي، سواء من حيث الإيقاع أو من حيث المفردات والتراكيب.

وهنا مطالع من ديوان ناصيف اليازجي:

لا تَبْكِ مَيْتاً ولا تَفرحْ بمولودِ   فالميْتُ للدودِ والمولودُ للدودِ
وكل ما فوق وجه الأرض تَنظره   يُطوى على عدمٍ في ثوب موجودِ[٦٠]

كَلّفتُ حَمْلَ تحيّتي ريحَ الصَّبا   فكأنني حَمَّلتُها بعضَ الربى
لا تَحملُ الريحُ الجبالَ وليتَني   كَلّفتُها حَملي فإني كالهَبا[٦١]

لكلِّ كرامةٍ زمنٌ يَعودُ   كما يَخْضرّ بعد اليَبْس عودُ
وإنّ الدهرَ يَبْخل بَعد جودٍ   وبَعد البخل نَنْظره يَجُودُ[٦٢]

---

(٥٦) مارون عبّود، «مقدمة تحليلية»، *ديوان الشيخ ناصيف اليازجي*، ٩.
(٥٧) المصدر نفسه، ١١.
(٥٨) المصدر نفسه، ١٣.
(٥٩) المصدر نفسه، ١٦.
(٦٠) *ديوان الشيخ ناصيف اليازجي*، ٥٧.
(٦١) المصدر نفسه، ٨٠.
(٦٢) المصدر نفسه، ١٥٨.

أتَعْلَمُ ما هاجَتْ بقلبي من الشغْلِ مخدَّرةٌ تَسبي بأهدابها الكحْلِ
غزالةُ إنسٍ لا غزالةُ رَبْرَبٍ رَعَت حَبّةً للقلب لا عَرْفَجَ الرمْلِ[٦٣]

عاج المتيَّمُ بالأطلال في العَلَمِ فأبْرَعَ الدمعُ في اسْتهلاله العَرِمِ
دمعٌ جرى عن دمٍ أو عَنْدَمٍ خَضِلٍ يسقي الركابَ ولكنْ ليس بالشَّبِمِ[٦٤]

ماذا الوقوفُ على رسوم المنزلِ هيهات لا يجدي وُقوفُكَ فارْحَلِ
تلك الأثافي في العِراصِ تخلَّفَتْ أظَنَنْتَ قَلبَكَ بينها فتأمَّلِ[٦٥]

لمن الخيامُ ومَن هنالك نازلُ أتُرى بِهِنّ ربيعةٌ أم وائلُ
كَذَبَتْكَ نفسُك بل غَطارِفَةُ الحمى قومٌ لديهم ذِكْرُ تُبَّعَ خامِلُ[٦٦]

لمن الهوادِجُ في عَراءِ الهَوْجَلِ تحت القِباب تَشقُّ ذَيلَ القَسْطَلِ
يَتتبَّعُ الآثارَ قلبي خَلْفَها فَلَوِ انْثَنَينَ وَطِئْنَهُ بالأرجُلِ[٦٧]

لئن كانت المطالع الثلاثة الأُولى التي اخترناها سهلة عموماً، فالمقاطع اللاحقة تنطوي على مفردات مهجورة لا يفهمها معظم المثقفين اليوم إلا بالعودة إلى القاموس وتاريخ العرب، ولم يكن يفهمها في زمن اليازجي سوى نفر قليل من أئمّة اللغة، من غير المسيحيين عموماً. لكن لا ريب في شاعريته المطبوعة التي تجلّت خصوصاً عند إطلاق عاطفته الصادقة، كما في رثاء ولده حبيب[٦٨]:

ذَهَبَ الحبيبُ فيا حُشاشَةُ ذُوبي أسَفاً عليه ويا دموعُ أجيبي
رَبَّيْتُه للبَين حتى جاءه في جِنْح ليلٍ خاطفاً كالذيبِ
يا أيها الأُمّ الحزينة أجْمِلي صبراً فإنّ الصبرَ خَيرُ طبيبِ

---

(٦٣) *ديوان الشيخ ناصيف اليازجي*، ١٤٥.
(٦٤) المصدر نفسه، ١٦١.
(٦٥) المصدر نفسه، ١٧٤.
(٦٦) المصدر نفسه، ١٨٤.
(٦٧) المصدر نفسه، ٢٠٥.
(٦٨) المصدر نفسه، ٣٩٣.

لا تَخْلَعي ثوبَ الحِدادِ ولازِمي   نَدْباً عليه يليق بالمندوبِ...
لكَ يا ضَريحُ كرامةٌ ومحبّةٌ   عندي لأنّكَ قد حَوَيْتَ حَبيبي

وتقف بعض حكميّاته بين أجمل منظوماته في الديوان، ومنها[٦٩]:

لَعَمْرُكَ ليس فوق الأرض باقِ   ولا مّما قَضاهُ اللّهُ واقِ
وما للمرء حَظّ غيرُ قوتٍ   وثَوبٍ فَوقه عَقْدُ النطاقِ
وما للميْت إلا قَيدُ باعٍ   ولو كانت له أرضُ العِراقِ
وكم يمضي الفراقُ بلا لقاءٍ   ولكنْ لا لقاءَ بلا فِراقِ
وما نَفْعُ الدراهم مَعْ جَهولٍ   يُباع بِدِرْهمٍ وقتَ النفاقِ

ومن حكميّاته المعروفة أيضاً[٧٠]:

يا بائع الصبر لا تُشفِقْ على الشاري   فَدِرْهَمُ الصبر يَسْوى ألفَ دينارِ
لا شيء كالصبر يَشفي جرحَ صاحبِهِ   ولا حَوى مثْله حانوتُ عَطّارِ...
إنّ الرياحَ تُصيب النخل تَقْصِفُهُ   وليس تَقْصف غصنَ الشيحِ والغارِ

ولعل أروع حكميّاته ما جاء فيها[٧١]:

دَعْ يومَ أمسٍ وَخُذْ في شأنِ يوم غَدِ   واعْدِدْ لنفسِكَ فيه أفضلَ العُدَدِ
واقنعْ بما قَسَم اللّهُ الكريمُ ولا   تَبسطْ يديكَ لِنَيْل الرزق من أحَدِ
والبسْ لكلّ زمانٍ بُرْدةً حضرَتْ   حتى تُحاكَ لكَ الأُخرى من البُرَدِ
متى تَرَ الكلبَ في أيام دَولتِهِ   فاجعلْ لرجليكَ أطواقاً من الزرَدِ
واعْلم بأنّ عليكَ العارَ تَلْبَسُه   من عَضّةِ الكلب لا من عَضّة الأسَدِ
لا تأْملِ الخيرَ من ذي نعمةٍ حَدَثتْ   فهْو الحريصُ على أثوابه الجُدُدِ

---

(٦٩) المصدر نفسه، ٢٤٥.

(٧٠) المصدر نفسه، ٣٦٠.

(٧١) المصدر نفسه، ٢٤٠.

وكما فاتت محرّري ديوان اليازجي العودةُ إلى ترانيمه وملاحظة التجديد فيها، هكذا فات هذا الأمر كل الذين كتبوا عن التجديد الأدبي واللغوي في عصر النهضة. ألبرت حوراني (١٩١٥- ١٩٩٣)، في كتابه *الفكر العربي في عصر النهضة، ١٧٩٨- ١٩٣٩* [٧٢]، لا يتناول النهضة اللغوية والأدبية والشعرية، علماً أنه حفيد يواكيم الراسي كما مرّ معنا، أحد أهم ناظمي الترانيم. وإذ يشير كمال الصليبي في *تاريخ لبنان الحديث* إلى ارتباط الانبعاث الأدبي العربي في لبنان بجهود المرسَلين الأميركيين[٧٣]، خصوصاً عالي سميث وكورنيليوس فانديك، عبر ترجمة الكتاب المقدّس إلى العربية بين ١٨٤٧ و١٨٦٥، إلا أنه لا يأتي أبداً على ذكر الترانيم. وعند كلامه عن ناصيف اليازجي، يقول إنه «كتب نثراً وشعراً على غرار الأقدمين»[٧٤]. لكن لا يتطرق البتّة إلى الترانيم العربية ولا يلاحظ بالتالي أن اليازجي كان أحد ناظميها، ولم يكن تقليدياً في ذلك كما رأينا، رغم أن الصليبي مثل حوراني نشأ في كنف الكنيسة الإنجيلية. كما فاتت هاملتون جب، في معرض كلامه عن الأدب العربي الحديث، ملاحظةُ هذه الترانيم. فرغم أن اليازجي «وقف حياته على بعث اللغة العربية والعودة بها إلى سابق مجدها»، حَكَم عليه بمحاربة «التجديد في الأُسلوب والمعنى»، مع «التنكّر لكل ما له علاقة بروح العصر»[٧٥].

وفي كتابه عن جبران حيث يعقد فصلاً عن النهضة الأدبية، يلاحظ خليل حاوي أن «الكتّاب المسيحيين، في سعيهم لهدم الحاجز القائم بين الفصحى والعامية، عبّدوا الطريق، عن غير وعي منهم، لخلق أُسلوب سهل وحيّ وطيّع كيّفه الكتّاب

---

(٧٢) ألبرت حوراني، *الفكر العربي في عصر النهضة ١٧٩٨ - ١٩٣٩*، بيروت، دار النهار ١٩٧٧. أصل الكتاب بالإنكليزية:

Hourani, Albert, *Arabic Thought in the Liberal Age 1798 –1939*, Oxford: Oxford University Press, 1962.

(٧٣) كمال الصليبي، *تاريخ لبنان الحديث*، ١٨٦.

(٧٤) المرجع نفسه، ١٨٧.

(٧٥) هاملتون جب، *دراسات في حضارة الإسلام*، ترجمة إحسان عباس ومحمد يوسف نجم ومحمود زايد، بيروت، دار العلم للملايين ١٩٦٤، ٣٢٣.

اللبنانيون في القرنين التاسع عشر والعشرين»[٧٦]. ويشير إلى الترجمة الإنجيلية للكتاب المقدّس كإحدى ثمار التراث الأدبي المسيحي، وإلى استلهام جبران لها في أُسلوبه المبتكر. لكن عندما يأتي حاوي إلى ناصيف اليازجي، لا يرى سوى تقليد لكتابة عصر الانحطاط، خصوصاً لمقامات الحريري اللغوية التي حاكاها اليازجي في *مجْمع البحرين*. ولا يجد حاوي في شعر اليازجي إلا القصائد التي حاول فيها أحياناً تقليد المتنبي، رغم أن تقليده اقتصر على التفخيم اللفظي، «فجاءت أبياته باردة وجوفاء ومتكلفة»[٧٧].

وفي تقديري أن حاوي أغفل ترانيم اليازجي والترانيم الإنجيلية عموماً عن عمد، واضعاً إيّاها خارج الشعر. وهو كان يعرفها جيداً كأُرثوذكسي من الشوَيْر تلقّى دروسه الأُولى في مدرسة قريته الإرسالية. وطالما كان يردد بتهكّم على مسامع أصدقائه كما في صفوفه الجامعية[٧٨] بعضَ الترانيم، ومنها ترنيمة اليازجي «صَرَخَ الأعمى ابنُ طيما»، وينظر إلى الشعر الديني كما لو كان «نظم عقيدة» أكثر منه شعراً[٧٩]. إلا أن شعر حاوي يحمل أثراً شكلياً واضحاً للترانيم، خصوصاً في اقتصاره على أوزان بسيطة غير مركَّبة وذات مقاطع قصيرة، مثل الرمَل والرجز. وإلى هذين الوزنين، يكاد حاوي لا يستخدم في شعره سوى وزن ثالث طويل المقاطع، هو الكامل. والواقع أن حاوي عوّل بكثافة على الرموز المسيحية في شعره، مستعيراً معظمها من التراث المسيحي الذي نشأ عليه. إلا أنه لم يفعل ذلك لهدف ديني، بل أعطى القصة الدينية أبعاداً وجودية شاملة تسعفه في بناء قصائده الرؤيوية الهائلة.

---

(٧٦) خليل حاوي، *فلسفة الشعر والحضارة*، تحرير ريتا عوَض، بيروت، دار النهار ٢٠٠٢، ١٤٠.

(٧٧) المرجع نفسه، ١٤٣.

(٧٨) طالما سمعتُ حاوي، كطالب لديه وصديق له، يردّد هذه الترنيمة وسواها انتقاصاً من اليازجي وهذا النوع من الشعر، خصوصاً في صفّ النقد الأدبي في الدائرة العربية (الجامعة الأميركية في بيروت) خلال النصف الثاني من الستّينات.

(٧٩) خليل حاوي، المرجع المذكور، ١٢٠.

في الشعر الإنكليزي كما في الشعر عموماً، نقع على هذين النوعين من استلهام الدين في الشعر. فهناك الاستلهام الحرفي لأهداف دينية أو روحية مباشرة كما نجد عند الشاعرة الأميركية إميلي ديكنسون (١٨٣٠- ١٨٨٦) التي جاءت قصائدها أشبه بالترانيم شكلاً ومضموناً[٨٠]، والاستلهام الرمزي لأهداف مركّبة، قد تكون روحية لكن ليست دينية بالضرورة، كما نجد في شعر تي. إس. إليوت (١٨٨٨- ١٩٦٥). ولئن كان حاوي قد وجد ينبوع إلهامه الرئيسي في شعر إليوت، فهذا لا يعني خلوّ شعر ديكنسون وما يشبهه من الروعة الشعرية. وخطأ حاوي هو نزعته الإلغائية التي جعلته يقصر مفهوم الشعر على ما يشبه شعره هو، مع استثناء الأنماط الشعرية الأُخرى من عالم الشعر. وهذه الإلغائيّة جعلته يُغْفِل ضروب الجمال في المعنى والنظم والشكل في الترانيم الإنجيلية التي عرفها على نحو لا يجيز له كباحث أكاديمي موضوعي أن يحدّ شعر اليازجي بديوانه المنشور من غير أن يأتي على ذكر ترانيمه.

صحيحٌ أن هدف الترانيم كان لإقامة الخدَم الدينية في الكنائس، وأن الشعب المؤمن الذي كان يشارك في إنشادها لم يهتمّ بأساليب نظمها ومزاياها الفنّية الشكلية – وهو، في أي حال، لا قدرة له عموماً على هذا النوع من التمييز – بمقدار اهتمامه بمحتواها الديني. لكن لا شك أن لجوء المؤسّسات التربوية في لبنان وسورية وفلسطين ومصر والعراق، وهي البلدان التي شهدت قيام الثورة الشعرية الحديثة كما ذكرنا، إلى جمع طلاّبها لإنشاد هذه الترانيم يومياً قبل بدء الدروس في العادة، أو أُسبوعياً في «مدرسة السبت» أو «مدرسة الأحد» الدينية، جعل ذوي المواهب الشعرية بين طلاّب تلك المؤسّسات، ومنها الكلّية السورية الإنجيلية (الجامعة الأميركية) في بيروت التي ضمّت طلاباً من كل بلاد الشام وبقية العالم العربي، يجدون في تلك الترانيم مصدر إلهام فنّي لما نظموه من شعر.

---

(٨٠) إضافةً إلى شعر ديكنسون، راجِع هذا الكتاب حولها:

Cooley, Carolyn Lindsay, *The Music of Emily Dickinson's Poems and Letters*, Jefferson (North Carolina): McFarland, 2003, 22–23 and 71–74.

لقد لاحظتُ شخصياً هذا التفنن الشكلي في الترانيم وأنا على مقاعد المدرسة[٨١]، حتى منذ المرحلة السابقة للثانوية. وهي مدرسة إنجيلية في بيروت مرتبطة بإرسالية أميركية، كانت تقيم اجتماعاً قبل الصفوف صباح كل يوم للترنيم والوعظ، مع مدرسة دينية صباح كل أحد. وكان الترنيم يحصل من كتاب إنكليزي. وقد بدأ ذلك قبل سنوات من معرفتي بكتاب الترانيم العربي أو حضوري خدمة إنجيلية بالعربية. كان ذلك مطلع الستّينات من القرن العشرين، وقد تزامن مع قراءتي ما أجده من شعر التفعيلة في مكتبة والدي، خصوصاً بعض أعداد مجلة *شعر* وسواها من الصحف التي تنشر الشعر. وكنت عندما أُشارك في إنشاد الترانيم الإنكليزية في المدرسة، أكتشف فوراً معادلها العربي، حتى إني كتبت ترنيمتين أو ثلاثاً بالعربية سُرَّ بها القس رئيس المدرسة ووزّعها على الطلاب في الاجتماع الصباحي لإنشادها. وكنت ذلك الحين، وأنا في بداية المراهقة، أكتب الشعر الموزون من غير خطأ في الوزن، وأنا لم أدرس التفاعيل في كتاب. وأدفع تلك القصائد إلى والدي الشاعر[٨٢]، فيندهش إذ يجدها خالية من أخطاء الوزن وينبّهني إلى عيوب النظم أو التجاوزات التي قد أقع فيها. وإذ تكوّنت لدي مجموعة من تلك القصائد الطفولية، بادر والدي إلى نشرها في كتاب أعطيتُه عنوان *قيثارة الضياء*. وقد احتوى شعراً عمودياً إلى جانب الشعر الحرّ، لكنه كله موزون.

مع متابعتي الكتابة الشعرية، صرت أشدّ وعياً للأثر الإيقاعي الذي أحدثته الترانيم لدي، وإلى جانبه المفردات البسيطة وعفوية التعبير وكذلك البعد الروحي أو الصوفي الذي وجدته ملائماً لتجربتي. ورغم ابتعادي نحو جيلين عن روّاد شعر التفعيلة، إلا أن الترانيم أحدثت أثراً إيقاعياً في شعري يكاد يتجاوز الأثر الذي أحدثته أشكالهم الشعرية لدي. وتقديري أنه شبيه بالأثر الذي أحدثته هذه الترانيم في شعر الروّاد أنفسهم، وهم أقرب عهداً إلى نشأتها وانتشارها. وهي أكثر كثافةً وذيوعاً من المحاولات

---

(٨١) أديب صعب، *هموم حضاريّة*، بيروت، دار النهار ٢٠٠٦، ٤٩-٥١ .

(٨٢) هو الشاعر والصحافي والمربّي وليم صعب (١٩١٢- ١٩٩٩)، وله: *حكاية قرن* (سيرة ذاتيّة)، و*الديوان* (شعر)، بيروت، دار النهار ٢٠٠١.

الخجولة التي ظهرت قبلهم مباشرة والتي أتينا على ذكرها، ومنها كتابة باكثير المسرحية وقصيدة شيبوب في مجلة حركة أبولّو. أما شعر «البند» الذي ظهر قبل ما يزيد على ثلاثة قرون من ظهور شعر التفعيلة فقد ظلّ بلا أثر في الحركة الشعرية خارج الوسط الديني الخاص، كما ظلّ مجهولاً حتى صدور دراسات قليلة حوله أعقبت انتشار الشعر الحرّ. وتبقى أقرب مصادر الإلهام زمناً ومنالاً إلى هذا الشعر ما كتبه المهجريون من شعراء الرابطة القلمية في نيويورك خلال الثلث الأول من القرن العشرين، وفي طليعتهم جبران ونعيمة، والذي وجد أكبر مصادر وحيه في ترجمة فاندايك للكتاب المقدّس، مع الترانيم التي نرى أنها تشكل جزءاً لا يتجزأ منها والتي سبقتها إلى العلن وعاصرتها واستمرت بعدها وعَرفت انتشاراً واسعاً في الشرق العربي، مهْد الثورة الشعرية الثانية أو الشعر الحرّ، عبر المدارس.

وكنت، إذ أقرأ لميخائيل نعيمة «تَناثَري تناثري / يا بهجة النظرْ / يا مَرْقَصَ الشمس / ويا أُرجوحة القمر»،[٨٣] وأقرأ ليوسف الخال «اليومَ مات صاحبي / عيناهُ نجمتانْ / بكيتُ فوق وَجْهِهِ / بكى معي المكانْ»،[٨٤] أستحضِر ذهنياً من كتاب الترانيم قطعاً كهذه (١٤): «أُبارِكُ الربَّ الإلهْ / ما دمتُ كلَّ حينْ / وفي فمي طولَ الحياه / تَسبيحُهُ مُبينْ»، أو كهذه (٢٩): «إنّي أُصَلّي شاكرا / إليكَ بالغَداة / فاسمع صراخي باكرا / واسْتَجِبِ الصلاةْ»، والاثنتان من نظم ناصيف اليازجي. ثم أتذكر أن يوسف الخال، الذي أسس مجلة شعر وحركتها، وهي التي احتضنت الشعراء المحدَثين وأَطلقت فلسفة الحداثة الشعرية وحدّدت معالمها، نشأ في جوّ تلك الترانيم، وكانت له صلة حميمة معها، وهو ابن القس الإنجيلي عبد الله الخال. كما كانت له علاقة وثيقة مع ترجمة فاندايك للكتاب المقدّس، وأُوكل إليه لاحقاً تنقيحها. وقد أشار أدونيس[٨٥] في مقدمة مستفيضة وضعها لمختارات شعرية من الخال إلى أن شعر

---

(٨٣) ميخائيل نعيمة، *همس الجفون*، ٤٧-٤٩.

(٨٤) يوسف الخال، *قصائد في الأربعين*، بيروت، دار مجلّة شعر ١٩٦٠، ٤٥.

(٨٥) يوسف الخال، *قصائد مختارة*، جمعها مع مقدّمة علي أحمد سعيد (أدونيس)، بيروت، دار مجلة شعر (لا تاريخ)، ٢٢ (من مقدّمة أدونيس).

يوسف الخال يمثل «فاتحة التجربة المسيحية» في الشعر العربي الحديث. وكان أدونيس نفسه قد نشأ شعرياً في مناخ تلك الترانيم في اللاذقيّة، حيث كانت أصداؤها تتردّد في الأجواء المدرسية والشعبية. وهذا ينطبق على فدوى طوقان، وهي من روّاد الحداثة الشعرية، التي لم تعرف من المدارس سوى مقاعد مدرستها الابتدائية في نابلس، لكنها اكتسبت ثقافة واسعة من مطالعاتها لاحقاً، خصوصاً تحت أثر أخيها الشاعر ابراهيم طوقان، خريج مدرسة المطران الإنجيلية في القدس التي علّمت أجيالاً من المثقفين الفلسطينيين والتي انتقل منها إلى الجامعة الأميركية في بيروت. ورغم أن ابراهيم نفسه لم ينظم الشعر الحرّ كما فعلت شقيقته فدوى لاحقاً، إلا أن شعره العمودي حمل تجديداً بيّناً في شكله ومحتواه. ويمكن تحرّي هذا الأثر الإنجيلي التربوي، المباشر وغير المباشر، لدى سائر الشعراء من حاملي لواء الثورة الثانية في الشعر العربي.

وما دمت قد انطلقت في ملاحظتي أعلاه من خبرتي الشخصية في مرحلة الدراسة الأُولى، فلسوف أتابع أني أخرجت هذه الملاحظة إلى العلن عندما كُلِّفت تدريس صناعتَي الشعر والنثر (Rhetorics and Poetics) في الجامعة الأميركية في بيروت خلال النصف الثاني من التسعينات. ورحت أتحرّى المحاولات التي سبقت الشعر الحرّ أواخر الأربعينات، فوقعتُ في الكتب على بعض جوانب مما ذكرت، باستثناء هذه الترانيم بالذات التي لم أعثر على ذكر لها في مكان كمحاوَلة إيقاعية قريبة من الشعر الحرّ، بل كأحد مصادر إلهامه. وأضفتها إلى تلك المحاولات من غير أن أنشر أي دراسة حولها. بعد ذلك أشرت إشارةً سريعة إلى أثر الترانيم في الشعر العربي الحديث ضمن دراسة لي حول «الأثر الإنجيلي والأنكلوسكسوني في وعي الأُرثوذكس وخطابهم»[٨٦]. وها أنا أكتب باستفاضة للمرة الأُولى حول موضوع طالما فكّرت فيه وانتظرت فرصة لمعالجته[٨٧].

---

(٨٦) أديب صعب، «أثر المؤسسات الأنكلوسكسونيّة في وعي الأُرثوذكس وخطابهم»، في: *الأُرثوذكس والإنجيليّون في المشرق العربي - قراءة تاريخية وآفاق مستقبليّة*، البلمند (لبنان)، منشورات جامعة

مجمل القول أن الترانيم الإنجيلية العربية كوّنت رافداً رئيسياً من روافد الشعر العربي الحديث، لا بل كانت من المحاولات الأُولى، بل المحاولة الأُولى الرائدة في تاريخ هذا الشعر، لا في أشكالها وإيقاعاتها الجديدة فحسب، بل في مضمونها الروحي ولغتها البسيطة أيضاً. وتشكّل هذه الترانيم كمية وافرة من الشعر الجيّد، تتيح النظر إليها كتجربة شعرية في ذاتها قبل دراسة أثرها في الشعر العربي الذي تلاها، خصوصاً الشعر الحرّ. وبعدما كان هنري جسب يتساءل بتشكيك(٨٨) عمّا إذا كان إيقاع الشعر العربي يستطيع استيعاب الألحان الغربية، وينطلق في إيقاعات وأنغام جديدة متحرراً من رتابة الموسيقى الشرقية، جاء ذاك النفر من ناظمي الترانيم الأوائل – ناصيف اليازجي وأسعد الشدودي وابراهيم سركيس ويوسف الأسير وسليم كسّاب ويواكيم الراسي وابراهيم الحوراني ورفاقهم – ليزيلوا هذا الشكّ

البلمند ٢٠٠٤، ١٠٩- ١٣٦. أيضاً: أديب صعب، «الأثر الإنجيلي والأنكلوسكسوني لدى نخبة من المفكرين العرب»، في: *هموم حضارية*، ٤٣- ٦٨.

(٨٧) عندما دعتني د. سارة بيناي من المعهد الألماني للأبحاث الشرقية في بيروت، نحو منتصف العام ٢٠٠٨، للمساهمة في المؤتمر الذي ينظّمه المعهد للانعقاد في ١٢ و١٣ كانون الأول/ ديسمبر ٢٠٠٨ حول المظاهر الثقافية واللغوية المتعلقة بترجمات الكتاب المقدس إلى اللغة العربية، اخترت العلاقة الإيقاعية بين الترانيم الإنجيلية والشعر العربي الحديث موضوعاً لدراستي. ومع فراغي من إعداد مراجع الدراسة وتصميم خطّتها وقطع شوط في كتابتها، عثرت في الإنترنت على عنوان كتاب لم أكن قد سمعت به، رغم صدوره عن دار بريل الهولندية عام ١٩٧٦، هو الآتي:

Moreh, Shmuel, *Modern Arabic Poetry 1800 – 1970: The Development of Its Forms and Themes under the Influence of Western Literature*, Leiden: Brill, 1976.

وعلى الإنترنت أيضاً قرأت من هذا الكتاب جزءاً من فصله الأول (٢١ - ٥٣) يشير إلى الترانيم الإنجيلية وأثرها المحتمل على الشعراء في سورية ولبنان. إلا أن دراسة موريه المذكورة تبقى كلياً خارج مصادر دراستي لعدم تأثّري بها، وحتى علمي بوجودها. كما أن دراستي تتوسّع أكثر في إيضاح أشكال الشعر العربي ودراسة الترانيم العربية والإنكليزية والمقارنة بينها والإضاءة على ناظمي الترانيم العربية خلال القرن التاسع عشر. لكني وجدت من الملائم للأمانة العلمية والموضوعية الإشارة إلى الكتاب المذكور.

(٨٨) Jessup, Henry, *Fifty Three Years in Syria*, 251.

ويجدّدوا في شكل الشعر العربي وإيقاعه، وقبل ذلك في مضمونه، انطلاقاً من انفتاحهم على الإيقاعات الغربية، ومن تجربة بعضهم الحياتية الجديدة. والتجديد في الحياة والفكر هو الأساس المتين للتجديد في اللغة والأدب والشعر. وتجلّى التجديد الشكلي على وجه الخصوص في إحياء الأوزان العربية القصيرة، وتنويع عدد التفعيلات، وفي ابتكار أوزان جديدة بعض الأحيان، وفي تسكين القوافي مع التقاء الساكنَين أحياناً كثيرة. إلا أن ناظمي الترانيم لم يعتدّوا بذلك الجديد الذي أدخلوه إلى الشعر العربي، لأن الأهداف كانت محض روحية. لو وعى ناصيف اليازجي، مثلاً، أهمية ما فعل في إيقاع الشعر العربي لدى نظمه الترانيم، لو تأثّر هو بنفسه، أي لو انطلق من تلك الأشكال المبتكرة ووسّع موضوعات ترانيمه لتتناول كل ما استطاع أن ينظمه، لحصلت الثورة الثانية في شكل الشعر العربي قبل قرن كامل من حصولها.

مؤرّخو النهضة، من جهتهم، أغفلوا عنصر التجديد الشعري في هذه الترانيم، بعضهم عن غير قصد وبعضهم عمداً. ورغم تقدير هؤلاء المؤرّخين للتجديد اللغوي الذي أحدثته ترجمة فانديك للكتاب المقدّس، أولاً لدى الكتّاب المسيحيين ثم لدى كتّاب المشرق العربي عموماً، عبر التعليم والصحافة والكتب والمحاضرات، إذ نأى الكتّاب عن التعابير والتراكيب اللغوية القديمة واعتمدوا «لغة الحياة» الحيّة مبتعدين عن «لغة الكتب» المهجورة، إلا أنهم أبقوا الترانيم خارج عناصر هذا التجديد اللغوي، علماً أنها سبقت ترجمة الكتاب المقدّس زمناً، ولعلها كانت من مصادر إلهام مترجِميه لاعتماد لغة معرَبة مبسّطة أقرب ما تكون إلى لغة الحياة اليومية لكي تفهمها كل فئات الناس. وها قد حان الوقت لإعادة الاعتبار الشعري إلى هذه الترانيم، واعتبارها جزءاً لا يتجزأ من لغة الكتاب المقدّس وأثرها في النهضة الأدبية العربية الحديثة.

125. RALF ELGER: Glaube, Skepsis, Poesie. Arabische Istanbul-Reisende im 16. und 17. Jahrhundert, Beirut 2011, 196 S.

126. MARTIN TAMCKE, ed.: Christliche Gotteslehre im Orient seit dem Aufkommen des Islams bis zur Gegenwart, Beirut 2008, 224 S. dt., engl. Text.

127. KIRILL DMITRIEV, ANDREAS PFLITSCH, transl.: Ana A. Dolinina: Ignaz Kratschkowskij. Ein russischer Arabist in seiner Zeit. In Vorbereitung.

128. KRISTIAAN AERCKE, VAHID BEHMARDI, RAY MOUAWAD, eds.: Discrimination and Tolerance in the Middle East, Beirut 2012, 124 S.

129. ANDREAS GOERKE, KONRAD HIRSCHLER, eds.: Manuscript Notes as Documentary Sources, Beirut 2011, 184 S. dt., engl., franz. Text, 15 Abb.

130. MIKHAIL RODIONOV, HANNE SCHÖNIG: The Hadramawt Documents, 1904-51: Family Life and Social Customs under the Last Sultans, Beirut 2011, 327 S. arab., engl. Text, 112 Abb., 1 Karte.

131. SARA BINAY, STEFAN LEDER, eds.: Translating the Bible into Arabic: historical, text-critical and literary aspects. Im Druck.

132. STEFAN LEDER, SYRINX VON HEES, eds.: Educational Systems in the Eastern Mediterranean: From Mamluk to Ottoman Rule (Arbeitstitel). In Vorbereitung.

133. MAFALDA ADE: Picknick mit den Paschas. Aleppo und die levantinische Handelsfirma Fratelli Poche (1853-80) (Arbeitstitel). In Vorbereitung.

134. VIVIANE COMERRO: Les traditions sur la constitution du *muṣḥaf* de ʿUthmān, Beirut 2012, 219 S.

Die Unterreihe „Türkische Welten“ ist in die unabhängige Publikationsreihe „Istanbuler Texte und Studien“ des Orient-Instituts Istanbul übergegangen.

Orient-Institut Beirut
Rue Hussein Beyhum, Zokak el-Blat,
P.O.B. 11-2988, Beirut - Lebanon
Tel.: +961 (0)1 359 423-427, Fax: +961 (0)1 359 176
http://www.orient-institut.org

Vertrieb in Deutschland:
Ergon-Verlag GmbH
Keesburgstr. 11
D-97074 Würzburg
Tel: +49 (0) 931 280084
Fax: +49 (0)931 282872
http://www.ergon-verlag.de
Stand: Juni 2012

Vertrieb im Libanon:
al-Furat
Hamra Street
Rasamny Building
P.O.Box: 113-6435 Beirut
Tel: +961 (0)1 750054, Fax: +961 (0)1 750053
e-mail: info@alfurat.com

104. AXEL HAVEMANN: At-tārīḫ wa-kitābat at-tārīḫ fī Lubnān ḫilāl al-qarnain at-tāsiʿ ʿašar wa-l-ʿišrīn. Al-fahm aḏ-ḏātī li-t-tārīḫ: Aškāluhu wa-waẓāʾifuhu (Arabische Übersetzung von BTS 90), Beirut 2011, 380 S.

105. MALEK SHARIF: Imperial Norms and Local Realities. The Ottoman Municipal Laws and the Municipality of Beirut (1860-1908). In Vorbereitung.

106. MATTHIAS VOGT: Figures de califes entre histoire et fiction – al-Walīd b. Yazīd et al-Amīn dans la représentation de l'historiographie arabe de l'époque abbaside, Beirut 2006, 362 S.

107. HUBERT KAUFHOLD, ed.: Georg Graf: Christlicher Orient und schwäbische Heimat. Kleine Schriften, 2 Bde., Beirut 2005, XLVIII, 823 S.

108. LESLIE TRAMONTINI, CHIBLI MALLAT, eds.: From Baghdad to Beirut... Arab and Islamic Studies in honor of John J. Donohue s.j., Beirut 2007, 502 S. engl., franz., arab. Text.

109. RICHARD BLACKBURN: Journey to the Sublime Porte. The Arabic Memoir of a Sharifian Agent's Diplomatic Mission to the Ottoman Imperial Court in the era of Suleyman the Magnificent, Beirut 2005, 366 S.

110. STEFAN REICHMUTH, FLORIAN SCHWARZ, eds.: Zwischen Alltag und Schriftkultur. Horizonte des Individuellen in der arabischen Literatur des 17. und 18. Jahrhunderts, Beirut 2008, 204 S., Abb.

111. JUDITH PFEIFFER, MANFRED KROPP, eds.: Theoretical Approaches to the Transmission and Edition of Oriental Manuscripts, Beirut 2006, 335 S., 43 Abb.

112. LALE BEHZADI, VAHID BEHMARDI, eds.: The Weaving of Words. Approaches to Classical Arabic Prose, Beirut 2009, 217 S.

113. SOUAD SLIM: The Greek Orthodox Waqf in Lebanon during the Ottoman Period, Beirut 2007, 265 S., Abb., Karten.

114. HELEN SADER, MANFRED KROPP, MOHAMMED MARAQTEN, eds.: Proceedings of the Conference on Economic and Social History of Pre-Islamic Arabia. In Vorbereitung.

115. DENIS HERMANN, SABRINA MERVIN, eds.: Shiʿi Trends and Dynamics in Modern Times. Courants et dynamiques chiites à l'époque moderne, Beirut 2010, 180 S. engl., franz. Text.

116. LUTZ GREISIGER, CLAUDIA RAMMELT, JÜRGEN TUBACH, eds.: Edessa in hellenistisch-römischer Zeit: Religion, Kultur und Politik zwischen Ost und West, Beirut 2009, 375 S., Abb., Karte.

117. MARTIN TAMCKE, ed.: Christians and Muslims in Dialogue in the Islamic Orient of the Middle Ages, Beirut 2007, 210 S. dt., engl. Text.

118. MAHMOUD HADDAD et alii, eds.: Towards a Cultural History of the Mamluk Era, Beirut 2010, 316 S. engl., franz., arab. Text, 32 Abb.

119. TARIF KHALIDI et alii, eds.: Al-Jāḥiẓ: A Muslim Humanist for our Time, Beirut 2009, IX, 295 S.

120. FĀRŪQ ḤUBLUṢ: Abḥāṯ fī tārīḫ wilāyat Ṭarābulus ibbān al-ḥukm al-ʿUṯmānī, Beirut 2007, 252 S.

121. STEFAN KNOST: Die Organisation des religiösen Raums in Aleppo. Die Rolle der islamischen religiösen Stiftungen (*auqāf*) in der Gesellschaft einer Provinzhauptstadt des Osmanischen Reiches an der Wende zum 19. Jahrhundert, Beirut 2009, 350 S., 8 Abb., 3 Karten.

122. RALPH BODENSTEIN, STEFAN WEBER: Ottoman Sidon. The Changing Fate of a Mediterranean Port City. In Vorbereitung.

123. JOHN DONOHUE: Robert Campbell's Aʿlām al-adab al-ʿarabī (Arbeitstitel). In Vorbereitung.

124. ANNE MOLLENHAUER: Mittelhallenhäuser im Bilād aš-Šām des 19. Jahrhunderts (Arbeitstitel). In Vorbereitung.

82. Türkische Welten 6. GÜNTER SEUFERT, JACQUES WAARDENBURG, eds.: Türkischer Islam und Europa, Istanbul 1999, 352 S. dt., engl. Text.

83. JEAN-MAURICE FIEY: Al-Qiddīsūn as-Suryān, Beirut 2005, 358 S., 5 Karten.

84. Istanbuler Texte und Studien 4. ANGELIKA NEUWIRTH, JUDITH PFEIFFER, BÖRTE SAGASTER, eds.: Ghazal as World Literature II: From a Literary Genre to a Great Tradition. The Ottoman Gaze in Context, Istanbul 2006, XLIX, 340 S. engl., dt. Text.

85. Türkische Welten 8. BARBARA PUSCH, ed.: Die neue muslimische Frau: Standpunkte & Analysen, Beirut 2001, 326 S.

86. Türkische Welten 9. ANKE VON KÜGELGEN: Die Legitimierung der mittelasiatischen Mangitendynastie in den Werken ihrer Historiker (18.-19. Jahrhundert), Beirut 2002, XII, 518 S.

87. OLAF FARSCHID: *Zakāt* in der Islamischen Ökonomik. Zur Normenbildung im Islam. Im Druck.

88. JENS HANSSEN, THOMAS PHILIPP, STEFAN WEBER, eds.: The Empire in the City: Arab Provincial Capitals in the Late Ottoman Empire, Beirut 2002, X, 375 S., 71 Abb.

89. THOMAS BAUER, ANGELIKA NEUWIRTH, eds.: Ghazal as World Literature I: Transformations of a Literary Genre, Beirut 2005, 447 S. engl. Text.

90. AXEL HAVEMANN: Geschichte und Geschichtsschreibung im Libanon des 19. und 20. Jahrhunderts: Formen und Funktionen des historischen Selbstverständnisses, Beirut 2002, XIV, 341 S.

91. HANNE SCHÖNIG: Schminken, Düfte und Räucherwerk der Jemenitinnen: Lexikon der Substanzen, Utensilien und Techniken, Beirut 2002, XI, 415 S., 130 Abb., 1 Karte.

92. BIRGIT SCHÄBLER: Intifāḍāt Ǧabal ad-durūz-Ḥaurān min al-ʿahd al-ʿUṯmānī ilā daulat al-istiqlāl, 1850-1949, Beirut 2004, 315 S. arab. Text, 2 Karten.

93. AS-SAYYID KĀẒIM B. QĀSIM AL-ḤUSAINĪ AR-RAŠTĪ: Risālat as-sulūk fī l-aḫlāq wa-l-aʿmāl. Hrsg. von Waḥīd Bihmardī, Beirut 2004, 7 S. engl., 120 S. arab. Text.

94. JACQUES AMATEIS SDB: Yūsuf al-Ḫāl wa-Maǧallatuhu „Šiʿr“. In Zusammenarbeit mit Dār al-Nahār, Beirut 2004, 313 S. arab. Text.

95. SUSANNE BRÄCKELMANN: „Wir sind die Hälfte der Welt!“ Zaynab Fawwāz (1860-1914) und Malak Ḥifnī Nāṣif (1886-1918) – zwei Publizistinnen der frühen ägyptischen Frauenbewegung, Beirut 2004, 295 S. dt., 16 S. arab., 4 S. engl. Text.

96. THOMAS PHILIPP, CHRISTOPH SCHUMANN, eds.: From the Syrian Land to the State of Syria and Lebanon, Beirut 2004, 366 S. engl. Text.

97. HISTORY, SPACE AND SOCIAL CONFLICT IN BEIRUT: THE QUARTER OF ZOKAK EL-BLAT, Beirut 2005, XIV, 348 S. engl. Text, 80 S. farb. Abb., 5 Karten.

98. ABDALLAH KAHIL: The Sultan Ḥasan Complex in Cairo 1357-1364. A Case Study in the Formation of Mamluk Style, Beirut 2008, 398 S., 158 Farbtaf.

99. OLAF FARSCHID, MANFRED KROPP, STEPHAN DÄHNE, eds.: World War One as remembered in the countries of the Eastern Mediterranean, Beirut 2006, XIII, 452 S. engl. Text, 17 Abb.

100. MANFRED S. KROPP, ed.: Results of contemporary research on the Qur'ān. The question of a historiocritical text of the Qur'ān, Beirut 2007, 198 S. engl., franz. Text.

101. JOHN DONOHUE SJ, LESLIE TRAMONTINI, eds.: Crosshatching in Global Culture: A Dictionary of Modern Arab Writers. An Updated English Version of R. B. Campbell's "Contemporary Arab Writers", 2 Bde., Beirut 2004, XXIV, 1215 S. engl. Text.

102. MAURICE CERASI et alii, eds.: Multicultural Urban Fabric and Types in the South and Eastern Mediterranean, Beirut 2007, 269 S. engl., franz. Text, zahlr. Abb., Karten.

103. MOHAMMED MARAQTEN: Altsüdarabische Texte auf Holzstäbchen. In Vorbereitung.

63. MONA TAKIEDDINE AMYUNI: La ville source d'inspiration. Le Caire, Khartoum, Beyrouth, Paola Scala chez quelques écrivains arabes contemporains, Beirut 1998, 230 S. franz. Text.
64. ANGELIKA NEUWIRTH, SEBASTIAN GÜNTHER, BIRGIT EMBALÓ, MAHER JARRAR, eds.: Myths, Historical Archetypes and Symbolic Figures in Arabic Literature. Proceedings of the Symposium held at the Orient-Institut Beirut, June 25th – June 30th, 1996, Beirut 1999, 640 S. engl. Text.
65. Türkische Welten 1. KLAUS KREISER, CHRISTOPH K. NEUMANN, eds.: Das Osmanische Reich in seinen Archivalien und Chroniken. Nejat Göyünç zu Ehren, Istanbul 1997, XXIII, 328 S.
66. Türkische Welten 2. CABBAR, SETTAR: Kurtuluş Yolunda: a work on Central Asian literature in a Turkish-Uzbek mixed language. Ed., transl. and linguistically revisited by A. Sumru Özsoy, Claus Schöning, Esra Karabacak, with contribution from Ingeborg Baldauf, Istanbul 2000, 335 S.
67. Türkische Welten 3. GÜNTER SEUFERT: Politischer Islam in der Türkei. Islamismus als symbolische Repräsentation einer sich modernisierenden muslimischen Gesellschaft, Istanbul 1997, 600 S.
68. EDWARD BADEEN: Zwei mystische Schriften des ʿAmmār al-Bidlīsī, Beirut 1999, VI S., 142 S. dt., 122 arab. Text.
69. THOMAS SCHEFFLER, HÉLÈNE SADER, ANGELIKA NEUWIRTH, eds.: Baalbek: Image and Monument, 1898–1998, Beirut 1998, XIV, 348 S. engl., franz. Text.
70. AMIDU SANNI: The Arabic Theory of Prosification and Versification. On ḥall and naẓm in Arabic Theoretical Discourse, Beirut 1988, XIII, 186 S.
71. ANGELIKA NEUWIRTH, BIRGIT EMBALÓ, FRIEDERIKE PANNEWICK: Kulturelle Selbstbehauptung der Palästinenser: Survey der modernen palästinensischen Dichtung, Beirut 2001, XV, 549 S.
72. STEPHAN GUTH, PRISKA FURRER, J. CHRISTOPH BÜRGEL, eds.: Conscious Voices. Concepts of Writing in the Middle East, Beirut 1999, XXI, 332 S. dt., engl., franz. Text.
73. Türkische Welten 4. SURAYA FAROQHI, CHRISTOPH K. NEUMANN, eds.: The Illuminated Table, the Prosperous House. Food and Shelter in Ottoman Material Culture, Beirut 2003, 352 S., 25 Abb.
74. BERNARD HEYBERGER, CARSTEN WALBINER, eds.: Les Européens vus par les Libanais à l'époque ottomane, Beirut 2002, VIII, 244 S.
75. Türkische Welten 5. TOBIAS HEINZELMANN: Die Balkankrise in der osmanischen Karikatur. Die Satirezeitschriften Karagöz, Kalem und Cem 1908–1914, Beirut 1999, 290 S. Text, 77 Abb., 1 Karte.
76. THOMAS SCHEFFLER, ed.: Religion between Violence and Reconciliation, Beirut 2002, XIV, 578 S. engl., franz. Text.
77. ANGELIKA NEUWIRTH, ANDREAS PFLITSCH, eds.: Crisis and Memory in Islamic Societies, Beirut 2001, XII, 540 S.
78. FRITZ STEPPAT: Islam als Partner: Islamkundliche Aufsätze 1944–1996, Beirut 2001, XXX, 424 S., 8 Abb.
79. PATRICK FRANKE: Begegnung mit Khidr. Quellenstudien zum Imaginären im traditionellen Islam, Beirut 2000, XV, 620 S., 23 Abb.
80. LESLIE A. TRAMONTINI: „East is East and West is West"? Talks on Dialogue in Beirut, Beirut 2006, 222 S.
81. VANESSA GUENO, STEFAN KNOST, eds.: Lire et écrire l'histoire ottomane : examen critique des documents des tribunaux ottomans du Bilād al-Shām. In Vorbereitung.

42. HARTMUT BOBZIN: Der Koran im Zeitalter der Reformation. Studien zur Frühgeschichte der Arabistik und Islamkunde in Europa, Beirut 1995, unveränd. Nachdr. Beirut 2008, XIV, 590 S.
43. BEATRIX OSSENDORF-CONRAD: Das „K. al-Wāḍiḥa" des ʿAbd al-Malik b. Ḥabīb. Edition und Kommentar zu Ms. Qarawiyyīn 809/49 (Abwāb aṭ-ṭahāra), Beirut 1994, 574 S., davon 71 S. arab. Text, 45 S. Faks.
44. MATHIAS VON BREDOW: Der Heilige Krieg (ǧihād) aus der Sicht der malikitischen Rechtsschule, Beirut 1994, 547 S. arab., 197 S. dt. Text, Indices.
45. OTFRIED WEINTRITT: Formen spätmittelalterlicher islamischer Geschichtsdarstellung. Untersuchungen zu an-Nuwairī al-Iskandarānīs Kitāb al-Ilmām und verwandten zeitgenössischen Texten, Beirut 1992, X, 226 S.
46. GERHARD CONRAD: Die quḍāt Dimašq und der maḏhab al-Auzāʿī. Materialien zur syrischen Rechtsgeschichte, Beirut 1994, XVIII, 828 S.
47. MICHAEL GLÜNZ: Die panegyrische qaṣīda bei Kamāl ud-dīn Ismāʿīl aus Isfahan. Eine Studie zur persischen Lobdichtung um den Beginn des 7./13. Jahrhunderts, Beirut 1993, 290 S.
48. AYMAN FU'ĀD SAYYID: La Capitale de l'Égypte jusqu'à l'Époque Fatimide – Al-Qāhira et Al-Fusṭāṭ–Essai de Reconstitution Topographique, Beirut 1998, XL, 754 S. franz., 26 S. arab. Text, 109 Abb.
49. JEAN MAURICE FIEY: Pour un Oriens Christianus Novus, Beirut 1993, 286 S. franz. Text.
50. IRMGARD FARAH: Die deutsche Pressepolitik und Propagandatätigkeit im Osmanischen Reich von 1908–1918 unter besonderer Berücksichtigung des „Osmanischen Lloyd", Beirut 1993, 347 S.
51. BERND RADTKE: Weltgeschichte und Weltbeschreibung im mittelalterlichen Islam, Beirut 1992, XII, 544 S.
52. LUTZ RICHTER-BERNBURG: Der Syrische Blitz – Saladins Sekretär zwischen Selbstdarstellung und Geschichtsschreibung, Beirut 1998, 452 S. dt., 99 S. arab. Text.
53. FRITZ MEIER: Bausteine I-III. Ausgewählte Aufsätze zur Islamwissenschaft. Hrsg. von Erika Glassen und Gudrun Schubert, Beirut 1992, I und II 1195 S., III (Indices) 166 S.
54. FESTSCHRIFT EWALD WAGNER ZUM 65. GEBURTSTAG: Hrsg. von Wolfhart Heinrichs und Gregor Schoeler, 2 Bde., Beirut 1994, Bd. 1: Semitische Studien unter besonderer Berücksichtigung der Südsemitistik, XV, 284 S.; Bd. 2: Studien zur arabischen Dichtung, XVII, 641 S.
55. SUSANNE ENDERWITZ: Liebe als Beruf. Al-ʿAbbās Ibn al-Aḥnaf und das Ġazal, Beirut 1995, IX, 246 S.
56. ESTHER PESKES: Muḥammad b. ʿAbdalwahhāb (1703–1792) im Widerstreit. Untersuchungen zur Rekonstruktion der Frühgeschichte der Wahhābīya, Beirut 1993, VII, 384 S.
57. FLORIAN SOBIEROJ: Ibn Ḫafīf aš-Šīrāzī und seine Schrift zur Novizenerziehung, Beirut 1998, IX, 442 S. dt., 48 S. arab. Text.
58. FRITZ MEIER: Zwei Abhandlungen über die Naqšbandiyya. I. Die Herzensbindung an den Meister. II. Kraftakt und Faustrecht des Heiligen, Beirut 1994, 366 S.
59. JÜRGEN PAUL: Herrscher, Gemeinwesen, Vermittler: Ostiran und Transoxanien in vormongolischer Zeit, Beirut 1996, VIII, 310 S.
60. JOHANN CHRISTOPH BÜRGEL, STEPHAN GUTH, eds.: Gesellschaftlicher Umbruch und Historie im zeitgenössischen Drama der islamischen Welt, Beirut 1995, XII, 295 S.
61. BARBARA FINSTER, CHRISTA FRAGNER, HERTA HAFENRICHTER, eds.: Rezeption in der islamischen Kunst, Beirut 1999, 332 S. dt. Text, Abb.
62. ROBERT B. CAMPBELL, ed.: Aʿlām al-adab al-ʿarabī al-muʿāṣir. Siyar wa-siyar ḏātiyya. (Contemporary Arab Writers. Biographies and Autobiographies), 2 Bde., Beirut 1996, 1380 S. arab. Text. Vergriffen.

20. WERNER ENDE: Arabische Nation und islamische Geschichte. Die Umayyaden im Urteil arabischer Autoren des 20. Jahrhunderts, Beirut 1977, XIII, 309 S.
21. ṢALĀḤADDĪN AL-MUNAĞĞID, STEFAN WILD, eds.: Zwei Beschreibungen des Libanon. ʿAbdalġanī an-Nābulusīs Reise durch die Biqāʿ und al-ʿUṭaifīs Reise nach Tripolis, Beirut 1979, XVII u. XXVII, 144 S. arab. Text, 1 Karte, 2 Faltkarten.
22. ULRICH HAARMANN, PETER BACHMANN, eds.: Die islamische Welt zwischen Mittelalter und Neuzeit. Festschrift für Hans Robert Roemer zum 65. Geburtstag, Beirut 1979, XVI, 702 S., 11 Taf.
23. ROTRAUD WIELANDT: Das Bild der Europäer in der modernen arabischen Erzähl- und Theaterliteratur, Beirut 1980, XVII, 652 S.
24. REINHARD WEIPERT, ed.: Der Dīwān des Rāʿī an-Numairī, Beirut 1980, IV dt., 363 S. arab. Text.
25. ASʿAD E. KHAIRALLAH: Love, Madness and Poetry. An Interpretation of the Mağnūn Legend, Beirut 1980, 163 S.
26. ROTRAUD WIELANDT: Das erzählerische Frühwerk Maḥmūd Taymūrs, Beirut 1983, XII, 434 S.
27. ANTON HEINEN: Islamic Cosmology. A study of as-Suyūṭī's al-Hay'a as-sanīya fī l-hay'a as-sunnīya with critical edition, translation, and commentary, Beirut 1982, VIII, 289 S. engl., 78 S. arab. Text.
28. WILFERD MADELUNG: Arabic Texts concerning the history of the Zaydī Imāms of Ṭabaristān, Daylamān and Gīlān, Beirut 1987, 23 S. engl., 377 S. arab. Text.
29. DONALD P. LITTLE: A Catalogue of the Islamic Documents from al-Ḥaram aš-Šarīf in Jerusalem, Beirut 1984, XIII, 480 S. engl., 6 S. arab. Text, 17 Taf.
30. KATALOG DER ARABISCHEN HANDSCHRIFTEN IN MAURETANIEN. Bearb. von Ulrich Rebstock, Rainer Osswald und A. Wuld ʿAbdalqādir, Beirut 1988, XII, 164 S.
31. ULRICH MARZOLPH: Typologie des persischen Volksmärchens, Beirut 1984, XIII, 312 S., 5 Tab., 3 Karten.
32. STEFAN LEDER: Ibn al-Ğauzī und seine Kompilation wider die Leidenschaft, Beirut 1984, XIV, 328 S. dt., 7 S. arab. Text, 1 Falttaf.
33. RAINER OSSWALD: Das Sokoto-Kalifat und seine ethnischen Grundlagen, Beirut 1986, VIII, 177 S.
34. ZUHAIR FATḤALLĀH, ed.: Der Diwān des ʿAbd al-Laṭīf Fatḥallāh, 2 Bde., Beirut 1984, 1196 S. arab. Text.
35. IRENE FELLMANN: Das Aqrābāḏīn al-Qalānisī. Quellenkritische und begriffsanalytische Untersuchungen zur arabisch-pharmazeutischen Literatur, Beirut 1986, VI, 304 S.
36. HÉLÈNE SADER: Les États Araméens de Syrie depuis leur Fondation jusqu'à leur Transformation en Provinces Assyriennes, Beirut 1987, XIII, 306 S. franz. Text.
37. BERND RADTKE: Adab al-Mulūk, Beirut 1991, XII, 34 S. dt., 145 S. arab. Text.
38. ULRICH HAARMANN: Das Pyramidenbuch des Abū Ğaʿfar al-Idrīsī (gest. 649/1251), Beirut 1991, XI u. VI, 94 S. dt., 283 S. arab. Text.
39. TILMAN NAGEL, ed.: Göttinger Vorträge – Asien blickt auf Europa. Begegnungen und Irritationen, Beirut 1990, 192 S.
40. HANS R. ROEMER: Persien auf dem Weg in die Neuzeit. Iranische Geschichte von 1350–1750, Beirut 1989, unveränd. Nachdr. Beirut 2003, X, 525 S.
41. BIRGITTA RYBERG: Yūsuf Idrīs (1927–1991). Identitätskrise und gesellschaftlicher Umbruch, Beirut 1992, 226 S.

المعهد الألماني للأبحاث الشرقية

ORIENT-INSTITUT
BEIRUT

BEIRUTER TEXTE UND STUDIEN

1. MICHEL JIHA: Der arabische Dialekt von Bišmizzīn. Volkstümliche Texte aus einem libanesischen Dorf mit Grundzügen der Laut- und Formenlehre, Beirut 1964, XVII, 185 S.
2. BERNHARD LEWIN: Arabische Texte im Dialekt von Hama. Mit Einleitung und Glossar, Beirut 1966, *48*, 230 S.
3. THOMAS PHILIPP: Ǧurǧī Zaidān. His Life and Thought, Beirut 1979, 249 S.
4. ʿABD AL-ĠANĪ AN-NĀBULUSĪ: At-tuḥfa an-nābulusīya fī r-riḥla aṭ-ṭarābulusīya. Hrsg. u. eingel. Von Heribert Busse, Beirut 1971, unveränd. Nachdr. Beirut 2003, XXIV, 10 S. dt., 133 S. arab. Text.
5. BABER JOHANSEN: Muḥammad Ḥusain Haikal. Europa und der Orient im Weltbild eines ägyptischen Liberalen, Beirut 1967, XIX, 259 S.
6. HERIBERT BUSSE: Chalif und Großkönig. Die Buyiden im Iraq (945–1055), Beirut 1969, unveränd. Nachdr. 2004, XIV, 610 S., 6 Taf., 2 Karten.
7. JOSEF VAN ESS: Traditionistische Polemik gegen ʿAmr b. ʿUbaid. Zu einem Text des ʿAlī b. ʿUmar ad-Dāraquṭnī, Beirut 1967, mit Korrekturen versehener Nachdruck 2004, 74 S. dt., 16 S. arab. Text, 2 Taf.
8. WOLFHART HEINRICHS: Arabische Dichtung und griechische Poetik. Ḥāzim al-Qarṭāǧannīs Grundlegung der Poetik mit Hilfe aristotelischer Begriffe, Beirut 1969, 289 S.
9. STEFAN WILD: Libanesische Ortsnamen. Typologie und Deutung, Beirut 1973, unveränd. Nachdr. Beirut 2008, XII, 391 S.
10. GERHARD ENDRESS: Proclus Arabus. Zwanzig Abschnitte aus der Institutio Theologica in arabischer Übersetzung, Beirut 1973, XVIII, 348 S. dt., 90 S. arab. Text.
11. JOSEF VAN ESS: Frühe muʿtazilitische Häresiographie. Zwei Werke des Nāšiʾ al-Akbar (gest. 293 H.), Beirut 1971, unveränd. Nachdr. Beirut 2003, XII, 185 S. dt., 134 S. arab. Text.
12. DOROTHEA DUDA: Innenarchitektur syrischer Stadthäuser des 16.–18. Jahrhunderts. Die Sammlung Henri Pharaon in Beirut, Beirut 1971, VI, 176 S., 88 Taf., 6 Farbtaf., 2 Faltpläne.
13. WERNER DIEM: Skizzen jemenitischer Dialekte, Beirut 1973, XII, 166 S.
14. JOSEF VAN ESS: Anfänge muslimischer Theologie. Zwei antiqadaritische Traktate aus dem ersten Jahrhundert der Hiǧra, Beirut 1977, XII, 280 S. dt., 57 S. arab. Text.
15. GREGOR SCHOELER: Arabische Naturdichtung. Die zahrīyāt, rabīʿīyāt und rauḍīyāt von ihren Anfängen bis aṣ-Ṣanaubarī, Beirut 1974, XII, 371 S.
16. HEINZ GAUBE: Ein arabischer Palast in Südsyrien. Ḫirbet el-Baiḍa, Beirut 1974, XIII, 156 S., 14 Taf., 3 Faltpläne, 12 Textabb.
17. HEINZ GAUBE: Arabische Inschriften aus Syrien, Beirut 1978, XXII, 201 S., 19 Taf.
18. GERNOT ROTTER: Muslimische Inseln vor Ostafrika. Eine arabische Komoren-Chronik des 19. Jahrhunderts, Beirut 1976, XII, 106 S. dt., 116 S. arab. Text, 2 Taf., 2 Karten.
19. HANS DAIBER: Das theologisch-philosophische System des Muʿammar Ibn ʿAbbād as-Sulamī (gest. 830 n. Chr.), Beirut 1975, XII, 604 S.